AMBUSH!

Colonel Knox sent Capt. Barry Norton to the site by helicopter to take charge and to assess the situation. Delta Troop was turned out, and four hunter-killer aviation teams were dispatched. A Troop was prepared to move in to reinforce them, a trip that would take two hours, at best.

Terry was right. He had disturbed the enemy, but they were about to pay for the ambush. Barry, an extremely competent officer, was appointed acting troop commander. He pushed the armored force forward and broke the ambush. The enemy scattered; they couldn't handle the shock action of the tanks. The new troop commander took over a very well-trained and cohesive organization, and they responded to him as if there had been no change of leadership. Their blood was up; the Gray Fox was loved by his troopers. More than a little revenge was involved in the fighting. Each time an enemy cell tried to stop and reconstitute, Barry brought in artillery. The Cobras on high said it was like shooting fish in a barrel. . . .

WHY A SOLDIER?

A Signal Corpsman's Tour from Vietnam to the Moscow Hot Line

Col. David G. Fitz-Enz, US Army (Ret.)

BALLANTINE BOOKS · NEW YORK

A Ballantine Book
Published by The Ballantine Publishing Group
Copyright © 2000 by David G. Fitz-Enz

All rights reserved under International and Pan-American Copyright Conventions. Published in the United States by The Ballantine Publishing Group, a division of Random House, Inc., New York, and simultaneously in Canada by Random House of Canada Limited, Toronto.

Ballantine and colophon are registered trademarks of Random House, Inc.

www.randomhouse.com/BB/

Library of Congress Catalog Card Number: 00-107753

ISBN 0-8041-1938-4

Manufactured in the United States of America

First Edition: November 2000

10 9 8 7 6 5 4 3 2 1

To
Impy

My West Highland white terrier,
who sat in my chair with me as I recalled it all.

Acknowledgments

I wish to commend my wife, Carol, for editing this work and correcting my inaccuracies. As an Army wife she is one of those selfless people who are all too rare in this progressive world. She raised three flawless sons and moved twenty-one times in thirty years, and she did it all with beauty and grace.

I recognize my brother, Dr. Jack Fitz-Enz, author and entrepreneur, who first read my manuscript and approved of it in most encouraging terms.

I acknowledge the late Col. John Elting, author and historian, and Lionel Leventhal, of Greenhill Books, London, England, for identifying the right path to follow.

I must thank Owen Lock, a fellow cold warrior and the man who insisted that this work be published, no matter how long it might take. His tenacity and encouragement were coupled with sound advice.

Mr. John Wayne Johnston, a notable professional photographer and teacher of the art, took my original photos, which were rather worn and shapeless, and gave them new life.

Republic of Vietnam

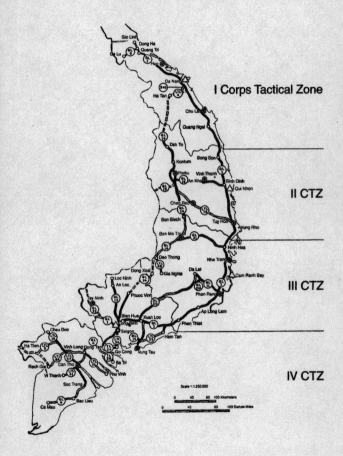

I Corps Tactical Zone

II CTZ

III CTZ

IV CTZ

Gio Linh
Dong Ha
Quang Tri
Ca Lu
Hue
Da Nang
Ha Tan
Chu Lai
Quang Ngai
Dak To
Bong Son
Kontum
Pleiku
Vinh Thanh
An Khe
Binh Dinh
Qui Nhon
Cheo Reo
Ban Blech
Tuy Hoa
Ban Me Thuot
Vung Ro
Ninh Hoa
Dao Thong
Nha Trang
Dong Xoai
Gia Nghia
Da Lat
Loc Ninh
An Loc
Cam Ranh Bay
Tay Ninh
Phuoc Vinh
Phan Rang
Bien Hoa
Xuan Loc
Ap Long Lam
Chau Doc
Long Binh
Saigon
Phan Thiet
Ha Tien
Vinh Long
Dong Tam
Ham Tan
Rach Gia
Go Cong
Vung Tau
Ba Tri
Can Tho
Vi Thanh
Phu Vinh
Soc Trang
Ca Mau
Bac Lieu

Scale 1:1,250,000

0   40   80   100 Kilometers

0   40   60   100 Statute Miles

Chapter One

Do what you can, with what you have, where you are.
TEDDY ROOSEVELT

My troopship sat at anchor within a mile of the Vietnam shore. For twenty-one days we had been at sea, and there wasn't a soldier on board who wanted to spend another minute confined within the gray steel decks, even if leaving the ship did mean landing on hostile ground. It was a dark, cloudy night before our landing, but we could see a dim outline of the shore illuminated by the light from artillery flares floating on handkerchief-size parachutes. "There, did you hear that?" 2d Lt. Lance Stonehanger said again and again at each new crackle, as a group of nervous novices leaned tight together along the damp railing. Most of them had heard rifle shots only on a range, and gunfire never sounded dangerous under those controlled conditions. Navy SEALs walked the decks all that sleepless night and threw percussion grenades over the side to ward off enemy skin divers. A mine attached to our ship's bottom would surely ruin the show planned for the morning.

By morning the Navy had tied a lighter to the side of the ship and strung a cargo net from the top of a rail down nearly a hundred feet to the lurching platform below. Well, it looked like a hundred feet or more to someone like me, who had never climbed down a net like this before. The infantry practiced on coarse fat-rope nets all the time, but my Signal

1

Corps battalion had never even seen one. It looked simple. The men, laden with an M-14 long rifle, forty-pound packs, fifty-pound duffel bags, and joint-stiffening fright, assembled at the top of the net. As a first lieutenant, my load was much lighter, only a .45-caliber pistol and full canteen.

However, as I peered down at the moving metal deck below, I experienced the same trepidation. I had been the acting company commander for the twenty-one-day voyage and so went first, along with my three other lieutenants. As soon as I swung over the rail I realized that my worry was well warranted. Three or four squares from the top I was slammed into the side of the mother ship, skinning my knuckles and nearly losing my foothold. From then on I crept along, staring ever upward at the face of my first sergeant, "Top," who was loading the next line of six. He looked very worried as he gave advice at the top of his voice and picked out men by name. At the bottom I became entangled and fell on my back against the hardest surface I had ever known, the unyielding metal plates of the barge.

My helmet hit the laminated deck last, broke free, and rolled into the hands of a sailor who fielded it like a grounder. He gave it back with a grin. "Is this yours, sir? You will be needin' it where you are going." His friends all snickered at his wit.

Once I was down the fear of the monster web was gone, and I encouraged the men as Top sent the first squads over the high metal railing in waves. My best combat cameraman, Private Murphy, was upside down twenty feet from what he considered his final resting place, with cameras swinging from around his neck in a stranglehold. Overwhelmed by their own predicaments, those on either side were unaware of his plight. He was pitiful, having already dropped his helmet, rifle, and bag, which thundered to the deck below. His arms flailed in big circles but made no contact. He would have been screaming if the camera straps had permitted him the wind. The ship moved up and a little to the side, and the back of Murphy's head banged against her plates. The thin leather straps twisted tighter as the cameras spun at the end of their cords. Lance went to the rescue, got above him, and hauled him upright, sticking Murphy's arms through the ropes. Breathless and draped from his armpits, Murphy encouraged the lieutenant to unwind the precious black cases that had nearly choked their master.

"Nice going, Murph. We have all enjoyed the acrobatics. You want to stop playing around now?" Lance said.

Safely on deck, Murphy grabbed his rescuer by the arms and said in a husky voice well beyond his eighteen years, "We don't ever have to do that again, do we, sir?"

Helmets rained down on the metal deck like bowling balls at terminal velocity and bounced twice at about shin height. In fact, anything loose or capable of being torn loose by the rope net quickly found its way to the ever-growing pile of debris on the barge. Cries of "Look out!" or "Watch it!" filled the air, along with many expletives. The lighter swayed and then wallowed, and we looked like an amateur chorus line as, knees bent, we held on to each other, tried to sort out the mess, and passed fragments back to their original owners. At last the 106 men of my company edged to the far side to await pickup by our landing craft. The remaining seven hundred of the battalion, who were about to follow, peered over the side at us and contemplated their own fates concerning the menacing contraption. A large cargo net, with our rations, field equipment, and ammunition, was swung out of the sky by the ship's crane.

The battalion executive officer, Major Marks, had kept up a constant chatter throughout the proceedings with an amplified loud hailer. His advice was neither correct nor helpful and I vowed to get him someday. A line of ten amphibious landing boats stood off a hundred yards waiting to pick up the remainder of the 69th Signal Battalion after it had negotiated the net. The landing craft were WWII type, about eighty feet long and eight feet deep, painted light gray with large white numbers on the side. They had flat bows that dropped open to form a ramp onto the beach, encouraging all to get off quickly. As the first one rolled up against our craft and the coxswain gunned the engine, which held her loosely to the barge, it did not look inviting. Another circus act was about to be performed by amateurs for the benefit of the spectators.

The first sergeant, J. B. Milrowski, a big man of few but significant words, organized the leap into the craft that banged relentlessly against the barge. He left the officers to their own devices and busied the men with throwing the half ton of equipment and duffel bags into the boat well. I made a giant step onto the slippery deck at the stern, slid a foot or so, and flattened myself against the wheelhouse. I vowed to stay there for the run to the beach.

Pitching the stuff aboard was the easy part. By now the remaining men realized what was in store for them and they shied away. Only a foot or so of damp metal edge stood between them and the sea. Once on that catwalk, they saw that the vessel's insides sloped sharply to the open floor that was deeper than the height of a man. The transfer would require one good, firm, lunging step, a turnaround, and one giant drop onto the layer of debris that had raised the floor by two to three feet. All the while the noisy chatter from Major Marks never stopped. Of the 106, two-thirds made it unscathed, and many lost firm footing for an instant and regained it just in time to lurch headfirst into a buddy who had already made the trip. Top, the last aboard, displayed with two jumps the way it should be done. "All correct, sir" was his only comment. Thank God for good sergeants.

Our boat swung out and started to circle in the bay while another performance continued, starring the other six hundred. Even though we had acquired our sea legs, a bobbing flat-bottomed craft was a new experience. At least the troops had learned while on the big ship to face away from the wind when seasick. Our battalion liaison team, which came over by aircraft weeks before, would be waiting onshore and provide us with a home that was at last stationary. An hour later, when all ten boats were filled, the flotilla strung out in a straight line and we went south for several miles until our transport ship was out of sight. I searched the shore for a landing site and the trucks that would end our transpacific journey.

"Where are we going, boatswain?" I asked when nothing obvious appeared along the endless beach.

"About another mile, sir. Over there near that point," he said, directing me to nothing of definition. "Sir, we will gather up in a flank formation and hit the beach together in about ten minutes."

Stunned, I said, "You mean assault? Isn't our team there to meet us?"

"Don't think so, just Charlie. Lieutenant, you guys ready?"

"Ready for what, mate?"

"Why, the war, sir."

My men had four magazines on their belts and one of them was loaded. The rest of the ammo was nailed in wooden boxes. We were told that it was to be an administrative landing, not combat. I yelled to Top to have the troops load their weapons immediately. Rather than giving the command, he stumbled his way to the stern and climbed up to my position. "What's going on, sir? Are we under attack?"

With my eyes now fixed on the enemy shoreline, I said, "Only by our own 69th liaison team; the beach is hostile." The troops didn't seem surprised—they thought it was a good idea to have a bullet in the chamber in a combat zone. By the time we were ready the sandy coastline was only yards away. All ten craft were in a perfect line; it was *Victory at Sea* all over again, and my combat photographers were shooting pictures of everything and everyone. With a forty-man combat photo platoon in the well that was equipped to document the entire war, it was the best-covered amphibious landing in the history of the Signal Corps. It was also the only amphibious assault by a Signal Corps battalion ever made in its hundred-year history.

The bottom of the landing craft bumped up on the beach. Everyone was thrown forward and my men collapsed on each other like dominos. A moment later the front gate dropped into the warm shallow water thousands of miles from home and we stormed ashore, just like in the movies. Fifty yards of sand stretched between us and a single-track road that paralleled the shoreline. I led a wallowing assault through the powdery sand and stopped totally out of breath at the edge of the road, the nose of my .45-caliber pistol pointing the way. Eight hundred men from ten tightly packed boats followed, eyes wide open, waiting for the first shot. They spread out over two football-field lengths. Then there was silence.

"Have the men dig in here and put the machine guns there and there," I told J.B., catching my wind and looking back at the boats that carried almost all our ammo. "Oh, yes, have a detail go back and unload the boat," I said, as if it were part of my nonexistent battle plan. A few moments later, in the boat next to mine, the battalion commander, Lt. Col. Harold J. Snead, marched forth with his staff backed by the unit color guard, which unfurled our orange and white flag beside the American flag. My photographers were there en masse. What a sight! The battalion banner of the 69th Signal was at war again. She had not missed a conflict since the Civil War, though she was a mere company then. Would her veterans be proud of this day? I think they would; the troops were magnificent in the confusion.

We sat in the sand the rest of the morning, and the colonel inspected our positions and ordered that we dig in deeper. Digging in sand was fruitless; it filled in as fast as it was tossed out. We saw no sign of the enemy or anyone else. Our left flank rested on the near side of a point. We had made a lot of commotion, complete with a great deal of disorganized yelling, but no gunfire. B Company reported movement from the point, which drew our instant attention. Slowly a few figures appeared and continued to advance along the rutted road. The order was passed to hold our fire. The "figures" quickly resolved into Vietnamese girls with their boyfriends. Vietnam being a former French country, the girls wore bikinis. Our visitors spoke a little English and asked what we were doing on the edge of the army rest and rehabilitation resort beach. Before long they were joined by men on motorbikes selling Cokes and offering to find girls for our outposts at very reasonable prices. They took American money, you see.

We had been at sea nearly a month and discipline immediately began to break down under the assault of the feminine bathers, who waltzed along our front line. Then a highly polished jeep with the marking of the 39th Signal battalion commander whizzed up, covering the troops with dust. It stopped in front of our colors and a pressed and starched American lieutenant colonel stepped out, straightened his blouse from under his pistol belt, and strolled purposefully into the sand. He wore no combat gear and sported an olive drab baseball cap with the oak leaf of his office embroidered on the front in silver thread. "I am Col. Sam Bonder, commander of the fighting 39th Signal. Who *are* you?" he asked Snead rather perturbedly. It appeared to be a matter of trespass. Had we crossed some invisible line on an unknown military map?

Lieutenant Colonel Snead, clearly not on his own turf, was very cordial and told the story of the fighting 69th. The two got on well since there was no dispute intended and they went off together in the Simonized jeep. Before leaving, Bonder assured our boss that we were in no danger, so we secured from our advanced state of readiness.

The girls were chased off by Major Marks. Strike two for him.

The C rations came out and we drew meals from the heavy cardboard cases. The food tasted much like the box. If not appetizing, it at least reduced the amount of weight we would have to carry. Our commander returned an hour later. Our advance party had never made it to Saigon; they were kicked off their military transport in Hawaii. Visions of remaining at the recreation area there at Vung Tau were scrubbed from our minds when a convoy of ten-ton Engineer dump trucks arrived in a cloud of dust. Climbing onto the standard army deuce-and-a-half trucks was always difficult, since the bed was a good five feet from the ground, but our transportation was a new challenge; the snub end of a granite-hauling dump truck was twice that high. The sergeants put big guys at the back end of the trucks' hoppers; on their stomachs, they stretched over the back end and, with great difficulty, pulled the others in. We were bound for the airfield, where a half-dozen C-130 cargoplanes came in after a short wait. We loaded them to overcapacity, being seated on the floor eight across, facing the rear. Webbed cargo straps were passed through our laps as restraints and the rear ramp doors were closed for takeoff. The heat was oppressive and sweat rolled down my face in a continuous rivulet, filling my eyes.

The inside of the airplane look liked Jonah's view of the whale. Everything was exposed to view to reduce weight and ease maintenance. It was generally a pale green with bits of color splashed here and there. The dark red webbed seating that ran the length of the fuselage remained folded up. Most emergency aids were housed in yellow cloth bags and hung on the firewall behind the cockpit. The major ribs, one every foot, encircled the cabin in rings and were run through with metal connecting rods six inches apart that ran the entire length of the bay. That was just the start. Hundreds of cables, electrical lines, and hydraulic tubes led in all directions. The floor was covered with tie-down rings and the raised roller tracks used to move large pallets of cargo in and out. Sitting on those protrusions called for careful positioning that required constant readjustment. We were miserable.

Takeoff was a kick. The four engines roared and there was no sound insulation to protect our ears. The airplane shuddered against the set brakes. Then the pilot released them at full throttle and we shot down the runway feeling every bump of the tires in the ruts of the dirt strip. We were in the air, and the four-inch strap across my chest stretched and bowed in the middle against the combined weight of eight straining soldiers. The air-conditioning came on and turned the humid atmosphere trapped inside from the ground into a thick, welcome, cool cloud. The sudden fog was so dense that I could no longer see more than a few rows. It was heaven. We only went eighty miles, to Bien Hoa air base in the interior, no more than thirty miles north of Saigon, the capital. The pilot greased it in and taxied to a metal-mesh hardstand.

The troops dragged themselves and their belongings onto the sun-baked apron. There, to my surprise, sat more dump trucks. The officers took seats in the cabs. I sat next to the driver, whose uniform was the same color as the dirt along the road. My perch gave me a commanding view of the Third World country. The French had built the air base and the road after WWII and no improvements seemed to have been made since. The village outside the fence was larger than I had expected and must have housed ten thousand people. No building was higher than two stories, and most had large wide open windows with no glass. Wooden shutters of bright colors were pinned back; they were closed only during the rainy season. The ground floors were all the same, open wall to wall into a general living area with a kitchen in the rear. Wooden or metal furniture sat on concrete floors, and as a rule a low wooden bed frame, large enough for two or more, was shoved into the corner. There was no box spring or mattress, just a wooden pallet. In the dirt between the road and the house, thin, small, dark-skinned people of all ages squatted, clad in the lightest of clothing. They were clean and interested in our passage through their world. We must have looked like aliens.

We were soon driving out in the jungle, yet no one seemed concerned about our safety. "Are there any Viet Cong around here?" I tried to make it sound like idle talk.

The driver's eyes never left the road. "Last week one of our guys hit a mine on this stretch, but we haven't been ambushed in a month or more, sir." He was totally unconcerned as we bounced along, eating dust.

Thirty minutes later we turned onto a sand track that led up a hill. The limp, dark green jungle opened up suddenly and we were at the top of a conical dome as big as a football field, with one large mahogany tree a little off center. We were literally dumped there, and the trucks departed. The same engineers who had brought us had scraped away the other trees and scrub and piled it all in a great tangled berm that circled this, our base camp. We had no water, no shade, and no neighbors.

The colonel claimed the tree and set up his tent and headquarters under it. The five six-man tents that we had dragged from the ship fitted his staff and served as the focal point for the battalion. He turned the establishment of the camp over to the adjutant. Capt. Redford L. Hammer, a favorite of the colonel's, was a genius, but his reputation was based solely on his high position in the graduating class of West Point of 1960. It was clear that his potential was to be realized during this campaign, he assured us all. Since my source of commission was Marquette University, I believed him. I remained the commander of the headquarters company until the real one arrived from his exile in Hawaii. Captain Hammer told me to set my tent on the base point, which he marked with the heel of his boot. "All other pup tents will dress and cover on it," he announced. A pup tent is a two-man shelter made up of two eight-by-six-foot pieces of waterproof dark green material that snap together and are raised into a peak by tent poles that come in sections. The sides are spread out and pinned down. After being propped up with the poles to a three-foot ridge, both ends are left open. My company area's fifty-three tents were set in place from mine in two perfectly straight lines, with an open lane down the center called the company street. Each tent was so close to its neighbor that the tent pegs interlocked. To the west, across the top of the hill, the other companies continued the construction until all four hundred were in a tight rectangle of corrugated olive-drab spikes. It was a great setup for Fort Dix, New Jersey, but had no place in a combat zone. One enemy mortar round anywhere would maximize its killing power. Disregarding our protests, the adjutant was proud of its symmetry and the powers above agreed. "Well done, Redford," our executive officer, Major Marks, said.

The perimeter defenses were dug in and sandbag filling became everyone's priority. A mess tent fly, the invention of Captain Hammer, went up across from my area. A beam was set on two ten-foot uprights, then a large canopy was stretched across and staked down tight enough to hold the ridgepole in place. The cooks got busy fixing a B ration meal: canned weenies and fried potatoes for eight hundred served with grape Kool-Aid warmed by the sun. The dehydrated potatoes came in large plastic bags and had to be soaked in water for twenty-four hours, but six would be enough according to the mess steward. Frying was no substitute for following directions, and the potatoes were as crunchy as plastic poker chips and had about the same flavor.

During the night we had our first experience of the rains common to Southeast Asia. I was lucky; the other half of my tent came from the chaplain, who had been invited to share the battalion commander's roomy quarters. Lying on my air mattress with my raincoat covering the windward opening above my head, I was snug. The rain hammered without letup and a river formed down the middle of my dirt floor. It ran and swelled until I felt movement, just a little at first and then, with a rush, I was buoyant and moved quite quickly out the other end of my tent and into the company street. I was not alone at midstream; my neighbors were there as well. Clad in shorts and combat boots—we slept with them on—we chased each other into the mess tent. As we organized in the dark, a great gust of wind inflated the canopy and, with the tension released, the large heavy ridgepole fell to one side. We looked up in disbelief as the sodden canvas roof settled gently on our heads.

In the morning things looked no better. It heated up rapidly and I experienced Kipling's "thunder in the sun." Our uniforms were designed for warfare in Central Europe. Vietnam had come on too quickly, and the "jungle fatigues" that became so popular were only in the hands of line infantry units. Our work clothing had become recruiting poster material because we were tailored down to skintightness. In order to roll up my sleeves I had to cut the seam free to just above the elbow and roll it to the middle of my biceps. The pants were just as tight but nothing could be done with them. On the olive drab fatigues, all our markings were in bright colors, just the thing for a parade. In Vietnam they were target material. First things first, though—latrines had to be dug. The conventional slit trench and piss tubes went into construction; sanitation is the most important part of field living. Our slit trench was a World War I design which called for a ditch to be dug a least two feet deep and twenty yards long with the spoil of dirt piled to the side. As the troops deposited feces they were to throw a shovel of dirt in, and as the trench filled to a depth of one foot it was to be completely covered and a new trench inaugurated. In our more modern version, diesel fuel was poured in daily and set alight. The smell was overwhelming if the wind was in the wrong direction, and a light stench always hovered over the home of American soldiers. Piss tubes were made of any piece of pipe at least four inches in diameter. A three-foot pit was dug and the pipe inserted at a sixty-degree angle, leaving about three feet sticking out of the ground. The pit was then backfilled with loose material like small stones or very light sand. These also smelled, but only within twenty feet. Both "conveniences" were outside the living area and quite near the perimeter defense. The big advantage to the stench was that it made them easy to locate in the dark.

Major Marks thought of himself as a field soldier, and in an effort to please his boss he constructed on one side of the camp an open-pit latrine of his own design that was exclusively for officers of the battalion staff. Rather than a long, thin trench that had to be straddled, his was a very deep square hole, six-by-six. Over it was built a wooden open-bottomed box with an appropriate hole in the top cover to accommodate users and a regular stateside toilet seat he had brought with him from his home at Fort Eustis. The box was surrounded by a plywood screen and had a front door with a half moon painted in OD truck-touchup paint. The whole outhouse, attached to two running boards ten feet long that spanned the pit, could be picked up and moved off the hole when it was burned every day. It was magnificent and the colonel said, "Well done, Major Marks; that's the kind of initiative I am looking for."

That evening the major obeyed the call of nature close to midnight. The camp was completely dark to prevent snipers from finding a target. Marks's night vision was not working because of the bright light cast by his Coleman lantern that had also come with him from the States. He marched straight into the bear pit. The entire camp was alerted by the battalion's deputy commander yelling from the bottom of the unburned pit, which had been very popular after dark with folks who were, indeed, not from the staff.

His cleanup was the topic of discussion the next morning at the headquarters briefing. When it was his turn to speak, he directed that white engineer tape be placed on pickets three feet high around all latrines. By nightfall he had inspected and insured that the telltale cloth tape was in place and could easily be seen. Around midnight the major repeated the journey to the little house on the prairie, as it was known by the troops. He confidently followed the strand of white cloth tape; pleased with his innovation, he even thought of writing it up for the lessons-learned bulletin. He was at full stride when the tape suddenly ended and he fell headfirst into his own invention a second time.

Unfortunately, the shit-burning detail had been running late that day and did not get to his special facility until well after dark. Because it was the *staff* latrine, they had been directed by the major to add sufficient fuel to burn the contents completely. The detail, with a reputation to uphold, doubled the amount of diesel, then topped it off with their own innovation, twenty gallons of gasoline. They lit a roll of toilet paper and threw it in from a distance. The flash, spectacular to even the untrained eye, was brilliant and, in the mild explosion, took the white tape on the edge of the pit with it.

The next night we received machine-gun fire that skipped along our northern flank. The entire camp panicked and opened up in all directions from the numerous bunkers around our perimeter. The remaining seven hundred, those not in bunkers, crawled into the company streets with unloaded rifles and began to call for ammunition. Our adjutant had directed that each company's supply be kept in a small sandbagged bunker at the top of each street, near the company commander's tent. The rifle bullets were in wooden cases, each of which contained two steel boxes sealed with a metal strip that required a key to open, like on a can of sardines. Loose cartridges were within. We had begged that the ammo be unpacked, loaded into magazines, and placed in the bunker for ease of distribution. The request was denied by our resident genius on the grounds that it was too dangerous to have it so readily available to troops who might steal it and hide it away for their own protection! His logic was lost on us, but it fit the Stateside rifle-range mentality. So there we were, in the pitch darkness, breaking open boxes and passing out handsful of bullets to figures who crawled by and grabbed. The shooting continued until dawn, every man prone on the perimeter and firing at anything and nothing. By dawn we had fired up our battalion basic load of nearly fifty thousand rounds, with not a single kill recorded. In fact, the original machine-gun fire had come from an American quartermaster outfit camped on the main road and, on hearing sounds from our unit a few hundred yards to the south, had fired at us in mistaken self-defense.

I was saved from the brilliant defensive planning of the adjutant the following day by two events. The first was the arrival of the missing advance party, fresh from its holiday in Hawaii. My company commander was one of them and he relieved me of command. I returned to being the platoon leader of the combat photographers. The second was an audience with Lieutenant Colonel Snead. He had returned from a short trip to Saigon and brought with him Maj. Malcolm Edgerton, the MACV—Military Assistance Command, Vietnam—pictorial officer. Major Mac, as he liked to be called, was a real soldier. He had learned the trade in WWII as an enlisted man and became an officer, on the field, in Korea. A big curly-haired man once known for his red hair, he was, when I met him, decidedly gray. Friendly and forthright, he spoke at ease with everyone, both above and below in rank. He wore a combat infantry badge that had been won long ago but still demanded respect. He was as happy to see us as we were to see him because the only other photo troops were the nine assigned to each division, who could not be touched for jobs outside their units. However, plenty of war was happening outside these units and it was going unrecorded, and the few guys inside the divisions were overwhelmed and needed reinforcement. My forty enlisted and four officers were badly needed, and he had an order detaching us from the 69th Signal Battalion for movement into the fray. We all left that afternoon for Saigon to expand his little photo laboratory. We never looked back.

That evening he spelled out the problem. He suggested that the platoon split up. One officer to the north with the 1st Cavalry Division, one to the south to support the American military advisers with the Army of the Republic of Vietnam, "the ARVN," and one to the 173d Airborne Infantry Brigade, which had no photo support but was involved in the bulk of the fighting then going on. I jumped at the opportunity to go back to the paratroopers. It was the perfect fit as well since I was the only airborne-qualified officer who was a combat photographer. The paratroopers were the elite of the infantry and did not like to have "legs," nonparatroopers, in their midst. Of course, I didn't object to jump status, which meant an extra $110 per month on top of the combat pay of $58 that every soldier in country received. With those additional funds, my wife and three sons could keep my entire regular monthly pay of $390 to live on back home in Illinois. It turned out that my needs were so few, I saved over $1,500 during my twelve-month tour.

The following day I left for Binh Hua, home of the 173d, with my own jeep and two trucks containing ten soldiers and all the photo equipment we could carry.

We drove back past the 69th compound, this time in comfort. My instructions were to go to the brigade headquarters and sign in as their new organic combat photographer. They of course were not expecting us, but that was my problem. The old air base built in French colonial times was substantial, similar in style to old California, but with a twist. The base was larger than the town. The buildings were light brown stucco and had tin roofs streaked black from rusted nail heads. The structures had not been cared for and were crumbling around the edges. Most had high ceilings and heavy brass fans that hung a few feet over our heads. The fans were rarely turned off and circulated the air and the dust equally.

The US Air Force shared the facilities with the Vietnamese Air Force, VNAF. The base was large because it also housed the families of our comrades in long low structures that must once have been warehouses for a very big French force.

The USAF took up residence between the permanent buildings and the airfield itself and built twenty-by-forty-foot wood-frame skeletons with corrugated tin roofs and screened-in sides. To that they added sandbagged sidewalls three feet high, enough for protection but still open to circulation. At least one hundred of these structures stretched alongside the ten-thousand-foot-long runway.

There was no evidence of the Army, and I stopped my little convoy in front of the operations building, puzzled by the lack of a mix of Army and Air Force on the rutted streets. "They are our protection, so you will find them on the perimeter, not on the main base," the American air force sergeant manning the counter told me. On the back of a flight plan form, he drew a map that took me back nearly to the front gate. Once there I followed his thin uninterrupted line around the end of the runway and across a swamp to a crude arch that I am sure must have once read HOME OF THE FRENCH FOREIGN LEGION. Now it held a newly painted red, white, and blue three-foot-high representation of the 173d's shoulder patch. Across the top was a tab that read AIRBORNE, an honor held by all paratrooper units. The body of the patch was a single white wing grasping a bloodred bayonet on a blue field. The 173d had not been in existence more than five years; before that it had belonged to the 25th Infantry Division, old Tropic Lightning, which was always at home in Hawaii. Now a "separate" brigade, the 173d was an experiment in the use of lighter forces which would prove to be very successful and spawn many others that would go on throughout the army in other campaigns. They had come from Okinawa as the first regular unit to be assigned to Vietnam, and so under their sign were the words FIRST IN. It was also the only American paratrooper unit in the country, and billets were sought in it by every ambitious officer with a career in mind.

There were only two Signal officer positions in the brigade and mine would be the third. She was an infantry brigade with two battalions, the 1st and 2d, and one artillery battalion. There were also an armor company, a cavalry troop, and an aviation company from the 82d Airborne Division (the bulk of which was still in the States). It was an international outfit because of the attachment of one infantry battalion of the Royal Australian Regiment, RAR, and a battery of New Zealand guns with its own aviation section of helicopters. An American support battalion brought trucks, riggers, supply, maintenance, and medics. An engineer company, Signal platoon, and headquarters company rounded out the force, making it self-sufficient. Everything was in tents of all sizes that had wooden floors of mahogany planks three inches thick. The tents had lost their dark olive color to the red of the dirt that covered everything, including the troops.

I stepped into the tent immediately behind the flagpole and announced our arrival to the sergeant at his field table, who was working on papers covered with orange-stained fingerprints. In his green T-shirt soaked in sweat, he didn't look like a proud paratrooper. "Beats me where you should report your arrival to, Lieutenant; everyone is gone on operations in the jungle." We agreed that the headquarters company would be a good start and since he was a part of it, he directed me down the main camp road, a hundred yards away to his own home.

The headquarters company commander was more receptive. He installed my people into a tent that would be both our workshop and barracks. He added me to a BOQ (bachelor officers' quarters) tent across the company street and I met my new roommates, who were on special duties.

The unit came out of the field the next day to refit and I was directed to the public information officer (PIO) for assignment. With his staff of four writers, he was housed next to the commanding general's quarters by the flagpole and had some space left over for visiting press. He was very happy to have us since he had no photo support at all. It was his job to portray the brigade activities to the outside world with a positive face and to record its glories. His name was George Washington Samson, the first black major I had ever met. He was perfect for the job, ebullient and the picture of a professional soldier. He smiled constantly. It was nice to work with a man who loved his work and knew that he was in the best unit in the whole country. "Any of my friends would give his left arm to be in my job," he said of all those who, in actuality, would kill for such an assignment. I knew just what he meant; my old friends would envy me, if it weren't for the possibility of my being killed or going missing in action. But we in the brigade weren't going to be killed; someone else might be, but not us. What drove us was the pure adventure of it all, and there it was at last, all around me, and I was overwhelmed to be a member. My only concern was that I not disgrace myself but become one of the brotherhood, a combat veteran of a very famous unit and become a part of its history. I would watch my step and do as they did, talk as they did, and succeed in my job as they did.

"Where did you get a name like that" soon became a topic. George practiced the pronunciation since he would be my sponsor and would have to introduce me time and again.

Mounting our first operation was a joy. According to the briefing given the previous night, it was to be an effort to secure the area around the village of Vo Dat sixty miles north, and enable the people to harvest their rice and get it to market before the Viet Cong could steal it for their army. The three battalions would be lifted in by helicopter and the rest of the brigade would come in by road. I spread out my cameramen in pairs of still and motion picture specialists among the formations.

I would go alone with Alpha Company, 2d Battalion, 503d Airborne infantry. They were a descendant of the 503d Parachute Regiment, "The Rock," which had jumped on Corregidor in WWII. I was to ride into my first battle in a UH-1A "Huey" helicopter with 1st Lt. Ramsey Connally and five other infantrymen. At the "snake pit," our loading ramp on the airfield, I was struck by the youth of the soldiers. In the movies, veteran infantry are rough, heavy-handed men who look at you through eyes that have seen great hardship that has turned them into demons themselves. As a rule they range from twenty-five to forty and look like film stars from start to finish. But I found that war and Hollywood have nothing in common. These were boys, just like my photographers, trying to survive and depending utterly on themselves and those around them to get the job done. They were not distrustful of their officers nor did they speak to them with hatred thinly masked in clever dialogue. We were all in it together, and it might take all of us to get each other back home safely.

I took their pictures as they relaxed on the hot steel-mesh pad, and they asked whether they could get a copy of my stuff after the operation or if it was forbidden to give up the images. They wanted to know if my pictures would be in the newspapers and joked about each other's ugly faces. They liked the idea of having their actions preserved by army photographers, soldiers like them, rather than newsmen, whom they distrusted. One youth confided in me, "I have seen those news guys before, they don't last long, one operation and they are gone, they can't take it. How long are you going to stay, Lieutenant?"

"One year, if this lasts that long," I replied, looking him

in the eye. I kept a slight grin on my old face. I was twenty-five and, in his eyes, well beyond his generation.

Before we took off I saw to it that my boys spread out among the waiting small groups and, once I had made a place for myself, walked around to see that they had received the same friendly reception. We went over the mission briefly and I reminded them not to try to take the "flag going up on Iwo Jima" again, but to take care of themselves and photograph faces, not explosions.

Suddenly the choppers began to crank up and I ran to my ride and jumped in. Once airborne, I was cool for the first time since the C-130 ride; the chopper had no doors and we were at six thousand feet, out of the range of small arms. I was in the middle of the wide seat against the firewall, with my back to the noisy engine. Next to me was Ramsey, who, recalling his own first operation, I am sure, was enjoying having a new guy tight beside him. Before long we began a rapid descent into an open area that I could see just ahead through the windshield, between the pilots. I heard two snaps behind my head and thought that the engine was making a funny sound. "What was that?" I shouted into Ram's ear, which was mostly hidden by his helmet.

"We just took a couple of rounds in the floor. It is going to be a hot landing zone." We had all heard it, but as a new guy I was the only one to record it. We touched down in a long line of ships and the first of our bunch was out before we settled. I was close behind the lieutenant and stuck there as we ran for the tree line. I thought of my advice to "take faces." I saw nothing but backs and my only thought was, don't get separated. There was plenty of rifle fire ahead of me and I had never run before half bent over at the waist, intent on keeping my balance. I shot a picture or two because the camera was in my hand and my .45 was in its holster, where it belonged. Those guys didn't need my added firepower. I didn't see much anyway except the figures to my front, waist-deep in grass, bobbing along at a pace a little faster than my own. When a man or two passed me, I felt a little more secure that I was in a bunch and not at the tail end.

There were 120 men in the lift, and I was just beginning to realize that we were in with the company headquarters as the company commander put his hand on my shoulder and pulled me his way. We settled into the wood and for the next twenty minutes organized into a cohesive fighting force. I was given a minute of the commander's precious time and told to stick close to his radio operator, the RTO, who was never farther than an arm's length from his captain, B. J. Lock. Grateful for his recognition, I did as I was told and contented myself with taking pictures of the goings-on in the small command group of five or six. The enemy melted away and we walked the low dirt dikes between the rice paddies for the next hour or two. In the open, I stopped momentarily and snapped away; I was a real combat photographer now.

After a couple of days I joined the brigade headquarters on the edge of a jungle-dirt airfield. It was Thanksgiving. The holiday was going to be celebrated briefly with a turkey dinner flown in from base camp at Binh Hua in marmite cans, French inventions from the Great War that kept hot food hot. It was our first hot food in about a week. I was living in a four-man tent with the PIO and two civilian reporters. One had come for the meal and would leave after chow with his human interest story, and the other was a veteran foreign reporter from Holland who had been in Southeast Asia for twenty years or more. Hans Grubber was internationally known and syndicated around the world. Wise in the ways of war, he always slept with his dirty boots on and his head resting on an inflatable pillow. Little impressed him, least of all me, so I was not afraid to ask silly questions. He said, "No one wins a war like this, but that won't stop you Americans from trying."

"Hans, how will it all end, with another Korean stalemate, and an American occupation for years to come?" I asked, hoping to hear that this was a possibility.

"I don't know. I doubt it; this is not a case of history repeating itself. You Americans like to wage war on other people's soil. You are a very dangerous people; you say one thing and do another. You are hard to predict. I predict that we are going to have a very good meal."

Around midday the food was set up on portable field tables, one large steaming can of hot food after another for twenty yards. In the headquarters the enlisted ate first and the officers followed with paper plates in hand. The well-known metal mess kit was not used there in the tropical heat since it couldn't be kept clean and was bound to cause disease. That meal we had it all, and I took pictures of the troops in line picking up one of everything. It rained so hard that even my still pictures showed straight traces of raindrops as they beat past the lens and mixed the mashed potatoes and gravy with the yellow corn and cranberries. I picked up my feast and walked to my tent down by the edge of the river that had been our airfield. By the time I sat down to eat, the rain had cooled it all to tent temperature. Like everyone else, I ate and thought of home.

To my surprise, General Westmoreland, the commander in chief of MACV, dropped by in a helicopter that had more antennas than machine guns. He was warmly greeted with a double hand clasp by Brigadier General Williamson, our commanding general. The helipad, once a green rice paddy, was at the time just stubble after the harvest, and they route-stepped to the briefing tent. There was great excitement to have the famous man with us on the holiday and the brigade staff shuffled around him with happy greetings. He was well-known, personally in fact, by most of them. He had a fondness for the 173d because he had commanded a similar unit, the 187th Regimental Combat Team, during the Korean campaign. He was also a paratrooper and had served with many in the brigade and may have been instrumental in assigning his fellow diners to their positions.

Though I had never seen him before, his face was familiar to me from television. He was even more distinguished in person, and I followed him as he passed among the enlisted soldiers and spoke of the holiday in fatherly tones. He was tall, a good six feet, and thin, with white hair that although short, showed below his hat. It had four stars and master parachute wings embroidered above the visor. In a deep voice that reflected great strength, General Westmoreland spoke directly to each man as if he were the only person there. He asked about the new M-16 rifle and solicited their honest appraisal of its performance in their hands. The press had been full of criticism because of problems the Marine Corps had had with it in the far north of the country. The paratroopers, the only ones in the Army at that time to be issued the new Colt weapon, said they loved it. Our G-2, the brigade intelligence officer, showed the general a captured report that read, "Stay away from the soldiers that carry the little black rifle." The M-16 was much smaller than the standard M-14, weighed half as much, and fired an elongated .22-caliber bullet that was much lighter and allowed the troops to carry more ammunition. "The Marines complain; they say it jams," the general said, hoping to hear our secret to good M-16 operation.

"Here is the answer to that one, sir." A sergeant held up a soap-colored plastic bottle, no more than four inches high, to Westmoreland's view. It was a container of Shake Well, so called because it bore no product name and the only thing printed on the container was "Shake Well."

"Tell those undisciplined Marines to keep the piece clean and use plenty of this," a captain in the background offered.

Westy smiled, his trip a success; he always learned something by going into the field and talking to the soldiers. "I knew I could depend on the Airborne to solve my problems," he confided to Williamson.

I took many pictures. I knew that the soldiers would like to have shots of themselves to send home. As Westmoreland left I saw my chance to take one for our commander, and I followed them toward the helipad as they strolled alone. I ran around the edge of the clearing to get in front of them and still stay some thirty yards away and rather inconspicuous. I temporarily lost sight of them, but picked them up again once I was in position to get a shot of their faces in intimate conversation. It was a perfect setup as they stood talking side by side and didn't move for several minutes. No one else was near, and the waiting helicopter sat clearly in the background, setting the scene. It was important that the surroundings look like Vietnam or the picture would lose its identity and look like it could have been taken anywhere. A few weeks later, back in the laboratory I had set up in Saigon, I stood in the darkroom and watched one of my technicians contact print my first rolls of film. It was all okay. I took the contact sheets with the filmstrip images no larger than the 35mm film itself, and with magnifying glass in hand and a red grease pencil circled the shots for printing that were in focus and had a content that merited transformation into an eight-by-ten glossy print. I remembered the last Westmoreland photo and hoped that it would be good enough to frame and present to my commanding general. There it was, and I put the magnifier over it in great anticipation. It was as clear as a bell and plainly showed the famous four-star standing with the Boss in conversation—as General Westmoreland stood directly in front of a piss tube and relieved himself.

I clipped the tiny print from the page of other miniatures, then went directly to the negative strip in the lab and did the same. "Anything come out, Lieutenant?" my lab technician asked, thinking that perhaps my first few weeks as a professional photographer might have been fruitless.

"Great stuff, all of it," I lied. The scissors destroyed the evidence of my massive indiscretion and until now no one ever heard of the faux pas. There was, however, one photo in the bunch that did rather well in years to come. I was sitting on the edge of a bomb crater made by a thousand pounder dropped from a B-52 and had taken several pictures of a soldier standing at the bottom when I realized that I had only one frame left on the roll. We had just completed a four-thousand-meter walk in the woods and the men of the infantry company were picking up their rations for the night and filing past me on their way to their night positions. I watched the tired and dejected line of men who seemed to be pitying themselves, when two black soldiers came plodding on, right at me. The leader was tall and wore multiple belts of machine gun bullets draped over each shoulder like Pancho Villa in a helmet. A pump shotgun in his left hand hung straight from the weight, and grenades were fixed to his belt. His uniform was curled from the heat and humidity and from being soaked through with sweat. His head was up and his eyes fixed in the distance, even though there was nothing but more jungle to look at. Two steps behind was his buddy, also black and half his size, and dressed nearly identically with the exception of the towel swinging from around his neck and the pack in his left hand. Though there was no war going on at that moment, there was no doubt that these two were warriors. The leader was stoic but the follower provided constant commentary, his mouth wide open below the sunglasses stuck to his face under a clearly too large steel helmet. Even though it was a still picture with no sound accompaniment, his shrill voice could be heard. To me they looked just like Brer Bear and Brer Rabbit from the *Song of the South,* discussing the briar patch in long verse. I took the picture and put a new roll in its place. That picture was printed and, I am told, General Westmoreland selected it for his office. It also appeared some years later in the *Pictorial History of the United States Army.*

It immediately became apparent to all of the platoon that our German Leica cameras and the super speed Graphflex's would not survive the moisture and dust of Vietnam, and most already needed repair. My platoon sergeant, L. Z. Whitley, perhaps the best leader I have ever known, came up with a solution. Go to the PX and buy a Nikon Nikonos underwater skin divers' 35mm camera. The Nikonos was made of heavy steel and had a wide-angle lens designed for close-up work that was perfect in the jungle, where we could never see more than thirty feet. Several of us bought them and never looked back. Old L.Z., and I called him that because he had nearly twenty years in the Army and a son in college, was a master at handling officers, lieutenants in particular. If I ever forgot the troops, he would remind me that they were the most important thing. "Without these troops, what have you got, sir?" would always bring me back to reality. Without them, all I had was a mission with no one to accomplish it. "Take care of the men and they will take care of the mission" only had to be said to me once. He was always respectful. He believed in officers and it was part of his job to train them. He hadn't been promoted in years, but during his time there finally made another stripe. I was proud of that black hero.

Back out on operations I attached myself to C Company, and shortly after landing on an air assault in a wide open, dry rice field, I fell in with the company mortar platoon and began a long walk into the jungle. We were strung out in a hot column on a search and destroy mission. That meant that we didn't know what to expect, but that someone, somewhere had looked at a map and said, "If I were Charlie, I would be there." Well, we were "there," but no one else was. I had never taken pictures of the mortars in action, but I hoped they might get the opportunity to do a little shooting.

When we took a little sniper fire up in front, the guns were set up just in case. The platoon leader came running back from his post with the company commander and said,

"We have a mission." The platoon routine was like clockwork, and in a minute or so they were in action. I closed in on the lieutenant and his map board for a shot of the action with his chief gunner. It was Lt. Paul Rob, my instructor from the paratrooper jump school and fellow member of the 44th Airborne Ranger Battalion back at Fort Benning. The reunion was quick and I moved back and took some pictures. What a treat it was to meet a friend so far from home.

Things were getting a little hotter up in front and, after taking a dozen shots, I decided to go forward. I was about fifty yards away when the enemy dropped several 60mm mortar rounds of their own nearby, and the noise of the explosions scared me to the ground, where I stayed until they let up. I went back to the scene of the impact but couldn't find the platoon leader in the confusion as the guns were being picked up and moved. The platoon sergeant called for me to join him and when I arrived I found him over what remained of Paul. The sergeant was bleeding or had Paul's blood on him. He stared at me and said, "It hit his helmet and glanced off just as it exploded. I know I saw it, but I don't believe it." The fury of the direct hit had destroyed my friend completely. I lost my breath. I could not recognize him and had to hold his image in my mind for a moment. There is no stopping war, but for me and the sergeant, we ignored our surroundings and gathered our comrade's remains for movement to the rear.

I had a motion picture guy with me on that mission and he was having trouble with the light. Our motion picture camera was a WWII hand-wound IMO that shot 35mm Ektachrome negative film. The film was for use on a lit soundstage, and the low light common in dense jungle put it right on the edge of usability. The film came to us in thousand-foot rolls but the camera could only accommodate hundred-foot spools. That meant that the cameraman had to use a changing bag to cut it into hundred-foot lengths and roll it onto the spools. He did that back at base camp before each operation. The bag was black cloth with two hand holes, and he did it all like black magic, as if he were going to pull a rabbit out at the end of the act. It takes thirty-three seconds to shoot one hundred feet of film, and he was always changing rolls at the worst possible time. "That is how we did it when I was at Bastogne," my major in Saigon told me. That didn't help.

It turned into quite a fight, and by midday we were calling for an Air Force air strike. A forward air controller in a box kite, something like a Cessna 150 painted silver and armed with only four spotting rockets on the wingtips, came in at one thousand feet and one hundred miles per hour. But he had some big brothers with him, five miles behind and at five thousand feet. He directed an attack of four Skyraiders, Korean War–era prop planes, to dump where the company commander requested. That did it, and all we had to do was move on. The sight of that silver bird so free of the jungle's grip made me vow to find that guy and ride above it all on the next operation. Two nights later, at the evening briefing in our forward headquarters, I spotted an Air Force major and introduced myself.

"Where did you get a foreign name like that, are you an American?" he asked in all seriousness.

"How would you like some bomb damage assessment pictures of all that hard work you are doing, sir?" I countered.

"Sure, you want a ride?"

That is how I met Harvey Crow, the friendly ALO. ALOs—air liaison officers—were attached to ground combat units to coordinate airpower in support of the guys on the ground. Harvey was bigger than I and had a full head of snow-white hair. He had been an ace during the Korean War, shooting down a lot of bandits with courage and precision. Even though the Air Force had its own combat photographers they were few in number, and he was a long way out from his air base home at Bien Hoa.

The next morning I met him alongside a small dirt airstrip after he had made a short trip to Bien Hoa for gas and rockets. We went in to see the brigade G-3 (the operations officer), an Australian infantry major. The two were pals and joked constantly while business was conducted. The Aussie was bigger than Crow and sported long, dark, wavy brown hair that had a bit of red. The length of hair and the unusual cut of his neat uniform made him stand out in the TOC (tactical operations center). In combat, the operations officer in the brigade is the key job, one sought after by all field grade (major, lieutenant colonel, colonel) officers. Giving it to the Australian was a vote of confidence in that nation's military profession. Our ally was experienced in jungle fighting and counterinsurgency. The Australians taught us a great deal, and we relied heavily on their combat troops who fought alongside our units. The difference in speech was a bit of a problem since we were divided by a common language. But those two had no problem communicating. So, armed with a bagful of maps marked with red circles, Harvey and I headed for his flimsy airplane. "I will preflight and you get into this." He threw me a fireproof Air Force flight suit with the shoulder patch of the 1st Air Commando Squadron on the right shoulder. "You can't fly in your fatigues; they aren't safe." Of course, judging from the frail appearance of the airplane, the clothing wasn't going to help much. In that plane the two seats were one behind the other and I climbed in the back. "I took the stick out so it wouldn't get in your way. Besides, if I get killed you wouldn't want to survive the crash out here in bad guy country," he confided. I would not let myself think of that possibility.

The plane had no windowpanes so I had a great view as we spun off the ground and out over the uninterrupted dark canopy. In minutes we were on station and he was calling into the radio, reporting our position, and looking for his helpers. "There they are." He directed my eyes into the bright blue sky at four black dots well above us. We flew in lazy circles, always looking down in search of movement. He spotted some friendly units and linked up with the infantry by radio. I didn't see anything, even when he pointed it out, but said, "Roger, I got 'em." I was feeling out of place, an occupational hazard for a photographer.

When we got the call, Major Crow was all business. No words were wasted and there was no time for chitchat with me. He tipped the nose of the little plane over and pointed it at some spot in the trees that looked like every other spot in the woods. He fired the first of the four white phosphorus marking rockets that went off the wingtip with little sound but left a thin trail of light-gray smoke. A blind man could see where they pointed and we pulled up and around, clearing the path for the mighty Skyraiders.

Those dots became full-fledged fighter-bombers and came in beside us one after the other, dropping cluster bombs on the enemy which went off like hundreds of flashbulbs. "Did you get it?" Harvey said, directing his commentary to me for the first time since the chaos began.

"I got it, any more coming our way?" I said into the microphone pressed against my lips.

"Plenty, Fitz," came the cheery reply into my aviation helmet.

He took me home to Bien Hoa. "We will spend the night there and the Air Force will develop the pictures." My last landing at the air base had been unsighted as I was in the bowels of the C-130 a month before. It was a huge complex and the airfield looked like one in the States, the field littered with high-performance jet fighters. After doing a victory roll over the active runway, the Skyraiders we had been playing with landed ahead of us. As jaded as airmen become, they always stop and watch landing aircraft; it's in the blood. "When I tell you, throw out that bundle behind you," Harvey said to me over the intercom. As soon as our landing gear hit the concrete toward the middle of the long runway, I pitched the heavy bag out the side window. It was a drag chute from an F-100 jet fighter that he had rigged to our tail with a forty-foot line. The canopy ripped out of its covering and billowed forth. A parachute like that would slow an F-100 in just enough time to keep it from going off the end of the strip; attached to our OV-1 Bird Dog, the chute stopped us dead in our tracks in front of the tower. The tower operator came on the radio and said, "It must be Harvey Crow, the friendly ALO."

After that I did quite a bit of flying as an aerial observer and branched out into Army helicopters on reconnaissance missions. The result was that I spent many evenings developing pictures, and it became obvious that I needed my own laboratory either at the air base or in Saigon. My platoon sergeant began to gather parts and so fell in with "the procurement squad," an ad hoc group of specialists, excess to the brigade's combat needs but essential to its day-to-day operation. The 173d had left its home station in Okinawa for a ninety-day "temporary" contingency assignment which had been extended time and again. They left all the big stuff behind—that is, anything bigger than a typewriter, and there were only a handful of those to start with. The band of procurement specialists roamed around the country and picked up things necessary for operations or the comfort of the troops while in the base camp area. A very efficient crew, they operated by day and, especially, by night, and often found items before they were reported lost. They thought of themselves as home builders and their motto was, "It don't mean nothing; it's all OD." Loosely translated the expression meant that everything was US Government–owned and it was immaterial who actually had control of an item at the moment. There was give-and-take, however; barter was alive and well. I never heard of money changing hands, and nothing was obtained for the sole use of the procurer; it was done for the overall well-being of the unit.

My platoon had control of one of the most tradable commodities in the country. In Saigon, my headquarters was the sole dispenser of the 16mm motion picture projectors handed out to units with a film account. Troops loved to watch movies from the States in the evening when they were out of the field. There were a limited number of the precious machines and my platoon sergeant let it be known that he had influence. Therefore, with the help of his friends he built a twenty-foot mahogany log tower with three water tanks, old bomb-transport cases, and a steel pipe plumbing system to feed a lab that he installed inside a "liberated" tractor trailer van.

One of the infantry companies needed lights for the tents that the returning field troops occupied after weeks in the jungle. Obtaining the light sets—wire, sockets, and bulbs—was child's play, and they were installed as soon as the large ten-man tents went up over their wooden floors. Tapping into an electrical supply was another matter. Rule number one was that we never found "not lost" goods within the brigade. A scout around in the daylight at the home of a quartermaster unit in Long Binh located a generator mounted on a trailer whose sole use was to provide power for the quartermaster unit's outdoor movie theater. That night, during the showing, our boys backed a small truck up to the generator that had been placed some distance from the field cinema to keep the noise of the machine from drowning out the film. Dressed in a quartermaster shirt, one of the team sat and enjoyed the entertainment with the crowd. When the first reel was about to end, he slipped away to the truck and alerted the driver to start the engine. When the projectionist shut down the projector to change reels, his feeder wires were disconnected at their source and our truck silently pulled away with his trailer following obediently behind. When the supply people attempted to start up the second reel of *Rio Bravo,* there was no joy because there was no generator. The frequent sudden appearance of "out of stock" equipment passed by brigade officers without comment, until one day the commander of the field hospital spoke to our deputy commander about a hospital ward generator that had disappeared on its way to the maintenance shop. That time the boys had gone too far. . . .

One night I was called out of the officers club—a tent with a bar made from artillery ammunition boxes. I met the brigade operations officer and Major Samson in the TOC and they asked me in utmost secrecy if I and one of my men could make a combat parachute jump in the morning and record it on still and motion picture film. I was sure we could and selected our place in the middle of two sticks of jumpers, one in the first plane and one in the second. It was a rare event; there had not been a combat jump since Korea and it was a very small one. All paratroopers dreamed of jumping into combat. Even during WWII there were only a few jumps and they were legendary. Any man who had completed one in combat conditions was authorized to mount a small bronze battle star on his silver jump wings. Only a small part of the brigade was going to make the jump and would be envied by the rest. We had jumped in Vietnam on a regular basis but only into areas that were safe havens. We did that to keep up our proficiency and to qualify for jump pay. For these reasons I had jumped with the ARVN Airborne several times and it was always a kick. The ARVN soldiers were of such small stature that their equipment weighed more than they did. On one such occasion several of the diminutive soldiers opened their chutes and went up instead of down when caught in the hot air rising at midday. I thought we would have to shoot them down like ducks.

I returned to my area and told Sergeant Pellaboy, a Filipino-American motion picture cameraman, to meet me at 0500 in my tent, prepared to go on assignment. I did not dare tell him about the jump for fear that it might leak out. For a parachute jump to be successful and not take a lot of casualties, the enemy must be completely surprised. When we arrived ready to go, my adrenaline pumping, the force was diverted to the helipad and we conducted an air assault via helicopter instead. I was bewildered until we slid into the south of the original area and walked through to the planned drop zone. There I photographed four-foot-high, fire-hardened pungi sticks pointing up at the sky that had been planted all over our landing site. Our combat jump had been canceled when the brigade had learned that newsmen in Saigon had compromised the operation. Though taken into confidence at the MACV briefing, they had spoken openly of the event in the bar of the Imperial Hotel and therefore informed the enemy. The remainder of the brigade might not have known of the jump, but the enemy did! If we had jumped as planned, our men would have been impaled on these skewers like fresh meat.

Out on a jungle airfield one day a Skyraider pilot did a victory roll after a particularly good job in support of the soldiers engaged on the ground, then plunged inverted into the strip, killing himself. An hour or so later an investigation team from his squadron came in to survey the tragedy and I photographed the wreckage. The squadron commander knew of my flights with the ALO and so I hit him up for a mission in one of his A1-Es. "Getting tired of that box kite of Harvey's, Fitz?" He knew I was. I tried to pull the wool over his eyes with a story about what great bomb damage assessment photos I could get if I were in the stick and made a real pass just above the ground. He knew a story when he heard it and said, "I don't believe it, but we owe you a real ride after all that stuff you shot from a thousand feet."

I suited up the next morning in the shed of the 1st Air Commandos. I had been given a proper flight suit and thin, brown fireproof leather gloves by my friendly ALO. The squadron topped that off with a white plastic flying helmet with fluorescent red strips and a seat-pack parachute. I looked the part. God, I loved it! My pilot was Capt. Fred Kubalac, an instructor pilot and the hottest guy around. Even though the plane was set up with side-by-side seating in the cockpit for a pilot and copilot, in Vietnam they used only a pilot. I had never seen the A1 up close, only in the air. When we rolled up in the flight line truck with the other three flyers who would man the stick of four that day, I was amazed at her large size. First employed by the Navy off of carriers in the Korean War and used as a close air support bomber for Marines on the ground, she was special because of the huge load she could carry on the fourteen stations under her broad wings. Her slow speed just fifty feet above the heads of the enemy increased her deadly accuracy. She therefore was armored underneath and had four 20mm cannons in the leading edge of the wings to strafe her way out. The cockpit was made of clear blue plastic and toward the rear was a compartment large enough to accommodate four stretchers. The A1 was the only plane of her day that could fly medical casualties off a carrier. The A1 sat on a tailwheel and was counterbalanced by the biggest four-bladed propeller-driven engine I have ever seen on a single-engine airframe.

It took two giant steps just to get up on the trailing edge of the wing and a walk of five more steps to reach the sidewall of the cockpit. At that point ten feet off the ground, I loaded myself with the help of the crew chief onto the very comfortable seat. Seated on my parachute I was strapped in like a baby in a car seat. I had the chief walk out to the tip of the wing on my side and take my picture to document the experience; no one would ever believe an Army air observer in such glory. In the photo, rather than a combat aviator going into battle, I look like an idiot, with a grin from ear to ear.

"If you have to jump, crawl out on the wing and slide off the back edge. Look out for the tail," Fred told me in all seriousness. I tried to imagine that as we taxied out to the active runway, but thought he must be just trying to have some fun with the new guy.

"Has anyone ever gotten out of one of these and lived?" I asked.

"Not that I know of," he replied over the intercom. He ran the monster up on the runway overrun area with the brakes set, then let her go. "This is the only airplane I know of that takes off at less than full power," my instructor pilot shouted. In the air she was beautiful, no instability as we climbed up to six thousand feet and met up with the wingmen.

"Why only half power on takeoff, Captain?" I inquired.

"If you give her her head, she will roll over from the extraordinary torque of the engine." The other capability that I did not know was that she could fly for four hours without refueling. On a combat mission a jet has about an hour of fuel from start to finish. We went on station at ten thousand feet and waited for a call for help. Our loitering pattern was a long racetrack oval. Then he said what I never expected to hear as I relaxed and thought of my days walking in the jungle below. "You want to fly her, Fitz?" broke my reverie.

"Yes sir, I do." I had never touched the controls of an airplane before and Fred knew it.

"Take the stick and put your feet on the pedals; you've got it." He let go of the controls, then got on the radio to tell the other pilots in the pattern that they were flying with an "army aviator." I heard their half-encouraging words through smiling lips. We spent an hour like that going round and round and even changed altitude. Sweat ran into my gloves and filled them to saturation. This is the only way to learn how to fly, I thought as I kept a death grip on the stick.

We got a call for action, Fred said, "Fun's over," and this ended the free flying lesson. In we went. Fred was all business and I stayed off the intercom, listening to the battle commands. We were number three, and I captured with my camera the two going in below and the one in front as we tailed in behind on our own attack. The pilot's eyes were fixed on the sight mounted on the dashboard in front of him. The cockpit was large enough for me to take his picture when I twisted in my harness. He pickled off the bombs and pulled out from fifty feet, and the g-force shoved me down into my seat like a giant hand. I couldn't move; I don't know how he did. On the fourth pass, just as we pulled out and all I could see was sky, I rotated the camera in my hands upward and put my head down to twist the knobs and change the lens setting. What a mistake. I couldn't resist the g-force, which pushed my head into my lap and hyperextended my neck. When we leveled off I had the worst headache and it nearly blinded me. I didn't tell the pilot.

"Did you get anything on that last one? I hit the target hard," Fred said as he looked over his shoulder at the destroyed jungle bridge.

"No problem, Captain."

That was not my only mistake of the day. On the way home the pilots decided to show the "army" some aerial acrobatics after we took turns flying under each other to check for battle damage. We did it all, chasing each other around the sky with classic fighter moves, the split-S, the roll over, inverted flying, then finished with something called a "hammerhead dive." My mistake was that I had gone to the Air Force officers club for lunch and picked my favorite, Hungarian goulash over rice. It returned with the last spin and I slid back the canopy window on my side and threw up. When I recovered my composure, I turned to the pilot. He was holding a shred of beef between the gloved fingers of his right hand. "You!" he said, nodding toward his hand. The airstream from the open window had not carried it out but around behind my head and his, depositing the lot on the windshield in front of him.

I felt better by the time we landed, but the gravy on the windshield limited his vision and hindered the touchdown. He said it was all his fault, he shouldn't have done that last maneuver. Neither of us believed it but he didn't broadcast my antics to the other pilots. We went to intelligence and debriefed the mission while the Air Force photo lab took my film for printing. At the end of the session the interrogator asked why we didn't report our battle damage. "We did not sustain any," Fred stated with conviction.

"Go check it out," we were told. Back into the truck, we rode out to the parking area as the heat rose up in waves visible to the naked eye. We were exhausted and really wanted the mission to end. I don't think I have ever been that wrung out, and it was a real effort merely to alight from the back of the truck and greet the crew chief who was waiting for us. He led us past the still black prop and under the wingtip, then pointed to several holes near the trailing edge. Fred said, "I did not feel a thing in the controls," and he looked to me for comment. I shrugged. According to the master maintenance technician, there were several more under the belly in the armor plate and a slew in the tail. Captain Kubalac patted the side of the warhorse, looked her in the eye, and said, "Good old girl, I am going to have a drink for you tonight."

I took pictures of her wounds. The crew chief handed me a wet rag and said, "Want to help me clean up the cockpit, Lieutenant?"

"How did you know it was me? I wasn't alone, you know." Fred did the paperwork and I serviced the old lady.

Back in the squadron headquarters the operations officer had my prints, and they were good but the commander did not seem totally pleased. He handed me the picture I had taken of the pilot looking through the bombsight. It was clear and sharp. I looked at him, a question on my face. "Air Force combat pilots don't wear glasses," he assured me. Fred had put his cheaters on before the attack. He handed me another of my photos that showed the captain with a cigarette between his fingers as his hand rested on the console. "Air Force combat fliers don't smoke either." By the time I left Bien Hoa I had logged twenty-five flights.

I have mentioned Sergeant Pellaboy, one of our photographers in a platoon of exceptional men, most of whom were under twenty. But Pell was extraordinary. At paygrade E-5 he was the lowest grade of sergeant and about twenty-five. He had joined the American Army voluntarily upon arrival in the States from Manila and applied for citizenship as soon as he could. He was very talented, and a natural eye for image-making led him to the camera. His looks had always been a handicap in the land of Europeans. He was not tall, just tall enough to get on active duty, about five feet three if he ever stood up straight, which he didn't. His legs were bowed and he looked like a kid from the ghetto who never ate properly. His skin was darker than that of most of his countrymen and his very thick, straight black hair stood straighter than he and sprung out of his helmet when he took it off. His eyes were very dark and appeared sunken by his heavy black eyebrows. His face was small with very high, prominent cheekbones. The dark skin under them was stretched and there was a dimple at the point of his chin. His mouth was rather large with beautiful white teeth that seemed to always be exposed in a grin that showed more pain than happiness. His English was not good and I always thought that I had missed the mark when laying out a mission for him. I would ask repeatedly if he understood and he always said, "Yees Sar," and never asked a question. In fact, he always got it right and even improved upon the original request. I liked to take him with me because I could protect him from marauding NCOs who picked on him because he was a natural target. On one hellacious day of air assaults, strings of helicopters were inserting infantrymen. I put him in the troop-carrying Huey while I lay facedown on the floor of a B-model Huey gunship. We must have hauled eight hundred men into the landing zone during that long morning. The enemy had opposed us from the start. I was feeling proud of myself for the work I had done under fire and thinking what a brave fellow I was. We went in again at two hundred feet and strafed the wood line ahead of the slick troop carriers as they landed in the midst of enemy fire and disgorged their seven combat soldiers each to the fray. Then I saw Pell. He was standing outside the chopper on the fat pipe called a skid, holding on to the inside edge of the open door with one hand and taking pictures with the other. As the empty airship lifted off nose-down, he reversed his stance like a wire walker and shot a picture of the men he had just put on the ground. He was totally exposed and offered himself up for the resulting pictures. That was bravery bordering on intrepidity.

When I saw him that night, I told him not to do that again because "you are too valuable to me."

"Yees Sar" was all he said. He ignored my advice though, I soon found out. An artillery battery commander came to see me at base camp. "Does Sergeant Pellaboy work for you, Fitz?"

"Of course, sir; all the photo guys are in my platoon. Why?"

"You had him with my battery in December when we went into D-zone, where we took a ground attack. The enemy made it as far as the parapet that Pell was photographing."

"I saw the pictures, Captain. They were great, I thought." I was expecting some negative comments and readied my support from Pell's past record.

"That little son of a bitch grabbed a VC by the ears, headbutted him on the nose, and knocked him cold, then he chased two more out of the gun pit. He went after them, and the only way we could stop him was by shooting the fleeing Charlies." My mild little man, who was the brunt of many jokes by the infantry, was magnificent! "I have a citation for him, the Bronze Star with V for valor. See that he gets it. My compliments to Signal Corps."

Some time later we were operating with the 101st Airborne Division, which had joined us with one brigade in the

Parrot's Beak, a hook of land bounded by a curving river that was known to be a large enemy base camp. At the end of the nightly briefing in the TOC, which was unusually crowded due to the presence of representatives from the Screaming Eagles, Pell walked out of the shadows in the back of the large tent to take Polaroids of the day's charts for the record, as he always did. Two 101st military policemen who were guarding the movement of their unit's display boards saw him come rather quickly through the departing crowd and jumped him. His wild little dark form, dressed in a jungle uniform that had no markings on it, caused them to think that he was a Viet Cong. He put up a loud struggle and yelled in such broken English that he sounded like anything other than American. With great difficulty, the Australian major and I rescued him, all of us ending up on the dirt floor.

To jump ahead a little and tell one more Pell story, in spring the brigade stood down for a few days for some rest, and Headquarters/A Company took the time to have an outdoor steak fry and beer-drinking feast. Near the mess hall—a low wooden building with screened sides—was a dirt veranda fifty feet square surrounded by a sandbag wall three feet high. It had been there for eight months and was badly deteriorating. Empty fifty-five gallon oil drums had been cut in half and lined up along the wall and filled with hot coals. Our cooks hovered over them grilling beef and pork. They were made happy to do the hotter-than-hot job for the free beer and the presence of the Red Cross "Donut Dollies" who were our special guests for the day. Sergeant Pellaboy was sitting on the wall minding his own business when a very large, drunken sergeant came at him from behind, spun him around, and hit him in the face, very hard, for no apparent reason. Then the sergeant realized he'd hit the wrong man and picked the little sergeant up. Pell broke from his grip and ran to his tent half a block away. I was summoned to our photo laboratory, which was parked behind the tent, by my platoon sergeant. "He is in the lab and he has his pistol with him, sir," L.Z. said. "He says he will kill anyone who comes in to get him." With that, the affair was put in my hands.

The back of the photo lab's tractor trailer was at least four feet off the ground and a metal ladder was the only way up. A back door was open and inside a maze of plywood partitions separated the darkrooms. There were no lights on. I had watched the scene in the movies: I was his leader and friend, and would go in and take the gun away and see to it that he got the medical treatment he needed. He trusted me. I crawled up onto the back deck in front of the open door and looked back at L.Z. and several of his friends, who lay behind cover on the ground. Clearly they had found a job suitable for the talents of an officer. I tried to remember the words of the actors from any number of films and television shows. "It is okay, Sergeant Pellaboy. It's Lieutenant Fitz. I am coming in," I said in a strong voice. No, I thought, call him Pell, friendly-like, man to man. "Pell, can you hear me?" There was no answer. Perhaps he had passed out. "Are you sure he is in here?" I asked L.Z.

Sp5. Stokes said, "I saw him go in and he never came out, sir."

I pleaded for Pell to come out and assured him that it was all a mistake and that I would protect him. The one-way conversation continued for some time, but I never got a response or heard a sound from inside. "Pell, I am coming in," I said finally as I stood up and stepped into the darkness beyond the door. It *was* just like the movies; a crowd had gathered around the end of the trailer, and I was the hero. One step inside and I heard the unmistakable sound of the steel slide of a .45-caliber pistol slamming forward and chambering a bullet. I backed off. It was no movie. Movies aren't real life and I wanted to live. I jumped off the back of the trailer and said to L.Z., "Get the military police; they are trained to handle this."

We all sensed the danger, highlighted by my rapid departure, and moved back into the tent as a group. While we waited for the MPs, Stokes, the nearest to the laboratory, yelled, "There he goes!" Pell had scampered down the ladder and run in the direction of the jungle. A search of the foliage near the perimeter was fruitless, then darkness fell. In the morning I was awakened by Stokes. "Sir, Sergeant Pellaboy is in his bed, asleep." I went to the barracks and there, on one of the ten cots covered by a mosquito net, was Pell, still in his dirty, wet uniform, sound asleep. "I found his pistol under the bed," L.Z. whispered as he handed me a rusty .45 that was still loaded.

"Wake him up, Sergeant." I was still a little ticked off from his chambering a round in my presence. It turned out that he remembered nothing from the time he was struck and, in fact, did not remember the blow at all. I took him to the medics, who at first thought that he was emaciated, but I told them that he always looked this way. They made arrangements for me to take him to the psychiatrist at the medical evacuation hospital in Long Binh a few miles away. Pell was very cooperative and answered all the doctor's questions while I filled in the details of the story. The medic said, "He has suffered a disassociated reaction that has brought forward his passive aggression."

"What does that mean in English, Doctor?" I inquired, lost by the contradiction in terms.

"Sergeant Pellaboy used to be a boxer. When he was assaulted blindly from behind, his mind took him back to the ring and some similar fighting experience. His initial reaction was to flee and when he got away he became paranoid, taking up the gun to protect himself. A strong blow to the head like that totally confused him and he reverted to the aggressive behavior of a boxer. When he was exhausted he slept, and on waking he lost all recollection of the event. He probably will never recall it."

"Would he have killed me if I had tried to take the gun

away—you know, an old friend just trying to help?" I asked out of curiosity.

"Absolutely," the doctor replied. "This isn't the movies."

I took him back to base camp, where I planned to rest him for a week or two; there was plenty of work to do cataloging and printing. I was quickly summoned to see the commanding general. I had never met the new CG but had seen him in action often and he was a sub caliber of his predecessor. Lieutenants don't merit but passing glances from generals and that was fine with me. I had enough trouble just trying to favorably impress majors and lieutenant colonels. I went to his tent, which was also his office. The aide met me, a lieutenant of superior quality, who placed me in front of the man in charge of the brigade. There were no pleasantries and I wondered why he was interested in the whole incident. Surely I had taken care of it myself. I pretty much told him that during my rambling account and finished with a quote from the doctor. "I doubt that anything like this will ever happen again." The general proceeded to tell me what a sorry officer I was because I could not control my men. "You should have taken that gun away and put him under arrest," he advised in ever louder tones. He raved on about prima donna photographers who pretended to be soldiers. Then I really got in trouble when I said, "You signed a Bronze Star for Valor for my sergeant."

He went white, and then red. "Where is he now?"

"He is in his quarters cleaning his pistol." My attempt to show that he was back to normal and quite safe was taken wrongly and the gray-headed old man exploded all over me. "You gave a lunatic a gun!" It was clear that he had not listened to a word of what the doctor or I had said. Rising slowly to his feet, he stuck out his arthritic finger. "I hold you responsible. Get out of here."

We went into the Ho Bo Woods on a search and destroy, or "hide and seek" as the men called it. After the entry by helicopter I left the infantry, which had only light contact with the Viet Cong, and watched them set up the brigade headquarters. Then a report came in that a tunnel complex had been found and the infantry called for support from the chemical team to root out any inhabitants. The team was known as the "crybaby platoon" because it used tear gas. I followed along behind as we trooped back into the woods. We joined an infantry outfit that pointed out the neat two-foot entrance flush with the ground and framed with small logs to keep the light soil from caving in the opening.

The chemical team covered the opening with a tarp and stuck the outlet pipe of a portable smoke generator through a hole in the tarp. The generator started up and blew a red smoke into the entrance at great pressure. "Watch for red smoke, boys; it will come out of vents and other entrances," Max, the platoon leader, yelled to the few milling soldiers who stood ready with loaded weapons like rabbit hunters searching the undergrowth. Red smoke came up in three or four places within a hundred yards. The team carefully covered the added holes. "Give them the tear gas." The team put on their protective masks and filled the complex. A couple of sniper rounds cracked in nearby and we all searched for the origin. I was getting very uneasy. Suppose that a bunch of VC, very angry, came popping up all around. I let my camera swing from its cord around my neck and pulled my .45-caliber pistol from its holster. I took it in my left hand and yanked the slide back, chambering a bullet, and let it slam closed. I had used a pistol ever since coming on active duty, it was the standard army officer's weapon, and I was very familiar with its operation. I didn't intend to use it but wanted to be ready. We were outside our position by quite a ways and only a handful of us were above the tunnels. I took the weapon in both hands and held the hammer back, depressed the trigger, and eased the hammer to the half-cocked position, the best of the three safeties on the gun. I lifted the thick brown leather flap at the top of my holster with my left hand and slid the pistol back in place. The gun went off!

We all froze. At first no one but I knew where the shot had come from but everyone knew it was very close. I felt a burning in my right knee. I was shot, by my own weapon. First I thought of the disgrace, then I thought of the court-martial charge of "self-inflicted wound in combat." How could I explain that it was an accident to my friends and family? No one would believe it—I didn't believe it! Max, standing next to me, looked at me with curiosity, then noticed that the bottom of my leather holster had been blown out like the end of a blunderbuss. He reached down, grabbed the edge of the bullet hole in my baggy field pants, and ripped it open. There was a faint red mark on my thigh just above the knee. The bullet had missed me and gone into the ground between my boots. Others walked over and examined the scene. "Nice going, Lieutenant," one soldier said. "They teach you to shoot like that in the Signal Corps?" I was speechless. After the near catastrophe, I locked the pistol in my footlocker. I carried a rifle for the remainder of my tour.

The caves proved to be empty except for two VC who came crawling out of a hole twenty yards away. The desire to fight had been taken out of them by the tear gas. All they wanted was fresh air and for the stinging in their eyes and throat to stop. Our soldiers simply took them by the arms and led them away like children. The crybaby team had not scrimped on the amount of gas they put down, and when they recovered the tarps from the entrances it billowed out into the damp jungle foliage and hung in the air nearby in invisible clouds.

I walked over and took a picture of one of the team in his mask, next to the generator. Suddenly my eyes began to heat up and my throat closed up, rejecting a remnant of gas. It got stronger. Like all soldiers, I had had many trips to the tear gas chamber during protective-mask training and knew too well what was about to happen. I was in the middle of a low cloud of the stuff and in a moment I would be as helpless as the victims that we had just captured. I ran off, the direction didn't matter. As I ran, it occurred to me that I might be running away from my own protection and into the sights of the snipers we had heard earlier. I stopped and tried to endure the vapors that hung around my face.

"What's the matter, mate, you lost?" came the welcome voice of an Australian patroller who was working the jungle like a cat. "You a part of that bloody gas gang?" He grinned. "What's the matter, won't they give you officers masks?"

Knowing I was safe with them, I changed the subject. "Mind if I stick with you guys and take some pictures?"

"Be our guest, mate, we are just working the edges and looking for trouble," he said. "Happy to have you along. We are a good-looking lot, much prettier than your pommy lot."

A few hours later they swung by our jungle headquarters and dropped me off just before dark. I went to the tent of the chemical platoon and saw Max, who was down to his T-shirt and shorts, airing out his uniform on a bush. "That sure is wicked stuff, hey Fitz? It lingers in your clothes and attacks you in the middle of the night." He never said a word about my near miss. He was an officer and, more important, a gentleman.

Christmas arrived and we all dreaded its coming. My tent was used as the depository for all the greetings and gifts sent to the brigade by ordinary folks at home. Anything addressed to the unit as a whole was deposited on the floor and began to fill the corner to the ceiling. Bags of Christmas cards, many from schoolchildren, and beat-up medium-size boxes wrapped in brown paper were left in our care until they could be distributed by Special Services and the Red Cross. The press at home may have vilified us and the war, but the American people had not forgotten that we were sent there to do a job, and they were grateful.

Feeling quite sorry for myself, I went to the officers club, which was crowded to overflowing; no one wanted to be alone with his thoughts that Christmas Eve. Well into the darkness of a black night, I walked back to my quarters along a muddy road that had deep trenches cut in both sides to carry the thundering rain away. I walked toward the only light, a spot on the little guardhouse at the main gate which housed a lone sentry who was as downhearted as I. As I got to within twenty yards of him he jumped out of his box, yelled a piercing scream, and fired his rifle twenty times, all that it held, into the ground around his feet. I dropped to the ground. An attack on the night before Christmas? When the firing stopped, the guard stood motionless and backed away from his post. There was no sign of an assault, or in fact any other movement, and we were in dead silence. Unarmed, I rose from the dirt and half ran to him, ready to drop again at any moment. I reached him as I heard others coming from all directions. There, in the sand and thick grass, was what remained of the biggest, scariest boa constrictor I had ever seen. Its body, the most visible part in the sparse light, was bigger around than my thigh and glistened with moisture from the swamp just beyond the gate. "He was coming for me" were the only words that came from the guard's mouth. He was so scared that he had not reloaded the weapon he still pointed at the serpent. He was replaced by another guard, who spent what was probably his most unforgettable Christmas Eve near the dead carcass until morning, when it was removed.

Our headquarters was only thirty miles from Saigon and drew every field-test experiment and research team that managed to find Vietnam from the States. Some were of great value. We were the first to have the new M-16 rifle and the M-79 grenade launcher. Whenever the geniuses appeared with a new superoffering, the photographers were called upon to document its success. The most bizarre was the Sniffer. "Did you know that the bedbug is the only insect attracted to man and that the bug can detect his presence at some distance?" the inventor said to me with great feeling.

"No. So what?" I replied.

"Well," he continued, "when they pick up the scent, they get very excited and jump around."

"Have you got bedbugs in that thing?" I asked, pointing to a contraption in a large, gleaming metal case at his feet.

"Don't worry, they are harmless," he assured me.

I had never seen a bedbug, and had only heard of them when my parents said, "Sleep tight, don't let the bedbugs bite."

"They bite, don't they?" I asked, exhausting my knowledge of the subject.

"Well, yes, generally. But not these; they are in the Sniffer." I stepped back. I had seen my share of bugs in Vietnam, and they came in many varieties, each more menacing than the other. They were everywhere, we didn't need to import them.

He lifted the backpack from the container by the shoulder straps and held it up for inspection. I stayed back and he continued with the briefing. "I put this container on my back like this," and he threw it around his shoulders and slipped his arms through the straps, mounting it like a soldier's field pack. From the bottom hung a black plastic hose that resembled a vacuum cleaner intake with a thin nozzle at the end in the shape of a crevice tool made by Hoover. "In the pack is a battery that supplies low voltage to a plate that is covered with live bedbugs," he went on. He adjusted the pack and pulled the nozzle up in front of him. He then placed on his head earphones that had a long wire coming from the top of the canvas pack. "Every five seconds, the end"—he pointed to the device in his hand—"sucks a sample of air from in front of the operator." He made a sniffing sound with his nose. "It sends the sample down the pipe to the bedbug chamber, and the bugs get excited at the prospect of a meal and begin to jump around on the electrified grid. That sends a signal to the earpiece in the form of a high-pitched tone, alerting the operator to the position of the enemy hidden in the undergrowth." When he finished, a bright smile wreathed his learned face. Clearly his device was a triumph of science. He pointed the thing at me and handed me the headphones for a listen. I very reluctantly leaned forward and heard the sound. I was now the target of hungry bedbugs and that made me shiver.

"Did you invent this, Mr. Moran?" I asked the bespectacled little man from some diabolical laboratory at Fort Detrick, Maryland.

"It was all my idea. It will save many lives, don't you think?" I didn't answer the scientist but instead said, "You plan to carry this out in front of an infantry squad in the bush while my people photograph it in action?"

"No." He paused. "I will train a man to use it and have *him* take it out on patrol while you document the operation. I am no soldier." Then, detecting reluctance on my part and invoking power from above to compel me to do his bidding, he added, "Your commander said you would do it."

"Okay, you find a volunteer patrol and we will go along," I said. I never heard from him again.

I had become friends with an infantry platoon leader who asked me to go along with his guys on the next mission. I told him I would join his operation in the field from a resupply helicopter on their second day out. I wanted to get some shots from the air as we were directed into a jungle clearing. I had taken pictures from the ground of the lone resupply ship coming in over the trees and now I wanted it from the perspective of the aircrew. One morning, while it was still dark, I walked the road to the helipad in the supply area where the choppers rested. We were not in the base camp but on an airfield cut out of the jungle by some French planter many years before. I was quite at ease for the first hundred yards but then began to get the heebie-jeebies. I couldn't see anything. I'd expected some light or sound from the supply dump to guide me but must have been a little too early. I began to walk a little slower and thought of back-tracking and waiting for some light. But when I turned around I saw nothing of my trail. I was stuck—all I could do was continue and hope to pick up some sign of activity. What if I was going in the wrong direction? I could walk into one of our own outposts and get shot by a jumpy guard. I thought of Stonewall Jackson, killed by his own troops when he was mistaken for the enemy in the gloom. My next step cracked a dry branch with a loud report and in an instant of fright that came involuntarily from deep within, I screamed at the top of my lungs. Get a hold of yourself, I thought as cold sweat ran down my back. Just then a voice called out from the supply pad just ahead and a flashlight beam caught me in the eyes. "That you, Lieutenant? You scared the hell out of me," the crew chief said. I wasn't alone in my fear, after all.

Once in the air we found our clearing with the aid of a soldier who popped a smoke grenade. On the radio I heard the ground controller say, "Call the color, Shamrock," using our call sign. "Red," replied the pilot. Identification was done this way as soon as the colored smoke poured out and started to rise. When they heard a helicopter coming in low, the enemy was known to throw smoke to divert him into a trap. I got my pictures and joined the company commander, who knew I was coming. "Nice to see you, Fitz. I will get you over to Bobby in a little while, but for now stick with me," he said in friendly tones, happy to see a new face. I took up a spot at the end of the command group behind a grenadier who trailed the commander by about five yards. We got into very dense "wait a minute" vines and twisted our way slowly forward. The man in front got tripped up, fell forward on his face, and accidentally fired his grenade launcher directly into the back of the captain. Snapping his head back, the officer went down as if hit by a sledgehammer. The 20mm metal ball of the projectile had hit him in the middle of his pack and flattened him. However, it did not go off. If it had it would have killed him and everyone in front of him for twenty-five yards. A safety feature built into the round required it to travel thirty yards before arming. The thick pack had protected him from the blow and left him breathless, with a large blue and red welt on his back between his shoulders. The grenadier, who liked the captain very much, was beside himself at the mistake. "Watch it, will you, Renalds," the recovered officer said to his very own grenadier.

Bobby Ray, my friend, was a graduate of Texas A&M, a part of the Cadet Corps, and a member of the governor's Guard of Honor. He was from a military family that dated back to the Civil War. His father and grandfather were West Pointers, but Bobby was not quite up to that and stayed in Texas, taking his commission from the Reserve Officers Training Corps (ROTC). But as he had been at the top of his class, he was offered a regular-army commission, which somewhat made up for letting the family down, and he was bound to prove that he was the best of his line. He was rather slight, about one hundred and forty pounds, and standing straight as an arrow at five feet eleven he looked like a toothpick. His blond hair was shaved nearly off and I knew it was kept like that even outside of Vietnam. He was confident and successful after six months in the grueling job of infantry platoon leader and I admired his courage that he had been known to demonstrate at any time. He took good care of his men and they thought him indispensable. He had won both the Bronze Star and the Silver Star by staying at his post in spite of slight wounds. As I sat on the ground with him, resting against a tree that evening just before dark in the wet jungle, he said, "You know, Fitz, that last gong [award for courage] could have been a Medal of Honor if it had been documented properly."

I got the picture. "You want me to stick to you and make sure the next one goes all the way, huh?" I was about two steps ahead of him. I'd had such requests before and was willing, but I feared that someone might get killed unnecessarily from such an effort. I said as much to Bobby Ray, and he assured me that any intrepidity on his part would be a lone action and would not endanger any of his troops, whom he truly loved. I believed him; he was a proven hero and a man of his word.

Four tiring days later the opportunity appeared. We came upon a small village of thatched houses. He reported to the boss, on the radio, that the village looked a little suspicious. He was instructed to check it out with his platoon while the remainder of the company swung to the far side. An open space of fifty yards separated the wood line we occupied from the nearest of the houses. No people were in evidence. A patrol came back and said there was a cement bunker in the open halfway between ourselves and the huts. We raised up and could see the mostly buried domed structure just above the chopped-rice straw to our front. It had a low chimney two feet across at the apex of the roof that looked like an air vent. We couldn't see the firing port; the stubble was too high. Since we were in bad-guy country, known more officially as a free-fire zone, and since no people were around, Bobby figured the VC had seen us coming and were in that bunker and other bunkers, ready to fight it out. "Got plenty of film in your camera, Fitz?" he asked. He called in his squad leaders and told them to deploy around the bunker in a semicircle and crawl up to within fifty feet. "I want you all to hold your positions and give me supporting fire when I need it. Stay down and wait for my command." He laid out his plan in detail. They were used to that kind of operation and took it somewhat in stride.

"Where is the best place for you to get a picture of that bunker," Bobby Ray asked once the troops had moved off. Figuring that the firing port was in the middle facing us and away from the village, I pointed to the left flank where the ground was a little higher, about twenty feet to one side.

"Good, take the platoon sergeant and get into position. I will assault it," he said.

"Are you planning to stand up and run at that thing, Bobby," I asked, hoping he had something else in mind.

"I am not crazy, Fitz. I will low crawl up from the other side, jump up on top, and throw these grenades down the air vent." He held a pair of baseball-shaped hand grenades and clicked them together. "That way you can get a picture of my face, right?" That nut had it all choreographed. The platoon got ready and I ate straw crawling to my assigned mark. I lost sight of Bobby and lay there raised up on my elbows until they hurt from the strain. Then in a flash he sprang up from the other side of the smooth white defense and pulled both pins at once with a twisting motion. The safety spoons flipped off either side and I took my first shot of him, his teeth gritted, as he counted to two and dropped the grenades into the vent hole. He fell on his face and the grenades went off with a terrific explosion. A dark cloud enveloped us all instantly. The material settled. We were all covered with shit. Single-handed, Bobby Ray had taken the village open-air latrine.

"That was no air vent, Bobby," I yelled, "it's the communal throne." I, for once, had the last laugh and I had it on film.

Back at base camp I received a visit from my boss, Major Mac, from Saigon. He wanted to see the handcrafted lab and assess our service. He was very happy with our production: six thousand still pictures and twenty thousand feet of motion picture film had been sent to the States in the previous thirty days. He carried with him the thanks of the Commanding General, United States Army, Vietnam, USARV, General Norton, and provided me with a copy of his letter that stated that we were in the field at his personal orders and would be shown every courtesy, consideration, and assistance. He also had granted us the privilege of wearing a black tab on our left shoulder above our unit insignia that read, in one-half-inch letters, COMBAT PHOTOGRAPHER. We were all thrilled with the honor, and Major Mac passed them out and thanked each man for the heroic job he had been doing. We all received a copy of the letter as well, which we were to carry and present to local commanders if we had trouble receiving support. I cautioned the troops after the major left to "only use that letter when it is absolutely necessary." A letter signed by the army commander is very powerful, but the farther you get from his flagpole, the less impact it has. It is better to try to be as good a soldier as you can and help out with fetching and carrying, thereby earning respect rather than just consuming the scarce resources of troops in the field.

Our next mission took us south, for the first time, and we surprised the enemy, who never expected to see regular US units operating below Saigon. The land was the delta of the Mekong River and therefore only a foot or two above sea level. There was just barely more land than water. From the air the surface below reflected back the strong sunlight. The flooded rice paddies with their irregular low dikes, and the twisting rivulets all heading south, to me resembled a giant stained-glass window in the making, the pane laying down while craftsmen filled in the last pieces. The colors were of the earth more than sky. Every hue of brown and green was found in the pieces, along with bits of bright blue from the sky. The texture of the spines was made delicate by banana trees with large leaves like elephant's ears but ragged on the edge, that nearly hid the large bunches of yellow fruit. Those windows had been worked on since before the great churches were begun in the western world. Vietnam was no starving Third World country nor was it overpopulated. The paddies below had fed most of Southeast Asia for millennia. On those windows, up to their knees in rich mud, saints and sinners tended the crops, plodding along behind water buffalo. The farmer's view of life is not of one conqueror after another, but of seasons, one after another, and they go on in spite of warlords. The people of that land were not backward, they were intelligent and educated.

As we prepared to land, supporting artillery and air strikes shattered the delicate glasslike surface, the artillery explosions catching the eye as black clouds with red-fireball centers spread close to the ground. A forward air controller, borne in a wide-wing Piper Cub, looked like a dragonfly skimming along with no apparent destination. I felt like a spectator on the top row of a great stadium who can just make out the players down on the green field. The two teams competing that day had few rules in their game, no time limit, and perhaps there would be no winner.

Again I was a member of a long column that got together after the air assault put us down. The enemy was moving away at high speed—they could travel much faster as they had home field advantage. The head of our column had significant contact, and we came in behind. I stopped at the medical point and took pictures of the wounded and the angels tending them. A medical evacuation helicopter (dustoff) was there to pick up the casualties, and as soon as it was clear another took its place. The last to leave were the dead, zipped into black body bags, and I left the demanding camera around my neck and helped load them. I wished them Godspeed.

Back in the column I crossed several feeder streams, with water up to my chest, and plunged in like the guys in front. The bottom was soft, sucking my boots off. A soldier on the far bank offered a hand and pulled me out. My camera was submerged, but since it was a skin diver's version of Japanese manufacture, a quick drying off of the lens was all that was necessary.

The soldier behind me emerged from the stream and tended to his own Nikon. "I didn't know these Jap cameras were waterproof, Lieutenant," he said as we dripped into the puddles forming around our sodden boots.

"Mine is," I replied. "I'll bet yours isn't." He looked into the lens and saw water behind it in the body of the black box.

One of his buddies looked at it and inquired, "Is that a goldfish bowl or a camera around your neck?" In the high humidity and heat I swear I could see rust forming.

"Why is yours okay, sir?"

"You can dunk all cameras into water but only a skin diver's will work again." I couldn't resist the straight line. My joke came from what a sailor told me once: "All ships can submerge; only the submarine can return to the surface."

We caught up with the unit that had been engaged in the firefight. They were resting on a piece of dry land, putting things back together. The others moved on ahead in pursuit, but I stopped to take a picture of the halted squad, ten or so men who were exhausted. They sat quietly reflecting on the current moment of terror that they had survived. One rather small soldier, sitting with his arms on his drawn-up knees, said to his sergeant, "We are all heroes, aren't we, Sarge?" To me that summed up the infantry soldier in combat—they *are* all heroes; some will get medals for special instances, but they are all heroes.

I made it to the brigade headquarters and found it in disarray; by mistake, they had been strafed by a helicopter gunship from the American 1st Infantry Division. It was hard to believe. The headquarters was not camouflaged and sat next to a very large helipad the size of a football field that was covered with cargo helicopters as big as trucks. The only injury was to the commanding general's cook, but there were bullet holes in everything, especially the tent I shared with the public information officer (PIO) and the surgeon.

I joined the Prince of Wales Light Horse, an Australian calvary unit mounted in American M-113 armored personnel carriers that sported .50-caliber machine guns and could act like light tanks. We were in a column of ten and I was in the middle with the captain, who wore a black beret and headphones rather than the American ballistic helmet. He pointed to it and said, "Our tradition demands soft hats and hard heads, mate." We were going out on the road to escort the land column which brought up the majority of our support and additional artillery.

We were returning to the headquarters area, rolling along the edge of the helipad, where men were unloading crates of gun ammunition, when we received heavy fire from the wood line on the far side of the open field. The commander ordered a flank turn into the field, directly at the enemy. The turn was so sudden and violent that I lost my comfortable perch on the back wall of the "track" and fell headfirst through the open hatch into the middle of the vehicle, where I bounced around like a golf ball in a tile bathroom. The Light Horse suppressed the incoming fire and the aggressors produced a white flag. The tracks pulled up one beside the other with their noses resting at the edge of the foliage on the far side of the field. An American captain, map in hand, stepped out from the brush in front of the Light Horse and asked my tank driver if he could point out his position on the crumpled paper. We had been attacked by a 1st Division infantry company that was lost!

I had one more encounter with the M-113 armored personnel carrier (APC) on that operation. The brigade had an organic unit mounted on the sturdy machines, D Company, 17th Armor. There was going to be a B-52 strike early one morning and the armored unit was going to exploit it from its position less than a hundred yards from the edge of the box the bombs fell into. My mission was to capture the explosions across our front and then ride with the tracks as they crossed the area after the attack, recording the scene for the bomb damage assessment (BDA) that would follow. I was excited; no one had done that in Vietnam with a ground-mounted camera. Just after dawn we drove all fifteen vehicles into position, first to prevent the enemy from escaping in our direction and then to exploit the havoc caused by the bombing. I took a half a dozen cameramen with me and we enjoyed the ride. "It beats walking," Stokes said as he held on desperately. There are no springs in an APC and we weren't on an improved road. We were in position by 0730; the attack was set for 0804. By 0803-and-a-half there was no sign of the enemy or the airplanes and we thought something had gone wrong. Speculation was rampant on the radio net when the entire world erupted right in front of us.

Dead on 0804, the first bomb struck the ground and a huge plume of dirt and fire went up to our right front and continued in a perfectly straight line past the front of our formation. The procession of the explosions rocked us back, knocked helmets loose, and deafened the entire crew. The cameras caught the first three hits and then the air filled with dirt and flying leaves and we all fell to the bottom of the tracks, covered in layers of debris. That went on, layer after layer, bomb after bomb. We covered our cameras and waited it out.

The B-52s made fourteen passes. We never heard an airplane or saw a condensation trail. The destruction seemed to well up out of the earth rather than rain down from above. When it was all over, which took longer than I expected, since the aircraft come in one after the other, we were in awe of airpower. A few enemy staggered out of the woods, blood flowing from their eyes, ears, and noses. They did not want to fight. We picked them up and sent them to the rear for medical treatment; then, abreast, the company moved out toward the target. Suddenly there was no jungle in front of us—it was gone! We stopped at the edge of an area roughly four football fields by two. The measurements of the box were as accurate as if drawn by a draftsman. And it was cleared, completely. Despite that, the armored carriers were unable to cross because the wet soil had turned to mush. We dismounted and moved in on foot, one trooper crawling down into a crater so large we could have put a track in it.

Later that day I took a helicopter over the site and took pictures from five hundred feet. It looked like the moon. Nothing survived inside the box.

Back at base camp I decided to visit a college classmate from Marquette University who commanded an infantry company in the 1st Battalion, 503d Airborne Infantry. A year ahead of me, he had sponsored me when I pledged Scabbard and Blade, a national honor society. Although an engineer by training, he had joined the infantry and was so good that he had been picked to command a company. I was very proud of him. He greeted me in the way I had become accustomed, "Lieutenant Fitzenses, with a name like that where do you come from? I have heard of you; you're that eccentric who goes around with a camera, right?"

"Right. I am. I make infantry officers famous."

"Well in that case come right in, you came to the right place." It was very nice to sit and talk to someone who knew me in another life. Constant combat was closing in on me and my circle was getting smaller and smaller. Life was so intense that my past life, family, and home were slipping away. Captain Barry Dominick, known as Nick, had all the attributes of a good commander: honest, well spoken, technically competent, and genuinely concerned about preserving the force. He didn't waste lives. He was not intensely interested in his own success but felt privileged to command. If there was anyone whom I felt comfortable with in a life-and-death situation, it was Nick.

My platoon sergeant, L. Z. Whitley, and Spec5 Stokes, my best motion picture photographer, decided that I did not have enough appreciation for motion picture taking because I had never attempted the art. I assured them that I had grown up on *Victory at Sea,* which led me to accept the assignment as platoon commander. I had never been a photographer, had no school training, and had never even owned a camera. All I knew was what they had taught me on the ship during the long voyage from San Francisco. "Don't be afraid of it, Lieutenant, we can show you here in base camp how to do it." Those guys were real psychologists. They didn't need a degree; they knew how to push my button. I couldn't let them think I was afraid of a camera. Of course I was.

The camera was heavy, eight pounds, and got heavier as the day went along. In the jungle, exposure was not a problem with the color studio film; I just opened it up and left it there. In the open it was different. The light meter was more complicated than the camera, and I struggled with the damn thing. The NCOs didn't make me use the changing bag because they rightly believed it beyond my capability. Instead they gave me the film rolled, expertly, on one-hundred-foot spools. Framing the sequence in my mind before I pressed the trigger meant a new way of looking at my subject. Holding the camera steady was perhaps the most important next step, and in attempting to do that properly, I began to develope an appreciation for my motion picture cameramen's chief problem. The camera, a hand-wound IMO, was a relic of the 1930s and could take the harsh conditions of Vietnam. Rule number one was, no fast panoramas. Rule two was, no 360-degree panoramas; they made audiences nauseous. Rule three was no shots of sky or boots.

The biggest drawback to the education of the lieutenant was that I could not see the results of what I had taken; there was no laboratory in the country that could develop color motion picture film. We sent all our thousands of feet of raw film to the Army Pictorial Center in Queens, New York. There they would develop the stuff and send a small portion, clips on five-minute reels, back to the cameraman. The purpose of the returned sample was first to tell him that his camera was working (sometimes thousands of feet were unusable because of malfunctioning cameras), and second, to show him how well he had mastered the craft. In the can was always a critique along with suggested improvements. The critiques, written by expert editors, were very helpful as well as a little hurtful. They were short and to the point and often the cameraman and editor developed a professional relationship because of personal notes of advice and comfort passed back and forth.

Stokes and I went on a mission together, he in one helicopter and me riding along in another, on an air assault. I was in a gunship and lay next to the door gunner on a floor covered with ammunition boxes. I framed the shot so that the muzzle of his machine gun appeared in the corner of the sequence and panned along the line of red tracer bullets as they poured like water from a lethal garden hose to the ground in a shallow arc. That day we had plenty of targets, and the thirty seconds of shooting time allowed by the hundred-foot rolls of film constantly caught me out so I missed most of the action. It seemed to me that I spent my time reloading—lying on my back, tearing old rolls out and jamming new ones in, shaking in unison with the violent vibration of the chopper. I thoroughly amused the crew, who had no end of fun on the intercom chiding my comic efforts to cope with the media. "How is the performing bear doing?" the pilot asked the door gunner, who smiled at my antics. I could see his mouth, the only portion of his face exposed below the dark green sun visor on his aviation helmet.

"You rolled him over on that last pass, Skipper. Do it again!" At least I was taking the tension out of their jobs. That mission was more a lesson in humiliation for me than in the making of a film epic. I learned what motion picture cameramen had to cope with, thereby fulfilling the wishes of my men and their sergeant. I'd known it wasn't easy, but until I walked in their combat boots, I really never learned an appreciation for the perils. In the weeks to come I put in my time and shot a considerable amount of Uncle Sam's expensive film. It was packaged up and sent to Mecca, then I waited anxiously for the critique print to return. When it came I was surprised to find that it had been accepted as official record. The last line of the critique sheet, however, referring to my helicopter gunship footage, read, "film shaky; recommend you use a tripod"!

After a mission with the Air Force, with whom I had taken a ride in an F-100, a jet fighter-bomber, I sat in with two airman photographers and debriefed the mission. We swapped war stories and they said they were tired of flying and would like some cross-training. I offered to take them out with me and my guys on the next helicopter air assault. They accepted. I thought, one week-long jungle march with us and they would happily accept the burden of air travel. The sergeants were young and eager. They were also very good technicians since the Air Force ran the joint photo training school that my boys attended, and both had been instructors before posting to Vietnam. They came armed with .38-caliber revolvers, a gentleman's weapon best used for committing suicide. I picked up two M-16s which had been left behind at a medical point, their owners no longer needing them. The airmen declined the weapons, said they were too heavy. For cameras, they carried the newer Filmo 16mm motion picture type powered by a dozen flashlight batteries carried in a belt. They could shoot much longer rolls of film and did not have to be hand-wound between shots.

I met the airmen at the snakepit pad early one morning, where they were a curiosity because they wore blue-and-silver Air Force chevrons on the sleeves of their old-fashioned cotton fatigue uniforms. I kept them close to me and afforded them some protection from the good-natured comments of the veteran paratroopers who milled around waiting for the liftoff.

My Air Force sergeants enjoyed the helicopter ride—it was a treat for them to be in a craft with the doors open fifteen hundred feet above the ground in a group of twenty aircraft flying in a very tight formation. Even on the way in there was plenty of opportunity for picture taking; the chopper beside us was only a hundred feet away and we could see the expressions on the faces of the passengers as they sat on the edge of the floor and dangled their legs into the airstream. It was hard to talk to the airmen because we were not wearing aviation helmets and so couldn't use the intercom, and the extreme noise of the engine combined with the wind noise made conversation almost impossible.

It was a big operation—an entire battalion of eight hundred was about to land and search for a prisoner of war camp believed to hold American soldiers. Everyone was determined to do their best to free their fellow soldiers. We all feared capture more than death.

The opportunity to film landing wave after wave was a motion picture bonanza, and my new land-combat veterans were taking advantage of the movement that surrounded them on the landing zone. When we moved out of the clearing and into the undergrowth, their mood changed and I could see a fear creeping into their movement as they trooped along in the middle of the long column. Bomb craters were all around and I pointed out the effect the Air Force had with 250 pounders. The Air Force photographers had always been at the release point, up in the sky, where the war was very impersonal. I had to remind them to take pictures of faces, not holes in the ground. Soon our movement had been spotted and the Viet Cong began to mortar our formation with just a few light rounds. We scattered and I lost track of one of the airmen until the fire had been suppressed. He rejoined us almost immediately. I was a little perturbed and told them to stick to me. "I dived into one of those Air Force foxholes," and he pointed to the bomb crater he had just photographed. "It seemed like the right place at the right time," and he threw a kiss to some Air Force god in the sky that had provided it for him.

After a day and a night I sent the sergeants back to the safety of their air base and continued on alone. I had moved to the 1st Platoon of A Company, 1/503d Paratroopers, and hooked up with 1st Lt. Brian Dodge, a gaunt blonde with high cheekbones that dominated his other features. Brian was tense; we were on the point and rather far out in front. A scout came back and reported a small village ahead on the far side of a clearing. He had seen a lot of movement and men carrying weapons. The company commander came forward and set the wheels in motion for an attack, which Brian's platoon led up the middle while the second and third platoons came in from the flanks. I moved with Brian to the edge of the wood line and we ran across the open field, not more than fifty yards. We took fire from the village as soon as we broke out into the sunlight. Suddenly my heart was pounding in my ears and my breath seemed to desert me. Even though I was a runner, that was the hardest race I had ever experienced. I even wondered, halfway across, if I could keep up. The enemy fled before us and we were suddenly in possession of an empty little town of fifty huts. As we searched we found evidence of our surprise. Food that was being consumed was scattered on the dirt floors and the cups of tea were still hot.

As our occupation continued, the commander ordered Dodge to push out the other side into the brush and take up a defensive position. That is when we made heavy contact. Just on the far side of the living area, the VC must have had a bunker complex with heavy machine guns set up in a military supply area. We had come in from the side that they had not expected to defend. The enemy fire went over the heads of the 1st Platoon and impacted in the center of town, where we were all standing around admiring a cache of weapons and ammunition. I rejoined Brian and crawled forward to a machine-gun position and took some of my best action pictures. Two troopers jumped up in unison and threw hand grenades that took out one of the enemy's heavy machine guns; several were still left. I moved down the line and clicked away. At one point I put my camera on a fallen log to steady it and took a photo of the expended rounds pouring out of the ejection port on the right side of one of our guns.

The man next to me took a heavy round in the pack on his back and it shoved him back an inch or two. He looked at me and smiled. "Missed me."

Another man was shot in the right shoulder, and his buddy tore open his sleeve. The rifle bullet went into the center of the ball of the muscle on the outside of his arm. It made a perfect hole of red and a trickle of blood ran slowly toward his elbow. "Goddamn it," the man said with a hiss at the end. He was angry, not because he was shot but because he would have to leave his buddies.

I pulled him toward me and got him to a squatting position as his pal put a white pressure bandage in place and tied off the ends. "Can you get him back to the medics, sir?" the squad leader pleaded. I nodded and we went back to the rear in a duckwalk. As we passed the busy platoon leader, he shouted to me to bring back some ammunition; his boys were beginning to "dig in." On the way back with multiple bandoliers of ammo strung around my neck, the swaying of the heavy load caused me to stop. I looked up and saw the enemy machine gun bullets shredding the banana trees' soft pulpy trunks. The debris followed the rounds exactly for a few yards before falling, as yellow slime, to the ground. That showed that the Viet Cong fire never got closer than three feet off the ground. If I stayed down, it was safe. I thought, if I just put my hand up I could catch a flesh wound and be out of this mess before I got killed. Reason quickly returned as I realized that one of those projectiles would tear my whole arm off if it even nicked my hand.

I reached Brian and he distributed my burden. A trooper took a bullet on the side of his rifle which rendered it useless. I gave him my weapon, he needed it far more than a photographer did. I took two more wounded back to the hut where the medics had set up an aid station, fifty yards to the rear of the action. The company commander yelled at me to guard the aid point and watch for enemy to the rear of his position. I found a rifle and lay down next to the village well, which was made of stone, and waited to fight a one-man battle. But the action dropped off as the other two platoons closed in from the sides and cleaned house. Suddenly there was movement in the trees in front of me and I raised my weapon. Two paratroopers stepped into the clearing and waved at me. B Company had arrived and I was out of the action, thank God.

We moved off and looked for a place to set up for the night. I picked a spot in the center of the headquarters group and began to dig a hole just my size for sleep and survival. It was next to a dead log that had twisted branches sticking out in all directions.

"You sure you want to sleep there, sir?" asked a tired young soldier ten yards away.

Not afraid to accept criticism from one I knew to be wiser in the ways of the field, I said, "Any suggestions?"

"You like bugs, sir?"

"Never have. What's wrong?" I searched the ground for red ants, the enemy of all humans, friend or foe. He came over and pointed at the branches of the dead tree with a stick and struck a big fat black millipede on it's back. It curled up and stung the stick repeatedly. The old wood was gray and had camouflaged the six-inch-long bug. A closer look revealed that the tree was covered with the disgusting critters. "Thanks, I'll move."

I was very thirsty, a common complaint after battle. I wasn't just thirsty, I had to find water and my canteen was empty and had been for several hours. I knew that the medics had some left over from the dustoff that always kicked off a bundle of supplies and water when picking up the wounded. We had not had a resupply for several days and wouldn't see another until the next day. There was water in the village but I was not taking a chance on getting dysentery. Most of the village Vietnamese had the disease in one form or other all their lives. I walked the fifty yards to the medical point when I finished my new night position. The two corpsmen were treating a few guys for minor complaints—fungus infections, diarrhea, insect bites, parasites, headaches, rashes, infected cuts, and fever.

"Have you got any extra water?" I asked a tall, very thin medic who had a particularly upbeat attitude about things in general.

"For you, anything, Lieutenant Fitz," came his cheery reply, which caught me off guard. He handed me the full canteen and advised me to drink slowly. "You don't remember me, do you, sir?" I didn't, except for the fun we had had together that afternoon. I looked at him closely. Why would I know a corpsman? He had to be referring to the past. I had never gone to the medics. The little group stopped talking and listened in on our conversation. He smiled broadly and showed a beautiful set of white teeth. "You were my stick leader at jump school."

For the first time, I looked above the left-hand pocket of the damp uniform that hung on him like an old sack. His nametag jarred my memory. "Holman, sure I remember you. You have changed." He had lost thirty pounds, like all of us, but the bright blue eyes still had that "can do" twinkle. He had been one of eighteen men in my squad during the three weeks of horrific training at Fort Benning, Georgia, nearly a year before. "Good God, how are you?" I grabbed his hand and shook it hard. It was a sudden relief from the darkness of our present existence and brought back vivid memories of bad days that didn't seem so difficult anymore. We reminisced and he brought me up-to-date. He was married and they were expecting a child.

"What a pleasant surprise! Did you know Lieutenant Rob was killed, before Christmas?" He didn't and said one of our stick was also dead, but I couldn't place the trooper in my clouded memory; I said I did and expressed my regret. Wrapping a healing hand around the biceps of my left arm and pulling it up and out for a better look, he said, "You better let me fix that arm, it could get infected. Did you get this in the fight, sir?"

"No, I caught it on a thornbush this morning." The thorn was two inches long and stuck in me like a needle. When I tried to pull away it had ripped across my muscle and gashed the skin. It stopped bleeding almost immediately. During the battle I must have opened it up again. There was quite a bit of dark red, nearly black, blood caked on my upper arm. "It doesn't hurt," I told him as he cleaned the wound and dressed it.

"Keep it covered as long as we are in the field and then expose it to the air," he said. "If you had gotten caught in that bush during the battle I would write you up for a Purple Heart."

"No thanks, Holman, those things are bad luck."

The next day we walked into an area near the battle and found that the Viet Cong had been protecting a vast tunnel complex. I followed the exploration team into the entrance large enough to take a small truck. It was concealed by a hut that had to be moved off to the side during operations. I photographed four paratroopers, arms linked, standing just inside. We found an old woman who said that she had been carrying baskets of dirt out of it since the Japanese occupation in WWII. After them, the French had searched for but not found the complex, as had Saigon government troops, who were often in the area but just as luckless.

After ten days I had exhausted my film supply and sat on the loading ramp of a jungle airstrip waiting for a plane to Bien Hua. A C-130 cargo ship was sitting nearby, waiting to reload, and I watched the crew preflight it for takeoff which should be within the hour. A very young paratrooper whose nametag read MANWARING was dressed in jungle fatigues and helmet, fooling around. He looked unusual because he did not have a pack, canteen belt, or weapon. A buddy had all those things and followed Manwaring around, speaking to him like a friend, answering the young man's questions. Manwaring would climb the four-step ladder at the side of the cargo bay toward the back of the airplane and then reappear at the open rear ramp, which was lowered to within three feet of the concrete pad. He would then take up a "prepare to exit" stance, yell "Go!" and jump into the air and as far from the gate as he could before crashing down on the hardstand in a very bad parachute landing fall, PLF. Manwaring would get right up, say something to his buddy, and repeat the process. When he spotted me he ran over and reported his name while saluting in a very stiff manner. Close behind, his friend ran up and stood at his side rather nervously. I returned Manwaring's salute. The soldier did an about face and returned to the PLFs.

His buddy stayed by me and said that the eighteen-year-old had had a little too much combat and had flipped out the night before, and he'd been assigned as his bodyguard for the journey to the hospital. "I can't stop him, sir. He is going to hurt himself, but he says he has to get ready for the jump today." Since the soldier seemed to have recognized me as an officer and person of authority, I walked over to him between jumps. "Well done, Manwaring. I want to see a little more rotation on that next one. It will be your last practice PLF until you chute up and join your unit." "Yes, sir," he answered crisply, and did his final fall which must have hurt. During my two tours of combat in that war, he is the only case of combat fatigue I ever saw and the sight is still with me. I hope he made it home.

I was sitting in our tent reviewing reams of photos and checking the backs to insure that the photographers had put complete captions in place, when the PIO, Major Samson, appeared with members of the press. He had several in tow and, after a short introduction, left them with me to take out on operations. One, a woman of superior quality, was dressed in an Abercrombie and Fitch safari suit complete with feathered bush hat and black leather boots with three-inch-high heels.

I had experienced the press before and, with two exceptions, found them wanting. Once gentleman of the press had tried to buy exposed film from my guys at the base camp; he refused to go forward and take his own pictures. Another tried to pay my cameraman to carry his camera for a week while he stayed behind and did stories about field operations from the comfort of the officers club bar. Still others would wait for a unit to return from the jungle and interview the men as they got off the helicopters. One trait seemed to be common: if they talked to ten soldiers, they only expressed an interest in those with something negative to say about the war or the operation. Soldiers quickly learned what the newspeople wanted and some would give it to them, just to see the reporter get excited and press them for more dirt. The troops despised the reporters, thought them to be cowards and scum of the earth. The more sensational the tale, the more reporters craved the story. When the troops spoke of loyalty to one another, or of the personal heroism of one of their leaders, that sparked no interest at all.

My own men had many stories to tell since they had seen so many parts of the war, but they were the wrong tales. They had seen the nobility of the common trooper and the love and respect he held for his sergeants and officers. But the reporters never saw the team aspect of the army in the field. They chose to pit one class against the other and pull out individuals who had been wronged or thrown into war against their will. When they met men who volunteered for the duty, and there were a great many in a Regular volunteer outfit like the 173d Airborne, they regarded them as fools and warmongers. That made them very unwelcome. Consequently the reporters were not trusted and the troops' stories would find their way back in letters. Those stories of the kindness our soldiers showed the Vietnamese, or of hours spent by troops building village waters systems, or of the number of good wells hand-dug during hours away from combat were never told by the reporters. They never spoke of our medics, who spent more time caring for the Vietnamese than treating their own men. I couldn't get a reporter to the orphanages sponsored by units or to watch the men teaching in local schools during their valuable time off. To the reporters, if the story wasn't negative, it wasn't a story, and the men resented that they were being made into boogeymen around the world.

But, I digress. Back to the lady reporter. The woman was not to be trifled with. She was demanding and dropped the name of every general of note. She insisted on going out with us on a short operation or "I would regret it." As she directed the men of my platoon, who at first had been intrigued by her presence, they slowly drifted away. They slid out of every opening in the tattered tent. Once alone, I began to tell her about my flying experience and the excitement of dive bombing. After hearing a few stories of wild blue yonder and handsome young pilots, she agreed that the air war was an aspect of the conflict in Vietnam little covered. By afternoon she was in the capable hands of the 1st Air Commando Squadron and set for a flight in an F-100, a long way away from me.

Today, the majority of the film and still pictures taken by army photographers lies unseen in the National Archives. Sadly, only a small portion of the war was ever exposed to the public back home.

Chapter Two

*The "constants" of morale in all Armies in all
times are loyalty, patriotism, discipline, unity
and determination: qualities that often
withstood disaster, but never withstood
favoritism, neglect and injustice.*
GEN. DWIGHT D. EISENHOWER

Lieutenant Colonel Snead arrived unexpectedly one day
from his post as battalion commander of the 69th Signal
Battalion, which had moved to Saigon since I left it nine
months earlier. He was tanner, thinner, and wiser. His command had grown from the eight hundred who had come over
on the ship to two thousand, far too large. He had taken the
Army headquarters by storm and picked up every small detachment and separate company in Saigon. He had given
those small units a home and provided better care for the
men than they could have gotten on their own. It meant that
they were now working as a team and therefore provided
better service to the Army in general.

"I have three good pieces of news for you, Fitz," he announced with great pride. "You have been promoted to captain, therefore you must leave this unit, and you have been
given a Regular Army commission." I was very happy to accept the promotion and I was ready to leave the line. In the
past month I'd found it harder to go out on operations. I had
lost a lot of weight and knew what tired really meant.

I had been commissioned as a Reserve officer and applied for the Regulars before leaving the States. In the early 1960s the majority of the officers were Reserve officers on active duty because the number of Regular officers in the army was limited by statute, in those days to about sixty thousand. It was common for as many as 80 percent of active officers to be in that status and remain so for more than twenty years. The advantage was that they could take a Department of the Army civilian position upon retirement and still receive the full amount of retired pay, and work toward a second retirement, a practice that was (and is) known as "double dipping." Therefore, after age fifty-five, they left the service of their country with two paychecks. That never appealed to me personally. I wanted to be a professional soldier, and that meant being a Regular. Regulars got better assignments, as could be expected, and could serve a full thirty years if they reached the rank of full colonel (0–6), longer if they made general.* All the West Pointers were Regulars and some distinguished ROTC graduates were offered Regular commissions. Even though I had been a Distinguished Military Student, my college grades were too low for me to be offered a Regular commission, and to get on active duty I had to settle for the Reserve status. While at my last stateside post, I had made an application and been called to Washington for a review-board competition. In the Signal Corps very few regular positions were open that year, and I joined five other applicants for the single slot. Dressed in a perfect uniform, I went to the Munitions Building on Constitution Avenue, site of the War Department before the Pentagon was built. When I visited, it held the headquarters of the Strategic Communications Command, a worldwide organization that provided the Army with long-haul communications. It numbered over twenty thousand and was in

---

*Not an easy thing because the number of general officers (paygrades 0–7 through 0–10, though no 0–10 slots were being created) was in those days limited to 3/4 of 1% of the number of Regular officers, i.e., 450.

fixed locations in some of the most exotic places on earth. I had been a member of that command in Japan, my first assignment. The white, stone-faced, three-story flat-roof structure hugged the avenue across from the Department of Justice and is today the site of the Smithsonian's American History Museum. The dark marble lobby was dominated by portraits of military heroes from the forties. It had been the office of General Marshall. As head of the War Plans Division the newly promoted Brigadier General Eisenhower had come to the building in early December 1941 to write the new plan for the conduct of the war. Gen. Mark Clark had been there before the war as a colonel, and his portrait hung in the wing that led to my destination. The halls were very businesslike and rather drab. Each office door was dark wood eight feet high with a rectangular transom above which allowed a little light to fall onto the granite floor of the passage. White milk-glass fixtures hung on blackened chains every twenty feet, with cracked electrical wire interwoven to sixty-watt lightbulbs that did little to dispel the gloom. The halls were filled with officers in suntan summer uniforms, and others in cheap suits were compelled to wear ties by the exalted headquarters they served. For the most part they had their jackets off, which were stuck on wooden coatracks that had huge unpolished brass hooks.

I asked a pretty secretary where the commanding general's office was located. She wondered why a lieutenant was looking for such rich company and I told her he was holding a board. "Second floor all the way to the end, take the stairs over there," she said, pointing a polished red fingernail at a door with frosted glass. Next to it was a men's room, where I stopped off to make one last check of my uniform and give a final wipe to the red-and-white signal flags on the collar. My silver parachute wings looked very sharp, and under them was the single ribbon I had received for the short month I spent in the northern provinces of Vietnam while on temporary duty from Japan. I knew that the general was a paratrooper from his picture hanging among the cluster along the wall. He didn't look very friendly.

It was a double flight of stairs and I took them slowly. The humidity added to the nervous perspiration that was building beneath my uniform jacket and I wanted not to sweat. The end of the hallway on the second floor was blocked off by a wood and glass partition. The transparent door had four-inch-high gold letters that announced COMMAND SECTION. It was clearly a warning, I thought: "Don't come in here unless you mean it." I felt safe going through since I had a letter of invitation. Beyond the door was a clutch of offices but only one was marked COMMANDER.

I was early, of course, but no earlier than the other four applicants. One of the two secretaries said hello and reached not for my hand but for my invitation. "What an unusual name, how do you say it?" she asked, because she would have to reproduce the sound exactly for the general.

The other secretary inquired, "Is it German or Irish?"

"Neither, it's French, from Alsace." She looked unsatisfied so I continued, "South of Strasbourg?"

"Oh yes! My husband and I were in Paris." She was cut off by the entry of Lt. Jim Shellburn, the aide-de-camp, who approached from the general's open door. "Hi, Fitz," he said, presuming my nickname and being a little unsure of the pronunciation of the whole thing. The other lieutenants visibly bristled, thinking I knew Jim and therefore had an unfair advantage. I didn't know three of the officers, but one, Tom Daily, had come from the same unit. The aide said, "The board consists of only the general. He will interview each of you. You can leave when he finishes with you and I will write to you with the results."

The first guy went straight in and Jim talked to us in the outer office about our careers and made small talk to fill the time. He was a very nice guy and kept our minds off the prepared answers we were all rehearsing in our thoughts.

I was the last to enter the inner sanctum for his ten short

minutes. I crossed the deep red carpet and stopped in front of the massive, dark wooden desk, saluted, and spoke my name clearly. "Have a seat," the old gentleman said, pointing to the large leather chair pulled up to one corner of his desk. His uniform blouse hung on the rack and he was only visible from the chest up, dressed in a tan shirt and a black tie that had a metal miniature of his unit patch in the middle. His face was older and heavier than in his picture. He looked just as grim though. He must have been in his mid-fifties and looked that and more. His black-and-gray hair was very sparse on top, but what there was was long and combed straight back in an attempt to cover the large, mostly bald, head. Great bags under his eyes made him look tired or sad. His hands were large and knitted together on the desk. He leaned forward when he spoke and asked the first and most expected question. "Why do you want to be a Regular Army officer?" With that he could sit back and listen to an answer concocted by the officer and designed to impress. I told him that my father had been a corporation man who devoted his life to the selling of road machinery. I wanted my life to count for much more. We went back and forth like that for the full ten minutes, and I left when he rose and thanked me for my application. He didn't seem very impressed with me, and I told Jim that as I was leaving. "Don't worry, Fitz, the real interview was out here in the office with me."

Colonel Snead had brought a new sergeant first class, John Millbank, along to replace me. "We don't have an officer on board yet to take your place and I have asked the 173d if they could have an NCO do your job for a while. You have a week to get him ready. I will expect you on the tenth in Saigon," he said as I walked him to his jeep.

The sergeant was a good man who told me that he felt he was in over his head. I took him out on an operation the next morning. I was reluctant to turn the job over, but all I could do was break him in fast and hope he would make his way on his own. His troops needed little direction; they were all veterans and looked to their leader for moral support and the creature comforts that were beyond their own ability or rank to procure.

To make the break-in period simpler we went out with the same unit I had just been with. I wasn't after pictures but wanted to demonstrate how to get along in the field. Millbank was attentive and very scared. He had never been in combat and never expected to be operating at the infantry-platoon level. Lt. Brian Dodge understood what we had to do and put up with our tagging along on the walk in the woods.

On the second day we were standing in a clearing with the platoon of forty men spread out, searching for weapons caches that had been reported by a local official in the nearby village. Things were slow and my replacement was with a squad on our outer limits. Brian was on the radio to the resupply helicopter, which was fifteen minutes out. The radio operator, Brian, and I were all looking for a trace of it in the sky when a Viet Cong soldier came up out of a camouflaged hole fifty feet in front of us. He exposed his body to his belt and reached back with his right arm, which held a grenade. We all saw him at once, our old combat eyes picking up the movement. Only the RTO and I had our rifles at the ready. We clicked off the safeties and fired too late to stop the arm from coming forward to deliver a bouncing, live, grenade. It went off as we all headed for the ground. Brian took most of it and was badly hurt. That resupply chopper was as good as a dustoff and he was on his way to recovery in minutes. I was not even scratched. The radioman stood next to me and watched his boss flying away. Then he said, "Could you get this out." He raised his trembling right wrist to chest level with his left hand. Two small fragments from the explosion were embedded in his wrist just above the bone end. I pinched them out with my fingers and dropped them on the ground between his bloodstained boots. He didn't make a face, but said, "God, I hope the lieutenant makes it."

With the platoon in disarray, we went back to base camp early. My new sergeant was grateful and we talked into the night about what he could expect. Lt. Joe Miller came to see me and offered us an opportunity to go out with the engineers. "Here is the mission, Fitz. Intelligence believes that the VC have constructed a footbridge across a tributary of the Mekong River north of here. They built it about two feet under the water so we can't see it from the air. We have had reports of troops walking on the water for some time and we think, since they aren't Christians, that it must be an underwater bridge."

"It's hard to take pictures of an underwater bridge, Joe, even though I am a Christian," I said.

"No, no! Come with us, Fitz." He was very excited. "We will find it and blow it up. It should be great for pictures. I'll make a nice big explosion, as big as you want."

"Sounds good, Sergeant," I replied. "It will be a great experience for you." Millbank was not so sure after his first outing.

"The plan is simple. We take ten engineers and three inflatable rubber boats and fly to an area just above where the reports say the crossing is. The jungle is rather thick there so we will slide down ropes and drop the boats in bundles. After we inflate the boats and attach the outboard motors, we will go down the river dragging grappling hooks behind. Once we snag the bridge we'll put underwater charges on it and blow it up. A helicopter gunship will be above for protection all along the river."

"How far away is the nearest friendly ground unit, in case the VC don't want us to blow up their bridge?" I asked.

"There aren't any friendlies in the area. If there were, the VC would dismantle the walking planks and we wouldn't be able to find it at all," Miller said, showing how cunning the little attack really was.

"Why did the boss pick you for this suicide mission? More importantly, why do you want me along?"

"I volunteered; it is a great chance, and you can document it for the record."

There it was, "storming the shithouse" all over again, and Miller was counting on a medal. If he pulled it off he would deserve one.

I was, like the others, rigged with a French seat, a tangle of rope was wrapped around my waist and between my legs, for the descent from the chopper which hovered unsteadily at sixty feet above the bank of the river. A metal snaplink connected me to a long rope that touched the ground, and with little instruction we all made it to the ground much faster than I expected. The slide was much more a barely controlled drop, and I landed on my feet, tail, and back of my head, in that order. Not wanting to give our unauthorized presence away until necessary our protective gunship would stay out of sight until we called for it.

The burly engineers had a very large hand pump, six times the size of one for a bicycle, that was used to fill the boats with air. Then the motors were attached, which was done in record time. The boats were of good size and took the passengers with no trouble. I can't say the same thing for the motors; one of the three would not start, which meant that the last boat had to be towed. Since we were going with the swift current, that turned out not to be a big problem. The problem was that we were deep in "bad guy" country and it was very quiet out there alone. After we'd been twenty minutes on the winding muddy river, a five-foot-long poisonous water snake came up alongside my boat and kept pace with us just a foot to one side, my side. He turned his head, which was held clear of the water, toward me and peered into the boat over the fat black-balloon side. I didn't make a move or shoot, for fear of missing him and puncturing the pontoon. Eventually, satisfied that there was nothing he could eat in the boat, he pulled away like a departing escort and disappeared. SFC Millbank stared at me and said, "Is it always like this around here, sir?"

"Pretty much," I replied.

Our leader spotted a lookout sitting in a tree as we rounded a bend, but the man ran away when he saw our approach. "He must be a guard," Miller deduced. We began to circle and soon grappled the foot treads of the underwater bridge. After that, everyone got very wet setting the charges before we climbed out on the bank for the big show. The bridge went up with a huge waterspout.

"I better get that chopper in here; they know we are here now," Joe said as he grabbed the radio and pulled the mike cord tight. Villagers just down river came running our way and we thought we were really going to earn that medal Joe had in mind. We took to our boats, and the chopper made a pass to show the enemy that we were not alone. The people ignored it and us and jumped into the river to collect the numerous dead and stunned fish that had floated to the surface. They smiled broadly and thanked us for the demonstration of a modern American method of fishing.

After that mission, I packed my belongings and said good-bye to the platoon. We had been through the fledgling period together and would never forget each other. The men still looked so young. Some of them really were. When I arrived at the 173d there were three soldiers living in our tent who were on their way out of country because the press had done a story on a wounded soldier who they interviewed in the field hospital. He was only seventeen and had lied about his age the year before when he entered the Army. There was an uproar in Washington and other seventeen-year-old troopers were identified in the ranks. They were to be sent back to the brigade's home in Okinawa until their eighteenth birthdays, and then would be allowed to return to combat.

Those three veterans were hostile; they did not want to leave their friends in Vietnam. They felt like deserters. "I'm no kid, I am nearly eighteen," one volunteered.

The ride to Saigon, in a jeep, took an hour. In my mind I climbed down from the plateau that I had occupied for the past nine months, and a new calm crept in by the time we reached the outskirts of the sprawling city. We crossed a bridge on the hard-top road that was busy with both the machines of modern war and putt-putt Lambretta motor scooter trucks stuffed with old women bringing produce to market. Next to the highway bridge was one of sturdy French construction that was three spans long. The first section had been knocked off its mooring by an explosion and dipped into the water two hundred feet from the shore. Thin brown men in plastic pith helmets and boxer shorts pulled handcarts at the edge of the high-speed road with their heads down, straining at the load. Here and there little policemen in white uniforms and patrols of ARVN military police stopped civilian traffic and inspected parcels and wagons.

Saigon itself could be a combat zone, but was not as a rule. The enemy used the city as much as we did and could not permit the chaos of war to disrupt the business that still sustained the nation. It was an uneasy safehouse. The city started with lean-to stands where one could buy just about any small item that could be stolen from the American PX system. The lean-tos were held up by flattened Budweiser beer can walls, label side out. It was the ultimate in outdoor advertising. Those soon gave way to small, doorless houses with rusted metal roofs and woven-mat sides. Only strings of colored beads masked the inside. The floors were dirt and watered with a sprinkling can to keep the dust down.

People moved in and out and along the road edge, dressed in baggy silk pants and loose, light-colored, shirts. Men and women alike wore low, tan, conical hats made from dried wide-bladed grass and held on by white elastic chin bands. The people looked very clean, almost scrubbed, and the children were beautiful and happy. They played with simple wooden toys and shyly stood a distance from American soldiers, who were known for their generosity. The soldiers were much bigger than the average Vietnamese and absolutely towered over the children, who didn't approach until enticed by a big hand offering candy. Many of the kids spoke a little English and a lot of French even though they were from the lowest class. There was no apparent malnutrition, and something always seemed to be cooking nearby on open charcoal fires. The women squatted over cooking pans and spoke to each other loudly in the singsong language that hurt unaccustomed western ears. The Vietnamese spoken word was hard for Americans to wrap their tongue around, and I knew very few who could speak more than a phrase or two.

The city itself began with permanent houses of concrete and light brown stucco. Toward the outskirts they were one story high but soon gave way to two floors. Only a few had glass windows; most had large, green wooden shutters that were pinned back during the day. The windows were very large and the ceilings were twelve feet high to allow even the smallest breeze to penetrate the four or five rooms per level. The floors were mosaic tile and extended out of the house onto wide porches that ringed three sides of the villas. Everywhere tropical vegetation was arranged by skillful hands into gardens both inside the properties and along the streets. Saigon was a colonial French town and one of the most charming I had ever seen. There was no clutter, everything was very neat. The main roadway was wide and paved. To each side was a row of tall mahogany trees and concrete sidewalks wide enough for bicycles and pedestrians. Each villa was surrounded by a low wall topped with decorative metal spikes. Large fat flowers of mostly red and yellow grew in pots or window boxes, and lazy banana trees five feet high let their broad, dark green leaves nearly touch the ground. But it seemed that with the departure of the French from the Paris of the East, the order and organization of the city garbage system had departed as well. Piles ten feet high were two or three to the block, which the heat and daily rain turned into rotting, sweet-smelling compost heaps. The smell of putrid vegetation and open sewers spoiled the image that the French had tried to impose on Vietnam.

Pedicabs driven by pumping men perched in front on worn bicycles wove in and out of traffic and competed with pretty girls on cycles for the side of the road. Everywhere French motorbikes and scooters left blue clouds of exhaust smoke that choked the commuters.

I was taken to the Khai Minh Hotel, the bachelor officers' quarters for the 69th Signal Battalion. It was only eight blocks from the center of town and across the street from the old Pasteur Institute, which was still doing research into tropical diseases. The hotel was six stories high and in two identical tan concrete buildings that sat at right angles to each other. There were no internal hallways, only stairways to balconies with metal railings provided the hundred rooms with access to the courtyard below. On the first floor was a sweltering dining hall and billeting office.

The Khai Minh had never been grand. Its only true luxury was a small one-room single-story house in the center of the court, which was the bar. The large courtyard was covered with square terra-cotta tiles and surrounded by a ten-foot stucco wall with barbed wire coiled along the top. The only entrance to the courtyard had massive iron gates and a guardhouse surrounded by a sandbagged wall three feet thick. The bags were showing their age and leaked little piles of sand onto the ground. An American Signal Corps soldier and an ARVN military policeman checked everyone in while keeping one eye on approaching traffic.

I was no longer a combat photographer or a platoon leader. My second night at the Khai Minh, I was relaxing at the bar with Capt. Jerry Raymond, who commanded the

280th Signal Company, a communications cable construction unit based at Long Binh. In the city we were allowed to wear civilian clothes in the BOQ area in the evening, so I bought a light green polyester shirt that stuck to my back in the heat of an evening that had no breeze. The ceiling fans in the bar turned so slowly they did little good. "Why do they bother to turn it on?" I asked Jerry.

"Well, it used to turn a lot faster until we invited the Australians over for drinks and a special service show," he informed me. They played mess games, a fine old British Commonwealth tradition. "You know, cabbage baseball, stuff like that," he said, trying to jog my memory. Cabbage baseball was played just like real baseball, but inside the mess. Instead of a ball, a cabbage was struck by a tennis racket and the runners were allowed to be blocked by the defense while they gathered up the fragments of the cabbage and threw the runners out.

"What has that got to do with the fan, Jerry?"

"They introduced us to a new game, designed for the tropics. It is called Grab the Blade, not just any blade, but the one painted red." I looked back up at the wobbly five-blade fan and gained a new appreciation for the one with a red tip. "The challenge for the player was to chug a beer while standing on the table, then attempt to jump up and grab the blade. Not just any one, only the red one could score a point for his team." I didn't ask the casualty rate. "Toward the end of the late night we improved on the game. Some drunk produced a steel helmet and it turned into 'Stop the Blade.'" The drunk put on the helmet, stood on two tables, chugged the beer, then stuck his helmeted head into the spinning fan, stopping it dead. A point was scored if the helmet was touching the red blade when it stopped. "I invented it," he said with the pride of originality. Those guys must have been very bored.

Lieutenant Colonel Snead came in with the staff trailing behind, as usual; he never went anywhere without them.

They took up a position against the far wall and called for quiet. I was taken forward by the adjutant and placed to the colonel's right. "Publish the order," Snead commanded. Standing there in civilian clothes, the colonel and his deputy pinned the twin silver bars of a captain on my polyester collar and the S-3, my new boss, poured a beer over my head.

"Speech," demanded the crowd of thirty officers, already howling at my sodden figure. "I would like to thank the commander for the ceremony; I didn't really want a parade in uniform like the rest of the Regular army. Drinks are on me!"

The first thing in the morning I reported to Colonel Snead's office at his headquarters, the first compound inside the main gate, to the left, on Tan Son Nhut Air Base. The base held many units, agencies, and headquarters. But it was dominated by the ten-thousand-foot runway and the large village in the middle that housed families of the RVN Air Force. In all there were ten thousand military from all services within Tan Son Nhut's confines, each group separated by its own defensive walls and bunkers. It was a park of tiny Fort Apaches; some even touched others. Ours was Camp Gaylor, named for the 69th's first casualty. He was not the first to die, however. Shortly after arriving in the war zone, Ron Gerry was accidentally killed by a bullet fired from the rifle of a fellow 69th soldier.

"Fitz, you are a Regular officer now; it is time to stop fooling around with cameras and begin your career." I was not surprised at the colonel's attitude toward combat photography; the specialty was not held in high regard by the Army. "I would like to give you command of a company but there is none open now. Instead you will be my assistant S-3 and operate the battalion control facility." The Bat Con tractor trailer van was parked next to the headquarters and connected to all the communications systems and circuits in the Saigon area. It monitored the status of and gave directions to installations, and it restored interrupted services. "It is the heart of my command and cannot afford any mistakes," he said. "You have a fine record and I expect you to go a long way as a Regular. You must think of the future. Where do you want to be in ten years? You need command of a line company, which is the only way to get to battalion command." He clearly had my interests at heart and was very sincere.

"I am quite content to leave that camera behind, sir; you were the one who put me into Photo." He had forgotten that I was not a school-trained photographer and had never intended to seek that line of work.

Happy with my agreement, he went on to explain how vital the Bat Con was to him and the role I was to play in the successful completion of his command. "Remember: no mistakes; I will make vital decisions based on your work." That meant that he would relieve people of their jobs and ruin careers based on my reports of their errors. "By the way, have you ever thought of changing your name; it could be bad for your career."

With my new silver bars, I checked in with Maj. William Pennella, who had been a captain on the boat over. He was unusual, a rather humorous-looking figure about six-feet-four, in the shape of a ripe pear, who stood in boots that must have been size fourteen. His head came to a distinct point which was accentuated by the tuft of black hair that stood straight up when he took his hat off. He had teeth with large spaces between the uppers. Inclined forward, they were visible when his mouth was closed. He was in his forties and not likely to see another promotion, even though he was one of the best operations officers I had ever known. The major had been at the top of the enlisted ranks when he received a direct commission to the grade of first lieutenant in his early thirties. He had complete mastery of all aspects of communications and a thorough knowledge of the men who provided them. His memory for technical detail was photographic and he liked to catch out those officers who tried to snow him with explanations that amounted to non-sense. Willy was friendly and intended to train me in his own image, no mistake. A picture of his wife—there were no children—was on his desk in a gold frame. A farm-town girl from Nebraska, she lived at home with her aging, retired parents until Willy's return. He planned to go to law school after his twenty years of army service, then run for local of-fice. Those who knew her said she was as mean as a snake and I wondered if Willy wasn't better off with us.

He took me out the side door after a pep talk and intro-duced me to my crew. My chief sergeant, the noncommis-sioned officer in charge (NCOIC) was Sergeant First Class Ziegler. The van, my office, was air-conditioned! The cool dry atmosphere calmed my fear and I thought, I could stay there the rest of my life. Sergeant Ziegler had not had an of-ficer since the commander had fired the last one a month be-fore. In fact, several officers had been fired in the previous nine months and there was no reason to think that I would last any longer. "The colonel demands accuracy and detail, and it is not always available," he cautioned me from the start.

Sergeant Rapp, Ziegler's assistant, was a chatterbox and eternal optimist. He was married to a German girl whom he missed very much, and kept busy to relieve his loneliness.

Then there was Sgt. Ronnie Rowbottom, a heavyweight about five-feet-five who was interested in the food of the country and was a walking restaurant guide to Saigon. He was the happiest man I ever knew and a natural clown. Out of several privates, one stood out, Bob Ratkey, the "Rat," a most unlikely nickname for that docile fawnlike blond boy. The others had given it to him and he didn't like it, but put up with it all day.

The Bat Con ran twenty-four hours a day on two twelve-hour shifts. Other American military elements in the city came up with their own identifying patches, which they had embroidered in town and sewn on the left pocket of their uniforms. My first act was to design one for my boys. *Batman* comics were making a comeback in those days, and I stole the black bat silhouette with blood dripping from a razor-toothed mouth. It fit our image; it was our job to rat on the mistakes of the operating elements of the battalion and to restore communication, by direction. I was regarded as the resident stool pigeon by my fellow officers. The guys painted BAT CAVE above the back door of the trailer and our morale went up a mark.

On the way over on the ship were many small detachments that were not a part of the 69th, even though they worked in some field related to communications. One, the 55th Cryptological Repair Team, which had forty enlisted and three warrant officers, was run by 1st Lt. Patrick Xavier Kelly of Boston. He was just what you would expect, very outgoing, a little heavy from the beer that he was devoted to, and very red-faced. Totally likable and rather offhand in his methods, he was not Colonel Snead's cup of tea. He treated the colonel as an equal, since he too was commander of an independent unit, even though there was no comparison in size. Once they had settled into a home office at Tan Son Nhut, Pat was invited to share the officer quarters at the Khai Minh. He saw Snead often at the bar and was always quick to give him advice or make a sarcastic remark about the 69th's latest failure. One day Snead stumbled across Pat's headquarters, a one-room sixty-foot building surrounded by barbed wire and protected by a heavy metal front door. Pat's unit repaired sensitive intelligence cipher equipment and was therefore restricted from visits by anyone outside its members or their immediate chain of command. In a good mood, Snead took the time to stop in and say a friendly hello. He knocked at the door and was greeted by a private who spoke through a small slit in the middle of the door. "Morning, soldier. I would like to come in and see your commander," Colonel Snead said in his commanding voice.

"Sorry, sir. No one is permitted inside." The private closed the peephole in the old man's face. That enraged the boss and he knocked again, this time getting a sergeant who in more diplomatic terms gave the colonel the same reception. The ruckus finally caused Pat, deep into his *Field and Stream,* to leave his swivel chair for the first time that day and go to the door. Pat recognized Snead and asked him his business, then denied him entry based on the fact that the colonel did not have "a need to know" what was behind the locked door. The confrontation went on and Snead finally turned and stomped off to his waiting jeep. Within the hour he returned with a piece of paper in his hand, banged on the door, and demanded to confront Pat again, face-to-face. Pat was enjoying the performance that he leveled at the colonel and was showing off for his troops, who liked their gruff boss very much. Snead ordered Pat outside and Pat said, "Certainly, sir." The much calmer colonel then presented Pat with the paper he had been brandishing, an order from the commanding general that read, "The 55th is reassigned to the 69th Signal Battalion."

"I will return tomorrow at 0730 for a command inspection," the grinning lieutenant colonel said. Pat lost, big time.

The girls of Saigon were unlike western women. They were the most petite of the petite. Most were under five feet tall and had a waist smaller than seventeen inches. They all had long black shiny hair and wore the traditional *ao dai,* black or white silk pants worn beneath a long jacket with a mandarin collar and long sleeves. The jacket descended to two panels, one in front and one in back, that floated freely to below the knee. Many of their faces were truly Eurasian from the French blood introduced during the previous two hundred years. Many of the young women had attended French Catholic girls schools and were absolutely charming. They were not prostitutes and were watched over by very protective middle-class families.

In a case right out of *South Pacific,* one of our lieutenants fell in love and wanted to marry one of the beauties, a Miss Huong. We never knew her by any other name; in time she was known as "our Miss Huong." Her parents permitted her to visit the Khai Minh on Sunday afternoon, after church, and she had a civilizing effect on the entire company of brother officers. Her jet black hair had never been cut during her twenty years and it reached to her belt. She was demure and glanced at one only briefly when shaking hands, lightly. When she walked across the stone floor of the courtyard on the arm of her young officer she was careful not to clack her high heels. She was fawn-footed. At lunch her meal was brought to her from the cafeteria line as she sat up straight on the forward edge of the only good wooden chair in the hall. Each Sunday, two other young officers would be asked to join her, Lt. Robert Matthews (her intended) and the colonel, for dinner. Her family felt that the colonel was a suitable chaperon. She wanted to meet other Americans, who were foreign to her. "I must learn about your country and its customs," she said in precise English with little hint of an accent. She spoke French as well and was a student of languages at the university. Her father was a planter and had taken over a plantation after the French had left. The rubber plantation was in the middle of the country, but her father had kept the family in Saigon since the beginning of trouble with the Viet Minh some years before. She knew little of North America, but had traveled to France once a year with her father and mother. She was concerned about the culture of the United States, knowledge of which she gleaned from American films dubbed into French and shown at university film festivals. She knew American film stars from the biblical epics that the nuns had shown during her cloistered years in middle school. Charlton Heston as Moses was her favorite, and she asked if any of us knew him. Bright as she was, she had no concept of the size and complexity of our homeland.

The usually noisy and profane atmosphere of the officers club dining hall changed to one of quiet composure during her presence, and men who had shown only rough ways regained civility even though they were not in her party at the corner table. She seemed to calm the "lords of the fly" who had taken on a different character in the absence of their own ladies. When in line for meals, one had only to say to someone who was cutting up that "Miss Huong is here." The phrase became a reprimand. Lieutenant Matthews and Miss Huong received permission to marry and her father decided that Robert would join him at the plantation rather than take his only daughter away to America. Lieutenant Matthews therefore decided to extend his tour to the end of his obligation with the Army and remain in Vietnam.

Less than three months remained in my own one-year tour, and I permitted myself to think of home and a return to the real world. Carol and I had written several times a week and we both had cassette tape recorders, which made correspondence nearly as good as a phone call. Once during the year, a two-week rest and rehabilitation (R&R) was authorized out of country. Free air travel was available to Hong Kong, Australia, Malaysia, Japan, and Hawaii. Like most, I was planning to meet my sweetheart in Hawaii, which was a favorite spot of Carol's. When I arrived back at the 69th, I expected to take my two weeks. The battalion commander, however, decided that the mission that pressed upon the unit was too vital to spare me and several others, who he referred to as key staff. My request was denied, but I was told that I could go over his head to Brigadier General Holeman, the Signal commander, who was a personal friend of our leader. I couldn't believe that I was vital. However, the colonel did not have the same high opinion of himself; he met his wife in Hawaii for the two weeks.

In the evening at the Khai Minh, after dinner, we would sit outside and talk over the day and drink something cold. Beer was popular, but cold Coke seemed to be the beverage of choice. It was so hot that it was difficult for our bodies to keep up with dehydration. One captain, a company commander, would always be found leaning against a lightpost with a tumbler of ice and scotch. I never remember him in any other activity no matter how hard I try. I saw him often in later years and even worked for him three times, and I still can't recall any contribution from him other than his smiling face every evening at the bar. Jerry Raymond would play his guitar and sing better than any professional. One night eight of us were sitting and talking when one related a combat story about Jerry. It seems that Raymond was leaving the compound at Long Binh one afternoon along the dirt track that led a mile to the main road for Saigon. He and his jeep driver were alone and halfway to the highway when a lone sniper took a shot at the speeding jeep and missed. "Is that it?" I remarked, surprised to find myself at the end of the heroic story.

Startled, the Saigon warrior said, "Yes. What did you expect?"

"He didn't go after him or go back and put together a patrol to eliminate the bastard?" I queried.

"No. Why?"

"He could have been killed," another chimed in. I could see I was not in the infantry.

One gets callused toward war and does silly things that only after the event send chills up the spine. Saigon was always the target for terrorist attacks. The VC's favorite targets seemed to be American Army trucks left unattended on the street. They would crawl under and attach a mine to the bottom, below the driver's seat, and wire it to the ignition. When the vehicle was started the bomb would go off, killing the driver, the passengers, and any bystanders. *Stars and Stripes,* the military newspaper, was full of warnings about the practice. I had the night off, a rare occurrence, and I drove my jeep downtown to the Rex Hotel. It was on the main street which bustled with traffic and pedestrians. At the time, Saigon didn't seem like a war town at all. It was more of an old-empire metropolis filled with locals in a hurry and street vendors at tables selling everything from toothpaste to flak jackets. If not for the brown army trucks and soldiers, Saigon could have been any peaceful market town in the modern Orient.

The Rex, once a first-class international hotel, had become a BOQ for senior officers and therefore a target. The first-floor shop windows, blown out by a bomb attack, had been replaced with cement block. That was also true for the second floor of the nine-story building. As a result it looked like a giant bunker. The main and only remaining entrance had been moved to the side, next to a considerable parking lot. Along the street's gutter, concrete pillars three feet high had been erected to prevent parking nearer than twenty feet from the pockmarked walls. The door was nearly invisible behind all the sandbags piled high, showing only a narrow vertical black slit to allow people to enter in single file. Military police in flak jackets and bulletproof vests and armed with shotguns stood watching the crowd like Secret Service agents guarding a president. Inside was even more grim since the bright tropic sun no longer penetrated. A number of temporary partitions spoiled the grandeur of the original design, and the once beautiful parquet floors were painted gray. The Rex was crowded, and I shouldered my way to the elevators which led to the best restaurant in the city. Combat officers who had somehow convinced their units that they had to go to Saigon for some compelling reason congregated at the elevator doors and looked up at the ceiling, waiting for the car to return. I crammed myself in with a contingent from the 1st Infantry. One of the tall, mean-looking lieutenants was wearing a buckhorn-handled Colt six-gun in a gunslinger's holster. "Howdy, Tex," I said. "Kill any varmints today in town?"

The others laughed, but Billy the Kid only curled his lip at the city boy he presumed I was. But I was safe; it was against the Code of Military Justice to shoot a captain.

The top floor was heaven. The area was divided between a roof garden and a handsome restaurant. I was hungry! Rather than a drink on the terrace, I got a table for one and sat back with the menu. I had come for only one thing, a big sirloin steak, the specialty of the house. The Vietnamese waitress, dressed in western clothes which made her seem totally out of place, said in broken English, "Yoou want a steek, sir."

"No, I want *two* steeks, medium, with onions and lots of fried potatoes." I don't know why they bothered to print the menu; everyone had "steek."

My two-steak order was not unusual, and she brought me the first one while the other was cooking. Perfect, the steak was like discovering sex; you knew you were missing something that everyone else knew about. I slowed my pace a little on the second one and actually raised my head and observed my fellow diners. Many ate alone, like pilgrims visiting a holy place after a long and lonely journey. Some were in ecstasy and smiled with eyes raised to God in thanks, no doubt remembering endless servings of cold C-ration ham and lima beans or beef patties in gravy. The C-ration beef was called hockey puck.

C rations came in thick, flat cardboard boxes which had to be ripped open with a bayonet, probably the weapon's only legitimate use in Vietnam. Inside were twelve individual meals in thin cardboard containers each half the size of a cigar box. On top of each box was printed in big bold black type the contents of the meal. To prevent the first people at the box from taking the favorites—anything with fruit cocktail or peaches—the box was always opened from the bottom to prevent revealing which were the good ones and which ones held the dreaded spaghetti and meat sauce. Rarely was the main dish, served in its OD can, ever heated in the field, even though heat tablets were included. Those were saved to make hot chocolate or coffee. English water biscuits, thick round crackers, with peanut butter, were the treat. In the field, no one looked forward to eating until driven to it by the long day and the stomach pains that always seemed to come before and after eating. Outside of sleep, food was a never-ending quest. I knew a guy so sick of C rations that he could no longer keep them down. He resorted to eating raw salted potatoes, which he munched on like apples. They kept him alive, just barely.

Every man in that room at the Rex was bound together by those little brown boxes, and we all recognized each other from aura of pure pleasure that glowed around each greedy gastronome.

After I'd finished my steaks, I couldn't believe it, but I heard myself tell the waitress to bring the dessert cart. There it was, banana cream pie! Even when I got a break from field rations and the cook at base camp prepared a hot meal, I never saw anything that resembled a dessert. Banana cream pie represents everything that is right with the world. And that one at the Rex was superb, thick and creamy, full of lovely lumps and as sweet as could be. When people are deprived of good food for long periods of time, they become solitary and sullen. But when they have consumed everything in sight, the old self returns and they are once again social animals. I left my private table and my angel of mercy—the waitress with the bad accent who smiled at the tip, the largest I have ever given—and slowly but steadily shuffled to the bar on the open roof. I wanted a drink I could think over. I asked the native bartender for his suggestion. "Something slow and warm," I said. A professional from the old days, when the guests were elegant ladies and gentlemen of means, he made the perfect selection and served me a large thirty-year-old Napoleon brandy in a snifter of cut glass. The man was a genius.

The drink carried me to the rail that surrounded the open

garden penthouse, and I leaned on it like a professional. If only I'd had my pipe and some Cavendish tobacco, I would have been totally content. I thought of my fear, on the ship during the long sea voyage, that I would disgrace myself in combat. I had passed that test and would not have to prove anything to anyone the rest of my life, not even me. The rail was crowded with others whom I guessed were harboring similar thoughts and, since I wore the patch of the most famous combat unit—by then transferred to my right shoulder, where it would remain the rest of my professional life—I could lean there and stare out blankly in the company of equals. A soldier wears his current unit insignia on his left shoulder, and reverses the one he wore in war to the right so that it looks back to days of fire and fear. In Vietnam all units but one wore not the full-color unit insignia but a camouflaged one in black and olive drab to reduce a soldier's signature and diminish his presence. My unit, the 173d was the only one to wear full-color in the presence of the enemy. We wanted to let Charlie know that he was facing the best.

The Rex was not the place for telling war stories—in fact, a sign over the bar read ONE WAR STORY IS WORTH A FREE ROUND OF DRINKS. As on nearly all nights, the sky around Saigon was lit up by artillery flares and carried the sounds of high explosives impacting in the distance. It was pretty to see the million-candlepower white phosphorous lights floating down gently in strings of four or five and then being snuffed out by the wet jungle beyond the city.

I stayed until my stomach said it was no longer hazardous to my health to move and returned to the slow elevator, one that had probably not seen maintenance since 1956. It was cool on the roof in the breeze, but on the street at midnight it was an oven. I found my little jeep among the big trucks and unlocked the padlock that held a heavy chain tight around the steering wheel. If I hadn't locked it, wandering drunks, late back to barracks, would have found her relative comfort irresistible and liberated her for sure. I plopped down in the seat and reached for the starter switch. At that moment I clearly remembered all the warnings of terrorist attacks and the newspaper pictures of mangled metal. Should I do the proper thing—climb out and crawl under the vehicle and inspect the undercarriage for explosives? I was an American; I turned the switch slowly and closed my eyes tightly, making a face in anticipation. Would the next sound be my last or would I just go home quietly? I went home quietly.

My old company commander at Headquarters Company, Capt. Norman Lee, gave up his company and became the battalion S-4 during my absence. He was perfect for that demanding job but had nearly burned out keeping a battalion three times normal size supplied. Though vital, he was allowed to take R&R with his wife in Germany. Norm's return coincided with the publication of the promotion list for major. Several captains in the battalion were on the list, which caused great celebration at the bar and led to much congratulation and to stories of how well-calculated careers had brought elevation to field grade rank. There are three categories of officers. The first is company grade, lieutenants and captains. Then (at the time, after ten or more years), comes field grade, major (0–4), lieutenant colonel (0–5), and ultimately colonel (0–6). Finally a few, less than one percent of the full colonels who began as second lieutenants, are promoted to the four levels of general (0–7 through 0–10), which occurs after the twenty-third year of service or later.

Norman had counted on promotion and needed it to retire at a decent pay level. But he was passed over and it came as a great shock to him. The once fierce officer, who had consistently demonstrated great knowledge and proficiency, lost his spark. "I am better than," and he would name one of his contemporaries, "in every way." As a rule, I agreed with him. It was particularly hard on the former enlisted man to talk to fellow captains who were young enough to be his son. I saw him in 1986 when I was visiting Washington, as a student at the Army War College, and he was getting off a subway train at the Pentagon. He was in civilian clothes, a retired major, working with a defense contractor. Norm was very cordial but I could see the hurt in his eyes that he had never kept up. He was more than good enough and I felt that the Army had missed an opportunity to retain a superior officer.

At first glance the man who took his place as commander of Headquarters Company and therefore directed the activities of the combat photographers might have seemed suited for the job. Unlike Norm, he was a school-trained photographer, a former sergeant who had been commissioned from the ranks. But he was the embodiment of being at least one grade too high for his ability. Sloppy and overweight, he was in constant need of a shave. Bombast was his style of leadership. Because of his age he was senior to all the other captains pouring into the battalion as replacements for the originals, who were all short-timers, those with less than two months left on their one-year tour. Worse, he had no desire to command. That is bad because, to command properly, one must want it very much since the responsibilities will wither even the strongest.

He preferred to take still pictures and his subjects tended to be Vietnamese girls rather than documentation of the war. Captain Lee had known of him in Berlin. Capt. Urie Minenski's family had been brought to the States from the Ukraine by his father just before the Second World War. Urie was born in America, grew up in New York City, and spoke several European languages. He looked foreign and used his appearance in the bohemian sections of Berlin to meet local women. He masqueraded as an American film director and snapped their pictures on the street while dressed in flashy clothes. He would then approach them and give them a line about being a talent scout for a future production. Urie had been run out of Berlin by the American command and was running a film library in Worms when he got orders for Vietnam. It was not a total loss as far as he was concerned. He spoke fluent French and in Saigon he could renew his old pursuits. At every opportunity he would sneak off to Cholon, the Chinese section of the city, and search for beautiful girls as "a photographer from *Playboy* magazine." He wasn't the only one. Many Saigon warriors used that approach, as all they needed was to purchase a cheap Japanese camera from the post exchange. The girls saw it as an opportunity to earn money and a chance to go to the States. Of course, they would have to give themselves completely to the nasty man, but competition was keen among the pretty women who were thick on the ground in the only cosmopolitan city in the country. Unfortunately for Urie, the troops didn't like his bragging and his private use of the photo lab to do his developing. He used his position like a hammer and treated the men as servants. He placed undue restrictions on their after-hours activities, presuming that they had the same low moral code that he enjoyed. As far as he was concerned negative incentives were the only way to keep the men in line, and he used military discipline with zeal.

One day I received a delegation at the Bat Con van from my old platoon. They weren't going to stand for any more of Urie's abuse and asked for my help. I had spoken to Urie before about his methods but he'd brushed me aside. I didn't want to rat to the Old Man about him because it would seem like I was still trying to run the platoon after leaving. Instead, I went to see the Signal Command's inspector general, a major, and suggested that since Headquarters Company had not had an inspection since arriving in country, while other companies had, they were overdue and could benefit from the experience. He agreed because it was easy to do; they were also billeted at Camp Gaylor.

The inspector general system, a Prussian invention that General Washington brought to the Revolutionary Army, was designed as an internal Army check on the operation of units to insure that the policies and programs set out by the major command were being followed to the letter. The IG, as he is known, reports to the commanding general only, insuring that no subordinate commander can unduly influence his inspection results. The officers and sergeants that make up the team—which descends unexpectedly on the element early one morning—are picked in Washington from the files. They must have a perfect record that shows integrity and job knowledge. It is a special detail which takes the officer temporarily out of his branch and designates him to be the conscience of the Army for a year or two. A unique insignia is worn on the collar in place of their old branch, and the sight of it makes unscrupulous men's blood run cold. Often, as a result of an IG inspection, the report will influence the commanding general to relieve commanders or cause charges of misconduct to be brought. The assignment as IG is rarely sought because it renders the designee a bit of an outcast. Nonetheless, it is a good experience and benefits the entire force.

I received another visit from the delegation a week later and they told me that the IG was in residence. I acted surprised. "We want to make a case against Minenski, sir," they said, "but we don't want to get in trouble."

They were afraid that he would get back at anyone who spoke out after the inspection was over. Twenty of them were ready to give the inspectors an earful. "You must organize your attack so it doesn't look like a mutiny," I told them. The IG sets up a time for personal problems and conducts the interviews away from the commander's oversight. "You must all go to see the IG as individuals, not as a group, and tell your own tales of abuse," I instructed them. "Make sure that each incident is covered in detail. He will get the total picture."

It is an ominous sight for the inspector to look out his door and see a line of downcast soldiers. It is always a bad sign and prompts him to look very deeply into the organization, across the board. As a rule few show up for the hour set aside for complaints, and the officer brings a book or magazine along to pass the time. That day the hour turned into an entire afternoon. It was not a pretty picture and most particularly in a combat zone where men's lives are at stake.

The inspector general was very impressed by the men and their plight and questioned Minenski as to the validity of the accusations. He went further and spoke to other members of the command during his investigation. Urie ran for cover and tried to press others to his side but found them unwilling to perjure themselves when the IG swore their testimony under the Uniform Code of Military Justice. The three-day inspection turned into a week. The mood at the officers club bar was electric in the evening, and Urie began to drink and protest his innocence, loudly. "They are all against me; they hate officers. All I did was try to keep them under control," he said, trying to enlist the help of the officer class. No one bought it. The report was furnished by the commanding general to Snead, who relieved Captain Minenski and wrote an efficiency report recommending that the officer never be allowed to command troops again.*

Captain Lee, by then maintenance officer because he had been bumped from his previous billet by a more senior man, had the responsibility to keep the electric generators running at the radio relay sites dotted around Saigon. The communications systems, both voice and teletype, were vital to the conduct of the war. It was over the military systems that

---

*In the mid-1970s I received a call in Stuttgart, Germany, while I was working an evening shift in the European Forces Headquarters Command Center. It was from SFC Urie Minenski, calling from the States. Not only did he not get promoted to major, in the reduction in force caused by the end of the Vietnam War he was reduced to his former enlisted rank, based on his record as an officer, and he was asking for my help. He still held a captaincy in the inactive Reserves and wanted me to write a letter to a board that was asking him to show cause why he should not be stricken from their rolls (which would affect his retirement pension and rank). The system worked!

orders were passed and supplies were requisitioned. They connected the foxhole to the worldwide system, back to the home bases that provided everything from personnel to medical resupply. They were used by commanders to report contact with the enemy and provided the information to higher authority, who made life-preserving decisions based on their content. The civilian telephone network was nearly nonexistent and, in any case, controlled by the enemy. The military teletype system was encrypted and therefore fairly safe from eavesdropping.

Obtaining parts for failing generators that ran continually was our biggest problem. Colonel Snead ran a very good network, the best I have ever seen, and Norm tried everything to keep the parts flowing, even resorting to horse-trading to make sure his boys were kept in operation. It was a never-ending challenge, and Captain Lee was expert at his job in spite of the disappointment he suffered at the hands of the promotion board. One day he told his senior NCO that there were machine shops in Saigon that made parts for generators similar to ours. "Our biggest problem is the worn-out crankshafts in the larger generators, right? Go find a foundry that makes shafts and have them fabricate a dozen for us." Like all great NCOs he did just that, and even worked out an agreement with the commodity command to sanction it as an experiment. There were no drawings or specifications, the selected manufacturer was just given one of the old shafts to duplicate. It took some time and careful monitoring to get the job done. The 1st Logistics Command appointed a project officer and the whole scheme was touted as a partnership between the host country and the US Army. It was not as easy as it looked and many hours were spent by Norman at the little factory to make sure that the proper grade of steel was used. A week became a month, and it looked like the assignment would never be finished. Lieutenant Colonel Snead began to doubt the wisdom of the venture and so did the Log Command. When at last the shafts were ready for pickup, they arrived in our maintenance shop in large wooden boxes packed carefully in straw to prevent damage on the ride across town. The first one was put in and it looked perfect. The generator was turned on and it nearly worked. The only problem was that it was too exact a copy of the worn shaft that we had supplied the manufacturer. It was, not to put too fine a point on it, an exact copy. We were the proud owners of twelve brand-new worn shafts.

One of those picked for promotion, Curtis Van Demere, threw a promotion party for his fellow captains. The ten of us were to meet at a famous floating restaurant, a large barge permanently tied to the main dock near the center of Saigon. I took off an hour early and strolled through town to the free dinner. Within a block I passed the Pasteur Institute for Infectious Diseases and stopped to read the large board on the black iron fence next to the main gate. It was a map of the country and had red dots showing where the plague had broken out over the past twenty years. That was very interesting because I'd thought that the disease had been stamped out. The dots were clustered around population centers and, in particular, around Hanoi and Saigon. Now I knew why we had to have shots. Next to the institute's gate, at the edge of the street, was a pile of garbage the height of a man. A dead brown rat was lying among the rotting vegetable matter. I wondered if it got there under its own power before dying or if a staff member put it there to add credibility to the map. The country was certainly diseased—we were given a half-dozen shots during deployment and took malaria pills daily. The river was so polluted that when one of our men accidentally fell in while unloading a ship, he was fished out and taken to the hospital for observation, his stomach was pumped, and he was fed antibiotics for a week before they would release him. Fevers of unknown origin (FUOs) were common among the troops, and I myself had night sweats for years after the war. Parasites were common. In the field each night, just before dark, we checked each other for leeches, horrible slimy black things that looked like large tadpoles that stuck to the skin and refused to let go. A lit cigarette applied to the tail would cause them to drop off just before the skin began to burn. They left a round wound where they had eaten the skin away, and sucked out a quantity of blood. Smashed with the butt of the rifle, they exploded bright red in all directions. For sport they might be lined up on a rock and smashed one after another, a source of much entertainment in the bush. I couldn't feel their presence because they anesthetized the incision with a chemical. They were commonly found around the top of the combat boot but also preferred the back, where they could only be found by a buddy.

Most Vietnamese in the countryside had several tropical diseases that they lived with all their lives, and our medics spent their spare time performing miracle cures on the villagers with simple western drugs. Bringing a sick child back to health was not only a joy to the parents, but it also made the corpsmen's day to see the kids playing again after just a week of treatment. Fungus infections were the rule for all of us and they were a devil to cure. In country they could only be controlled, not cured, and when one left, a packet of medicine went home in the luggage. Hepatitis or mononucleosis frequently attacked those who ate local produce and the treatment was nearly as bad as the cure. Once a week the casualty went to the hospital and received huge shots, many cc's of gamma globulin, in the rear end. The victims were easy to identify—they couldn't drink alcohol or sit.

Two blocks farther down the tree-covered street was the headquarters for the entire war effort, MACV, a joint operation which had officers from all services and our allies passing in and out of the gates. Just before I stepped off the curb to cross at the corner, a black Ford sedan rolled around the corner rather slowly and my eyes met those of Ambassador Henry Cabot Lodge, who was in the backseat. He smiled and gave me a little salute as he passed. That was nice, I thought. What a pleasant man to make a little gesture like that to absolutely nobody.

Across the street was an old hotel, of white concrete, MACV, that was set well back. Five stories high, most of its windows had been covered over or bricked in and painted white. It had a complex of smaller houses clustered around and was heavily guarded, clear out to the street. The roof was a forest of radio antennas. Little of the frenzied activity could be seen from the street and I was never allowed inside.

A friend, Capt. Roger Craven, worked there for the general in charge of logistics, the G-4. Roger was one of the most intelligent men I have ever known and was particularly valuable for his foreign language skills. He spoke French, Vietnamese, Chinese, and several dialects of Arabic. He was a political historian as well, and highly cultured. His parents were French immigrants, first to Canada and then to Boston. They had owned a barbershop and hairdressing salon. Neither were educated but they saw a spark in Roger early and sent him to *the* university, Harvard.

He was in the Quartermaster Corps and helped with the daily briefings given to the senior staff of generals who ran the war. Roger was not an impressive military figure and tended to be a little unkempt and overweight. He had no use for physical exercise and preferred his books and the pursuit of knowledge to games. It was easy to get him started in conversation at the Khai Minh in the evening after the nightly dog and pony show—the big MACV briefing every night at seven o'clock. Mostly he talked about international politics. He always took the side of the underdog, explaining the nation's character and history before explaining why it did what it did. He was a true Renaissance man and threw in bits of art and music along with the analysis.

I wanted to serve in Europe after the war and had always been fascinated with Napoleon and Wellington, whose lives and works he knew well. "With a name like yours, what else could possibly be of interest to you? It is in your genes,

Fitz," he explained. He knew the origin of my name, and after hearing that Colonel Snead had advised me to anglicize it said, "Don't you dare. Who would you be without your name." Because of his privileged position, I asked him to explain the strategy behind the war effort.

Roger was a chart holder. That is, each briefing consisted of presentations by the many principal members of the staff, covering every aspect of the war. The topics ranged from civil government to the delivery of B-52 bombing raids and covered the north and south as well as Cambodia and Laos. It was all laid out. Throughout the briefing Roger was out of sight in the doorway of a closet, with two three-foot-high acetate-covered charts showing the state of resupply. And, because the G-4 presented last, Roger heard the generals' candid discussions.

Roger said that one night they got stuck into a debate on the conduct of the war. My sensitive and knowledgeable captain friend listened for more than an hour, hoping to hear a clear plan with well-defined goals. Instead he heard a rambling diatribe based on the past service of the participants in the Second World War and Korea. "They didn't have a clue what this war was all about. They seemed to think that if we just put enough troops in and conducted normal combat operations in the areas they controlled, we would be victorious. After all, we always won. They took the politics out and tried to run a purely military campaign. But they accepted the direction from Washington pundits that gradualism was as good as any other method. What did it matter? We were destined to win or at least force a stalemate, like Korea. They accepted the casualties as a part of war. The wars that they had fought had much more carnage. There was no overall national strategy designed to win," Roger said.

He carried out the last presentation and placed it on the stand, like a pretty girl announcing the next act at a vaudeville show, and pointed while a slick briefer interpreted the numbers. His eyes were filled with tears when he thought of all those soldiers in the field fighting while the nation and its military leaders dithered. His boss, a very nice man, who liked Roger, was trying to do his best, and noticed the young captain's plight. After the conclusion the general came up to Roger and asked him, "What is bothering you, son?" They were very close.

"You all have no idea what you are doing," he blurted out, not now caring about the tact normally due a general officer. "You have no strategy and have made no attempt to apply the operational art of war."

"I know, Roger, don't worry about it," the old man said, "we are bound to win."*

As I walked on, the genteel architecture of the villas and Catholic churches mingled with the quiet of the suburban neighborhood to calm me as I continued toward the city center. The bustling traffic kept to the main boulevard three blocks to my right and I could see it each time I completed a block. I passed the Rex Hotel and wished Curt had picked it for his party. The restaurant he chose was known for good food and also for terrorist attacks on parties of unsuspecting soldiers and civilians. I passed through the red-light district of Saigon "tea bars," where the girls charged outrageous prices for their cup of tea, which they rarely drank. The buyer was treated, with no additional charge, to a trip upstairs to heaven. When I saw the floating restaurant in the twilight, lit up with colored Chinese lanterns that reflected off the wide river, I was glad I came.

We were all in a party mood. We were pleased that the board had picked Curtis for the field grade and were sure we would all serve together again and again in the years to come. The talk was of our families and how we would have them with us at our next posting. Several of us had orders

---

*I thought about the conversation each time I passed the headquarters and, in my naive state, I agreed that we were bound to win. Only after attending the Command and General Staff College and the Army War College did I appreciate the wisdom of the quartermaster captain.

for Fort Monmouth, New Jersey, home of the Signal Corps.
We were going to attend the corps' Career Course that began
the next January; we would be assigned other duties until
the six-month school began. We looked forward to resting in
our own quarters surrounded by each other and living the
high life in New York City.

The food was mainly Chinese and we picked through the
multiplicity of dishes on the menu, in the end ordering the
Genghis Khan banquet, which served the entire party and
literally filled the big table with exotic dishes too numerous
to name. It was an all-we-could-eat supper and I had a lot of
everything. A truck from Curtis's company picked us up
around midnight to convey our swollen bodies back to our
billets.

The next night I was stricken with the worst stomach
cramps and diarrhea I have ever had. There was no thought
of going to work in the morning and I lay on my bed only
briefly between trips to the toilet which, thank God, was attached to my room. I was sure the illness was temporary and
I medicated myself with the help of friends, who brought me
several medicines from the post exchange. I tried pills little
and big; potions pink and white; nothing stopped the flow or
the pain. I was drinking soft drinks and fruit juice in an attempt to abate dehydration. On the fourth day I felt a little
better and went to work, but spent the day running across
the street to the latrine. Always a believer in self-medication,
I sought the advice of friends rather than the medical community, which was at hand but not very appealing. What did
I need with them? I was strong and had survived nine
months of combat operations. I was no Saigon Warrior. By
week two I was no better and was finally taken to the hospital by my sergeant when I was too weak to resist. "I don't
want to lose you, Captain. I am tired of breaking in replacements," he said in comforting me. They didn't bother to admit me, it was too common an ailment. Testing revealed that
I had a raving case of amoebic dysentery. "Nice going, Cap-

tain," the doctor said, clearly a self-inflicted wound in his mind.

Lt. Sam Demming had been exiled to Nha Trang after several missed steps as a communications center officer. His first mistake was handing out to people without proper clearances unclassified traffic with classified messages in the stack. His second mistake was his inability to change the combination to a safe properly, thus, accidentally, locking it permanently. His third strike was the midnight procurement of a forklift from the Air Force and then changing its identification number to 007; James Bond was very popular at the time. The finding of the forklift, before it was lost, wasn't that bad, but being caught driving it by the air police with a pallet of beer stolen from their club was inexcusable, even stupid.

There is a block on the officer's efficiency report labeled "Judgment." Sam got a one out of a possible five and a new assignment as the officer in charge of the radio relay site near Nha Trang, the gulag of Southeast Asia. Once a staging area for combat operations, it had recently been given to our South Korean allies and served as an emergency airfield and communications site. "There is no way he can get into trouble up north," the colonel said one morning after the departure of the unfortunate junior officer from West Point. The site continued to operate normally and the boss decided to go up for a visit, so a hop was arranged for him on a cargo plane that was delivering supplies to the Koreans. Sam was sent a message to meet the aircraft and take the commander to see the relay site on top of the signal hill.

Those lonely radio installations were always located on the most inaccessible points because the signal required line of sight. When putting in a long-distance system, the land was profiled on a map to insure that no object interrupted the transmission path. Even tall trees could soak up the energy and reduce the signal strength to a level too low for intelligible reception at the distant end.

The signal hill at Nha Trang was precipitous, nearly eight hundred feet above the surrounding plain. The two trucks that serviced the crew of ten at the station suffered from fatigue and lack of maintenance and were deadlined at the announcement of the visit, and Demming was relying on the Korean Army for essential transportation. That morning they reneged and could not offer him any hope of a vehicle for support that day. Like any innovative young officer, Sam overcame that.

The colonel was accustomed to very good, even VIP, treatment when he graced a unit of his own with an inspection. As a rule the local commander met him with a polished jeep and a driver to match. They would first call on the local combat commander and go to visit customers, where the Old Man could see the quality of service delivered by his element. After all, the Signal Corps was a service organization, not a fighting unit. The only fighting it did was in safeguarding its own sites, which occurred all too often in Vietnam. Next he would go to the station and meet the soldiers and see to it that they were well cared for. That was always the easy part. Snead was an expert in equipment maintenance and he would pore over the radio gear and ask questions designed to show that the officer at the unit knew as much as they did about the operation of critical components. Before Colonel Snead left Saigon, I would brief him on the statistics for the past several months, pointing out the strengths and weaknesses of the unit's performance. (The detachment at Nha Trang had done a good job.) Lastly he would go over the vehicles and generators in enormous detail. The Old Man knew his stuff, and any survivor was damn good. The colonel expected a pleasant day away from Saigon, where he was under the watchful eye of the many critics who subscribed to our service.

He stepped from the ancient C-123 Air Force cargo plane onto the hot steel mesh of the temporary strip near the port city of Cam Ranh Bay. He was dressed in his finest starched tropic-weight jungle fatigues and shiny black boots, which were a little out of place in the real field and made him stand out next to the aircrew in their oil-stained flying suits. Looking like a drowned cat in a hand-washed uniform that was soaked by the heavy rain of earlier that morning, Second Lieutenant Demming stepped out from behind tall pallets of ammunition that lined the edge of the ramp. Not a good example, the colonel thought to himself as he greeted the officer with a smile and a good, firm handshake. "Well, Sam, how is it going? Your reports look good," he said to put the lieutenant at ease.

"Yes, sir. All is well here. I think you'll have a good day."

"Where is the jeep, Sam?" the colonel asked, looking in vain for the appropriate transportation. "I couldn't get one up here in the sticks, sir." The colonel understood, since his was the only American unit in the area.

Sam led the boss away from the apron and around the little mobile tower that controlled local air traffic, sticky mud caking the shiny boots and ruining the polish his maid labored over each night. "Here we are, sir." Sam pointed to a sixty-four passenger bus parked in front of them. The commander took several sidesteps to locate the small truck or similar vehicle that must be parked just the other side of the gigantic empty bus. "You mean that bus is my transport for today?"

"Yes, sir. It's nice and roomy," Sam said, trying to make a joke out of the whole thing.

"Where are your trucks, my boy?" The colonel was almost at a loss for words.

"Oh, they are deadlined, one for tires and the other has a blown engine. The hill and the rough roads take their toll up here without a motor pool to see to them."

"Don't you have an agreement with your customers to help you out with motor maintenance?" the colonel asked. That was a common practice among detached units. "Why, aaah, yes, sir. They give me replacements when mine are broken down." That was the wrong answer. The Boss never belabored questions or gave advice, he just stuck it in his memory bank and kept moving.

"Where is the driver, Demming?" It was a policy that officers never drove in the Army. There were two good reasons: They usually worked as they rode, and if there was an accident, the officer would not be held wholly responsible for any serious mishap.

"Well, sir, I couldn't spare a man from his duties." It sounded good but didn't wash. The colonel reluctantly climbed aboard and Sam took his place in front of him, like Ralph Kramden of the Gotham Bus Company for a trip down Madison Avenue.

"Our first stop is to see General Kim, the local Korean commander." Sam's choice of words, "first stop," was unfortunate. The colonel turned red at the thought of pulling up in front of the Korean commanding general's office in a large empty bus. Snead was very much into image.

The folding doors closed at the pull of the handle and the air brakes released with a "shhh." Snead pulled at the brim of his hat, a very bad sign. It was a nervous tick that always denoted a very unhappy man. They rumbled slowly out onto a red-dirt road deeply rutted by tanks, and the bus lurched around as they negotiated their way past the Korean guard, who saluted the lieutenant colonel perched alone in the front seat. The colonel returned the salute, feeling foolish and very alone in the cavernous bus.

A Korean Military Police light truck came up behind and turned on its siren and red lights as it passed. An escort, the boss thought, well *that* is a nice touch. The MPs stopped short once in front and got out. They boarded the bus and arrested the driver for stealing the vehicle from the motor pool. At last the colonel got a ride in a vehicle of more appropriate size. And it took him right to the commanding general's office, just as planned—where he was at a loss to explain the behavior of his lieutenant.

My Waterloo came shortly after the bus incident. One evening, just after I arrived at the Khai Minh about eight o'clock, someone called from my control office to tell me that we had lost the major system that fed the US Army headquarters on Tan Son Nhut Air Base. I gave them preliminary instructions on a plan for restoration and called for a driver and jeep to return me to the Bat Con. Before leaving I told my boss and passed on to him the directions I had given for restoration. An explosion along the main drag out of Saigon had brought down a string of multipair cables and injured people in the street nearby. I passed the scene on the way out and noticed that no signal repair trucks were on the site, nor were any on the way from Camp Gaylor.

When I entered the van my controllers were in a heated discussion with the company commander who had the responsibility for the span. He told my people that he didn't need any help or direction on how to do his job and directed my sergeant to butt out. I took the phone and told Capt. Melvin Orr the extent of the damage and not only to repair the break, which would take some time, but to reroute communications traffic over several other systems and preempt lower-order circuits that were still in operation for the higher priority stuff that fed the headquarters. Mel was a nice guy but didn't like taking instructions from a "photographer," as he put it. I held my ground and wrote down his words in the running log.

He ignored me and went about his business and told his people not to report anything to the Bat Con; he would take care of it himself with the battalion commander. When the periodic reports failed to come in on time, the C Company controllers got quite arrogant and told my guys to piss off. Things went from bad to worse and in the morning I was called to the battalion commander's office to answer the charges of incompetence leveled by Orr. My boss, Major Pennella, stood beside me silently, as the colonel blamed me for the slow restoration and misdirection. This was no time to back down, and I spoke slowly and directly to the colonel as to the incident of the previous night and provided quotes from my logs, which I placed forcefully on his desk. I remember saying that Orr's account was bullshit and that his picture at the company level was not sufficient for him to go it alone. Major Pennella, an old friend of Snead, just smiled and nodded. The colonel said, "One of you is going to get relieved, what do you think of that, Captain?"

I resorted to the professional answer, "Yes, sir," and stood looking Snead in the eye.

"That's all," he said, without changing his demeanor, and we left the ring.

"Fun, isn't it?" Pennella said as he peeled off into the quiet of his own office. When I got back to my office in the van my guys were up and wanted to know how it went. They had been through it before. In the past the officer never returned; he went directly to the gulag. I told the story rather more dramatically than it had occurred. My presence meant to them that Captain Orr had met his match and so had the colonel. My sergeant, Ronnie Rowbottom, summed it all up in his soldier fashion: "You have bullshitted the chief bullshitter. You are the survivor, Captain." At my Waterloo, in spite of my French name, I was the British.

I paid a visit to the Army headquarters on the air base one day to say good-bye to Maj. Malcolm Edgerton, who was leaving. He had completed his year and that, added to his service in Korea, gave him four years of combat. He was cheery as usual and we spoke of the hundreds of thousands of feet of motion picture film and the contribution he had made to history that was stored in the National Archives. He was gratified by the work done by the brave young soldiers, most of whom were in their teens. It seemed to us that one day they were in high school thinking of fast cars and pretty girls and the very next day they were given the responsibility of documenting the history of their country. They worked alone for the most part, in the shadows of great events, which at the time were significant only to the men around them. It would take time before their contribution was realized. Like Matthew Brady's neophytes of the Civil War, who first brought the camera to the battlefield as an instrument to record history, our boys continued their tradition. Brady's people were civilians and because of their crude equipment were static, shooting scenes after the fact or individuals and groups at rest. The modern combat photographer was a soldier who got into the thick of the action.

Combat photography came of age during World War I. Just before the war, America's Signal soldiers shot motion picture film of Lieutenant Selfridge, a Signal officer and first military pilot, with Orville Wright on the first military aviation flight from the top of the hill at Fort Myer, Virginia. They crashed, killing the officer and injuring Wright. The mishap occurred at the edge of the Potomac River on what today is Arlington National Cemetery.

Fort Myer itself was named for the first chief of the Signal Corps, Albert Myer, inventor of the military flag-signaling system used by both sides during the Civil War. Myer had been a medical doctor and first used mirrors during the Western Expansion to communicate across the plains and deserts. His flags during the day and torches at night were so successful that a new branch of the Army was formed in 1863. The new corps, regarded as cavalry, was given the facing colors of the American Dragoons—orange piped with white—who had been disbanded prior to the war.

The first balloons used for observation were given to the Corps, so it was natural that when the Army bought the first military aircraft, six years before the war in Europe, it would go to the Signalmen. Early pioneer pilots of note therefore, Eddie Rickenbacker, Hap Arnold, Billy Mitchell, and all the rest, were Signaleers before the formation of the Army Air Corps at the beginning of the war. The first American pilot wings showed an eagle in flight holding two signal flags in its claws.

The shaky black-and-white films of our troops in the Ardennes were an improvement over the film shot of Brig. Gen. Blackjack Pershing hunting Pancho Villa in Mexico. Pershing realized the importance of the motion picture and took combat photographers with him to Europe. In our age of images, which instruct our television audiences today, those early films make history alive the way no book could ever do.

During World War II, young soldiers with motion picture cameras were first to climb aboard Allied bombers to record the effects of daylight bombing. Assessments of the crews' accuracy were often exaggerated and film was quickly developed to give a truer picture of the deviation to be expected by mission planners. As a happy spin-off of field-photo documentation we amassed a library of motion picture film of every aspect of the conflict, which was seen by the public in newsreels and on TV after the war in *Victory at Sea*. What better way for the veterans of the wars to explain to their families the hardship of what they had done? The men who fought the wars deserve the accolades brought to the screen by the young soldiers who hung in there with them, camera in hand, who froze their youth for us.

I accompanied Lieutenant Colonel Snead out to Long Binh's Camp Gerry one day to see the place where I had spent my first night in country. I expected a change but was overwhelmed by the city that had grown up on top of the hill. Give an American soldier some time and access to materials and in his spare time he will construct a little America. We are not a people that takes on the customs of others. I couldn't find a vestige of the old tent village. The camp looked like a tract of ranch houses modified with screens along the length of their low side to make up for the lack of air-conditioning. The smell of the open latrines was gone because flush toilets had been installed. The dusty streets were glazed with Pentaprime, a black oil-extract similar to driveway coating used in the States.

I was dropped off at Jerry Raymond's company for lunch and a game of volleyball between the officers and the enlisted. The colonel continued on to my old home at the 173d Airborne to inspect my former photo platoon headquarters. He thought it best that I not go along.

When he returned four hours later my replacement was in the back of his jeep, along with his personal belongings. I pulled the sergeant aside and asked what was up. Sgt. John Millbank said he had been relieved. The Old Man had gone to the photo company headquarters after the demise of Captain Minenski and been briefed on the health of the operation in general. He noticed the drop in production from my old unit and went to see what had happened. The problem was that not much had happened. He found the photographers all in base camp and living conditions that appalled him. Cameras were rusty, trucks were deadlined or should have been, and the laboratory was not functional. John complained that he couldn't get space on transportation to the operational areas. I was not surprised. Sergeant Millbank was not a paratrooper and therefore unacceptable to the noncommissioned rank of the 173d. He was not an officer and therefore had little access to operational plans. The PIO, who had been so helpful, and the original commanding general had left, and their replacements had other priorities. The sergeant had been placed in an untenable position and he paid the price.

Capt. Jerry Raymond commanded a company of cable construction men, some of the strongest and most difficult to discipline in the Corps. It was their job to string the heavy cables along the roads around the capital and out along the highways north of the city for twenty miles. They were equipped with line trucks similar to those seen along the roads in the States that set the poles and hung the fat black cables that carried communications to every office, detachment, and headquarters. It was not only a thankless job but a backbreaking one. The troops felt little identification with the war until someone sniped at them or cut one of their lines in the middle of the night.

Captain Raymond had a complement of one hundred and twenty of the great apes, a term that made them fighting mad. In fact, they were very intelligent, and the brightest of them all was the cable splicer. Many of his men had worked for the telephone company before being drafted and were well schooled in their work by both civilian employers and the Army. Jerry's unit strung four-hundred-pair cable for the most part—that is, a line that contains eight hundred tiny copper wires coated with colored plastic. They are bundled in groups of fifty and within that bunch many subtle shades insured that one color was soldered to its perfect match in the next span. If soldered properly, the pairs do not cross even though a splice is made every quarter mile. After testing out each pair as the job goes along, the two ends are coupled together and they are covered with a waterproof case and sealed. It is time-consuming work that makes me admire the linemen every time I look up at a phone line and see the wad in the cable that looks like a boa constrictor that has swallowed a pig.

In the old city the French had run their lines through ceramic pipes installed under the sides of the main streets rather than on telephone poles. Much of the system had collapsed over the years and was nearly unusable in spots. Raymond's men were given the task of installing one of their giant cables into this system from MACV headquarters to United States Army, Vietnam (USARV), a distance of six miles. It took the effort of the majority of his unit and employed his only remaining cable splicing team, nonstop. While the majority reamed out the mud and pulled the reluctant snake through the underground conduit, the splicing team worked in half-submerged manholes, up to their knees in water. Colonel Snead, like Pope Clement egging on the painter in the Sistine Chapel, asked daily, "When will you finish, Raymond?"

The answer was always a reluctantly given, "Soon, sir."

That dialog had been going on for more than a month and Snead was about to leave the country to attend the Army War College. He didn't want to leave with the project undone on his watch. In normal circumstances it would have been a near-impossible task, but the colonel didn't see it that way. "It is a straightforward job," he would tell Jerry as they stood on the street looking down at the splicer in the depths of the manhole.

"Yes, sir," Jerry would admit, then stall for time. Distinguishing the many pastel shades of coated wire was difficult in the poor light. What Jerry never told the Old Man was that he was cursed with the only color-blind cable splicer in the Army.

At last I was going home. I was driven through the ornate pillars of the air base entrance and did not stop at Camp Gaylor. We continued past the numerous compounds, each ringed with sandbagged bunkers and a guard in helmet and flak jacket, who, very exposed, leaned against the side. It was too hot inside and they had plenty of time to duck and join their weapon which rested, unattended, in the open firing window. Some waved; they knew a short-timer when they saw one. It was like being kissed by a chimney sweep on your wedding day, and I bestowed good luck as I passed by. I was dropped off in front of a compound near the airstrip that was surrounded by a ten-foot-high chain-link fence. It was well guarded to protect the travelers, who had turned in their weapons. There was only one small man-size double gate, like an air lock. In between was a processor who asked for my travel orders. None entered without credentials; it was the holy of holies: there was no sneaking through. Once inside, one remained until the following day, when the Freedom Bird left. Officers were taken aside to a low, metal-sided one-story building just inside the fence. The enlisted went to one of three identical structures according to their place in the alphabet. In the space between the four was a crushed stone courtyard where a crowd of two hundred milled around. They had been processed the previous day and were waiting for buses to take them to their 707 and departure. I am sure that each in my group looked at them and envisioned themselves there the following morning, kicking at the stones and watching the sky for the arrival of the commercial airliner. Once the plane was inbound, the buses would load and take them to the ramp. The airport was known to be mortared periodically and takeoff was as immediate as possible.

Inside, large fans in the four corners sat on metal stands, blowing the humid air around in a vain attempt to cool the squat hall. It did little other than ripple the packs of paper and blow them on the floor.

I stood in line at the wooden counter faced with raw plywood, in front of a large letter F, with several others. It was a simple drill and we all showed great patience; there was nothing else to do. It would be a long day and I hoped that after administration was over there would be a place to relax and read a paperback book or get a good quiet meal with the others. I knew that out in the jungle nothing had changed, and my thoughts went out to the men there as I heard a flight of helicopters lift off and head out. God, I was lucky.

Suddenly someone, and then another, yelled, "Get down, get down!" Veterans, we all hit the dirty concrete floor at once. Forty guys all trying to find the lowest, safest point inside a flimsy building that gave little protection from any serious attempt to destroy it and us. The sides were nothing but insect screen and I could clearly see from my very own spot on the floor, next to the counter, the crowd in the yard heaped one on the other. Some, with wild eyes that had been so content a moment before, darted for a better place to hide. No one threw himself over a buddy to save his friend's life at the cost of his own.

What's happening? I thought in my spinning mind. It is our 364th day of 365. I didn't hear any shooting or explosions. I had heard the roar of a Skyraider, but the enemy didn't have any airplanes. The yelling continued. I braced myself for something terrible and pressed my face to the cool floor and covered my head with my arms. A banging and clattering noise grew louder and seemed to enter the room on the other side of the counter, then stopped. "All clear! All clear!" shouted the officer in charge of the processing center.

Reluctantly I rose and stuck my nose over the counter along with everyone else on my side. There, resting against the outside of our fence, was the front half, engine, cockpit, and torn wings of a Vietnamese Air Force fighter-bomber. The huge, black, four-bladed propeller, bent over on each end like cardboard, had torn a hole in the high fence and come to rest harmlessly in front of the gang getting ready to leave. The Skyraider had been making a low pass over the field and struck a power line, sending it skipping along the roofs of the numerous buildings of the family-housing barns. As it came straight at our group in the open, they had watched and realized that there was no place for them to hide in the next few seconds before its final impact. Along its route, pieces broke off and the fuel cells ruptured, setting fire to the long houses. If the missile had gone another twenty feet it would have killed most of the Americans trapped between the fence and the center.

People got up slowly and silently in the yard. The engine sat in front of them and smoked. Another yelled, "Look!" and everyone went halfway to the ground again. "No, up there." One man was pointing at the sky. It was the TWA 707, on its final leg. The buses and firetrucks arrived simultaneously. "A Skyraider, of all things." I was probably the only one in the two planeloads of Army troops who had ever ridden in one. Had it come to say good-bye?

The next morning it was our turn. We gathered and looked at the sky, some for another crash and others for our magic carpet. We loaded without incident. The plane was a marvel.

It was clean, dirt- and dust-free. No matter how well I washed, the red dirt was in my pores, and I stained the white doily on the headrest of my seat when I grabbed it to sit down. I was well forward and on the aisle. The flight attendants were like angels, neat and pressed with hair shades other than black. They had round eyes. Their hands were soft and white. The smell of the streets, sweet and heavy, was gone and replaced by that of the perfume worn by the ladies. The changes were a culture shock for me. The plane was quiet and when someone did speak, it was low and reverently. The airtight doors were closed and sealed before we were all seated. While the aircraft taxied, the crew scurried about getting the passengers strapped in and the bags stowed. We swung hard to the right, the four engines roared, and the tires bumped. The nose pitched up and the huge landing gear obeyed the hydraulic pumps and stowed themselves away. A mighty cheer went up that nearly blew out the windows. We were safe, we had survived. The pilot rolled the big plane over and said, "Take a look, boys, for the last time. Welcome home." Tears of relief rolled down my cheeks, unwiped.

As soon as we leveled off at thirty thousand feet over the South China Sea, the gray-haired colonel in front of me reached under his seat and pulled from his bag a new bottle of Johnny Walker Black Label whiskey. He twisted the cap off slowly but purposefully. He elevated the bottle like a priest offering the sacrament at mass, admired the color, and took a drink. Those nearby, his parish, watched the ceremony. He offered it to them with a blessing, "To all those we left behind." It passed between the immediate seats and came back to him. A lovely, polite flight attendant approached and said rather sternly, "There is no alcohol allowed on this flight," and reached for the bottle. The senior officer with ribbons from three wars on his chest looked her dead in the eye and said, "Now listen, little girl. You go back to your seat, sit down, and leave me very much alone."

"Yes, sir," she said.

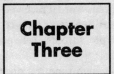

Chapter Three

*To a certain extent a man must merely believe
in his luck and figure that a certain amount of
good fortune will bless us when the critical
day comes.*
GEN. DWIGHT D. EISENHOWER

When I was young, the idea of being a soldier was exciting. I thought of all those who had gone before me and remembered Norman Rockwell paintings of intense faces with eyes fixed on some great goal that seemed beyond reach. To be an officer was an honor that filled me with dread, that all eyes were on me and that I dare not let anyone down. But to be a paratrooper was a joy. Those silver wings put one not only in plays of history but at the top of a profession. Now that the ceremony at the auditorium was over and I at long last sported silver parachute wings, it was time to open the orders and off I would go to join the Special Forces. The Green Berets, just made famous by the song and the book, were soon to be immortalized by none other than John Wayne in a Hollywood movie. While in Japan on my first tour of duty I had been an aide-de-camp to the visiting commanding general of the Signal Corps, and his executive officer had asked upon his departure if he could do anything for me. "Yes, sir," I said. "I would like orders of transfer to the Fifth Special Forces group in Okinawa, who are on their way to Vietnam." "Great," said the colonel, "I will take care of it, Fitz." A man of his word, I received orders that sent me to jump school at Fort Benning, Georgia, with assignment to follow. All Special Forces troops were paratroopers and volunteers.

There was just enough time left on that glorious day to get to the tailor shop and have my white embroidered parachute wings and airborne tab sewn on my work uniforms. I hoped there wouldn't be a long line; I had to compete with other members of my class who didn't want to be mistaken for "legs" (non-airborne-qualified soldiers) a moment longer. There was nothing worse than being a leg on that day. The seamstress at the counter could see my anxiety as I handed over the pile of uniforms. "It will be a couple of days before these are ready, Lieutenant," she said. "But I could do your glider hat patch now if you want to wait."

"Thanks, I'll wait," I said with great relief.

"Do you want a blue flash for your wings, too?" My God, I had forgotten the powder-blue cloth oval, the background for my wings. It proclaimed, "Here is a trooper who is currently being paid to jump out of airplanes, not just one who has been to jump school."

"Yes," I shot back. She sold me one then, along with a few more if that one ever got dirty. I still have the extras. Out in the car, on went the flash, an added bonus. Another short ride to personnel and I would be done for the day. I parked in a dusty parking lot next to a WWII-era wooden barn of a building and tried to keep my shiny jump boots clean as I leaped up the broken steps into the hottest building on earth. Late in the afternoon is a good time to go to personnel. The crush is over, the clerks are ready to go home, and a late customer gets quick service. A Spec4, one of the clerk Mafia who actually runs the Army on a daily basis, offered his assistance. I gave him my details and he disappeared into the files for my records. All I needed were my orders to Special Forces school at Fort Bragg, North Carolina, and I would be on my way in just in a couple of days.

He returned with my class yearbook, which I had completely forgotten. I had put an X in a block when I arrived and paid the seven dollars along with several other outlays in that blue fog that goes with "in processing." It was twenty pages of group photos and stock pictures of days gone by. A cartoon section mocking the instructors, students, and instruction was both poignant and funny. The last one was a classic and I thought of it often as my own career progressed long after the school had ended. It showed a four-star general (0–9) settled at his desk with clouded thoughts looming in the background. Within the cloud was the doorway of the school reception barracks with a sign above that read REPORT HERE FOR JUMP SCHOOL CLEARANCE. His chest full of ribbons, the general was writing ". . . and in writing my memoirs; Normandy, Bastogne, Inchon . . . they all fade away as, once again, I recall the most horrible and terrifying experience of my entire career . . ." How true. Why is school always more difficult than the real thing?

I looked up to see the clerk approaching with my folder. "Here you go, Lieutenant," he said as he dropped it on the well-worn, scratched counter. Not skilled at reading the jumble of abbreviations, I asked for a translation. "Well let's see, sir," as his eyes wandered from my face to the clock on the wall behind me. "You are assigned to the 44th Airborne/Ranger Battalion, Fort Benning, Georgia, with assignment pending."

"I was expecting SF school," I said, a little irritated.

"You may still get it, but not today, Lieutenant," and he glanced at the clock once more. I was ready for a long conversation about the system and what was liable to happen, but he was not. "Take these orders. You are the new assistant adjutant in the school battalion over in the Airborne area," he said. "Stop back in a week or two and maybe we will have something for you."

Orders in hand, I turned to see the sergeant in charge standing at the door with keys in hand. The door was so decrepit that locking it seemed pointless. Not at all impressed by a brand new paratroop officer, he grinned. Assistant adjutant, that was a personnel job, not something for a Signalman on his way to war. The war was going to be over in a few months, just like the conflict in the Dominican Republic that I had missed a few years ago. As adjutant I would be in charge of a bunch of clerks. I didn't know anything about personnel and didn't want to. The drive home across the post was slow and uneventful as I went over and over the disappointment.

The next morning I reported to the battalion area I had just left as a student and met 1st Lt. Paul Rob in the headquarters parking lot. I knew him but he didn't recognize me. I had been one of the many unknowns that he trained. Even though we were the same rank he had considerably more going for him. He was eight years or more older with a deeply rutted face from many years in the field. He had come up the hard way, as an enlisted for seven years, and was a graduate of the Officers Candidate School. More important, he was a master parachutist with over a hundred jumps in all conditions. I was nothing to him, and I knew it. Besides, I needed all the friends I could find. "Morning," I said with a new guy nervousness. "I am just checking in to be the assistant adjutant." He extended his hand and said, "Do you know where to go?"

Surprised that there was a little infantry grin attached, I said, "No." I expected some crack about being a Signal officer lost in the wrong area, but none came. I guess he thought that I was just another guy stuck in a training outfit just like himself. He pointed to a small squat building with a sign that was far too large, and said, "Good luck. What's your name?" Embarrassed at the obvious oversight in not recognizing the well-marked headquarters, I said, "Call me Fitz," hoping that my nickname would be easier to recall and one he might remember at the club or during an officers' call. Paul was a gentleman, but he looked like a movie version of a professional killer. I would meet many like him in the next few years but he was a real relief that morning, and I needed his kind touch just then.

The sign, flanked by a large, garish, colored crest and the words RANGER and AIRBORNE in the boldest possible lettering, announced that the building with peeling paint was the home of the training battalion. I opened the screen door and the usual piercing call of "Attention!" yelled by the private sitting just inside door made even me jump at its ferocity.

"Carry on," I said in a much quieter tone, since we were not in an auditorium but a very small chamber filled with metal desks, wall to wall.

"Can I help the lieutenant?" said a senior sergeant approaching through the maze. It was indeed the old Army when they addressed one in the third person. Trying to hold back my amusement, I said that I had orders assigning me as the assistant adjutant. That brought the typewriters to a dead stop. Those words, if correct, meant that I could be the new boss. The sergeant hesitated for just a moment in his stride but, hoping that I was in the wrong place, almost instantly recovered his composure as he reached for the orders. His eyes shot to the left side of my collar, but instead of the union shield of the Adjutant General Corps that should have rested there he saw the red-and-white Signal flags. I knew he was disappointed, so I smiled at him and asked to see the adjutant. "He is in with the boss right now. Would the lieutenant like a cup of coffee?" It was going to be a long day and an even longer couple of weeks if I remained in the third person. It was already a hundred degrees in that box, and hot, strong coffee had no appeal. The adjutant came in with long noisy strides and muttering to himself, not uncommon, I was to find, after meeting with the Old Man. He paid no attention to me and began to translate the wishes of the battalion commander to the sergeant in slow staccato phrases.

"Sir, this is your new assistant," the sergeant said, pointing to me.

Capt. Marty Ziegler was tall and thin and wore the shortest haircut I had ever seen. I could see his red scalp though a burr of black hair. He was flushed with stress and I knew that his high color would not come down when he found out about the qualifications of his new right-hand man. With relief I noticed that he was Infantry, a little out of his element as well, I hoped. "I'll be right with you, have a seat in my office. Sergeant, put another desk in there for the lieutenant." Marty's office was sparse but it had a fan so large that it blew me into a corner. It was great! In an obvious hurry, he said, "Have you met the Old Man?"

"No, sir," I said, surprised at his first words. Why should I have to meet such an important leader?

"Let's go," he blurted in an early effort to get my show on the road that hot morning.

We went through into another world. Lt. Col. Roger M. Johnson II had been a lieutenant on the big combat jump at Normandy and his office was a tribute to that Longest Day. Since he was totally absorbed in his *American Rifleman* magazine, I had a moment to take it all in. On the coatrack was his WWII tan jumpsuit with the red, white, and blue patch of the 82d Airborne Division on the shoulder. The suit was complete from the gleaming brown jump boots to the steel helmet covered with a camouflage net. The starch in the uniform broke the spell—I'll bet that only at Fort Benning had that suit ever looked like that. The walls of the very large office were laden with plaques, pennants, and posters. Pictures of old comrades were neatly lined up with present portraits of generals whose young faces were duplicated in the fading prints of old. I got the picture—they were all wearing stars and he was still hoping.

From the look of him he had long since been passed over. He had a dark-red complexion and a drooping face which matched his late-forties frame. He sat sideways to us with his feet resting on a pulled-out drawer of the wooden executive desk that was as highly polished as his boots. His badge of office, the colors of the battalion, were draped behind him along with the American flag. Above, on the wall, was a large set of simulated silver master jump wings and above that an even larger Combat Infantry Badge. On the wings were three bronze battle stars granted for his participation in the roughest fighting of that bygone campaign. On another coatrack, one for the present, a clear plastic bag held his Class A blouse, which was covered with multicolored ribbons. As could be expected, everything from the Silver Star on down were arranged to proclaim that I was indeed in the presence of a hero.

"Sir, this is Lieutenant Fizzen, your new 'quitters' officer." Struck by this new title, I was speechless.

The lieutenant colonel whirled around and said, "Signal Corps, hey?" I knew it would catch up with me, the only noninfantry officer in his battalion, and he appeared not to be grateful. No pleasantries were offered and I didn't even try to correct the mangling my name had taken.

He went right to the point. "I have given you a very important job, Lieutenant. We wash out fifty percent of each class because they don't have what it takes to be a paratrooper. That is split evenly between failure to meet physical standards and inability to master the training requirements. However, we lose another ten to twelve percent to quitters. Did you know that?"

It was my first chance to speak to the great man. I looked him straight in the eye and said very crisply, "No, sir," but I was not surprised.

"I want to know why, and you're going to tell me. Understand?"

"Yes, sir."

"Keep me informed of your progress." He returned to his previous posture and the magazine fell open once again. That was our cue to leave.

My next instruction came from the adjutant, in our office. "Think about it, and give me your plan by the end of the day."

"Why pick me for a job like this? I don't have the experience in the schoolhouse to critique training. I just graduated yesterday, sir."

Looking down at the stack of papers too large to be satisfied in one day, the captain said, "He has tried to get the answer before and used the school staff, but he thinks they were wrong. I suggested that he get a new guy, somebody from outside the infantry, to confirm or deny what he has been told."

"What has he been told?" I asked, hoping to get a running start.

Cracking a grin, he said, "That would be cheating, Lieutenant. See you at 1600 hours." He returned to the business of the day.

Quitter officer, I thought—that won't look good on my record without a lot of explaining. But I had to agree, no one knew better than I why someone would give up after struggling through those three weeks of ups and downs. Like so many, I would have quit every other hour, every day, but I kept myself going by always waiting until the next break to turn in my equipment. By the time next break came, I had distracted myself and let the feeling pass.

I walked the half mile to the training area and stood in the shade to watch the new class go through the ritual physical training hour from a safe distance. I had a real job on my hands, an important one, but who ever would have expected the Airborne school, which had been turning out determined men since 1942, to ask a Signal officer to answer such a serious question? I had to do it right, and guidance was deliberately absent. At the end of the hour, I heard the chief instructor announce, "If anyone wants to quit, just walk up to the instructors' hut and turn in your equipment, no questions asked."

I had heard that statement many times before and always felt that it was genuine and a little cynical. That they really didn't "need" me, or any of us, was the impression given by the invitation. But clearly the battalion commander did not want the decision to quit to be quite so cavalier. I followed the class across the ground-week area to the tower-week grounds. The covered bleachers held the whole class of four hundred, and I stood at the end in the dirt with some instructors to watch the demonstration. I would have enjoyed the show if it hadn't been for the task on my shoulders. After my hellos, I spoke to an old Signal Corps sergeant who had dogged me during tower week as I attempted to master the 250-foot free tower. He had a particular interest in seeing that an officer from his branch be the best, even better than those from the combat arms. At the end of the week I wasn't the best, but I was good enough to get out from under him. The demonstration progressed through all the skills each man would have to master, and the instructors finished by dropping a dummy dressed in a chute that did not open from the top of the tower. With that thud and puff of Georgia dust, the class was invited once again to quit, and "Just turn in your equipment" at the open-ended army truck the men would pass on their way out.

Sergeant First Class Young, my mentor and fellow spectator, said, "Every time an officer quits, ten enlisted soldiers join him within an hour." I was amazed. He continued, "You think that an officer is unseen by the soldiers in a school, don't you, sir? Well, they watch you like a hawk, and if you show weakness or express fear it just amplifies their own. Everyone is afraid that they won't measure up, and if *you* can't take it, they fall a little further. Remember, Lieutenant, don't ever disappoint the troops."

At little before 1600 hours I had a plan and I hoped it would fit what was required. I expected to brief the Old Man, but the adjutant took it instead. I started, "When a soldier quits, he is sent to personnel without any hassle and waits for orders to a new assignment. That's it, the end. I propose to set up shop in the personnel office and interview all grades away from the jump area, but not to speak to any of the jump committee or look at any of quitters' school evaluations. I want to keep the interviews sterile and non-threatening. I don't plan to make any transcripts, only notes as to my impressions and root causes for their failure in their own words. I will rely heavily on my own experience but will try to remain as objective as possible. At the end I will provide a written report and a short briefing."

The adjutant nodded. "Go see Sergeant Markowski at the post out-processing center and have him set you up. You have two weeks."

That is what I like about the Army—no long discussions, just simply-stated objectives with a lot of trust implied, and plenty of opportunity to fail. Sergeant Markowski was reluctant to have his well-oiled machine disrupted by some outsider. So, after some name-dropping, I ended the discussion by telling him that I would see the soldiers after he had finished with them. He gave me a small break-area room decorated with war surplus vinyl kitchen chairs and Formica-topped tables. Against the wall was an oversize, rust-stained refrigerator that looked like a coffin standing on end. Barely supported by the warped, water-marked, brown linoleum floor, it tilted to the left. The light-green room had the usual ragged fire evacuation plan stapled to the wall by the only door, complete with faded red arrows pointing to the end of the corridor. A good fire was the only hope for the building. In addition to the life-saving advice, there were black-and-white photos in thin black frames, presentations of awards and certificates given by a sturdy colonel in the traditional "grip and grin" pose. One dirty window let in the blazing sunlight. Well, I had picked the place so I was stuck with that oven of a room.

My first client was led in before noon. His first words I

would hear many times: "I thought I wasn't goin' to be hassled, sir."

"I'm not here to change your mind or fix any blame," I said. "I would just like to know why you decided that Airborne life isn't for you." I scrupulously avoided the word "quitter." After some beating around the bush I got his story: He had received a letter from his girlfriend that said if he went Airborne she would leave him.

"Well, sir, she said she only likes 'Legs.'" As improbable as that story seemed, I was stuck with it.

Right behind him a slightly older soldier came in slowly. He had a little limp. He was truly disappointed in himself and told me that he had developed shin splints and just couldn't see getting through any more long runs. If he went to the medics they would put him on a medical profile, give him a couple of weeks of barracks duty, and then he would be recycled. I understood his position; the thought of getting ill and having to start over again with no guarantee of completing had haunted me and most everyone.

Next came a second lieutenant of Artillery, my first officer. He was from Texas A&M and had just finished the basic gunner's course at the home of the Field Artillery, Fort Sill, Oklahoma. He was a sky diver with lots of experience and never thought that he, among all his friends in the class, would be on his way out. I found his story incredible. He said, "The thirty-four-foot tower was my undoing." When he surveyed it on the weekend before class began, he had scoffed at the massive structure, which was built on top of numerous telephone poles. But he had not jumped it; when his time came he stood in the door, looked down, and froze. I had seen it happen, had worried about it myself, but I had never heard of a sky diver refusing. It seems that he could jump from a plane without fear, but that tower was attached to the ground and he could not will himself to test the parachute harness; he felt sure that he would slip out.

A private whose meeting had been preempted by the arrival of the lieutenant reported stiffly with his best salute and took his seat across the chipped Formica. "I just didn't know what I was getting myself into, sir. I did pretty good in basic, it was a snap for me. I'm a real good shot," he said, pointing to his sharpshooter medal. "My buddies were at the top of the class, too, and they all signed up for Airborne. My drill sergeant thought everyone ought to be Airborne and he got me into this class with a little pull. Sir, I stuck it out for the first week, but I have been looking at that 250-foot tower for a week and I just can't do it." To the lieutenant it was the act of jumping from a thirty-four-foot level, and to the private it was being released by unseen hands in a parachute that was already inflated, high above the ground, that grabbed his insides.

Day after day they came in with one story after another. Some were very straightforward and others seemed to have missed their calling—they should have been novelists. Ernest Hemingway would have been proud of one private, who read me a letter from his mother. It seems that he wrote every day about his experiences and described, in particular, the morning physical training hour, which he found very grueling. Often he was unable to do the exercises to the satisfaction of the instructors, who would shout at him and make him do even more. His name had become known by them all, and all day they would single him out for even more physical punishment. He found the long runs in the morning beyond his personal endurance and fell out on every one. Such a display brought him still more attention, even a personal trainer, Sergeant Lucas, a man of prodigious size and strength who attached himself to the suffering soldier. He read me the letter. "Son," it began rather abruptly, "your dad and me are really unhappy by your letters about the tough time they are giving you at that jump school. They shouldn't treat a dog like that and you should tell someone over there to stop it. If it don't get no better for you, you should quit before they hurt you and put you in the hospital." It was signed, "Your loven Mother."

"Did you show this to anyone?" I asked very quietly.

"No, sir; I was going to but they said, 'Put your stuff on the pile and go to personnel.'"

"Why don't you give it to me; I will take care of it." He left happy that he had gotten out of another bad situation in his troubled life and I read the letter for myself. Written in pencil with large rounded letters, it was rather smudged and looked like a note written in haste by a schoolboy. It was an obvious forgery. Thank God, he didn't have a chance to show it to Sergeant Lucas, who had long ago lost his patience with quitters.

My heart broke one late afternoon when a very young would-be trooper sat in front of me with tears in his eyes and told me that his dad and uncles had all been Airborne and that he grew up on the stories of great times and great friends they had told over and over. He had felt a legacy being passed down, one that had become a burden at Fort Benning, far from the warm setting that had spawned his dreams of manhood.

"Why did you quit?" I asked, the only word that seemed to fit.

"I don't know, sir. I am just afraid I will never be able to pass the swing landing trainer. I have been at it all week and they told me today that I am going to be recycled. What is the use? I just don't have the coordination I should have. How can I go home, Lieutenant?"

What a spot for an eighteen-year-old kid. "Go call your dad; he will understand. He probably had trouble with the same damn thing; it's hereditary, not your fault," I said it to him with great authority in my voice. "You will be back after you talk to your dad," I assured him. To my surprise, he seemed to respond to that tin-pot analysis and departed in a little better humor.

There was bound to be a classic. Private Pitch was mine.

He was very straightforward, nearly self-righteous. "My wife and I have been praying about this school ever since I entered it last week and God told me last night that I should quit."

"Is this the first time God has spoken to you?" I asked out of curiosity.

"No, sir."

"Did God tell you to enter jump school also?"

"No, sir; that was my wife's idea."

"Did she know that paratroopers get paid more than other soldiers?"

"Yes, sir. One of her friends told her." Clearly the motivation provided by his God had transcended his wife's need for money. "Did God speak to both of you?"

"Ah, no sir. Just me."

"Does she believe that God speaks to you when there is a problem?"

"Yes, sir."

"Soldier, she is a very trusting woman. You are very lucky to have her."

When my two weeks were up, I gave the briefing to the Old Man. The hot weather had not broken and I was sweating through my tropical-worsted tan shirt as I waited. The written report was very short and so was the briefing. In other assignments I'd had, I would never have gotten away with such brevity, but there in the home of the type A personality I felt safe. The adjutant would lead the way and later pick up the pieces. "The colonel is not a man to be trifled with," advised the battalion executive officer, who was to be present at the briefing. The major, the oldest major I had ever met, was the second in command and would only assume command in the event of death of our leader which, from the healthy sound of his roar, was never going to happen. I checked my uniform for the last time and slid the note cards into my pocket. I had memorized the presentation and put the written report in a bright orange—the Signal Corps' color—folder. If anyone ever looked for it in the future, it would stand out from all that light infantry blue that buried the post.

"Let's get this over with." The adjutant pointed toward the closed door to the inner sanctum. The lieutenant colonel sat upright and ready to do battle behind the camouflage-cloth-draped meeting table with its eight leather-wrapped chairs.

I started with a restatement of the mission, just for safety. Then I said, "The student became totally immersed in the training and to him time stood still. In that time warp, that only the student entered, every task became enlarged and seemed insurmountable. Yet because others around him with the same background and experience were able to complete the same tasks, it led the trainee to believe that he could do it as well, eventually. However, when a soldier allowed himself to isolate himself mentally from the others, his natural fears took over and he was very likely to quit if faced with a task at which he had only marginal success. Therefore, *any* hurdle could be some individual's downfall. Something as simple as physical training could be as frightening to one trainee as the 250-foot tower could be to someone else. I recommend that the entire cadre and the student leaders be briefed on the importance of identifying those who are quiet and appear withdrawn and that such soldiers be paired up with a buddy from his own stick who is doing well, to carry him on."

The colonel looked at the adjutant but spoke to me. "Don't you want to change the training schedule, the attitude of the instructors, the content of the lessons, the arrangement of the students, the layout of the training areas, the positioning of the towers, or the color of the goddamn grass?" His voice and color had begun to rise as he spoke, though his eyes never left the adjutant's recoiling features. Turning his attention to me, he said, "Why, that sounds so simple, Lieutenant. You would think that any idiot who had been around this school for years would have already mentioned it." Having never been let in on previous attempts to answer the question, I regrettably said in my imposed ignorance, "Oh, then you already know that, sir?" I attempted to continue with an apology for parroting others, but he cut me off and looked again at the other two persons in the room. *"I* know that, Lieutenant, and now *you* know that, but believe me when I tell you that no one else knows that. Do they, Captain?" His eyes swung to meet the adjutant's.

"No, sir" was the adjutant's almost whispered reply.

"That is all, Lieutenant." The Old Man held out his hand for the orange folder. Grinning in triumph he handed it to the captain and said, "Put it in a blue folder." I left instantly. Put it in a blue folder, I thought. What a compliment.

Sitting in the glow of victory at the little desk pushed against the wall in the captain's office, I let the big fan work on drying me out; clearly it was not capable of cooling me off. When I saw the captain's face across the room, it occurred to me that I should go to the club for a swim with Carol and the boys and let my report seek its own level of interest while I hid out for a while. I looked down. On my 1940s-style black iron telephone was a bright yellow note that read, "LT, your orders are in." Perfect, I thought. I will be out of here before the training committee can get its hooks into me and discredit my conclusions.

At out-processing my treatment was a little more cordial than it had been two weeks earlier. I knew everyone there and had shared the horrors of that god-awful building. I knew that there would be no grip and grin photo of me and Sergeant First Class Markowski to grace the walls, however. The nameless clerk who had first presented me with the bad news of my posting to Fort Benning was a nice kid by the name of Bouts. This time he was cheerier than when we had first met over the counter. Service was instant. "Here you go, Lieutenant, they came in this morning." He handed me the usual seventy-five copies of thick, white, low-grade paper. Why we received so many copies every time we moved was beyond me and everyone else I ever spoke to about the issue. At the completion of each new assignment there would be a desk drawer filled with unused orders, even though I had made a real effort to unload them on every individual who ever even hinted that he might need one. Clerks always encouraged us to keep them "for your own records," as if we'd need them for our defense counsel in some punitive hearing yet to come. The warning was always the same and you heard it from everyone. As a result, after thirty years I have multiple copies of every transaction, an entire era of Army nonhistory in a steel footlocker that still resides with me. No one has ever expressed an interest in any of them.

Without even looking, well aware of my shortcoming at deciphering orders, I asked Specialist Bouts to do the honors and read the sweet news out loud that I knew would translate: 1st Lt D G Fitzenz is assigned to the 5th SF, Republic of Vietnam, with training en route at Ft Bragg NC.

"It says here, sir, that you are going to Fort Ritchie, Maryland, to some kind of support command. It don't say nothing about Special Forces or Vietnam." My heart stopped. How could it be? I had pulled strings—the head of the Signal Corps himself had stepped in and started the ball rolling. When Bouts saw the pain on my face, he sought out Markowski at once.

"That's right, Lieutenant," Markowski said. I did not see any sympathy in his eyes. I thought I caught a hint of "I just got even with you for interrupting my well-oiled machine."

"Who can we call to get this straightened out?" "We," it seemed, was the wrong word.

"You have to call your branch in Washington, sir," Sergeant Ski said, removing himself from the proceeding. I could see I was condemned. Taking on Washington by phone was beyond even the powers of an Airborne first lieutenant. As resignation began to rise, I asked where Fort Ritchie was and what was done there.

"Never heard of it" was the response from everyone in personnel. I began to worry. What are they doing to me, doesn't anyone know there is a war on and we should all be needed there? "I see here in the special instruction that you need an unusual kind of security clearance," my friendly sergeant said. Clearly he was beginning to enjoy the moment in an otherwise humdrum day.

Another visitor at the counter chimed in, "Fort Ritchie, that is a spook post outside of Washington." I immediately pressed him for more information but the well was dry. "Spook" was army slang for Army Intelligence service, but the term was never used by anyone in that line of work.

"It's near Washington; you could go see branch on your way there, Lieutenant," my concerned clerk advised.

In the car, the boys stuffed in the backseat of the two-door Falcon, Carol read a short passage from the *Officers Guide* as we ran the road to Washington. " 'Fort Ritchie, located in northern Maryland, has adequate housing, schools, commissary and PX facilities.' Well, that sounds nice," she said. She'd never been too keen on Fort Bragg and the aftermath I'd hoped would follow that assignment. Of course, she knew about Vietnam and the inevitability of an assignment there, but anything to postpone its becoming a reality was welcome. All other posts in the *Officers Guide* had long paragraphs describing their life and work in some detail, so it was a bit ominous that nothing else followed. I had been to Washington as a high school student, while visiting my brother, Jack, a naval officer, but I knew little of the layout. Therefore I headed for Fort Myer, adjacent to Arlington Cemetery and the Pentagon. I packed the family into the visiting officers' quarters there and we walked through the National Cemetery that bordered the post. It was Carol's first encounter with the rows of white headstones. Many years later she would become an "Arlington Lady," attending the funerals of my comrades on behalf of the Chief of Staff of the Army and Army families in an effort to comfort the bereaved. That volunteer duty, performed by a handful of Army wives, takes place at every ceremony whether for a president or a private.

I found out that officer records and assignment were located at historic Fort McNair, across the river in old Washington. At the time it was quite beyond my ability to imagine that I would one day command a brigade headquartered in the antebellum, red-brick buildings just inside the black iron gate made from old cannons. That day, however, the guard directed me to "Tempo B," one of many blocks of WWII-era "temporary buildings," crammed with the Army's personnel center. The numerous two-story blocks were connected by a continuous wood-floored causeway that steamed in the usual summer heat and humidity. People were everywhere, a slow swarm of uniforms and civilian attire. Clearly I was in clerk heaven. If those guys at the Benning outprocessing center excelled, personnel at Fort McNair was their reward. I could tell the residents from the visitors. Visitors were in crisp Class A splendor, hoping to impress assignment "detailers" and get the assignment they wanted. I doubt if it ever worked, but why not take the chance. I was certainly no exception and still on jump status to the end of the month, so I had it all together. Burdened with a blouse and tie and brilliantly polished jump boots, the hat in my hand showing the glider patch, I was prepared to beg my way out of Fort Ritchie. I had been advised by Sergeant Ski *not* to point out that a patron had directed my assignment to Special Forces. Those who did so might have their files stamped PI—political influence—a distinction not at all suitable for a lieutenant.

I reached the door marked SIGNAL CORPS and checked myself out in case something had been liquefied in the heat. Inside, the air-conditioning nearly knocked me over. One of the infamous little old ladies in tennis shoes was plopped in a steel swivel chair eating something that resembled a sweet roll. She looked very experienced as she quickly sorted and then dispatched the large stack of mail that overwhelmed her olive-drab desk. Behind her was a long open room containing four rows of identical desks overcrowded with clerks, all with their heads down, totally involved in their work and unaware of the din. Drab filing cabinets leaned one upon the other along the length of the walls. Telephone cables and electrical lines hung down from the ceiling over each work area, giving the place the appearance of a turn-of-the-century sweatshop. Not only was the room crammed with office paraphernalia, a mix of officers, enlisted, and civilian clerks worked with seemingly no separation. Without exception there was a paper stuck to everyone's hand. The telephones never stopped ringing even though it looked like most people already had a receiver mashed between their left shoulder and ear.

The cigarette smoke was too much for the window air-conditioners and a cloud of haze hung at about head height that had a smell common to public transportation. The room was painted light green; all rooms in the Army were light green. Apparently a study by psychologists on the effect of color upon the victims of combat fatigue after WWII showed light green to be the shade that most eased their suffering.

I finally broke the receptionist's obsession with her breakfast and inquired about my sudden change of orders. "You need to see an assignments officer, Lieutenant. That would be Major Springfield, he handles the F's. That's a funny name you've got, is it spelled right?"

"No, ma'am; it has a hyphen between the *z* and the *e*.

She looked totally bewildered and said, "What's a hyphen, honey?" I looked back at her equally stumped, not knowing where to start that journey into the English language, but she stepped right in and said, "Major Springfield is that tall man down there." She pointed at a humped-over figure who was speaking on the phone and writing from a standing position. His hair was longer than that of the officers at Fort Benning and he was considerably heavier than those outside Washington. His few ribbons showed that he had been in the Korean War but there was nothing of distinction. I squeezed between the people and furniture, taking many little steps in the general direction of my goal. He saw me coming, waved a friendly hand, and pointed at a nearly empty chair against his desk.

"How are you doing, Lieutenant?" He stared at my nametag and sorted me through the F's in his mind. Most of the people whose files he dealt with daily he had never seen, except for the poor quality, full-length, black-and-white photo stapled to the inside of their record folders. Those pictures made everyone look like a stiff laid out for the newspapers after a 1920s bank robbery. Each folder also had a name board in white plastic letters with our vital statistics. Signal Branch was known for telling lies to get us to take whatever assignment they had in mind for us. If a guy hadn't a clue about the job he had just been given, they would say that he needed the assignment to broaden the basis of his career. If he had been doing the same thing at each assignment, they said they were sending him to another such assignment in order to take advantage of his expertise, thereby setting him up for success. In reality, the assignments officers filled slots that came open at the same time as men became available.

Major Springfield was friendly at the start and then stealthily transformed into my confidential adviser, the man who knew best. He explained that an assignment to an outfit outside my branch was not good for the career. "You will lose valuable time while your contemporaries are learning the guts of big-time communications in assignments that prepare them for command." What he didn't say was that he had a slot to fill at Fort Ritchie and not in Special Forces. As

I put my case, his patience began to run thin rather quickly and, even though I kept bringing up the new war, I could see I was stuck with the assignment. I weakened, and he knew he had me when I asked what the job at Fort Ritchie was going to be. "Sorry, I can't discuss that here. Do you have the special clearance yet?"

"No, sir." I was dead and we both knew it was over. As an olive branch he took down my volunteer statement for service in Vietnam and said he would keep me in mind. I left the room and the building complex with a heart as heavy as the humidity. In retrospect, a few years later I found that Major Springfield *had* given me good advice. In the long run, and in most cases, Special Forces assignments hurt careers much more than they ever helped them. But it would have been fun.

Fort Ritchie turned out to be as elusive as Brigadoon. I found a state map that showed a general area for the installation but no road appeared to connect with it. We drove through Frederick, Maryland, and inquired at Fort Detrick, but the gate guard didn't know any more than that it was about thirty miles north, past Emmitsburg, Pennsylvania. "It is in Maryland," I told him.

"Well, maybe so, but it's still past Emmitsburg, Lieutenant." We drove out of town to the north and passed the giant antennas of the Moscow Hotline and accompanying building complex, which showed no windows. We had no idea that we had just passed the headquarters of my future battalion command, and our little boys stared unknowingly at the high school on the other side of the road where they would each graduate. We entered Pennsylvania next, and there inquiries led us off to the left, back into Maryland. There were no signs to direct motorists to the fort, no strips of run-down stores specializing in pawning, auto discounts, or army surplus, and none of the sleazy bars and blood donor stores that always preyed on the young soldier.

At last, running low on gas, I stopped just short of reentering Pennsylvania for the third time. "Yap, I know where it is," said the attendant at a Texaco station. He pointed behind the station to a little side road that wound through the hamlet of Blue Ridge Summit, Pennsylvania, which was just a dozen old run-down, large-frame houses. "No matter what, don't leave that road, and it will take you there," was his solemn advice. He took my money cheerfully and I could see he had given that advice before.

Carol mentioned how pretty a spot this was and asked if the fort was much farther; we were all getting restless. The road didn't show much promise, but we had no choice—our gas station attendant appeared to be the only inhabitant ever to have seen our Brigadoon; he was rather old and the station was Macintosh's Texaco. The road alternated between dark-green forest and great old Victorian houses. Carol thought that something great must have gone on there when we passed a large railway station on a single track. It matched the houses for quaint charm and was the center of what little activity there was. We were steadily climbing and the air began to cool but there was still no sign of Army activity. Passing cars bore no bumper stickers that granted access to Fort Ritchie and there were no olive drab trucks to follow.

Just when I had convinced myself that we were lost, we plunged over a ridge and there it was, in a green crater huddled around two small lakes and shimmering in mountain mist. As we all cheered, I rushed our little car down into the valley. From above the installation seemed small, no more than a half mile across, with no large buildings. It was walled in by a green mountain peak that rose a thousand feet to the pinnacle and was topped with a large red-and-white signal antenna. The gate was an arched stone affair that held a massive black-iron Victorian grill. The sentries were a pair of military policemen in Class A green uniforms with white cross-belts and gloves. Their greeting was precise and they directed us to the stone guardhouse adjacent.

We were expected, and in a few minutes our sponsor, Lieutenant Parsons, arrived and led us to the officers club and our temporary family quarters. The club was a jewel that matched the rest of the picturesque post. Made of native beige stone and great wooden beams, it featured a large center hall. At one end was a fireplace that reached forty feet to the timbered ceiling, with a hearth fifteen feet across. The hardwood floor was ringed with reception rooms and a bar that looked through a glass veranda onto the miniature lake and noncommissioned officers club on the other side. The great hall, roughly forty by sixty feet, supported a balcony that encompassed the open space on all sides with a light, wood-paneled balustrade. Lining the balcony were guest rooms, and one suite with a kitchen was ours until our quarters and household goods could be married together. After months of travel and school, this was heaven in the heather.

The next morning Lt. Bob Parsons and wife, June, showed up for breakfast in the dining room. Our boys were interested in the lake and asked if they had any children of their age, boys preferably. Carol was immediately in conversation with June about quarters, shopping, schools, and the other wives.

I was ready to explode. "Bob, what goes on here?"

"Nothing goes on here," he said calmly.

"What do you do?" From the shield on his collar, I could see that he was an Adjutant General Corps officer.

"I am the assistant adjutant so I don't get involved in the mission, Fitz."

With a glint in my eye, I said, "Assistant adjutant? I can do that."

"I will take you to your in-briefing and you will get the whole picture there." Then he changed the subject. "Did you know that Mamie Eisenhower shops in our commissary?" he confided to Carol.

After lunch, Bob drove me around the little nine-hole golf course that doubled as our parade ground and helicopter landing field. The first four holes were the flattest I had ever seen. On the far side was a tiny stone castle built in the shape of an Engineer Corps insignia, with two small square towers just large enough to house the office of the commanding officer and his deputy. "In the basement the Bureau of the Budget meets every year to finalize the president's plan; they like the seclusion," Bob said. The name-dropping was just beginning. "Henry Kissinger was an army private here when this was a training area for the Intelligence Corps. General Vernon Walters was a second lieutenant here about the same time as well." Curiouser and curiouser, I thought. We went to his office and I received my picture ID badge and a list of security clearances I had never had before. He turned me over to an escort who took me into the operations center across from the commander's office. So far all I had seen was barracks made of much more substantial stuff than wood and many very small office buildings made of stone and arranged in rows like fingers. They were all attached across the back by an enclosed corridor several blocks long. What a strange-looking place. I sat alone in the briefing room.

"Welcome to the National Underground Command Center," read the first color slide. Under that startling acknowledgment was a picture of a large, wooded, cone-shaped mountain with a bunch of wildly shaped antennas bristling from its top. I was intrigued. I had heard of Cheyenne Mountain, in Colorado; I had never heard of this place. The narrator said, "This has been a classified location for the president and members of the government to operate from in case of a national disaster since it was completed in the mid 1950s. Recently its existence has been disclosed to the public, and if you look to the right on the road to Emmitsburg, you will see that the trees have been cut around the parking lot to reveal the tunnel entrances." The narrator made it sound like they were a common tourist attraction. I had just driven that road and seen nothing. "Of course, you have to know what you are looking for," he said with a little chuckle. The briefing went on at length and buried me in the Cold War.

After work, Carol saw the plastic badge on my shirt and said, "So you know all about the mountain." She had met several army wives that morning who had ruined the best story I had to tell her in years. She then went on to tell me the important stuff. "The quarters are lovely, the commissary is really nice, and the Parsons have two boys," she said enthusiastically. "We are having dinner at six in their backyard." She expressed no hint of interest in site "R," or Raven Rock, as it was known among the inhabitants of the post.

I was soon to discover that except for the battalion commander, I was the only paratrooper in the outfit of forty officers. It might have been staff heaven or the old folks' home, but it was no place for me with a war going on. My worst thoughts were confirmed when I realized that there were only three lieutenants in the whole command. My company commander was Capt. Bobby Joe Lipscomb, from Virginia, and he was tall, dark, and handsome. He had a Hollywood smile and was very friendly and outgoing. He was also my next-door neighbor, occupying one of the four town houses in our building, one of a dozen like it in the family housing area. He had a wife and toddling son. Captain Lipscomb was a kind, sensitive, and deeply understanding man who took it to extremes. When he was told that his reenlistment rate, that is the number of his enlisted men who chose to remain in service when their three-year hitch was over, was low, he turned over the running of his very large three-hundred-man company to me and devoted his time to improving his statistics. That was in the days before the all-volunteer army was dreamt of, and drafted civilians, as a rule, returned happily to civilian life without even a thought of becoming Regular Army. Bobby Joe planned to charm them. Every one of the younger soldiers was interviewed in the Old Man's office. That was not an uncommon procedure but it was usually done informally by the executive officer and the first sergeant, and only those cases that hung on the edge were referred to the commander for the final push into permanent army life.

Not so in Bobby Joe's company. He would prowl through the barracks day and night with his list of potential "lifers." Once Bobby Joe collared a man, he was cajoled along the corridor to his impressive office and laced with free coffee. The talks could go on for hours. At times I believe he used sleep deprivation and brainwashing tactics that were still in the news from Korea. He achieved some success, but the collateral harm he was doing was destroying both the company and, more important, the first sergeant. Jean Claude LaGrange was our top sergeant and the best I have ever known. He was right out of Napoleon's old guard. So tall that he bent forward a little, he proudly carried a large hawk nose on his ruddy face. He cultivated one of the few mustaches I had seen in that time of Prussian-hairless stereotypes. Very thin, he was almost as gaunt as the survivors of the march from Moscow in 1812. But he was a soldiers' soldier and did not like to have his troops harassed. When at last Top could rescue a soldier from the clutches of the CO, the boy was usually visibly shaken. Top would send the lad off to the enlisted club with one of the clerks as an escort and nursemaid, buying them both a beer. In spite of the heart-to-heart talks LaGrange had with his captain, the badgering went on and on.

One day, when the Boss had gone golfing, the two of us sat in my office and talked of military history, at which we were well versed. I mentioned that I wanted out of that chicken outfit and of my aspirations for service in an elite unit in Vietnam. A veteran of WWII and Korea, he sympathized. I told him that I had volunteered and hoped that my statement wasn't lost behind one of those filing cabinets in Washington. He suddenly lit up, his whole craggy face turning up in a broad smile, and said, "All officers should get combat experience. It makes them appreciate the troops." I agreed, the conversation became much lighter, and he seemed to warm to me more and more. "Just where did you make this volunteer statement?" he asked.

A few days later the captain received a call from his friend, the adjutant, while we three were having our usual morning meeting to review the reenlistments. During the call, the broad white-toothed smile, the hallmark of Bobby Joe's personality, vanished, and he began to stutter as his eyes shot about the room in a wild attempt to focus. "I never volunteered for Vietnam. Why would I do that?" he blurted into the phone. I made eye contact with my very favorite first sergeant, and he said, without any danger of being overheard by the captain, whose mind had left the room for some blood-soaked battlefield, "Let that be a lesson to you, Lieutenant. Don't fool with the troops."

We had been short of money most of the time, but back in the States our Army pay seemed to evaporate. I remember one Sunday, we went to church, and after stopping at the corner store for a newspaper and a candy bar, I paid the clerk with my last paper dollar. It was only the twenty-fourth of the month; it was going to be a long six days to payday, but we would survive, as we had done before. It was my fault—I couldn't leave Japan without raiding the PX for one of each kind of oriental trinket, and this put us well into debt.

My job at the underground command center was interesting. The site was enormous. From the parking lot, the twin entrances, a hundred yards apart, looked like railway tunnels. They were a full thirty feet high and rimmed with white cut stone. Roadways two lanes wide led into the cool darkness and down to over a thousand feet below the top of the mountain. The Center had been blasted out of green granite. They said it took years to make the cavern. I rode into the Center on a bus with my fellow moles, as we called ourselves, and lined up inside to pass security. It was refreshing inside and a real relief from the summer heat that never penetrated its depths. Surprisingly spacious, one never got the feeling of claustrophobia. Well lit, the revolving glass and brass doors were replicas of the ones at the Fair department store on State Street in Chicago that I passed through each Christmas during the shopping season. But instead of the bustle and the smell of the perfume counter I remembered from the grand store, we were greeted by long empty corridors and light-green Army paint, just like in the Pentagon in Washington.

As a very junior officer I was entrusted with the position of "tour officer." Many folks from the various establishments of the federal government would be brought to the alternate office provided them in case of a national emergency. They were each entitled to a walk-through and encouraged to familiarize themselves with underground operations. I shepherded only minor officials and staff members; the big shots were cared for by others. If one was very important, a helicopter brought him the thirty-five minutes from D.C. A little lower down the scale and a chauffeur-driven car made the three-hour journey. If the functionary was destined for my attention, an old Army bus with all the windows open dragged the parties to my doorstep.

By the time they were in my care each one was ready for the snack bar. I always started and ended there. It was a walking tour and it was important to get the audience on my side that very long day. Everyone was looking forward to plunging into the science fiction of a city under the earth. They were shown the environmental systems that sustained life, and segregated bunkhouses for men and women that were fitted with steel army cots. There was a medical ward and tons of survival gear in storehouses. Mostly there were offices, not unlike the crammed ones they had left early that morning. I led them up and down, round and round though the labyrinth like an early monk in the catacombs of Rome.

"Let's go see the offices of the bigwigs," I said when their eyes began to glaze over. "This would be the office of the secretary of defense," I said as I opened a door that looked like every other door. It was only slightly larger than the other chambers, and I confided that "This is also his bedroom" while pointing to the steel cot in the corner, its army blanket wrapped tightly around a thin mattress. Crestfallen, the visitors would agree that life postevacuation would be no picnic, even for the leaders. Foot weary, I usually finished the day with a nice sit-down in the briefing room which restored their spirit. They had all seen the movies *Seven Days in May* or *Fail Safe* and had a strong hunch that a Doctor Strangelove lurked about the premises somewhere.

They were on the spot that would rule what was left of the world in a nuclear war and that alone made it very impressive. I turned them over to the watch officer and he put on a "dog and pony" show worthy of the menace we faced in the Cold War. Two hours later they were once again pumped up and ready to do their part to fight communism. Twenty-three years later the site was part of my brigade command; I made the trip by car, not by helicopter, and was toured around by a young successor. Remembering my own discontent, I offered him a good job once his sentence was served.

The summer dragged by. It was easy to let go and join in the slumber of Sleepy Hollow and the Van Winkle family, the home of Support Command. As the president moved the first regular forces in number into that faraway place, the news was beginning to fill with Vietnam. Just when I was ready to make another trip to my detailer in Washington, Bob Parsons called and said, "Its here, your orders to the 69th Signal Battalion, Fort Eustis, Virginia."

"What has that got to do with the war, Bob?" I asked.

"You're not going over as an individual replacement, you are going with a unit. That's good, Fitz; if you fly to Saigon as a replacement, they will assign you against a combat loss and you will be thrown into the fray, literally," he said with genuine concern in his voice.

"I never heard of the 69th. Are they Airborne?" I guessed they were not.

"Nothing in the orders requires a jump qualification, so I doubt it."

"When" was the only thing left to settle.

"It says no later than the first of October. That's next week. Can you make it?" Bob's voice cracked a little. We had become very good friends and our families had already gotten close, the way Army families do in the cloistered life common to small posts.

"I'll make it. I'll be in my quarters if you need me. I will pick up the orders this afternoon and start the out-processing. Can you get things started?"

"Sure thing, buddy. No problem. You better tell the colonel, though." He hung up, leaving me with the telephone in my hand and my head spinning.

Carol knew the moment I came through the door that the time had come. "My orders are here, and I leave for Fort Eustis and then to Vietnam by the end of the month," I said, getting the essentials out all in one burst. We hugged very hard and rocked for a long time.

"Well," she said, "I knew it was going to happen and nothing could stop it. I just wish it wouldn't come so soon." Her words choked off and she couldn't speak for some time. Army families are very tight, and the five of us, though apart, would maintain ourselves as a unit through it all. I never for a moment thought I would be killed, but I knew that Carol was not so sure and I tried to reassure her of my invincibility. I am afraid, though, she saw herself a young widow sitting alone for the rest of her life; I was a little accident prone.

The colonel, promotable, John Kelsey, understood that I had volunteered but felt I should have let the Army choose the time and place. "I can stop this, Fitz," he said to me as I entered his office and was seated in one of the two big armchairs in front of the stone fireplace in his dark-wood-paneled chamber. Clearly it was going to be a father-son talk, and I appreciated his interest. "I have been there," the veteran of two wars confided. "I know you don't want to miss your chance, but remember our history—this one is going to last long enough for all of us to get all the war we can stand. You need command and I would like to give it to you, here, now, Fitz." The offer was flattering, but I was beyond it and it did not turn my head. I just could not take the chance that he was wrong and miss my chance to be a warrior.

I read the efficiency report, the last piece of paper in an avalanche of paper that I received in thick files to be hand carried to my new unit. There was no time to mail them on to the 69th. My battalion commander at the Signal Support Command was a Special Forces lieutenant colonel of Infantry who had just returned from Southeast Asia. He was six foot six and the comment I can remember that he made on the report was that I was a "very neat small officer." Everyone was a small officer to that guy. At that moment I knew I had made the right decision to leave Rip Van Winkle's last outpost.

Carol and I drove south through Washington in near silence. I was on a great adventure and couldn't stop myself from thinking of other soldiers who had traveled down the same road past Gettysburg, Antietam, Bull Run, Fredericksburg, Cold Harbor, and Richmond. I did it in four hours; they did it in four years. I could see why men of all ages left the comfort of home and went easily to war. Women, mothers, girlfriends, and wives don't have the same perspective. They witness only the preliminaries and the aftermath of the distant battlefield, a place they will only read about. They tend to see it as a place of termination and are afraid for their men and for themselves. A young man's view is of excitement and purpose that transcends the wait and boredom of everyday life and enrolls them on the honor roll of events. They want to be able to say, "I was there." They know that some will suffer, but they are certain it won't be them.

The highway turns left at Richmond and the fort was just fifty miles away, near Hampton, Virginia. I finished my thirty-year career only twenty miles away at Fort Monroe, the island fortress that witnessed the battle of the Monitor and the Merrimac. We slipped through the gate of Fort Eustis and found the headquarters of the signal battalion in the early afternoon. Carol was not staying, she should be back with the boys before dark. Our good-byes had been said the night before in our bed, deep within the confines of our home. There in the street I unloaded the single suitcase, my name stenciled on the side, now my only possession. I had given up all else. Neither of us could bear the parting; we'd been together since grade school. Besides, there was nothing left to say. I promised to write continually for the year that would have no end.

I stood and watched the little blue Ford with Carol at the wheel, truly alone for the first time in her adult life, roll away. I stood in front of a one-story, pale-brick, glass-fronted building with the colors, a three-foot-square orange flag trimmed in white, snapping in the sea breeze. Not much activity for a unit on the move, I thought as I walked in and reported to the adjutant.

"You're the last one in," he said with a big smile; the roster was finally full. "The colonel is in and you better see him now before he disappears again." Lt. Col. Harold Snead was the boss and had been for two years. He was from the Class of '48 at West Point and a third-string football player, some would say on a two-string team. His early years on active duty had been spent as a unit football coach in the brown-shoe Army and he was well connected. The story was that he went to Washington and volunteered the whole battalion for service in Vietnam. Not only had he spent the end of WWII in school, he had missed the Korean War as well. Now heading for the twilight of a mediocre career, he was not going to let history pass him by. Small for a football player, he made up for it by strength of will and a great deal of skill. He was the strongest force in the battalion and had weeded out officers who, he thought, would not meet the challenge to come. A friend in Washington, at assignments branch, had done the transfers and assigned new folks with good potential to his command.

Snead was set. I was the only unknown as he reached across the desk and greeted me. "This eight-hundred-man battalion is headed for war," he said very dramatically. "That is classified secret," he told me in a much more intimate tone. Then came the bad news. "There is only one job left in the Sixty-Ninth, and no one else wants it. We are a field army signal battalion, the only one on active duty, and therefore have the largest combat photographic platoon in the Army. You are its platoon leader. Congratulations." I had done it again. This was one step below "quitter officer." Unconcerned about my qualifications, not caring that I did not even own a camera, he went on, "I want an officer who can lead that bunch of prima donnas and keep them alive." That said it all. I accepted. "Where did you get a name like that?" A purely rhetorical question, I thought, so I evaded giving an answer that would require far too lengthy an explanation.

"They call me Fitz, sir," and I left it at that, which seemed to suit him just fine.

As part of Headquarters Company, I went to check in and draw my combat equipment for the deployment, which was to start in forty-eight hours. The headquarters commandant, Capt. Norman Lee, was Jewish and married to a German girl who had remained in Berlin. A gray-haired officer from the school of hard knocks who had started out as a radio operator on merchant marine ships during WWII at the age of thirteen, he had been an enlisted soldier and won a commission through the Officers Candidate School. It meant a great deal to Norman Lee to have command of a company. With his elbows on his cluttered desk and with one hand in his thinning hair, he looked at my youth with utter despair. "I am going on ahead of the battalion by aircraft in the advance party. You are going to take the company by ship from San Francisco." I then understood why he looked so disapprovingly at me; his 106 men, forty-four of whom were in my platoon, were going to be trusted to a youth nearly young enough to be his son. "Do you think you can do that, son?" he said, knowing that I would give him the flip answer.

I did. "Yes, sir."

His eyes rolled and he reached for a bunch of papers, handed them to me, and we went to work. I got a break around six and went to the mess hall. There was no time to make it to the officers club and back, for my marathon had just begun. The mess hall was part of a barracks building that had everything under one roof: three stories high, it had forty four-man rooms, a supply room, company offices, and a recreation area with TV, table tennis, and pool tables. The vending machines had been emptied by the troops, as could be expected just prior to the move. This modern army's stomach traveled on junk food. The washers and dryers on each floor never stopped spinning since the order was that "all underwear will be olive drab and will be inspected along with each man's personal baggage." The idea behind this was that white underclothing would blow a man's cover in the jungle. Of course, in Hampton and the surrounding area the sudden unfashionable switch blew our cover. Our highly classified departure was advertised by the olive drab clothing now worn by ordinary citizens; soldiers don't spend an extra fifty cents to run the laundromat machine clear of dye after use.

Like all mess halls, the dining area was segregated to allow the officers to sit together in seclusion and discuss business. There I met the other lieutenants who would make the odyssey with me. The most memorable, perhaps, was Jerry Raymond, a football player from New Mexico. He appeared a little older than twenty-four, my age. He had a break in service, having returned to civilian industry when his two-year obligation was over. He and his wife, Grace, had a young boy and girl, and the army life of travel and separation was a threat to their family life, which they cherished. During his time with IBM—and I never found out how long that was—he found that corporate life provided even more disruption and left little room to do anything of significance. The service didn't pay as well but it was never short on giving out responsibility. Jerry had arrived the day before and already established himself as a competitor: he had to make up for time lost. A backslapper and hand-wringer, he greeted me as I have never been approached before, or since. "Hi, I am Jerry Raymond, what's your date of rank?"

Date of rank was never an issue between lowly lieutenants, and I stammered that I couldn't remember. "Sometime in January, why?"

"Just checking. What job did you get?"

"I'm the photo platoon leader, it was all that was left." With that the others at the big dining tabled cheered. They were relieved that someone else had finally been stuck with it.

"And you will be a great one." Jerry laughed and shook my hand again with even more vigor than the first time.

Even the other three lieutenants in the platoon, who had been to pictorial school and majored in film studies in college, were glad to welcome me as their leader. "It is one of those jobs you can't win at," a rather inarticulate second lieutenant told me. "The platoon is filled with guys who want to be immortalized taking the picture of the flag going up on Iwo Jima, and the colonel wants the platoon to immortalize the 69th."

"That is the way it has been for the last two years," another officer said. "I am glad I am getting out of this chicken outfit." I soon found out that half of those present were not accompanying the battalion overseas. They had been hand-picked to leave and none of them was sorry to miss the war or the colonel. He was known as "No-chance Snead," the terror of the Signal Corps. If anything went wrong on your watch, he would get himself another boy. I didn't subscribe to that style of leadership, but when lives are at stake, and they would be where we were going, Colonel Snead may well have been right.

The next evening meal, and our last at Fort Eustis, was at the officers club. We were joined by the ladies, who were still there waiting for the last minute and the last good-bye. The colonel's wife was charming and took in the new offi-cers as if we had known her for years. In spite of the carping I had heard from those who were being left behind, I got the feeling that night that 69th Signal was a top-notch unit that would do its best. To the great surprise of the Boss, the offi-cers he had rejected bought both him and his wife going-away presents. A crack in his manner appeared briefly as they presented his wife with a piece of silver for her table, which they would all remember as an "island of refuge in a sea of hostility." To the commander they presented a new hat, claiming that his "needed an oil change."

He came right back with, "I am going to miss you boys, but not much." The Army is a great place because of the fre-quent movement. If you get a boss you can't stand, be as-sured that one of you will move within the year.

The party went late—there was no sleep for anyone that night. After midnight the officers recovered to their units and began the last of many inspections. Officers' baggage was not inspected; we were gentlemen. As a result some rules were bound to be broken. The first sergeant, J. B. Miller, known to all as "Top," had prepared the company, so the other lieutenants and I met briefly to fan out with the NCOs. Within the headquarters, the troops were divided up by work departments. Headquarters Company serviced the three line companies that provided long-haul communications to large field units and connected them to the Army's central command headquarters in Vietnam. While the majority of the 69th worked at terminals and relay sites or in communications centers that processed the thousands of written messages or operated telephone switchboards and network control facilities, Headquarters Company provided the means for them to do their job. Our job was administration, personnel services, operations, intelligence, supply, and maintenance, and the company contained a separate combat photo platoon.

Segregated by sections, the troops had been isolated in different bays of the barracks and dismantled everything they intended to take in a display which lay on the floor in front of the owner. Anything not necessary had to be left behind. Not only was the soldier expected to carry his own belongings, he would also help with unit equipment needed for survival in the jungle until we married up with the major items that had been shipped earlier. The "300" trucks, with their signal huts perched on top filled with radios and teletype equipment, had been driven to Savannah and loaded on commercial ships for the long trip through the Panama Canal and the South China Sea.

The inspectors were looking for consumables, extra stuff that the soldier was afraid he couldn't get replenished. Excess quantities of candy bars, cigarettes, toilet items, magazines, peanuts, and canned hams or salami from well-wishers back home were forbidden. In 1965 alcohol was still the drug of choice, and since we were going by a US Navy chartered ship, no booze was allowed. However, the American soldier is most innovative and the men presented us with a challenge. The "amnesty boxes" scattered throughout the barracks were empty; the men were going to make us find it all. Top and I hit the photo platoon and he led me to the first find with a nod of his head; he was giving me first blood. Rolled inside socks were miniature whiskey bottles.

There was also a canteen filled with gin. I know because I took a sip from every one. Top opened any aftershave that was caramel colored and found sour mash, one hundred proof. Several wooden tent poles had been drilled out and filled to the brim. Large-mouth opaque plastic bottles of developing fluid held smaller bottles of vodka submerged inside. Vodka was a favorite; it leaves no telltale odor. My prizewinner was an old sergeant who had a long plastic hose filled with white lightning wound around his legs, which was invisible underneath his baggy field pants. In the cooks' section, notorious for its drinkers, inspectors found that the cooks had decanted theirs into large plastic bags and flattened them between the folds of blankets. A sharp lieutenant, a veteran of the deployment to Europe, threw the blankets on the floor, saying, "We won't be needing them ten degrees from the equator." The aroma of Red Label filled the room. From that point on we each searched with a bayonet, probing every soft bundle and breaking many hopes for a drunken sea voyage.

Weapons were our primary concern. Patton may have carried ivory-handled revolvers, but those below the rank of general had to survive with issue firearms. Even though a good old country boy professed to be a much better shot with his old squirrel gun, he would tote an army rifle on that there hunt. It wasn't the gun that was the problem as much as it was the ammunition. Calibers must be standard because nothing else is heavier than bullets. When you don't need them, they're too heavy to carry around, and when you do you aren't carrying enough.

No civilian clothes were permitted in a combat zone. As we progressed, the troops who had not yet been inspected witnessed what we were doing and began throwing items in the amnesty boxes. Our work began to go a little faster and by three in the morning we had finished. I had a feeling that some of the stuff would reappear when the men said goodbye to their families. Outside in the parking lot the warm night was lit up by the headlights of family cars and the blue glow cast by the overhead street lamps. A line of Greyhound buses sat nose to tail. Dressed in uniforms of blue-gray highlighted by white socks, their drivers gathered together and smoked. The drivers were totally unconcerned, as if they were taking the high school football team to an away game. The families gathered near their soon to be departed men and spoke in low tones, waiting for the starter to begin loading. The battalion executive officer, Major Fukashima, said, "If you are all in order, Lieutenant, get this show on the road." Major F was an outstanding leader and would be sorely missed. He had just returned from a one-year tour in Vietnam and was posted to another unit in the States as soon as we left. He was a first-generation American-born Japanese from Hawaii and had spent the last fifteen years on assignments without his family. It was an old tradition with oriental officers in the Army, that they spent their careers away from home, only returning a few times a year on leave, providing children with a more stable life. I had never met anyone who had lived that lonely a life before, and after the war I never met another who chose to continue the tradition. Times and the Army were changing.

I gave the signal to Top and he gave the command for the men to fall in and file onto the buses. Then only the officers were left on the tarmac and the atmosphere thickened with heavy hearts and the smell of diesel fumes. Wives, children, and sweethearts pressed against the sides of the grimy vehicles and reached up for a last touch. Some of them looked at me and their faces, blue-gray and drawn, fixed me in place for a moment. They might be receiving a condolence letter in my handwriting and they wanted to remember my face. I knew that I would not recall their countenances when I told them of the last moments of the life of a soldier who was then staring down from the bus window. In previous wars, the War Department sent families of the missing and dead a very brief telegram of the news that hit like a hammer.

During the war in Vietnam it would be different; each victim's next of kin would be notified in person by an officer or senior NCO. I and many of my friends would take on that duty during breaks in our tours; a most unforgettable experience.

As I walked around the four buses for the last time, I felt my dog tags swinging under my shirt. We had been scrupulous with each man to insure that his records were correct and that we knew who in the world cared for him. The tag, with only the most vital information stamped in raised letters, would start that ball rolling. The pre-combat training program included instructions on "what to do in the event of the death of a soldier on the battlefield." A charming representative of the Adjutant General's grave registration section gave the instructions. He was a career army undertaker and delivered a rather matter-of-fact discourse. His only training aid was a pair of notched metal tags just over an inch square, which he dangled from a silvery necklace. "The unit commander will insure one of the identity tags, known as a 'dog tag,' is removed and provided to the graves registration section of the AG office." The tags he held aloft clinked together, a tiny death knell. "The remaining metal tag will be placed into the open mouth of the deceased. The tag will be held vertically between the upper and lower jaw with the notch at the top between the center incisors." Thankfully he demonstrated on himself, straining to allow adequate space for the metal wedge. He inserted it briefly and removed it quickly before gagging. "Then crush the lower jaw, forcing the tag deep between the two large incisors." Rather cavalier he continued, "This will insure that the tag will not become separated during transport of the remains." With that he gave himself a mock uppercut on the chin, leaving us to imagine the dental damage. No one objected to the macabre demonstration, stunned within our own thoughts. Each saw himself in a wet, muddy jungle looking at a face that now said good-bye to the family. The image remained with me for a long time, more than any other training I had received. Could I do it, would I have to? When the boys from graves registration took charge of the remains, they would insure that as few as possible would be unknown. This practice began during the carnage of the Great War and has been refined with each conflict since.

I mounted the lead bus, took the place in the first row that had been saved for me, and told the driver to go. As prescribed, we slipped through the front gate at four o'clock and headed back up the road that I had just descended, to Washington and Dulles International Airport. To maintain the secrecy of the movement the battalion had been scheduled to slip out of Hampton Roads by different routes and airfields. The other three companies left from Richmond, Norfolk, and Fredericksburg. The commander and his staff, although a part of my company for administrative purposes, were leaving from Washington's National Airport. There, near the Pentagon, the Boss's friends could see him off to war in a more fitting and memorable way.

Most slept but I could not. What an adventure, and I was in the catbird seat watching the sun come up through the big glass windshield. We arrived on the auto ramp for departures and stopped in front of the TWA entrance. I went inside as the troops and all that baggage were unloaded on the sidewalk. It was eight o'clock on Monday morning and I bypassed the long line at the counter and hailed an airline official in her dark-blue livery. I told her who I was and the mission I was on and handed her a bundle of 106 tickets. She stared at me in disbelief. By then my men were stacking up behind me in full combat gear with steel helmets, field packs, and long army rifles. The polished floor was soon covered with dark duffel bags and the pile grew uncontrollably before her eyes. Clumps of civilians circulated around us in an attempt to join the lines of passengers of their own kind. "I assume that TWA has been expecting us. Do you have a charter agent?" I asked in an attempt to help.

"You can't stay here, we have all these people to board," she said as she tried to get me to go away and find my rightful place.

Other airline representatives crept out and told me I must put the men back on the buses, but the Greyhounds had returned to their kennels and we were in TWA's hands as I pointed to the tickets held together by rubber bands. It was obvious that they'd had no warning of our arrival. An Army full colonel from the Pentagon accompanied by some friends of similar rank walked up to me and asked for the battalion commander. I told them that he was not with the company but, along with the staff, was leaving from National. The colonel was as perplexed as the ticket agent. "We have come all the way out here to bid him bon voyage," he said, as if it were my fault. Clearly caught out, the field grade officers changed their attitude and began to talk to the sergeants and soldiers, a rare occurrence for men who probably hadn't seen a real soldier for years. The fraternization picked up the troops' morale in the middle of that mess and cleared the way for me to resume negotiations with the carrier.

The airport manager arrived with a handful of uniformed security police. My tickets were behind the counter and a huddle had formed around them. The scene was getting ugly, there was no space in front of the counters, and I heard one older man telling his wife that we were there to take over the airport. He must have seen the movie *Seven Days in May*. Another man walked up to me, broke in, and asked if we were part of the force that would seize the capital and the TV stations and put an end to the war. The airport manager took the man aside to assure him that this was just a summer troop movement that was having a little problem. The chief ticket taker emerged from the huddle and said curtly, "You are indeed on the regularly scheduled Monday morning flight to San Francisco. Take your men outside to the parking lot and away from the counter." The man said he would call me when they were ready. Then he asked, "Are those guns loaded?"

Angry at our treatment, I said, "Not yet." I was about to make a scene and fall in the troops with much pomp. I could already see the headline in the *Washington Post*. After all, the Army expects lieutenants to screw up; it would understand. But my commander, luxuriating in the lounge at National Airport, would surely swing.

The airport manager took our side and moved us in an orderly fashion away from the ticket counter and across the main lobby to the doors at the far end. There we were placed on several transporters to wait the remaining hour in comfort before boarding. The first sergeant made the rounds and gave the security lecture one more time. "What if someone asks us who we are and where we are going?" someone inquired.

Ever resourceful, Top said, "Tell them that you are the 33rd Underground Balloon Corps Company going to Disneyland for training." That got a laugh and the point across at the same time.

I had expected some kind of charter arrangement, so the news that we were regular passengers surprised me. At last the transports came to life and propelled us to a stretch-707, where the back hatch gaped open, waiting for us. I stepped into the aft cabin and was greeted, as expected, by a beautiful blond flight attendant who handed me one hundred and six boarding passes. "Here, give these out as they get on," she said with no other greeting. I looked into the cabin and discovered that rather than sitting in a block of seats, we were interspersed the entire length of the airframe. The men filed past and the other officers helped get them seated. The movement on board was a shambles.

Another attendant came up to us and said, "Those long rifles won't fit in the overhead racks."

The blonde was losing her company composure. With arms folded she said, "Well what are you going to do about it?" Before I could answer, she added, "Don't you take your hat off when speaking to a lady?"

"No. I am under arms." I was wearing my .45-caliber pistol. We were just about to get very ugly with each other when the airliner's captain arrived. Like most airline pilots he was a Reservist and therefore from both worlds. He grabbed a rifle and maneuvered it under a seat with great difficulty. Everyone fanned out and did likewise to help the soldiers get settled.

Suddenly an elderly lady in a fur hat and matching coat screamed at the top of her high-pitched voice, "These men have guns!"

The captain was off in a flash and seized the handset from the wall. "This is your captain speaking. We have the pleasure today to welcome on board some American soldiers. Their guns are not loaded and are perfectly safe. Please help to make their trip a pleasant one." *That* was composure! Order was restored, and an attendant who had been forward came up to me and asked, "Is it true that you are all going to Vietnam?" In spite of all our efforts, it had taken a pretty girl just two minutes to wangle a secret out of one of my boys.

We landed in San Francisco in the early afternoon and there the passenger agent had been warned of our arrival. We deplaned last and nearly destroyed the seats while retrieving our weapons. We were literally dumped onto the tarmac and stacked up against the terminal wall facing the airplane. The troops' morale sank in the sun as we gulped the fumes from the taxiing jets. No one had come to meet our flight. I found a phone and called the Oakland Army Terminal. After many dry holes, I reached the transportation motor pool manager, who had never heard of my unit. "I haven't any buses until tomorrow, all I have is open-topped cattle trucks, Lieutenant."

"Send them; I have got to get these troops off the hardstand," I said in desperation.

"They will be there in an hour," he promised. True to his word, six dark-green tractor trailer trucks snaked around the apron and picked us all up.

What a great ride. It was a beautiful, clear day as we crossed over the Oakland Bay Bridge. The view from the open trailers was spectacular, much better than inside a closed bus. The men, jubilant at the sight, waved at their fellow travelers, and folks in cars seemed amused at their antics.

Oakland Army Terminal dates back to the Philippine campaign at the turn of the century. It hugs the water on the west side of the south bay and is made up of loading piers and wooden warehouses large enough to hold commercial airliners. The last civic improvement had been made during WWII, when they painted the leaning buildings a rose beige. There were no troop barracks; no one stayed there long enough to warrant the buildings. Since the Korean War the terminal had moved freight to support troops stationed along the Pacific Rim and in Hawaii. The whole battalion fit into one giant room, and the concrete floor was packed with steel bunk beds. A balcony above the office space on one side was reserved for officers. The accommodations were the same, just a little higher up. I went to the phone and called my brother, Jack, who lived in Walnut Creek. His wife answered and said she didn't know when to expect him but would give him a message. We spoke briefly; she was not a supporter of the military.

I settled the men, reported our presence, and spoke to some of the officers from A Company who had just arrived in buses from the airport in Oakland. They told a similar story. Their organization was twice the size of ours and they had not enjoyed the change of planes in Chicago. At least our trip had been nonstop. About dark I found a bed and crashed for the first time in two days. In my dreams I saw a bright light and a crowd of soldiers yelling my name.

Suddenly I was roused by a strong flashlight beam that I

tried to ward off. "That's him!" a man said. "Fitz, wake up; your brother is calling" were the first discernible words.

Alarmed and thoroughly confused, my head buzzing, I said, "Get that damn light out of my eyes."

"Are you Lieutenant Fitzins?" the duty officer insisted. "Your brother is on the phone."

"I don't have a brother. Leave me alone," I lied, in no mood for that nonsense.

"Get up; he says it is a matter of life and death," the duty officer announced.

"I'll kill him, where's my gun." I reached for the pistol belt slung around the bedpost. Still dressed, I melted to the floor; I was absolutely disoriented after only fifteen minutes' sleep. Holding on to the bunks, I followed the courier to the steep wooden steps and clattered down. The receiver swung from its cord on the pay phone. I snatched it and yelled, "What the hell do you want!" Startled by my greeting, my brother held the conversation while I reached for civility. A former Navy officer, he had located me by going to the top and working his way down until he talked to an enlisted man in the motor pool. The one thing I remember was his saying, "Don't worry. I have purchased a life insurance policy on you that has no war clause. We will all be taken care of," he assured me with a bit of triumph in his voice.

"What do I get out of it?" I inquired. My older brother was betting with a conglomerate that I was not going to make it.

"Well—you get peace of mind."

"I had peace of mind until you called."

In the morning we packed up and headed for the docks on foot. The officers in a leadership position went on board and met the captain in the wardroom. He was pushing sixty and rather overweight. A good sign; he appreciated good food, the only thing we had to look forward to for the next twenty-one days. We were briefed by the US Navy liaison team that acted as go-between for us to the Merchant

Marine crew of the permanently chartered USNS *Upshur*, named for a naval admiral who was a hero of the last great war in the Pacific. She had been a commercial cruise ship until the Navy took her over in the fifties and had her stripped of luxuries. The majority of the rooms had been converted into open bays, and the game rooms were gone, as well as the duty-free shops and the swimming pool. However, the air-conditioning was in working order. The officers mess was the old first-class dining room, but it was no longer ornate. The large staterooms up top were for the officers, and the troops were confined to large rooms filled with canvas beds. There was a sick bay and a canteen store counter that offered shaving gear, candy bars, cigarettes, and malted milks. How they came up with that combination I will never know. She was large, seven hundred feet overall, painted many times in light gray with a black smokestack striped in blue and yellow. Like all ships I have ever been on, there was a sweet, cold smell in the passageways.

The complement aboard was to be just under three thousand. The 588th Engineer Battalion was nearly as large as the 69th, and we were expecting the 97th MASH—mobile army surgical hospital—shortly. The engineer outfit was brand new and commanded by a classmate of Snead's, Lieutenant Colonel Chambers. In a properly staffed engineer battalion he would expect to have a complement of three majors, a dozen captains, and twenty lieutenants. He arrived with one captain and thirty-four lieutenants, most of whom had been commissioned in June of that year. Snead was amused.

The Navy team consisted of one well-worn lieutenant, equal to captain in the Army rank structure, and four Navy ratings, sergeants in army terms. Stowed away from the Regular Navy, they seemed uninspired, and I wondered what they had done to be exiled into our hands. The Navy's first words were, "There will be no alcohol on this vessel." They gave us the daily rituals—boat drill, mess drill, man overboard drill, ships details, and inspections. The spread of disease was rapid in closed spaces and the specter of mass mal-de-mer was also discussed. The MASH unit had forty-five Army nurses and required special handling, to use a nautical term. We were required to conduct a 100 percent muster within twenty-four hours of departure. If the roster presented to the ship's company did not match perfectly with the head count, we would return to Oakland and start all over again. Lieutenant Colonel Snead assured the captain that his unit would not be the cause of such a drastic action. We got the message.

In the meantime, the troops had been loaded by the sergeants and I went out on deck and joined the officers at the rail. The Navy knew how to do things right. On the end of the dock a military band struck up "Anchors Away" and "As the Caissons Go Rolling Along" as we shoved off. There was one great advantage to going to war by ship. As soon as the ship was free of land, the one-year combat tour began and combat pay, fifty-eight dollars a month, started. Those who arrived in the combat zone by air began their time when the wheels touched down in Vietnam.

Eighty feet below, between the ship and the pier, the dark-green water boiled. I could feel the vibration in my shoes as the ship's turbines throbbed for the first time. An airliner hurtled past just above our heads, its wheels extended, on the glide path for the international airport at the south end of the bay. A long line of strong white strobe lights, which reached out into the water on pilings, signaled the end to their voyage and the beginning of ours. On our port side, "When the whiskey is gone the port is always left," Navy men-of-war stuck their prows beyond the mooring and strained for the open sea. As narrow as razors, they were not at all like the bulky troop carrier we inhabited. We had no need of their escort on our passage; there were no U-boats in our path. Next to the Navy were ships of the steamship lines, and I hoped to point out the liner that I had taken from Japan, at government expense, with my family less than a year ago. No luck, the SS *Cleveland* was not at home, but her sister ship was and I waxed on about her glories. My last passage was free; this time I would have to pay double.

We passed under the Bay Bridge and everyone commented to the effect that "We didn't come within a hundred feet of scraping her bottom." Out the other side, San Francisco was lit up by the sinking sun. We all joined in pointing out landmarks and telling tales. The seafood at the shoreline restaurants dominated our comments.

Major Marks, our new executive officer, promised to treat us all to lobster thermador on our return. His offer was not taken seriously, nor was anything else he said. A tall thin man with a large head, he was the toady of the Old Man and ran to him at every opportunity. A rusty container ship twice our size, its decks covered with multicolored metal boxes, momentarily blocked the view. To starboard, Alcatraz looked like a ship tied to the red buoy off her tip. I wanted to see the Presidio, the Army fortress that guarded the harbor entrance. And there it was, in Spanish white stucco and red tile roofs, still on duty. It was clear that we were going to meet a tramp steamer that was closing on us rather quickly under the Golden Gate. She gave us a warning blast on her horn and we responded with the correct number in return. It was the first time we had heard *Upshur*'s voice and it startled us, to say nothing of the drivers above on the car span who were unsighted. It seemed to me that we had just left the dock, but an hour had passed.

The sea closed behind us and the mist came up in front. The ship began to pitch and roll gently. The first sergeant met me on the stern after dinner and reported that all was correct below. "Ready to start, sir. I'll lead the way down." We both wanted to get the muster over with.

The ship's troop decks were A and B, which were at and below the waterline, respectively. There were eight compartments from front to rear on each deck. C deck was for the crew, stowage, equipment, and the running gear. Below that were the fuel, water tanks, and ballast.

My troops were all in one compartment of their own, B/8. We were on the whip end, above the propellers, or screws, and at the end of the air-conditioning lines. Top took me to a hatch which led to a nearly vertical ladder that ended three decks below. How the men carried all that baggage down there I could not imagine, but I didn't ask. Top preceded me, facing away from the ladder and grabbing the rails with his palms reversed. I had seen Mister Roberts do that in the movies and it looked natural. Faced with real life, I mimicked Top, but at a much slower pace. A fall would be very embarrassing and surely land me in sick bay.

The men's compartment was one big metal box filled with a forest of steel poles three inches thick, each strung with four beds. The top one was a mere two feet from the overhead. I could not see the lower ones for all the humanity and luggage piled tightly. There was no open area at all to hold a meeting, only narrow slits that allowed one to pass sideways. I beckoned J.B. back into the stairwell.

"How do you plan to do this?" I asked, knowing that he must have a plan.

"Beats me, sir." The instructions were "to physically see each man individually and have him sound off with his name, rank, and serial number while you check his picture ID card against his dog tag and roster number from these sheets. You can't let anyone leave or enter during the count and you must insure that there are no stowaways."

I noticed right away that there was no "we" or "us" mentioned in the requirements. "Okay, have each man get in his bunk and we will follow a strict pattern so as not to pass a man twice." He did not look thrilled so I asked him if he had a better way. He shrugged and we began. After an hour it was clear that it was not going to work. Not having much knowledge of the sea, I did not know that there was a group of rocky islands ahead. I did notice that the swaying was increasing. We retreated to the ladder-way once more.

"We need a new plan, sir," Top said, pointing out the obvious.

"Here it is," I said, talking to him like a quarterback in a sandlot football game. "Take all that debris in the aisles and pile it on the beds, then have each NCO gather his own section around him and account for each man. When they are ready, I will stand at this hatchway door as they lead their boys past, one by one, and return to their holding area. You check the roster and I will verify the dog tag and ID card with the face."

I did not ask for his opinion but I got it just the same. "Moving all the stuff up for the muster and back down again for the night is not going to be a treat, Lieutenant." When he called me by my rank, I knew he was passing me a signal of disapproval.

"They have twenty-one days to get the baggage straightened out. We have a few hours to get this damn roster correct," I responded. "I will be on deck when you are ready." I knew he did not need or want my supervision, and I retreated. I stepped onto the wet deck. I had forgotten how dark it is at sea. Although I could not see the water I could feel the turbulence, and I looked for handholds to get me to the rail. The fresh swirling air was a relief after the closeness of the chamber below. It took longer than I expected and the bells told me that it was after midnight. I was alone.

J.B. grabbed my arm and yelled above the angry sea that they were ready. "This better work, sir; the men have had it." I stood at my designated post and got a handhold on the edge of the hatch. The picture had changed. The troops were down to just their shorts and the temperature was hot and steamy. The compartment pitched and rolled more violently than the deck. For the first time I picked up the smell of vomit. That good Navy chow that had been consumed so greedily had come back to haunt us. With each pitch the stern breached and the propeller cleared the water slightly. With the resistance against the blades reduced the screws spun at much higher revolutions, like a car up on blocks. The whole compartment shook for a moment before the tail end submerged once again into a deep wallow. The rolling caused the rifles, hung by their slings, to swing out in unison into the path of the troops as they began to sidestep toward me. We need not worry about stowaways in those conditions; no one would have willingly remained in there.

The plan was working and the troops were quiet except for their recitation. We had reached one hundred when Private Nance's turn came and he planted his feet in front of me on the heaving deck. He gave me his card on the upstroke and held out the dog tags still secured around his neck. He spoke out loud and clear. I took a look at the picture ID on the downstroke and raised my eyes to his, and he threw up on me. The first sergeant was frozen. That did it, one hundred and one was close enough. "Well, Top—all correct, put the men to bed, I will report." I pivoted to the ladder and climbed to the top, the aroma with me. I burst out on deck, skittered to the rail, and threw up into the wind.

In addition to the forty enlisted men in the photo platoon, there were three lieutenants besides me. The officers shared a stateroom high up and in the middle of the ship. It was a spacious room with two portholes and two built-in leather-covered couches that became beds. The other two bunks were buried in the wall and swung in place at night like Pullman berths on a train. The cabin was painted a Navy shade of the Army's light-green, a tad darker. The deck was red linoleum kept shiny by the Philippine cabin boy, who I rarely saw but who always left everything in perfect order. They spent their life at sea just like the sailors and retired after twenty years to a life of great comfort back home, maintained by their pension that goes a long way in that poor country. Most important, we had our own head which, on the first night out, was commandeered by 1st Lt. Bill

Williamson, whose complexion matched the walls. We had gone to basic officers school together at Fort Gordon, where we became friends. I had gone to Japan, and he had expanded his horizons and coupled his degree in cinematography to an assignment with the Army Pictorial Center on Long Island that produced all the Army training films and the television program *The Big Picture*. The Center had originally been owned by the commercial movie industry, but it was abandoned for Hollywood in the thirties. Bill's wife, Ginger, and their daughter, Emi, had gone home to Montana for the year and he was said to miss them very much already, although it was hard to tell with his head in the toilet. Tall and thin with dark wavy hair, Bill bore a striking resemblance to the actor Henry Fonda, something that was mentioned by everyone who met him. The comparison would make him blush, which only added to his plight. "See, just like Henry Fonda!"

"I never saw Henry Fonda that color," snickered Norm Deiver, one of my second lieutenants and fellow roommate. He was from southern California and talked about his sailboat and trips to Catalina Island in a force eight gale. He loved the sea but was not keen on war. His degree was in journalism and he had picked the photo platoon to expand his knowledge so he could land a big job in the media when his two years were up. He was clearly scared of the thought of combat and had never expected to experience it so soon after his commissioning that June. I told him that I would need an officer to remain in the rear to run the lab and do the administrative work. He was most relieved to hear that and accepted.

That left only Lance Stonehanger, who was a book in himself. He was from Miami and lived with his mother, a lady of some reputation. Lance was the most handsome person I had ever seen and his personality was as winning as his looks. He was six-one with a permanent dark tan and thick black hair. A thin nose almost too small for his high checkbones and square jaw combined with light-blue eyes to attract the girls everywhere he appeared. A white toothy smile never left his face.

He had been raised by a succession of his mother's gentlemen friends, who provided Lance with expensive diversions. He was accomplished at cigarette-boat racing, water-skiing, gliding, and polo. Most of all, Lance loved women, all women. He said that during his college breaks he was a beach boy at some of the most beautiful grand hotels on the sand. Since we were unfamiliar with his use of the term, he explained that he searched the verandas near the pool and approached ladies who seemed to be searching for some diversion from the stress of the world. It usually started with an offer to put suntan oil on places they could not reach. He seemed to prefer older women, women who had been "neglected," as he put it. He would offer other amenities and they were often grateful enough to show great generosity. One story I will never forget was of an aging widow who preferred to lean on the windowsill of her fashionable suite dressed only in a top and wave to her friends at poolside while Lance attended from behind with services that thrilled her. However, Lance was no soldier; he was not taking the whole thing seriously. But his charms would be wasted on our commander, I told him for his own sake. "Your primary mission is to avoid contact with the Old Man at all costs," I told him. No fool, he took the advice to heart and I doubt that Snead ever knew that Second Lieutenant Stonehanger was on active duty.

Our battalion commander was installed in a suite, and the surrounding staterooms were inhabited by his staff of majors and senior captains. A small party consisting of his operations chief and a few others had been left behind to close out our buildings at Fort Eustis. Its members were going to Saigon by military airlift to prepare the new area for the battalion. The muster had not been a problem in the end and we began to settle down into the ship's routine.

The majority of cases of seasickness cured themselves within forty-eight hours, but some never fully recovered. To the inhabitants, the vessel was known as the USNS *Upchuck*. Daily inspections began in earnest every morning after breakfast. Snead was a master inspector. Day after day he made the rounds of each of the troop bays and demanded improvement. I had to agree with him, in this confined space the lives of the men could be made even more uncomfortable if diseases were allowed to fester. In addition to cleanliness, Snead used the inspections as a tool to bind the unit together and get it to work as a team. That kind of skill would be needed in war when Snead was not around to enforce teamwork. He made himself very unpopular, but that was a price he was willing to pay for results. He added competition to the drill by offering to give the "Best Compartment of the Day" the privilege of entering the mess hall first at all meals that day and permitting it longer on-deck time. Both prizes were in demand. Out of fairness, he did not spread the accolade around; it had to be won.

I believe in positive incentive and we went after the title with a vengeance. Jerry Raymond saw the advantages as well; not only did we want to win for the sake of the troops but we both wanted to become known to our new boss as the kind of officer who could be depended upon to deliver. Impressing our commander was a full-time job. With the help of my very good NCOs, we organized the mountain of baggage into uniform stowage that was easy to inspect and gave the appearance of neatness. One NCO came up with the idea of putting the rifles together in groups of four and hanging them upside down from the top rung of each bunk. They looked organized, were easy to account for, and easy to inspect. Such innovation pleased the inspector and led to our first winning of the prize. Until then Jerry had won it twice in a row. The troops liked to win and step to the front of the line. They no longer had to be driven by the sergeants and took over the ever escalating competition between A/6, Raymond's compartment, and our own.

By the halfway point in our voyage the colonel resorted to using a flashlight and doubled the time it took to inspect the space. On one occasion Snead invited me to join him on his hands and knees under a bunk against the wall where the deck met the bulkhead. He shone the beam on a black speck where the two joined and asked me if it was "dirt or chipped paint." I said paint. He then invited the first sergeant to join us on the floor and asked him the same question. Top also opted for paint. "I can see you are both in this together. It is dirt, gentlemen, and don't you forget it. I am surprised at you, first sergeant, letting a lieutenant lead you astray like that, with all your years of experience."

Top took up the challenge. "It's paint, Colonel." The men were enjoying watching the three of us, with our butts protruding in the air from under the bed, in a high level of debate.

Snead drew a folding knife from his pocket with great difficulty, opened the blade, and began to scrape at the dark spot. "I know dirt when I see it." He shone the light on the spot once more, which had been enlarged by his efforts.

"Put the light on the blade, sir," J.B. urged. Orange powder was clearly visible on its edge. "You were right, Colonel! The rust on this ship looks just like dirt." We won "best compartment" again.

No matter the circumstances of a sea passage, it is a great experience. On deck the solitude of being out of sight of land day after day changes the way you look at your home, the earth. The sheer size of the ocean and the power of the wind, water, and sky overwhelm the senses. The ship that seemed so large and powerful against the dock is dwarfed by the expanse of the surface of the water. The plowing bow scared up flocks of flying fish that breached, glided a hundred yards three feet above the surface on transparent wings spread straight out to the side, then plunged back in nose first. In spite of our size we left no tracks. The sea was indifferent to our presence. Although we were going twenty-four knots, our progress was imperceptible. Time was marked only by the sun and the calendar. I spent most of my time against the rail looking at nothing and remembering the hours I'd spent as a boy watching my favorite TV documentary, *Victory at Sea*. I could hear quite clearly the "Guadalcanal March" and visualize the black-and-white image of the sea rolling in front of the camera. When I looked over the side, the water seemed to invite me to jump in so it could close over me. As a child I had a recurring nightmare that I was in the dark water and about to be run over by a great metal ship that was so tall that I could not see the top of the monster. Now I was riding that throbbing juggernaut and passing over the skeletons of other ships of war that lay deep below with their crews. They had also gone to war.

The combat photographers were the only ones to conduct live training on board. We had brought our cameras and a few chemicals. The cameramen crept about the ship taking pictures of everything in an effort to begin our documentary. I took the opportunity to learn the business from my experts. I could not hope to lead from behind. The first thing I learned is that everyone wants to have his picture taken if it is going to flatter. The second thing I learned is that everyone wants a copy. I would use that knowledge in the field; it became the basis for our operation. It never failed and allowed my folks to reenter units time and again if on our return we freely passed out glossy eight-by-tens. I know they were sent home to the family, proving to loved ones their subjects' valor and the hardships endured. On board ship, even the tiny contact prints that we used to evaluate our work were given out to rave reviews. The contact print is only the size of the 35mm film itself and to be appreciated has to be viewed with a magnifying glass. When we reached our first port, Guam, they were stuffed into letters written long before and mailed home as proof of passage.

After sixteen days at sea we were admitted into the harbor for a twenty-four hour replenishment stop. The troops had visions of girls, bars, and booze. The officers had not been so deprived. Although alcohol was forbidden, a number of bottles of whiskey had somehow come aboard in the officers' kits and were rationed out sparingly in the evening behind closed doors in the staterooms. There was not enough for parties and the Navy was always on the prowl. When we were invited to join the field grade officers, who were totally underemployed, the scent of sour mash was unmistakable. The nurses had provided diversion, if only in the hearts and imaginations of those who engaged them in endless conversation. On occasion our own Lothario, Lance, would politely ask that his three roommates not return to our crowded cabin for an hour or two for the sake of a lady's reputation. We obliged willingly, knowing that as payment for our cooperation, a tale of true romance would follow the brief encounter. He was particularly taken with a pretty young woman who reminded us all of Mitzi Gaynor from *South Pacific*. Our Mitzi would not make it back, though. She was killed in a mortar attack on her hospital a few months later.

The troops spent a day at Gab Gab Beach and drank enough warm beer to make up for the two weeks on the wagon. Back out at sea, the boredom returned and the men queued up the entire length of the A deck passageway, some five hundred feet, leaning against the wall and creeping slowly to the canteen for a vanilla milkshake. Some would take their drink to the end of the line and consume it as they began the process anew. "It takes about an hour or so, Lieutenant. Do you want me to get you one this time around?" one of my photographers asked.

Murphy was the youngest of my folks, just eighteen.

The smell in the passageway put me off. Even though it was covered with sawdust, the evidence of seasickness was mixed in despite the constant cleaning and renewal. The gray steel walls were becoming a prison by the time we entered Asian waters, and everyone wanted out. I was looking forward to our passage through the Philippine Islands. I had read of Douglas MacArthur's adventures there when he was a second lieutenant and aide to his father, who was the governor general. He had been riding on a remote jungle trail when attacked by two bandits. Douglas killed them both with his .45-caliber pistol. He described the primitive people and their villages of grass huts and roaming livestock. I checked the charts for our path and the next day at first light was on deck to see the land rise out of the sea. In some places the route was quite narrow and I strained to see human activity but in the day and a half that it took to pass by the many islands I never saw another person or boat, just the occasional primitive dock protruding into the water a few feet.

In the South China Sea activity increased both on board and at sea. We were in the shipping lane and every few minutes a new ship appeared. A day out of port we picked up a Navy escort, the first destroyer I had ever seen underway. She was sleek and fast, changing station first on one side of us and then the other. We felt important. Plans to dock picked up and the inspections stopped. About dusk we approached land, a gray-green hedge that went the length of the horizon off our bow. We moored in an estuary a mile offshore with several other ships that looked just like ours. When called upon, our ship would proceed up the channel about thirty miles to the port of Saigon for unloading.

The next morning a Navy party boarded and gave us the plan. Several ships were ahead of us and since we did not have any cargo, we were to be taken to the beach the following day and make our way inland by road. We organized all that day while Navy SEALs walked along the rails and periodically threw percussion grenades over the side to discourage enemy divers from attaching mines to our bottom. The year before they had seriously damaged the USS *Card,* a small WWII jeep carrier, while she sat at anchor. We could see Vietnam. The next day we would be engulfed by her sweaty arms.

Chapter Four

> *To be a successful soldier you*
> *must know history.*
> GEN. GEORGE PATTON

I received a commission as a second lieutenant from the Reserve Officers Training Corps at Marquette University. My first exposure to the ROTC program had been at Marmion Military Academy, a Catholic high school. The discipline provided by the Benedictine monks, Marist Brothers, and the United States Infantry had made the college senior program a breeze. I had selected a commission in the Signal Corps because my eyesight was not good enough for the Cavalry and I was left with a choice of Signal or Engineers. The Engineers were dominated by West Pointers, and I knew that over the length of a career I could not compete with such a strong fraternity. Even though I had taken Corps of Engineers ROTC for the last two years, my instructors, who were all from the US Military Academy, told me that I would be a second-class citizen in that branch of the Army.

I was provided with one issue of uniforms with the exception of a mess dress. It would be six years before I could afford to buy that one. Enlisted soldiers were provided their uniforms but officers had to buy them after their initial issue. We were given a small allowance of forty dollars a month to maintain and replace them, as well as a housing allowance of ninety dollars (for second lieutenants) if we were not living in government quarters. Our basic pay of $222.30 a month was less than half that paid to college graduates in industry. After Social Security was taken out, there wasn't a lot left. I remember Major Knowles conserving his pipe tobacco to four ounces a month and telling me that I would never be rich no matter what grade I achieved. "The life of the Regular Army officer is one of genteel poverty," he confided, "but what an adventure! As an officer I can walk with kings," he said. In years to come I walked behind a couple.

Our first son, David, had been born while I was in college, and Carol was pregnant for the second time. I left her temporarily in Aurora, Illinois, with the folks, and went to Fort Gordon, Georgia, the new field home of the Signal Corps, for a six-week officer basic school. I couldn't afford to fly so I left Chicago by train for my first visit to the South. I was happy, dressed in suntan pants and shirt adorned with the gold bar of a second lieutenant on the right side of my collar and crossed red-and-white signal flags on the other. The trip was long, a full day's rolling and thinking. It had been such a struggle to get to this glorious day that I couldn't believe all the obstacles were gone and I was really beginning the thirty-year career of a professional soldier. To retire, one must complete twenty years, but I never intended to spend less than the maximum allowed by law. That early decision made the years to come much easier. Most of my friends were constantly reviewing the future and vacillating over getting out, tempted by the lure of big money that was well within their reach. I was content on that train and remained so every day of the years to come, no matter where it took me. My year group of officers commissioned that spring numbered seventeen thousand. Thirty years later less than one hundred were left on the last day.

I got off in Atlanta and quickly changed trains, riding the Georgia Railway the final hundred miles to Augusta. It had been a fast, slick journey to that point, but this Georgia rail line was something out of the past. The steam engine and three massive brown-and-black cars were turn-of-the-century, and the seats were wooden with ornate curlicue metal arms like old park benches. It was Sunday, and the few passengers were well dressed. I headed for the last car, as I liked to look out the back at the track and countryside as I was yanked along. A conductor intercepted me and said, "Lieutenant, we are going to put you right up in the front car, that is where the officers go on my train." He was the first person to call me by my rank, and I realized that I was no longer a civilian, even off post. I loved it and followed him as he took me aboard and seated me. I watched out the window and he did not seat another person, even those who appeared quite distinguished. This was the life—I was somebody, at last. We pulled out of the main station a half hour late but no one seemed concerned. I swear that that railway car had square wheels. We literally bumped along at half the speed of the previous train. The soil was dark red in many places, a shock to a boy from Illinois, where the dirt is rich and black. How does anything grow here, I thought in my naiveté. Soon we were crossing cotton fields and for the first time I saw Negroes, a northern term, clustered around scrawny plants and dragging long white bags along behind. It was hot in the train, even with the windows open, but those poor people out in the sun picking cotton must have been suffering. In the north, I thought, farmers would have used a machine. But I didn't dwell on their plight long as I was getting close to the end of the trip, and after today my life would never be the same. The conductor entered the car and announced in a loud voice that it was getting close to supper time. "I am going to stop this here train in the next town and the crew is going to have their meal. It is a nice little town, my hometown, folks are friendly and have prepared food for my crew and a little extra for those of you who like fried chicken. The price is very reasonable, and don't fret about having enough time to finish. We are not leaving until you all have had your fill." I got his drift, even if I didn't quite understand every word of his sugary accent. We stuttered to a stop at the little old station, which must have loaded Confederate soldiers on board during the siege of Atlanta. Pretty young southern belles with big smiles entered the train with large baskets covered by checked cloths. They charmed the passengers into buying more food than they had planned. I was no exception. It turned into a rail picnic and, true to the conductor's word, we did not leave for a good hour from that shady spot picked out especially for the subsidizing of his kin. The food was delicious and so was the company of fellow passengers who talked freely to this stranger. Up north that could not have taken place. I was beginning to like the South and the southerner very much.

We finally arrived in Augusta, a town that had remained untouched by Sherman's march through Georgia. It was said that the Union officer in command there had a sweetheart in the city, so he spared it. I dragged my heavy B-4 suitcase off the high metal steps of the iron passenger car and stopped on the platform for a moment to get my bearings. The conductor came up behind me and said, "First time in Augusta, Lieutenant?"

"This is my first time in the South," I confessed. "Where do you think I could find some transportation to the post?"

He motioned down the platform to a little man in a white shirt and dark pants. "Tiedder can take you out there in his cab." Another relative, I was sure, but any help at that point was fine with this Yankee. The driver tipped his hat and took the heavy burden that was making me sweat just looking at it. I followed him like a rich man. I'd never had anyone carry my bag for me before.

The broad entrance into the rather large station was divided down the middle by a thick metal bar. Above was a sign, WHITES, on the other side was another sign, COLORED. I saw only blacks alighting from the last car, my choice if the conductor had not ushered me forward with such grace. They trooped down the platform and around me. So it was not my celebrity status, but my skin color that set me apart. Inside, even the twin water fountains against the back wall had signs. My town had only one black family, who I knew from school days. I thought nothing of race. I couldn't believe what I saw.

In the taxi I looked out on the charming city, which didn't last long as we were soon out in the red clay and going through a gate guarded by a black military policeman. I wondered how many black police there were in Augusta. The post was named for a Confederate corps commander, General Gordon. It was a sprawling installation, five miles by twenty-eight, just the kind of place to run long-range communications cables and radio systems. The main post, where all the business was done and troops were housed, was a good three miles square with a mile-long parade field in the middle. At the head end was a semicircle of large white frame buildings two stories high. The center one had mock white columns and a sign, HEADQUARTERS. Inside I met the officer of the day.

"You're a day early, Lieutenant," said the captain duty officer. "Is that your name?" he said, pointing to the black-and-white plastic nametag on the pocket flap of my tan uniform shirt.

"Yes, sir."

"Is it spelled correctly?" He had a touch of a southern accent and had never seen a hyphen before in the middle of a last name. "Well in this man's army, we don't hold with such practices. Get it changed. They sell nametags in the PX. They do it while you wait." He had no trouble pronouncing it because he only referred to me by my rank. He made me feel un-American, a little like the blacks on the train.

He assigned me to a BOQ (bachelor officers' quarters) nearly at the other end of the parade ground. "Just go down the first street until you reach the officers' training area, and report to the company headquarters CQ [charge of quarters]." I didn't ask about getting a ride—the duty officer seemed hostile—so I grabbed my fifty-pound bag and started out into the heat of the evening, which seemed to increase as the day wore to a close. My route took me past a solid row of barracks buildings made of the same painted white wood, which were arranged like hotels on a Monopoly board, but each block was named for an Army hero rather than Boardwalk, Atlantic Avenue, or Marvin Gardens. The soldiers were recruits and had just learned how to salute. Clearly their drill sergeants had convinced them that the worst thing they could do was to speak to an officer. There were many on the single sidewalk, on Sunday evening, their only free time. Every few steps I was greeted with "Good evening, sir," said with trepidation in a loud, clear, high-pitched voice followed by a very stiff and exaggerated hand salute. That compelled me to carry my big bag in my left hand all the way as I returned the honor with my right, nearly every time my left foot hit the ground. By the time I arrived both arms were tired and I was dripping with sweat.

The salute is viewed by most civilians as a burden that acknowledges another's superiority. I have often heard from civilians, "Why should I give such homage to a stranger? How do I know that he is a better man than me if I don't know him? He should have to prove himself to me first before I give him such servitude." The answer is that one is merely giving a traditional military greeting. The salute is not for the man but the rank, the office that he holds in the structure of military society. Officers salute each other as well, and on occasion I have seen a senior salute a junior who in battle has performed with courage. I have done it myself. A private who holds the Medal of Honor would receive a salute from a general. It is regarded as an honor to render a salute, and only a soldier is authorized to give a salute, not a civilian. One thing a soldier who has become a prisoner gives up is the right to salute. It is an honor to receive a salute, and it must be returned with an appropriate greeting.

The BOQ was better than a barracks, but not by much—two men to a room in a two-story wooden building without air-conditioning but with a common latrine. The bugs had first claim to everything; they were long-term residents. I intended to be there only a week or so until I could find a place to rent in the city for my family. The Officer Basic course for the Signal Corps was similar to those conducted by all branches for the new officer. It was six weeks of study on the equipment and mission of the Corps. We learned about radio, cable, and telephone field communications equipment and their deployment in the field. We were a service branch that called itself the Combat Branch of Command and Control. Gen. Omar Bradley's quote "Congress makes a man a general but the Signal Corps makes him a commander" was posted everywhere. It was true—if a general can't communicate his desires, he is not in command. Our job sounded simple, but under field conditions or combat the challenge was enormous. Other branches looked upon us as the smart guys who understood "all that electric stuff" they would rather not have to deal with. Steeped in the electrons we might be, but we also had to conduct ourselves as soldiers, not Bell Telephone representatives.

I found a place to rent, a redbrick ranch-style duplex off-post on Tobacco Road, the location of John Steinbeck's novel. It was in a development put up primarily to rent to soldiers from the post. My neighbors were members of my class of forty, many of whom were married. I bought a car, a little Falcon from the local Ford dealer, for fifty dollars a month. While at school we received an extra ninety dollars a month TDY (temporary duty) pay, which would continue until I got to my permanent unit, in Japan. I was in fat city. I never had that kind of money in my life and I was going to need it with another child expected to arrive in September. Carol liked the two-bedroom house, and she felt secure now that we had a salary and a future. Poor girl, she hadn't had anything new except for maternity clothes in two years. She was still using the supply of cosmetics she'd hoarded during her school days, but she was a natural beauty and didn't need much help, I told her. What an asset she became to a young officer—pretty, and willing to help out with social duties. Though shy, she made every effort to overcome it. In nurses' training they had included a course in charm, which only enhanced her in the role as an officer's lady who, though unpaid, would be expected to play a large part in the military society and in support of families of all ranks.

We both went with our classmates and their wives to get our identification cards, our ticket to all benefits. With that card the post exchange, commissary, hospital, travel, and officers club were available. In the Army they didn't say "Show me your papers," it was "Do you have an ID card?" It opened all doors. It had a picture of the holder and a seal of the United States. Very official, it had to be carried at all times, like a security blanket. The class was headed for "overseas" and the medics had a field day getting us ready for living in foreign lands with all the inoculations known to man. Our son, David, hated the Army medics—"they shotted me."

I didn't like exercise outside of games, but I had to become proficient because I was going to paratrooper school in a few short weeks, a course of instruction that lived on physical fitness. The whole class was required to pass a proficiency test before we graduated and so I had a group to help me through the change of lifestyle. The most rigorous activity, outside of the push-ups and pull-ups, was the one-mile run. At the time, running a mile was unheard-of outside the military. There was a standard one-mile-in-seven-minutes run, in fatigue uniform and combat boots, with no stopping and no walking allowed. One ran, even if only in place, until the day came that it could be done in seven minutes. Those boots were like lead; each weighed four pounds. Most of the class hadn't taken the PT test since ROTC summer camp the year before and the run area was a pathetic scene, sweating lieutenants strung out around the oval in the middle of the company area, gasping for air in the humid Georgia heat.

We were exposed to all the hazards of military life, but the trip to the tear gas chamber was the least popular. Most of us enjoyed shooting and field exercise, where we spent the night in tents and put in long-haul communications. Once a year everyone in the Army was required to test his personal protective mask, which prevented chemical agents, nerve agent, mustard gas, and all the other hideous killers from debilitating one on the battlefield. The test was conducted using a rather harmless tear gas. In a corner of the post was a metal one-story building with no windows and a door at each end. Inside was a can of burning agent that filled the forty-by-twenty-foot space with a cloud of tear gas. The test was a confidence exercise designed to convince the soldier that the mask could protect, and therefore he had nothing to fear from a chemical attack if he did not panic and put on his mask correctly. To prove the point, we each reviewed the procedure for donning the mask and then went into the building as a group and stood around inside for ten minutes to show that we were okay in a toxic environment. Inside, we were given a lecture given by a Chemical Corps officer. The gas burned any exposed skin and I could feel my neck and hands beginning to heat up and itch; the concentration was very high. At the end of the talk each of us had to remove his mask, one at a time, recite his name and service number to the chemical officer, and walk out the door at the far end. If anyone didn't believe that we had been in a hostile environment before, he did by then. The gas went up my nose and down my throat as soon as I inhaled to speak my piece. It was as if there were a miniature explosion in the back of my throat. My eyes slammed shut. My nose ran while the skin on my face warmed up with prickly heat. I said my bit with remarkable speed and needed help to find the door. Before I could get outside, my mind had shut off and all I could think of was getting away. On the dry grass outside, we were all helpless for a good ten minutes. My eyes teared uncontrollably and the inside of my mouth burned worse than my exposed skin. Within twenty minutes the effects were gone and only the vivid memory remained. When I got home that night I had some funny stories to tell Carol and David at dinner, which was waiting for me on the table. They enjoyed the antics that I acted out and she said my account was so vivid that she could feel the effects herself. What a storyteller I was! Within a few more minutes, David was coughing and Carol's eyes were burning. I began to feel a tingling in my nose and soon we were all crying in the confined space of our dining room. My heavy cotton uniform had soaked up enough agent to make me reek of the stuff, and I ran outside and took most of my clothes off on the driveway. There, out on the lawns of the neighborhood, stood my classmates, down to their underwear and combat boots, ripping off their shirts and pants and hanging them on tree branches to air out.

I was a barely qualified Signal Officer when we left Gordon and headed for Airborne school. A very pregnant Carol rode the hundred and fifty miles past Atlanta and south to Columbus. Fort Benning, the home of the Infantry, was a huge installation, much larger than Gordon, which conducted training for the Queen of Battle, as the Infantry branch was widely known. I was only interested in the paratrooper training which had begun there during the Second World War. Paratroopers are all volunteers and therefore the elite of most modern armies. They come in all varieties, not just infantry. Paratrooper units are made up primarily of foot soldiers, but they require the support of the other branches to accomplish their mission of "vertical envelopment" behind enemy lines. Therefore they all jump in together and fight as a combined arms team. The school lasted three weeks so we needed to find a temporary place to live on the local economy. That community is always in turmoil with people moving in and out, but I found a one-room motel apartment with kitchen. Our neighbors were in similar short courses and we fit right in as soon as our suitcases were unpacked. The guy next to us was in the third week and gave me all the tips I needed to get through with minimal trouble.

Monday morning I was standing tall, in the dark at 0400—four AM—in front of 42d Company, along with over four hundred other would-be jumpers. There were fifty officers, most lieutenants, many of whom took up the leadership positions. I was appointed stick leader of a twenty-man squad, the average age of the men being nineteen. Each platoon had four sticks and there were six platoons. There was a handful of sailors, Marines, and airmen in the ranks, since the Army is the only service to provide airborne training. The other services qualify a few of their own each year to work with paratrooper units. As a stick leader I was responsible for my men's welfare and expected to motivate them by example. Inspection of both the uniform and the general health of each man was first each day. Boots had to be polished to a deep, glassy shine and the uniform was to be spotless and starched. As a rule officers had their high-top black boots polished at the PX for two dollars a day, and the men who did the job guaranteed their work. Enlisted in general did their own, which took most of the evening after training. That combined with their cleaning of the barracks prevented them from going out at night. The other factor that controlled those hell-raisers—and hell-raising is synonomous with paratrooping—was that they were very tired after an absolutely exhausting—both physically and mentally—day.

As the sun crept up, we ran, at double time, in formation and in step, to the training area half a mile away. It was such a relief to get clear of inspection that the run was not a problem. All instruction at jump school is done by sergeants. Even the officers are expected to take direction from those men because they are the best. Only the occasional cadre officer is seen and that is only when something has gone wrong, beyond the reach of the sergeant. Our officer instructor was Paul Rob, a master parachutist, one who wore a silver star above his wings surrounded with a silver laurel wreath. It meant that he had been on jump status for a number of years and had many—in his case over one hundred—jumps to his credit and was a qualified jump master. We would see him at the end of the course, standing in the open door of the aircraft, sending us all out safely into the air high above the ground. He had once been a sergeant and had earned his commission the hard way. Fate brought us together again in Vietnam, where I had been present at his horrific death.

Physical training was conducted at the highest energy level I had ever experienced. It was one hour of calisthenics, stripped to the waist, on a field of sawdust. Every exercise was to be done perfectly, mimicking the instructor who performed on a dais three feet above the ground in the center of the formation. Roaming sergeants picked out the weaklings and the inattentive for special attention and extra training. In addition to strength, the paratrooper needed mental alertness to cope with the emergencies that could occur in the air which required instant and correct action if he and his fellow jumpers were to arrive safely on the ground, ready and able to fight. In addition to the training that morning, a physical fitness test was administered once we were warmed-up properly. By nine o'clock we had taken our first losses—sixty members of the class were put in a special remedial physical training course, never to be seen again by the 42d Company. For the most part it was inability to do the seven perfect pull-ups that caused soldiers to fail. Upper body strength was very important, since it is used to steer the parachute. I completed mine out of fear, not strength. I lost my first stick man to the pull-up bar.

Clad again in starched shirts and steel helmets, we ran to the tower-week area for orientation. Nearly in the center of the old fort is a giant field with three 250-foot-tall "free towers," each rigged with four iron arms at the top. If the average building story is ten feet high, the tower is the equivalent of a twenty-five-story building. They were particularly awesome to us because we knew that we would be falling from the top of them. Time was consumed with the process of getting the now-reduced class into the stands that hugged the edge of a small area near the base of one of the structures. We all sat at attention, shoulder to shoulder, with our helmets in our laps. Over a loudspeaker, an unseen narrator directed our attention to the four sergeants in full battle gear to our front. "These paratroopers are here to demonstrate to you what will be expected of each of you during the course. Pay close attention. If at the end of the demonstration you do not feel that you can complete these tasks, you are encouraged to quit. To terminate jump status, report to the trucks at the end of the stands. You will receive orders for another assignment and will leave the school within the hour. To be a paratrooper is a voluntary calling." He made it sound like a vocation, perhaps the priesthood.

The demonstration began with a man donning a military parachute and its reserve chute, and then the forty-pound pack and the rifle. In addition, the equipment bag, another twenty-five pounds, was strapped to his side, bringing the total equipment to nearly one hundred pounds. Now I knew why I had to be so physically fit and why sky divers are not necessarily paratroopers. We might be as free as birds once in the air but there was a lot of ground travel before we got to that stage. Most of the early program seemed to be possible, but then we were introduced to the thirty-four-foot tower which had a mockup of the center portion of a cargo airplane fixed to its top. It had an open side door and from it extended four steel cables that ran a hundred sloping yards to a low dirt ridge six feet in height.

"I direct your attention to the top of the tower." An instructor in a white T-shirt and black baseball hat waved to

Bien Hua "snake pit" pad, Operation Hardihood, May 1966. Combat photographers Airmen First Class Benell (left) and Winter (right), 600th Air Photo Squadron, receive final instructions from photo platoon leader 1st Lt. David Fitz-Enz before an air assault during the first joint photo mission.

Vung Tau, May 1966. Paratroopers wait to be loaded on choppers at an intermediate pick-up point close to their landing zone for an air assault. C Company, 1/503 Parachute Regiment, 173d Airborne Brigade.

Paratroopers load for an air assault from an intermediate site near the battle. Note the combat motion-picture photographer at right. C Company, 1/503 Parachute Regiment, 173d Airborne Brigade.

The company executive officer (right) of a combat unit just off the chopper. The unit is under fire from the wood line. A Company, 2/503 Parachute Regiment, 173d Airborne Brigade.

Vo Dat, November 1965. Squad leader on a hot landing zone gathers his troopers for an assault on the wood line. A Company, 2/503 Parachute Regiment, 173d Airborne Brigade.

A machine-gun crew fires at a dug-in Viet Cong position thirty meters to their front. Fifteen Viet Cong were killed in the attack. 1st Platoon, A Company, 1/503 Parachute Regiment, 173d Airborne Brigade.

War Zone D, January 1966. Paratroopers from 173d Airborne crawl toward their objective with a minimum of cover. A Viet Cong tunnel entrance is seen in front of Signal Corps combat photographer Sp4. Dan Peksenek. (Courtesy of Sp4. Bernie Zawaoki)

Plain of Reeds, 1200 hours, January 3, 1966. Paratroopers cross a deep stream under sniper fire as they close with the enemy. Recon Platoon, HQ Company, 2/503 Parachute Regiment, 173d Airborne Brigade.

Paratroopers in battle under fire from Viet Cong at the edge of a village. 1st Platoon, A Company, 1/503 Parachute Regiment, 173d Airborne Brigade.

Paratroopers move in to attack the entrenched enemy. Senior medic Sp4. Gerald Smith is in foreground. A Company, 1/503 Infantry Regiment, 173d Airborne Brigade.

Platoon leader calls a cease-fire. He keeps his men down as he awaits the arrival of 2d Platoon, which is pushing the enemy back into his position.

War Zone D, November 1965. Called "The Mad Bomber," this chopper of the 173d Airborne Brigade is dropping mortar rounds on the enemy to relieve a fire base that is under attack, while the resupply choppers go in to drop off more ammunition.

An 81mm mortar crew puts the gun into action as the company commander calls for fire fifty yards in front. Left to right: Sergeant Tate, PFC Ronald Mill, PFC Ulysses Colemen, PFC Frederick Park, PFC Guthrie. Weapons Platoon, A Company, 2/503 Parachute Regiment, 173d Airborne Brigade.

Two miles south of Vo Dat, III Corps area, 1330 hours, November 26, 1965. Paratroopers of the 173d Airborne Brigade coming in after a morning-long search-and-destroy mission. 1st Platoon, A Company, 2/503 Parachute Regiment, 173d Airborne Brigade.

Phuoc Long, near Song Be, April 1966. Signal Corps combat motion-picture photographer Sp5. Eugene Randon on a search-and-destroy operation in the jungle. 1/503 Parachute Regiment, 173d Airborne Brigade.

Thanksgiving dinner served during a rainstorm in the jungle next to a dirt airfield. HQ and A Companies, 173d Airborne Brigade.

Bien Hua, U.S. Air Force Base, November 1965. David G. Fitz-Enz in the flight suit of the 1st Air Commando Squadron, while wearing the green hat of an army paratrooper. (Courtesy of Sp4. Bernie Zawaoki)

Bien Hua, U.S. Air Force Base, January 1966. 1st Lt. David Fitz-Enz, Platoon Leader Combat Photographer, 173d Airborne, just before takeoff in Skyraider (A-1E), 1st Air Commando Squadron, USAF, on a bomb-damage assessment mission. (Courtesy Capt. Carl Light)

Soldiers' sleeping arrangements for the voyage on the troop ship to Vietnam.

An infantry platoon moves out to the helicopter pad for an air assault against the enemy.

Cam Da, Vietnam. Paratroopers pass by an exposed tank-trap ditch while the Prince of Wales Light Horse of the Royal Australian over-watches. 2d Platoon, A Company, 2/503 Parachute Regiment, 173d Airborne Brigade.

Vong Cam Da. An elderly Vietnamese woman receives part of para-trooper Sergeant Conner's C rations while her grandchildren look on. This is an important photo because it shows the soldiers as they were, friendly to civilians, not baby killers. Notice that the people are at ease. 2d Platoon, A Company, 2/503 Parachute Regiment, 173d Airborne Brigade.

Vung Tau, May 1966. Paratroopers move out on an ambush patrol to reestablish contact with the Viet Cong. 1st Platoon, A Company, 173d Airborne Brigade.

Paratroopers take a short break to reorganize but are still on the alert for Viet Cong snipers. Recon Platoon, HQ Company, 2/503, 173d Airborne Brigade.

Near Landing Zone English, May 1970. A shot-down helicopter has bullet holes in the blade. The crew chief wraps duct tape around the prop, which allows us to fly home. Operations Section, 124th Signal Battalion, 4th Infantry Division.

Combat engineers watch the riverbank for signs of an underwater bridge.

Vietnamese children in boats watch as PFCs George Allen and Arthur Tate look for an underwater footbridge behind enemy lines while on river recon. Bridge Platoon, 173d Engineer Company, 173d Airborne Brigade.

Plai Grang Special Forces Camp, May 6, 1970. Cavalry troopers prepare for an incursion into Cambodia. A Troop, 1/10 Cavalry Squadron, 4th Infantry Division.

Troop commander of A Troop, 1/10 Cavalry, 4th Infantry Division leads the line of tanks abreast into an attack on an NVA company.

East of Landing Zone Precarious, II Corps, November 1969. A tank is mired in enemy territory. An armored cavalry vehicle provides over-watch while we wait for the M-88 tank retriever. B Troop, 1/10 Cavalry Squadron, 4th Infantry Division.

The 1/10 Cavalry Squadron digs in at its command post at Landing Zone Meredith.

The author, Col. David G. Fitz-Enz, brigade commander of the 1101st Signal Brigade, 1987. (Official U.S. Army photo)

the crowd. A microphone was attached to his shirt and the squared-off muscles of his massive chest were visible in the bright summer sun. "Stand in the door," came the clear jump command. One of the combat troopers shuffled into the doorway and he slammed his hands on the outside of the metal jam. "Go!" The trooper jumped up into the air, out and away from the tower, and fell straight down like a big rock fifteen feet before the webbed riser straps snapped off his back and jerked him up nearly back into the tower. Holding his tight body position, he swung violently from side to side as gravity propelled him at high speed down the cables to the waiting arms of a catcher on the dirt berm.

There was a gasp from the audience. Not the kind you hear at the circus, when the high-wire act performs a death-defying feat. But one from the soul. Then the company fell silent. The men didn't even look at one another. Three hundred and forty volunteers heard the instructor say, "Most of you will make twenty of these during the first week of ground training. It will teach you to exit the aircraft safely flying at one hundred and sixty miles an hour and twelve hundred feet above the ground." His voice was firm, but our resolve was beginning to wane. It seemed that it was not enough to master the apparatus, we now imagined ourselves flying at the speed of sound and plunging into space. "Stand in the door!" he barked once more.

The second jumper, concealed in the mock body of the airplane, yelled, "No, Sergeant!" The jump master reached into the darkness and pulled the next jumper forward. He was a mess, his helmet was on backwards and his leg straps dangled unconnected between his legs. The heavy metal connectors, which were to keep him from sliding out of his chute, clanged as they swung freely behind his knees.

"Connect those leg straps, trooper! Don't you know you will fall to the ground with the same aerodynamic characteristics as an army footlocker?"

"I ain't a goin', I'm scared," he said as his knees banged visibly together. The company laughed uncontrollably at the antics in the tower.

"Stand in the door!" he was told again. The jumper reached in his pocket and humbly handed the jump master a piece of folded white paper, urging him to take it with a little bow. "What is this?" the instructor demanded. "I don't have time to read that. Stand in the door!"

"It is a note from my mother, she wants me to be excused. I have to go home. My aunt died."

The instructor took no more guff and put the man in the door once he was properly attired. But instead of two riser connections from his shoulders to the cable, only one was hooked up. The crowd didn't notice it until the man jumped, screaming, and rode the line down to the end, spinning and bouncing, shaking his fist at the tower and hollering, "You pushed me! Mama, help me! Mama, help me!" The demonstration was a success—even I could see that the apparatus was safe.

"I direct you to the 250-foot tower in the center of the field," said our unseen ringmaster. There, three jumpers were standing in the sand and being rigged to white silk parachutes which were already deployed from their backs while the fringe was snapped into a huge metal hoop that looked like a giant needlepoint ring. Each man was then snatched off the ground and pulled up slowly to the top of the tower arms. They dangled under the canopies like weighted puppets with their hands above their heads, gripping the riser straps. It took a full thirty seconds to reach the top and stop. They were blowing in the Georgia morning wind. The students leaned back in unison as they carefully watched the three men go to the very top, twenty-five stories up. Suddenly the thirty-four-foot tower, which had struck us just moments ago with its danger, was eclipsed by that new specter. I could not even imagine the sight those men saw while blowing around helplessly on thin strings. A member of my stick sitting next to me said, "Are they going to be all right?"

I didn't answer. All I could think of was, Am *I* going to be all right up there? I wondered how they were going to make a joke out of that one; it looked far too dangerous.

"The free tower is designed to accurately portray the final 250 feet of an actual jump." At that he released the first jumper, the chute billowed with air, and the soldier fell at fourteen feet per second to the ground and made a parachute landing fall (PLF) in the dust at the foot of the monster. He got to his feet with the help of a ground staff member and walked off the field, unhurt. The second jumper, deliberately rigged with a malfunction, was released. A shroud line, one of sixty white nylon cords that connect the canopy to the trooper's risers on his shoulders, had been thrown over the center of the rigged-up chute. It divided the silk above him into two small domes, like a woman's brassiere, therefore it was called a "Mae West." It did look queer, two little chutes instead of one big one, but no visions of Miss West came to mind; I was too concerned with the jumper's well-being. Of course, I saw myself under that peculiar wonkey canopy because that is the kind of thing that happens to me.

That jumper descended a little faster and hit a little harder, but he also got up and walked away. If that was supposed to have been the comic relief for the big tower, it missed its mark. No one even chuckled.

The third jumper's chute failed deliberately, and he plummeted to the ground like the footlocker mentioned before. As he fell and we gasped, the voice said, "This is a dummy, not a real man, and demonstrates how important it is that you learn your new trade and are always mentally alert to your equipment and that of your buddy. The dummy hit with a thud and a puff of dust. "He wasn't paying attention when he exited the aircraft. I am sure that this will not happen to you."

We silently filed out of the stands, passed the trucks that had been waiting quietly, and fell in for our first hour of paratrooper training. I lost my second man to the trucks. I hadn't had a chance to speak to either of them. The class was down to 315 as ground week began. Ground week, the first of three, was held across the street from the tower-week area where we had the demonstration. Therefore those 250-foot monstrosities were always in view. The objective for what remained of the morning was to get at least one exit for each man out of the thirty-four-foot tower before lunch. Thirty-four feet was chosen because that is the worst height for those who suffer from acrophobia. Above and below that level, I am told, they aren't quite so fearful. But one didn't have to suffer from the fear of height to resist jumping off a three-and-a-half-story building, and the staff knew that. If each one of us did it before lunch, the rest of the day could be devoted to perfecting the exit rather than letting fear build until someone cracked. It also meant that those who couldn't do it would be eliminated and not waste more time.

The proper exit isn't a matter of just blindly hurling yourself out the door. The main parachute is opened by the lines that remain attached to the airplane. A tight body position must be maintained to prevent arms and legs from becoming entangled in the sixty white nylon shroud lines as they snap out of their rubber-band retainers and allow the chute to take the air. In addition, the chin has to be held down against the chest to prevent the head from being slapped between the riser webbing as it is drawn taut at the end of the shrouds. The mind must continue to function throughout. If at the count of four, from the time of leaving the door, the opening shock is not felt, the right hand will violently pull the rip cord on the reserve chute and a life will be saved. Back in 1942, during the experimental days of the first test platoon, one jumper was bet that there would be such fear at the moment of the actual jump that his mind would be not at all functional. To prove that it would be, the jumper was asked to say something complicated rather than just blindly count. He did—he yelled, "Geronimo!" But for us, yelling anything but one thousand, two thousand, three thousand, four thousand would earn us a hundred push-up penalty, and worse, a reputation among the numerous instructors that was truly not worth the error. They would "bring smoke" on anyone who did not fit the program. That is, the offender would do so many extra push-ups and deep knee bends that smoke would rise from his internally heated body. Any slight infraction or lapse would cost ten push-ups. The punishments might seem silly to an outside observer and be painful to the offender, but they were beneficial to mental alertness. In the split seconds it takes for something to go wrong in the air, a thinking, well-trained man could save his life or that of a buddy.

During training hours, one moved when he was told to move and never moved on his own. No time was wasted and no one was in the wrong place. It was as if I were a part in a large mechanical clock laid out on an open field, and I went up and down and round and round to the "tick-tock." One click too many or too few to the right or left would gum up the whole works.

There were three mock towers, each with an open door on either side and four cables running down fifty yards to the recovery point. Once the process started, men were pouring out of the elevated doors with only seconds between them, first out of one side, while four more took up positions on the other and went out moments later. The tower kept filling and emptying as troopers in groups of four stood on the steps leading to the thirty-four-foot level on the jammed open staircase built between the four massive telephone poles that held the mockup of the airplane. Those not chosen to jump or those just finished ran the trolleys, four at a time, back up to the jump master in the mock door, who snared them with his metal skyhook and pulled the straps inside. Others stood on the dirt wall at the end of the run and disconnected the jumpers, who ran back to the tower judge, a sergeant who graded each performance and critiqued their last exits.

As a stick leader I was chosen as one of the first to go. That was okay with me, I wanted to get it over with. At the parachute harness rack, I was shown how to strap in. It was simple and almost second nature. At the base of the tower the first four waited. I was one of them, in fact number three. We were safety-inspected by an instructor. "That is way too loose and comfortable, Lieutenant," he said, and he grabbed the take-up tabs for the leg straps and literally pulled me off the ground. The viselike clamp between my legs took my breath away. It also drew my shoulders down and bent me over like an old man. Naturally my head was pulled forward and down by the offending harness as well. "Head up, Lieutenant. Look like a leader!" He smiled a little. I took on the appearance of a vulture on a perch as I stepped up on the stairs. "Now don't forget—next time, pull the leg straps *tight,* you will thank me later. You'll see," he said as he sent me stomping up the three flights of steps.

We popped up through the rough floor and found that the inside looked nothing like an airplane. It was a simple shack with exposed two-by-fours, and the walls, rather than aluminum skin, were the backside of unpainted wooden siding. Only the outside looked like an airplane. Thin light came from the slit in the forward wall, used by the jump master to see that the cables were clear, and the two holes floor-to-ceiling on each side that served as airplane exit doors were openings to nowhere. I did not feel like a paratrooper at all at that moment, but more like a foolish daredevil goaded into a prank, and I wondered if I would lose my nerve once I was balanced on the edge. I had not been known in my young life for taking chances or leaping off or into things much higher than a kitchen table. The most daring thing I had done was drive my father's Oldsmobile at 106 miles per hour down a two-lane highway. When I finished that stunt I didn't tell anyone, and never did it again. I had broken my leg on a motor scooter, not a motorcycle, when I hit a dog that was chasing the front wheel. "Don't think of breaking anything now," I told myself. Between the two guys in front of me I could see the field below, and it was so far down that as the heat waves came up I could actually feel the air between it and me like a semisolid block. I wished it would hold me up a little, but I knew I would slip out of my harness and slice right through that air like a knifepoint and stick in the ground while cracks formed in every bone. The harness was helping me concentrate—it hurt—and I hoped that when the risers were connected it would take some of the pressure away from my crotch. The jump master handed me the straps that were fifteen feet long and holding the trolley back, outside on the cable. It didn't help—the added weight of the trolley only pulled me toward the door and I now had new stress forces which caused me to lean my curled-up weight backward on my heels. Quasimodo was about to jump from the cathedral tower, and I could feel the hump on my back. Wouldn't it be so much better if the straps were shorter and there was no slack? Then I could ride the cable like a circus performer, gliding above the crowd, taut and under control. Why must I free-fall half the way to the ground first? I thought. The first man received the command, "Stand in the door!" He did, reluctantly, and put his hands on the inside of the jamb and leaned out just far enough, with his head up, so that only his nose was visible to birds passing by. The instructor slapped him on the back and yelled, "Go!"

He went, but he didn't jump, he slid off, with a slight bend in the knees that brought his head back and banged his helmet on the leading edge of the floorboards as he passed by, ringing his bell.

The jump master turned to the man in front of me and grabbed him by the chest straps. "Jump! Don't fall! You got it?" The man nodded vigorously and the front of his helmet came down on the bridge of his nose and stayed there. He had to cock his head back and to the right to see at all. It wasn't all bad, it helped him take up a good door position and kept him from looking down.

Suddenly he was gone and there was nothing between me and that hole in the wall except for a sharp left turn. I was riveted to the instructor's face. I saw his mouth move but didn't really hear the words "Stand in the door!"

I remembered to put my hands on the outside of the tower, but rather than shuffling into position I crept, raising my boots off the planks in a tiptoe fashion and searching for the floor by feel, gently, as if it were made of eggshells. I wasn't going to look down for the edge and was sure I would simply sneak out the door by mistake. Although the top portion of my body obeyed, that part below my belt remained safely inside, several inches from the edge. "Put your toes over the edge, heels on the inside!" he demanded.

My foot movement, though rapid, was minuscule. I expected to get poised and then the command would come. It didn't happen that way.

On my way to the threshold he yelled, "Go!" and slapped me on the shoulder. His touch was electric and, shocked, I pitched out into free air for the first time in my life. I had never jumped off a diving board or out of the hayloft into the safety of the water or the haystack. I felt like a large rock plummeting straight down to destruction. I looked straight ahead, my head and neck locked, and the bottom dropped out as I pitched forward and saw the ground rushing up. My stomach passed my heart and was in the roof of my mouth. I fell a story and half toward the hard ground and was snatched up by those straps between my legs, and with little help from my shoulder connections. It knocked my breath into my closed mouth, but my lips were sealed. Four giant bounces and I was riding like a kid on an amusement ride toward the gatekeeper. I liked it.

Flushed with a wave of adrenaline, I ran past the snatchers and back up the field with a sense of accomplishment. I posted myself in front of the grader, grinning from my feat. Sitting on his chair, which was impaled on a metal post set in the ground at an angle which allowed him to see the door without craning his neck, he didn't see my triumphal countenance. Watching the next performer and scribbling on a pad, he spoke without ever looking at me. "You didn't count, your feet were wide apart, your arms were out, your head was up, and you failed to jump up and out. Give me twenty push-ups and do it again." The only thing I did right was obey the law of gravity.

It took me twenty-two exits to finally pass during ground week. Major General Gibbs, the chief of Signal Branch, told me of his experience when I met him a year later. He felt that it was important to test an officer's courage before combat. "In my day, young officers were required to jump horses over ever higher barriers. Then we adopted airborne forces at about the same time the horses disappeared. So I sent as many as would go to jump school, knowing that they would probably never serve on jump status, to see if they had the right stuff for command. I did it for so many years that I began to feel ashamed that I had not done it myself. So, at age fifty, and a one-star general, I enrolled. As a general I was given my own private instructor, which is no great honor. He dogged me all day, every day, and made me do it all and then some for the benefit of all to see. I had a lot of trouble with the thirty-four-foot tower. I couldn't get a passing grade. At the end I held the record for most exits from the tower, forty-seven. It took all week, and at night the doctor treated me for burns. The metal edge of the quick release assembly had rubbed all the skin off the center of my chest. Just the thought of that still makes me hurt."

After twenty-two exits, I could identify with the feeling. My faults were common ones, but the one I committed most was failure to count out loud. Without it the chance of using the reserve chute during a combat jump was small. As I watched my stick I heard lots of things yelled out—among them "Help!" and "Noooooo!" and "Ohhhhh shit!"—but only rarely did the jumpers count. A medic in my stick, Private Holman, always yelled, "Mama, one thousand, two thousand, three thousand, four thousand." Holman later treated me in Vietnam. There were those who would not go, and the instructors never ceased to amaze me when it came to handling the problem. Sometimes they would back off a little and, with their boot planted in the middle of the would-be jumper's back, shove the man out. With others they would simply pull the man away from the door by the risers, turn him around, disconnect him, and send him down the steps with orders to report for dismissal from the school. How they separated the sheep and goats I never knew. Those literally booted out of the tower were fine and finished their training with no further trouble. However, the instructors saw something in the others that told them they would never make safe jumpers.

I made it through ground week and on the following Monday morning, driving to class through the front gate in the dark, I could plainly see over the dark outline of the trees the 250-foot towers over a mile away, lit by the red aviation warning lights at the very top, daring me to try. They sent shivers down my spine, and cold sweat formed at my collar and ran down to where I pressed myself against the car seat. I was alone in the dark and I did not want to do it. I had watched all the previous week, during breaks, as the class members a week ahead of us were sucked up to the top and released. They floated down, blowing away from the structure and out of sight as they made contact with the ground. They lost all identity at the top of the tower and all looked alike. Each made several trips. How would I cope?

Of my two problems that week, the swing landing trainer was the other. Standing on a platform twelve feet high and hooked to the three-inch-thick risers connected to the top of my shoulders, I swung off and oscillated back and forth like a kid on a big children's swing without the benefit of a wooden seat. The instructor let me go at the top of the swing and I crashed down into a sawdust pit, trying to hit, twist, and rotate all at the same split second, absorbing the shock with my boots and the side of my body. It took coordination and mental alertness. It took time and repetition. Once, twenty years later, I went back for a high overhead on the tennis court during a game of doubles with some civilian friends. I jumped and did a scissors kick, bent back too far, and did a somersault, quite by accident. Upside down in the air, the swing landing trainer took over and I made a back parachute landing fall, to my surprise. I rolled and popped up to a standing position, unhurt, with the racket still in my hand, ready for the next shot. The other three stopped, mouths open, letting the ball go, and I won the point. "Any paratrooper can do that," I assured them.

By the time we moved on to the big tower, I was somewhat ready. But the stick leader position went against me this time. "You are going to be the ground safety officer, Lieutenant," the black-hatted official told me. "After each man is rigged up, you take this safety line, loop it over the rigging ring, walk it up to the jumper, and connect it to his harness. When he takes it off at the top of the tower and drops it, retrieve it and put it on the next jumper. You will be the last to go at the end of the week." Didn't he know that I had to do it *now*? I had thought of nothing else all weekend. I was all ready, had talked myself into it. It gave me no sense of well-being to watch my classmates, one after another, performing the high flying act safely. In the heat and dust the tension grew. On the third day the wind came up and changed direction as one student was dropped. Rather than floating away from the giant steel girders put together like an erector set, he was blown into the superstructure a hundred feet above our heads. His chute and lines wrapped tight around the members and he was stuck, swinging twenty feet below the hangup. Two instructors jumped on the gray metal ladder on one of the legs and climbed like firemen toward the helpless trooper. I couldn't see what possible help they could be. It took time for them to reach him. There didn't seem to be any danger of the lines untangling themselves and dropping him, but there was no way he could climb up to the girder, either. He was silent but unhurt. I marveled as the rescuers walked the beams like cats, arms out for balance, to a spot above him. Everyone on the ground, students and cadre, watched breathlessly, like an audience at a circus rehearsal. One of our own was up there. When the two gained a position directly above him they sat facing each other, and their leader on the ground with a loud-hailer broadcast to the jumper, "Just relax." He assured the trooper that everything was all right.

I wondered. I had hooked him up to the safety line just a moment before, but he had cut that loose before the drop from the top of the tower. His only hope was in his rescuers' hands. If they couldn't hold him, he would fall and the parachute would not have time to reinflate before he hit the dirt. There was no reserve on a tower jump; it was too low. The unfortunate man was too high for me to see his face but I could hear a bit of a whimper, and I wondered if it was from him or me. Everyone in the class was thinking the same thing, "There but for the grace of God go I." Those who had already performed the deed were relieved, and those of us who still had to do it were stricken; if it happened once, it could happen again. We had all witnessed what happened when a previous man pulled the safety line too fast as one end passed over the steel rigging ring and it wrapped tight around it as if it had been deliberately tied in a knot. That guy had to be lowered very slowly back down to the ground and rigged with a new safety line. Like a yo-yo he went back up to the top for another try. If his chute had been pulled out of the clips around the ring by a downdraft, he would have been left hanging by the snarled safety line, which might

have been pulled free by the weight of his fall, and he probably would not have survived.

The two strong-armed men above the trooper, who had
now become a pendant, began to pull him up to the narrow
beam, hand over hand. As he watched his rescuers, he
helped by climbing up his own shroud lines, aptly named, I
thought. They all got together with the help of great upper
body strength, and he crawled onto the cross member, holding on with both arms and legs. He was disconnected from
his harness and the offending chute was cut loose and
dropped to the earth. The instructors walked and the trooper
crawled toward the fixed ladder fifty feet away, high above
the observers, who were breathing again. I had never seen
anything like that and was surprised when the head instructor grabbed me and we went to greet the jumper. There,
waiting for him, was another chute. While the officer in
charge was talking to him in a low voice, carefully, the man
was shaking his head in agreement to whatever it was he
heard. We hooked him up again and he was jerked off his
feet on the way to the top of the structure. "What did you
say to him?" I asked the captain as we watched him ascend
like an angel.

"I told him that his last decent was a 'no go' and he
needed a 'satisfactory' this time."

My wife, Carol, had been shopping in the commissary
that afternoon. She was one week overdue and not happy.
When she waddled out to the parking lot with our sixteen-
month-old, David, and a cart full of groceries, she looked up
and saw the man waving around in the breeze just under
halfway down. She knew I was there that week. It was
bound to be me. Everyone in the lot stopped, watching. They
all commented as they gathered together. "Those guys are
crazy," one woman said. "My man would never be so foolish." Carol's man was. She delivered our second son, Timo-
thy, that evening.

Friday afternoon I gave up my safety line job and became a jumper once again. Between Tim's birth and my experience of the week, I was numb. It was peer pressure and the weight of my lieutenant's bars that made me do it. I stood, catatonic, as I was rigged under the large white umbrella. I had seen over a hundred men pulled off their feet and strung up, but I could not imagine the feeling until it gripped me. I was captured by the cable and zipped upward at a much higher rate of speed than anyone else, I thought. It was like seeing Cinemascope for the first time. The world below me went away, and I ascended like a heavenly being. It was a near-death experience as described by Prince André in *War and Peace*. Flying above the trees at high speed toward my Maker, I felt free. I came to sudden stop at the twenty-five-story level. From the ground I heard the familiar voice of the instructor that had rung in my ears all week. "At ease in the harness." The words billowed up. I was more than just reluctant to let go of the riser straps on my shoulders and put my hands behind my back, and had to be told twice to do so. I then realized that I had no confidence in my equipment—knowing that I was held in place by the strength in my arms, which were seized and had been ever since I left the ground. I obeyed, but let go with one arm only. "Are you listening, jumper number three?" That was me! As I let go with my remaining vise grip, I felt myself drop. I was sliding out of my chute! Did I forget to connect my leg straps? My slide stopped an inch later as the leg straps took over and I was grateful for that painful pulling between my legs. Jumpers one and two were now visible to me, on my level, high up and blowing gently in the wind. It was much cooler up there and not at all unpleasant. I could see half of Georgia, pine trees and red dirt spread out in all directions. The place was as flat as the back of my hand and I looked for the road in from the main gate where I had feared this specter for the last two weeks. I had conquered. The other two were given their last rites and let go.

"Jumper number three, release your safety line!" came the call. I disconnected the large metal snap from one side and let it go. It swung far out into space and hung below the ring twenty feet in front of me. I had learned not to pull it over the ring too fast or it might get tangled. I eased it over the galvanized metal bar and it took off for the ground by itself. I looked down and released the other end on the front of my chest and for the first time saw the ground. I had not actually looked straight down before, only out. I saw my shiny boots and realized that the ground they enjoyed so much was far, far away. I was scared all over again. Look up, look up, I heard in my head. Take up a prepare-to-land position. I forced my knees together and pulled up on the risers, taking my weight off of the leg straps. I was next. Nothing happened.

"We are experiencing a power outage on the post, jumper. Relax in the harness." There I was, at the top, all alone, and no safety line. A strong gust of wind could blow me out of the ring and I would fall with a chute probably half inflated. "Enjoy the view, jumper, of beautiful Fort Benning, home of the Infantry," I was told by a confident voice over a loudspeaker. I wanted to yell, "I am not Infantry!" but I was not going to move a muscle, not even my diaphragm. After ten minutes I was told that they were going to attempt to bring me down slowly on the main cable that had taken me up. I keyed on the word "attempt." Very slowly, riding the brake, I was lowered by gravity. I did not enjoy it. The tops of the big green pine trees fell even with my eyes and a minute later I felt the ground under my feet. I was greeted by that same captain I had spoken to earlier in the week. He hooked another safety line on and said, "We have power again."

I was snapped off the ground a second time and by then had lost all feeling except that I wanted to jump this tower so badly I could taste it. I was angry. "Why me, you bastards," I said out loud, but no one could hear me as I reached the top once again. This time it went like clockwork. "Take up a good landing position." My parachute landing fall in the deep dust and dirt at the bottom was no picture, but it was good enough.

It was a great weekend. I was through with the awful training, the two longest weeks of my life. Most of my stick had made it through and we had done it with each other's help. I wanted to quit many times but always told myself I would do it at the next break. When the break came I just went on to a little more, promising myself that I would walk away at the end of the day. So it went. The others did the same. Each of us had our own boogeyman to defeat. Buddies got buddies through and so it would be in times to come, in war. No successful man is an island. The buddy system was preached every day. "Never leave a buddy, here or anywhere" was the spirit of the paratrooper, and it made Airborne work. We all learned that if we were wounded, we would not be left behind.

Jump week, the last week, was free of physical training except for a short run around the airfield to show that we were not injured or infirm. I suited up in my gear after picking out a main chute from the stack at the end of the riggers' tables. A rigger is a quartermaster soldier who packs the parachute for the jumper. It is all done in a hangar with many flat tables connected together to form a line sixty feet long. With the backpack lying on one end, the shrouds are laid out in untangled lines to the canopy, which has been fluffed out and folded into a pack at the other end. Carefully, the rigger then pulls the lines into the backpack, neatly running the lines in bunches into the wide rubber-band retainers. At the end, the silk canopy is set on top of the banded lines and a covering of brown canvas is closed with shiny steel pins that are attached by a cable to the static line of yellow webbing. The system is simple, designed by the Safety Parachute Company, which guaranteed that it would always open. If it didn't, one was encouraged to return it for a free replacement! Each rigger packs one more chute than is needed. When the jumpers have picked up the chutes of their choice, the rigger will jump the only one left behind. Quality control, Army style.

Tension was high as we helped each other into the now very familiar and confining equipment. It didn't seem as heavy, but that's because I was in shape. The only other officer in my stick, Lt. Jimmy Hude, was uncertain about everything every day, so I was a little surprised that he was still there on jump day. He wasn't talking, a bad sign. I was running at the mouth, but his answers were short and to the point. The mood of the instructors changed. They were human, checking out equipment and speaking like friends interested only in safety. We took our places for the briefing. I was proud, standing there with those strong men. They all looked older than when I had met them fourteen days ago. We were down to eleven. It was a pity that so many, with such high hopes, were not among the survivors. The briefing room was a hangar of great age. Put up hurriedly during 1942, the corrugated metal siding was streaked with rust from the steel nail heads that almost held it together. Is this what it was like in Britain, just before Normandy? So many had gone before me, there at Fort Benning, before they jumped into history. Would there be a war before my years were up, and would I join the roll call of combat paratroopers listed on the plaques up on the forward wall of the room? Above the names of the dead on the wall were full-color depictions of the patches they wore on their shoulders. Each crest had the word AIRBORNE across the top. There was the screaming eagle of the 101st, and the red block of the All American 82d. There were golden talons, white wings, and blue dragon heads. Which would be mine? In the center was a large emblem showing the famous circle of red, white, and blue with a glider and inflated parachute that each of us would wear on his hat, and under that was a giant pair of silver wings. The sign under it said it all: ONLY FOR THOSE WHO

DARE! Present at all Airborne sites were the words ALL THE WAY, our motto.

Long wooden benches, the seats of which were six inches higher than normal with backs that were high and set well back, were made for oddly shaped men attached to parachute packs. We rested against them rather than sitting like normal folks. I really had no fear, the training had done its job and I knew I could jump. I wanted to do it. It was jumping into space, which now did not seem unnatural. The jump master finished his review of the jump commands and their hand signals, used because the noise of the uninsulated airplane might drown out his voice. They were the ten-minute warning, two-minute warning, get ready, stand up, hook up, sound off for equipment check, stand in the door, and, finally, Go!

The Air Force was next. Our pilot was from the Air National Guard and commanded a C-119, or Flying Boxcar. Even though he was not full-time Air Force, his skill level was said to be just as high. He was older and he had made too many trips to the mess hall in his long career. His gray-green flight suit did not clash with his gray hair and was stretched out in the middle, giving away his paunch. A hint of double chin completed a picture that was not off a recruiting poster. He told us about the characteristics of the 119, a twin-tailed brute of an airplane with two enormous propeller-driven engines. "I will sound a loud klaxon horn if we are about to crash. When I do so, exit the aircraft as soon as you can hook up." These things must never crash, I thought—look how old it is. He went through several other in-flight emergencies, which was just part of the routine. Then he said, "If you are being dragged behind the aircraft." Wait a minute, I thought, no one ever said anything about being dragged behind an airplane at 160 miles per hour twelve hundred feet off the ground. Jimmy and I looked at each other at the same time, and I mouthed the word

"Dragged!" I saw myself flying along facedown, arms out like a bird, sixty feet to the rear.

"If you are being dragged behind the aircraft," he said quite simply, as if it were an everyday occurrence, "put your hands on your head to tell us that you are conscious. We will cut the static line and you immediately pull your reserve." No one moved except Jimmy and I. Had we missed this part during the last two weeks? Now I knew what they meant by staying mentally alert. "If you are not conscious, don't put your hands on your head and we will attempt to pull you back into the bird." What was this, "Humor in Uniform" from *Readers Digest*? He was serious. No one asked what would happen if the "attempt" failed! We didn't want to know any more at that point. Would they foam the runway and let the dragged trooper skip along like a yo-yo on a string until he stopped by running into the rear of the slowing 119? That ended the briefing. There was no request for questions from the floor.

We filed out to the line of sad, old planes, which were leaking hydraulic fluid on the concrete hardstand. All I could think of was that we were all volunteers, and now I knew why. No one in his right mind could be forced into that airplane. Of course, peer pressure loaded us on board. I took up the first seat next to the door and Jimmy plopped down next to me. He reached under his red cloth bucket seat that had been pulled down from the bulkhead, found the white paper bag, and threw up. The engines had not even started and my Airborne buddy was airsick.

It would be a twenty-minute flight along the Chattahoochee River and, unlike an airliner, the rugged craft jumped and lurched. The pilot banked and climbed at radical attitudes, throwing his passengers around. We strained against our seat belts and each other, trying to maintain an upright attitude while being bundled up in far too much equipment. Airsickness struck several, including, for the second time, my partner. As the sick looked for a place to put the bags the loadmaster said, "Take it with you. Don't leave it on my clean airplane." So they stuffed the bags into the top of their shirt. Not a good idea; it would probably revisit them on the way down.

Mostly the men stared at the men seated opposite and tried to find a comfortable position. There was none. I kept going over in my mind the steps to getting a strong exit from the open door. If I didn't, I would be bounced along the outside of the fuselage, which could tangle my lines and result in disaster. I knew that if they did get twisted I would have to bicycle with my legs, causing a spin, which would straighten them out. The only restriction on board was that we had to keep our right hand over the silver handle to the reserve chute on our chest. The smaller parachute, used only when the main malfunctioned, was spring-loaded and if the handle was accidentally snagged it would open inside the airplane. My hand never left the handle.

Clad in white T-shirt, field pants, and glistening black boots, the jump master tightened his Air Force parachute. It was lighter and allowed him to move freely. Hooked to the overhead by a safety line, he opened both side doors and gave the ten-minute warning. We were all so uncomfortable by then that we longed to get up and get the weight of the equipment off our backs. Holding on to the forward edge of the door, he stuck the upper portion of his body outside the airplane and looked for the drop zone. The prop wash of the engine rippled the skin on his face and gave him a horror mask like some monster from the movies. He didn't just glance out, but hung there for the next few minutes. It was impressive. He was watching the red smoke that had been set off in the DZ (drop zone) by the safety officer, which showed the attitude of the ground wind. From that he and the pilot would set up the approach. If the winds were above fourteen miles per hour, the jump would be scrapped. The drop zone was a mile long and several football fields wide, devoid of trees or other hazards. A legend had it that there was an open well, a mere two-foot opening, that jumpers swore they had seen from the air but could never find once on the ground. If one landed dead center, he would disappear, chute and all, without a trace. There was no shortage of scary stories going around, but they were all pushed aside at the two-minute warning.

"Stand up!" came the call. With difficulty but resolve, I got to my feet and turned toward the rear of the aircraft. "Hook up!" I pulled the flat metal connector on the end of the static line from my chest and snapped it on the fixed cable, just like the one on the thirty-four-foot tower. I threaded the safety wire through the hole and bent it over, which prevented the hook from disengaging by accident from my lifeline. "Sound off for equipment check!" Since I was first in line the jump master checked me out, and the guy behind, the famous mal-de-air kid who had three bags to take with him, checked my backpack. "Stand in the door!"

The shuffle we had been taught was the only effective step as the plane pitched and rolled, side-shifted, and dipped as it lined up. They were all violent movements that defied walking. I made it the three feet forward and made a right-angle turn, seizing the edge of the open door. My boots found the threshold and the tips rocked forward, verifying that they were outside the fuselage. My stick, packed front to back, pressed against me and I leaned back into Jimmy's solid weight. The forms of ten men held me in position, we were like one. I heard "Go!" and felt the blow on my back from the jump master. I propelled myself up, and the "out" was done for me by the prop blast from the engine. I was free. Weightless, I rolled onto my back and saw the underside of the giant tail boom pass above me. I even counted. And when I got to three thousand, a strong hand gripped me by the shoulder. Four thousand was never heard, by God; it was choked off in my throat as my harness rode up. I looked up to see who was holding me. I knew from the force that I was being dragged behind the mighty aircraft. To my surprise a beautiful green parachute billowed above with the sun shining through the small hole at the apex. It was deathly quiet.

I felt great. Everything worked just like they said it would. There was no fear because there was no feeling of falling. I was flying in a private vehicle across a clear sky and with no restrictions. All around me were fellow parachutes from my plane and others—we filled the sky. From there we looked like solo balloonists floating in long lines staggered a little above and a little below. I took a peek at the ground, which held no fear and was dotted by a few men. The semi–tractor trailer trucks at the edge of the open DZ seemed toylike from a thousand feet. It was time to pull a riser and steer in their direction. Everyone had the same idea—shorten the walk. Why walk a half mile with all that heavy silk when one could land beside it. Just above me I saw a man coming at great speed right at me. He hit my canopy and I could see his big feet on top of my chute. I yelled, "Get the hell off!" He began to run and I saw his deep footstep impressions as he went across the top of my chute and off the other side. Nearby, two others collided at eye level and tried to push each other away with their arms rather than pulling opposite risers and spinning away. An instructor on the ground with a megaphone reminded them of the procedure, and they parted. Suddenly there was another offender crossing the top of my chute and I repeated my instructions. The only sound was the cussing and swearing from outraged buddies having near collisions as we neared the ground. I took up a full slip by doing a double pull-up, put my feet together, and looked straight out as I saw the tops of the big green pine trees draw level. The parachute landing fall that I had practiced never happened. I hit the ground like a sack of Idaho's big baking potatoes thrown into the back of flatbed truck. "Bang!" I hit with my boots, my knees, and my face.

That was the fastest thing that had ever happened to me. One second I had the plan all set in my mind and the next my mind was stuffed into the back of my helmet. There was no time in between. I'd never tasted Georgia's red soil before. I knew it wouldn't be great, and it wasn't. Rather musty, I thought. I collected my thoughts and then ran through all systems: no pain. I got to my feet as a wave of euphoria swept up and down my body. My mind was as clear as a bell and I jumped around getting out of the harness and rolling up the lines. I was giddy. A smile broke out that I couldn't contain—everyone was my friend. I laughed and joked with anyone nearby. What a great feeling! Nothing could touch me now.

I found Jimmy nearby, and he had been attacked by the barf bags stuffed in his shirt. "Well, at least it is your own barf," I said. He should have released them when he got straightened out at a thousand feet, but he forgot. "Stop complaining, at least you're not airsick anymore." We made another jump that day and one the following day. I looked forward to them and to experiencing that nearly indescribable feeling that took over me once I was on the ground.

It took five jumps to qualify and get the silver wings. Jump number four was a full-equipment trip. We suited up with pack, ammunition, and rifle. I weighed so much that I had to be helped up the loading ladder into the rear of the airplane. I was last that time; I would rather have been first. Pushing the stick out the door with all that stuff on was a real challenge. The unstable floor beneath my boots threw me around, and every bit of strength I had was used to keep my weight forward against Jimmy.

Georgia in summer is unbelievably hot and humid. I was soaked with sweat that had turned cold in the airplane at altitude, and I was chilled until I started the run for the door. In the air, I saw one of my men slide off the DZ to the left and head straight for the medical ambulance. His chute blew past over the roof but he didn't. He hit the side of the van right on the big red cross, bull's-eye, then he crumpled to the ground while his chute draped over the top and rippled in the wind. A medic went to help him up, and just as he did the wind inflated the canopy and it pulled him out of the corpsman's grasp and up to the roof, leaving him on the red cross painted on the top. He lay there for just a few seconds when the chute billowed once more and dragged his motionless form off the top, then dropped him to the ground on the far side. At least there were medics in attendance.

The winds were blowing up the DZ, and as the last man I ended up against the trees at the far end. I was so far out that I could not even see the trucks at the parking area. I picked up an armful of chute and lines and plodded for the transportation. Loudspeakers urged me and others to get off the DZ quickly; the DZ is a dangerous place and no time should be lost evacuating. I was struggling—the sun pushed me down from above and my legs were losing their strength. I was dehydrated. I never saw the trucks, but came to in the hospital. "You have a bad case of heatstroke, Lieutenant. You are going to stay with us for a few days," said an Army doctor. Great, both my wife and myself were inmates.

I was put on two weeks of light duty and released. My class graduated without me, and I was miserable. But the worst was yet to come. The adjutant of the school said, "You are on orders for Japan and you are past your report date. I can't hold you any longer, you will have to go without getting in your last jump." Without the final jump I could not get my wings, and so I left Fort Benning trained but not qualified.

Carol checked out of the hospital with Tim, and all four of us drove quietly home to see our folks before going to Japan. In those ancient times the airline regulations would not allow an infant of less than three months to travel. So Carol and our two sons remained behind as I drove across the country to California. Other than running out of gas in Wyoming the ride was uneventful. My heart was broken without those wings—in the eyes of the Army I was still a leg. I stayed with my brother for a day in San Francisco and he painted my portrait. Fortunately, it has been lost.

Chapter Five

*Persuade by accomplishments rather
than by eloquence.*
GEN. GEORGE C. MARSHALL

Since my car had been shipped to Japan, upon my arrival in California, my older brother, Jack, drove me from his home in Walnut Creek to Travis Air Force Base in the valley. I was traveling on a Military Airlift Command airplane, my first experience with anything outside of commercial travel. The Air Force maintained a fleet of prop-driven airliners in those days. They could haul either cargo or passengers. They ranged from the huge C-124s with two decks to the famous DC-3s. The passenger terminal at the large base looked much like a commercial terminal except that it was very small, only two clerks at the counter. The agents were regular Air Force women and very professional. The airlines were flying Boeing 707s on the polar route to Japan, which took ten hours, but I was taking the scenic route by DC-6. It would be great—first to Hawaii, then to Wake Island, and finally to Japan. The flight time for the trip was over thirty hours, with a night in Honolulu. The DC-6 was the same plane that John Wayne flew back from Hawaii in *The High and the Mighty.*

I was a little nervous about flying over all that water and remembered all the films I had seen of crash landings at sea and of passengers floating around for weeks in rubber rafts.

We flew in uniform and my fellow travelers, mostly officers, were from all services. I was lucky that they did not schedule me on a troopship, which was the normal way for Army personnel to cross the wide Pacific. I was very excited at the prospect of adventure. I walked out to the silver, four-engine, propeller-driven plane and climbed aboard from the same spot where General MacArthur had taken off for Washington after his relief by President Truman. He had made the trip in a DC-6, in 1951, the first time he had been in his home country since 1937. I didn't plan to be gone that long.

Inside, it didn't look like an airliner. The interior skin was not exposed like the C-119 of recent experience, and it was insulated. The seats, covered with rough royal-blue cloth, were all facing to the rear and had a little padding. Yellow bags with survival gear were stuffed under each seat. The spindly aluminum legs of the seats were held to the tracks in the floor by brass pins for easy removal and instant conversion to cargo space. The seating was two by two on both sides of a narrow aisle. I was next to the round window and my seatmate was a Navy lieutenant commander. He was very distinguished-looking, gray hair, in his early forties. The seat belts consisted not only of a lap belt of dirty white webbing, but it also had the two shoulder straps that connected to the clasp at the waist. Like the cockpit crew, I fastened myself in for the takeoff. My favorite film was *South Pacific,* and I felt like Lt. Joe Cable, going out to the war in the deep Pacific and meeting people from exotic cultures. The crew chief, a sergeant of great age, ran through a lengthy explanation of ditching procedures that I would have missed on a commercial flight. I purchased an in-flight meal in the terminal. It was contained in a flimsy white cardboard container nearly as large as a shoe box. I wedged it under my seat along with my Mae West life preserver. The box lunch was sealed with scotch tape and very heavy. My brother, a veteran of military air travel in the Orient, made sure that I ate a large meal before boarding. We expected to be aloft for more than twelve hours, and with my reputation as a professional eater he knew that I would be chewing on the box before we arrived.

The long, slow climb out took us over San Francisco at ten thousand feet and it was after we were out at sea that we finally reached twenty thousand feet. I held off breaking the seal on the lunchbox until we were told that we had passed the point of no return. I never saw food that I didn't like until I ate a Belgian lasagna in 1984. Two ham sandwiches, an orange and banana, a can of juice, three chocolate candy bars, two packages of chocolate chip cookies, one coke, two packages of potato chips, a pack of spearmint gum, some beef jerky, and a piece of fruitcake—just what I would have ordered. Perfect, all my favorites. Waste not, want not, I ate it all, to the surprise of my seatmate. During a waking moment he offered me the remains of his box. I accepted it gratefully and finished it off as we circled over Schofield Barracks, Fort Shafter, Pearl Harbor, and landed at last on Hickam Airfield. The names were history itself. I followed the senior officers (higher-ranking members always got off first), when I was hit by the humidity right in the face. I was in Class A coat and tie. Before I walked the twenty yards to the old terminal I had perspired through my shirt. A ride on a dark-blue school bus to the BOQ only made it worse, but the smell of perfume from the huge number of flowers that covered the base told me I was in another world. Except for pockmarks on the mess hall's outer walls, which had been barely covered with plaster, there was no longer evidence of the attack that had occurred over twenty years before. It was late afternoon and we would be back at it early the next morning. Before dark I took a swim at the club beach, just outside the opening to Pearl Harbor, and watched a submarine pass into the narrow channel. I had only seen subs in black-and-white films, but the real thing was longer than I expected and more graceful as it silently slipped by. The mile-long waterway was only wide enough to accommodate one large ship at a time, and I could see how the Japanese could bottle up the American fleet easily in that deathtrap. Now I was going to serve in the country of our former enemy.

Dressed in a fresh shirt and tie, carrying my blouse, I climbed back aboard, vowing to return to that heavenly dot in the great ocean. We droned over the endless Pacific all day. From the air Wake Island, our refueling point, looked more like a passing ship than an island. It is shaped like a horseshoe surrounding a bright blue lagoon. The water is only knee-deep for miles and the orange and red coral was visible from the air. One side had an airstrip, in the middle was a parking pad, and on the other side were three flat-roofed cement-block buildings about the size of ranch-style houses. There was a permanent party of twenty airmen and hundreds of seabirds. Wake is ten feet above sea level and has less than a hundred small palm trees. I remembered the film that told the story of the American fighting men who attempted to defend the strip of sand. All of them were killed. I spent the two hours there walking the beach, always within sight of my airplane. Little had changed since the war. I crept inside some of the bunkers that ringed the island. They still contained the remnants of empty ammunition boxes rusting their way down into the sand floor. Outside in the surf were the tilted, burned-out wrecks of Japanese landing craft. It was my first visit to a modern battlefield and I was all alone to conjure up its ghosts as I looked out through the bunker's slits. A few days before, an Air Force C-124 pilot had attempted to reverse its propellers while landing, but this had failed to engage so it was sitting belly-deep in water off the end of the parking area. While I was digging around in the past, everyone else was involved in the present, offering solutions to the retrieval of the C-124.

On the wall of the operations shack was a metal plaque commemorating President Truman's presentation to General of the Army Douglas MacArthur of the fourth oak leaf cluster to the Distinguished Service Medal (DSM). That was for his defense of Korea. The DSM is our nation's highest award for achievement. MacArthur was also the holder of the nation's highest award for heroism, the Medal of Honor, for his defense of the Philippine Islands. He and his father, Arthur, were the only father and son to have won it. His father's was presented for heroism in the Civil War. Between the two, they served from 1862 to 1951, his father ending his career in Manila as the governor general. The son only broke his service for five years, as Marshal under the Philippine government just prior to the beginning of WWII. I was about to serve in the military theater the MacArthurs had built.

We finally made it to Tachikawa Air Base in the early evening. I didn't know exactly what date it was, since we had crossed the international date line somewhere that long day. I was met by a Japanese driver in a shiny black American sedan. American cars were known as yank tanks because they were twice the size of Japanese-made autos. My driver spoke excellent English. "Sir, I am Kato. I will take you to Camp Zama. It is a two-hour drive into the countryside. Welcome to Nippon."

"Tachie," as the Americans called it, was on the edge of Tokyo. The air base looked very American in the blue light of the street lamps. It was a little America, with sidewalks, curbs, and signs in English. But when we passed through the gate into the Oriental evening, that all changed; we were in the neighborhoods. Few buildings were over two stories, three being tops, and all had brown-tile roofs and wood-frame sides of more or less natural color. The doors were all sliding, most with glass panes to the ground. Some were still rice paper and the illumination of TV screens came through them as a blue glow. Though it was night, the streetlights and gay neon signs on the little storefronts made everything quite visible. What struck me most was that the writing was in Japanese, in several different scripts; I couldn't read anything. To me the words seemed more like designs than writing, which made the area seem like a magical kingdom.

There was no space between shops and dwellings, everything was a jumble of buildings. It was raining, just a drizzle, and the neon lights of the storefront plate-glass windows reflected on the wet pavements. Most inhabitants were walking and bowing. They nearly all wore traditional dress (this is the early 1960s) and clumped along in white socks, on wooden sandal-like shoes that had wood blocks underneath. It gave them a short, clicking gait, which was further hampered by the long skirt of the kimonos worn by both men and women. The inch-thick blocks kept the Japanese out of the puddles. Perpetual smiles seemed to be on everyone's faces and the passersby were interested in me. As our car stopped every few yards in the traffic, pedestrians, mostly women, would dip slightly and peer into the car window from a foot or two away, chatter something in Japanese to a friend, and clatter away.

The younger the woman, the brighter the costume. The young men, school-age, were generally in white shirts, dark pants, and black peaked caps. Rarely did I see a lone figure; they were always in groups of at least two and mostly in parties of three to six. The women carried babies on their backs, wrapped tightly and tied on in front with cloth bands. The little ones were all fat and raven-haired. It was impossible to tell the sex of the children from dress or haircut.

Between the roadway and the storefronts were open drainage ditches, a foot across and a foot deep, which ran with black water. One sudden turn and the front wheel would drop in and the car would likely remain there. Everything I saw was very clean. A complicated scent hung in the air, a mixture of fresh-cut vegetables, steam, and fish. Little restaurants, open to the street, were crowded. Some locals stood outside and with twisted chopsticks ate a mixture of noodles and vegetables from high-sided, ornate little bowls of blue and white. It was all very animated. No one moved slowly, they all seemed to be in a hurry, but not really headed for any particular destination. The only things I recognized were the Coca-Cola signs, which were in red and white, though the familiar word was written in Japanese characters.

During the final fifteen minutes of our drive the villages strung out a little but the traffic never let up, a mixture of tiny cars and motorbikes of varying horsepower. The only vehicles bigger than my sedan were the dump trucks piloted by young boys training to be kamikaze. Wooden blocks were screwed to the floor pedals, and still the drivers were barely visible in the cabs. There were no Japanese driver's licenses in those days and everything was backward for me because the Japanese drove on the left side of the road. Bicycles were everywhere but, that late in the evening, mostly leaning against racks. We passed through the town of Sobidi Mi, a cluster of houses around a railway station, and Kato said, "Sir, Camp Zama, next stop." The road went through the center of the post and there was a big gate on both sides. The gate guards were American soldiers and Japanese national police in dark-blue uniforms too large for them. They looked tiny next to the military police.

I spent the night in the officers guest quarters. The room smelled of sandalwood. Though very tired, I lay in bed and absorbed the atmosphere. I was a very long way from home.

In the morning a rap on the door and a tiny childlike voice from the hallway roused me. "A very good morning to you, sir. I have your fooding," came the call over and over again, until I responded. When I did, the door pushed open very slowly and a diminutive girl with short black hair cut in bangs peered in, revealing only one eye. "Breakfast, sir," she said as she padded in on her white socks. She carried a tray with a western-style menu and placed it on my lap. Then she giggled, bowed, and left. I must have been a sight. What a life, and all for a second lieutenant.

When dressed in my best uniform, I walked out the front

door to see the new country. It was heavenly. Camp Zama had been the home of the Japanese national military academy before the war. The emperor, on his only trip outside the palace in Tokyo, had been the guest at a graduation there during the war and a large stone with the imperial name cut into its face stood on the site of the former reviewing stand. The post had been especially prepared for his visit, a singular honor, and the resulting landscaping was now enjoyed by the conquerors.

The guest house was high up and I could see most of the installation. Zama was built on a hillside covered with hand-manicured trees ten feet high. They were full, rounded on top with thick dark-green leaves, and backed with giant, nearly black, fir trees. All the structures were painted in shades of green as well, and were nearly invisible in the morning mist. Brilliant flower beds were fitted between the roadways. Kato arrived and escorted me to the car, then drove me one block to the headquarters of the United States Army Forces, Japan. I'll bet no new officer arriving at Fort Dix, New Jersey, ever enjoyed my lavish lifestyle.

The headquarters had been constructed by the Americans during the Korean War and was a miniature of the Pentagon in light gray concrete rather than Portland stone and in two instead of five stories. It was already showing its age, and dark streaks ran down the sides. Colonel Ball was chief of the Communication Command, which provided long lines to all the US forces on the islands and overseas links east to units stationed in Korea, south to Southeast Asia, and west to Alaska, Hawaii, and Washington. His history, which I was given prior to meeting him, showed that he was West Point 1940, had served throughout the war in Europe, and by 1944 was promoted to lieutenant colonel. In 1950 he became a colonel and was married to Missy, the daughter of a well-known colonel of Coast Artillery from Fort Monroe, Virginia. He was ready for promotion to general officer. To me they were Army aristocracy. The adjutant, Captain

Watanabe, a nisei, or first-generation American-born Japanese from Hawaii, escorted me in for an audience. The colonel was a portly gentleman with a burr haircut. He was very much at ease—I was merely another young lieutenant, one more for his officer corps of fifty. "Your name is very unfortunate, young man," he commented as he read my short background. I had had many things said about my name and was prepared for most, but this was a new one. "We can't call you 'Fitz' here, I already have one, your new boss, Captain Fitzsimmons. You will have to be David. You are going to be a radio engineer here, building a new system." This was not good news. I had a degree in business.

The only confusion my Christian name caused was for me. In the office, which I shared with the captain, I always answered when someone was addressing him and I didn't respond to "David" at all. My new boss, commissioned at the Citadel, was an Army brat whose father had been an old friend of the colonel's. Captain Fitz was a brilliant electrical engineer and headed the project to install a new tropo scatter radio network, which was on the leading edge of technology. He was also the ideal-*looking* officer—tall, strong, handsome, and very sure of himself. He was happy to have an assistant, but soon found out that I didn't have a clue when it came to engineering. He had other helpers in the office, though, and resigned himself to training me; there was no other choice. His patience was amazing. He gave me stacks of material on the specifications for the system, which covered sixteen sites spread out among Japan, Korea, and Okinawa. The contract was with Nippon Electric Company, and it was nearly ready to go on the air and eliminate the thousands of miles of cable that had been the backbone of communications since the end of WWII.

I moved out of the guest house the next day and into a modern BOQ built just out of sight on the other side of the post. It was one large room, very comfortable, with maid service. A Japanese woman who looked to be about fifty took care of several rooms. She was one of six maids in the new building, which had communal bathrooms. Each day she cleaned and tidied the room, washed and ironed my clothes from the previous day, and put them away. With that kind of service, I only needed two sets of clothes. Each day I found my uniform, underwear, and the socks I had just worn back in my cabinet. She and her friends spoke no English so we had only a nodding acquaintance. She was there seven days a week. Late one Saturday morning I was in the shower when she and the other maids joined me, their arms filled with dirty clothes and a box of Tide. They paused in the open door to the shower room and each made a greeting in Japanese and bowed several times while I turned my back and said, "Hello," hoping they would go away. They disrobed completely, came in, and washed the clothes of their patrons on the tile floor under the showerheads, which were on full blast. They were not at all put out by the encounter. It was a never-to-be-forgotten experience for me. I knew about public baths and had glimpsed them in some movies, but this was like an out-of-body experience. I was trapped in the corner. They were all very well into middle age, and former peasant women who had spent their youth in the rice fields held no allure. They were not ignoring me, either—each in turn would steal a glimpse, and if I caught an eye she would giggle and titter with the other matrons. Their smiles were ear to ear. I thought, this has probably happened before, in fact it is more than likely a daily occurrence for the other residents. Now that I was a man of the world, I should take it in stride. I was mature and so I relaxed a little and finished; I even did a little singing. I took my soap and barefooted quite comfortably past the pile of clothes and women huddled in the middle of the floor over the drain. Their short stature and well-fed figures made them look more like modern-art lumps squatting over the wash than women. I even managed a "Good-bye girls" as I reached for my robe on a hook next to the sink. I shaved around the corner at the washbasin, and left with a wave of my hand, very sophisticated and worldly. I met two other officers in the hall who were obviously headed for the shower. "Don't fall over the maids," I quipped.

"What do you mean, Fitz?" one asked. "Are they in there again? It is off limits to us then." He pointed to a sign I had missed on my way in since I didn't have my contact lenses on prior to entering. "You didn't go in there, did you?"

"No, of course not," I lied.

As the lowest-ranking officer, the only second lieutenant in the unit, I got the worst extra duties. I didn't mind, I loved everything and remembered what Major Knowles had told me before I left college. "Take the jobs no one else wants and do them very well. Your superiors will take note of your can-do attitude. They are always looking for someone who won't complain." I was always upbeat and said, "Thanks," to any opportunity; I was an optimist. So it was that the company commander, a first lieutenant from Texas A&M, gave up his additional duty as honor guard commander, suggesting to the colonel that it would be good training for me. With my military school background and the fact that I had been the drill team commander in college, it was a natural for me. The total guard consisted of five platoons who dressed in special uniforms and formed up in front of the headquarters whenever high-ranking visitors arrived. The guard was graded by the commanding general after each performance, and my platoon was the worst of the bunch. My eight years of experience in drill and ceremonies made up for my lack of engineering knowledge that was so obvious on the job. Within the month we had won the first-place slot and led the formation.

Noon, November 22, 1963, occurred during the night in Japan, so when I woke and turned on the radio, I heard that our President had been shot. It was the weekend, so I dressed in uniform and went to the officers club for breakfast and the company of other mourners. We were so far away and, with no television, all we could do was listen to the broadcast account piped in on the loudspeaker from Armed Forces Radio. Was it harder for us, without the images that were repeated endlessly on the TV at home? The news was shocking, gut-wrenching. In the club, the Japanese waitresses were all crying and avoided our eyes as they served breakfasts that we only poked at but did not eat. All units in the Far East were placed on alert, and I went to the communications center and read the official account coming over the wire from the Pentagon. The local Japanese had seen the news on television and they took it to heart. In a way, they mourned even harder than we. For weeks after, they would stop Americans on the street and express their condolences in broken English or in Japanese accompanied by many low bows. They named streets and squares in honor of our fallen leader. They were very sincere and that's when I realized that the war was over and the Japanese were grateful for our presence and the security we provided their nation from the Communists. Our defense of Korea was proof of commitment. The Japanese were helpless after WWII, easy pickings.

The honor guard formed up in the afternoon and the three giant-size post flags—the American, Japanese, and United Nations standards—were brought out of storage and hoisted to the top of the poles, then run back down to half staff. Each was so large that the tip nearly touched the ground. They were so heavy that if the wind reached fifteen miles per hour they bent the poles, so one platoon stood by, day and night, for the next two weeks to take them down and replace them temporarily with normal-size ones when the wind blew too strong. As a result, I spent hours sitting and watching those flags waving in the wind, my tribute, wishing I was home.

My own family was on its way. Tim was old enough to travel and they were booked on a commercial flight to Tachie. I didn't have much money since most of it went home. It was only a week before Christmas and we were fortunate that they could come before the holidays. I rented a little Japanese house on the economy in the village of Sagami Ono, a block from the Army hospital compound and ten miles from Camp Zama.

I went to Yokohama, a two-hour drive, to shop for Christmas presents. I didn't want to buy anything from the PX, I wanted everything to be Japanese. Yokohama was not like Tokyo. It was a provincial town with a big shopping district. Hundreds of little shops were stuck one to the other, and the smells of the open food market were heady and drifted over the entire district. The open sewer added a magic of its own. Some buildings soared to five stories and traffic was a solid pack. People were nearly standing one on top of the other but the atmosphere was gay. Few occidentals were seen on the streets and I, though not tall by our standards, stood out above everyone. I had been learning Japanese and could speak enough to buy "stuff" with some ease. In Yokohama the shops were brighter than in the village near Zama, painted red or yellow and hung with paper mobiles or Japanese lanterns covered in black characters edged in white on red tissue.

Japan is very formal and correct. Ritual is deep in every conversation and action. All the shops were wide open to customers, as it was considered an affront to cause a buyer to open a door, as a door was looked upon as a barrier to be crossed only at personal invitation. To insure that one knew one was welcome, a plaster cat of yellow with black stripes called Miniki Nekko was always somewhere near the entrance, one front paw raised to beckon. The story goes that an old man was not doing well, in fact starving, because customers failed to be attracted to his merchandise. So his cat sat in the window and waved at passersby, who were so intrigued by its antics that they were drawn into the shop. The old man prospered, and ever since, shop owners have displayed the icon to free enterprise in their establishments to conjure up similar success.

I found that many items were in my price range in Yokohama; the dollar was trading at 365 yen to one dollar (today it is about 100-to-one). I picked out a dark, wooden, carved jewel box from the northern island of Hokkaido for Carol that played a Beethoven theme. It was very precious. I found a heavy black silk kimono with birds in gold thread which reversed to red and gold. It had a gold lamé obi waistband six inches wide with a bow in the back. The shop owner threw in a pair of thick white shoe-socks. I bought a red "happy coat" for David, which all Japanese children wore in the house. It had a black collar and funny little cartoon characters running up and down the front. He also got a plastic dump truck filled with colored blocks. For Tim there was a stuffed black bear with long shaggy fur and a white muzzle. I found a fireman's jacket for myself. It was very thick cotton, in the traditional pattern of red and black with a white circle on the back and the character for "number one man" in black a foot high. Each man on the firewagon had a different designation according to his job and position on the team. The coat was heavy so it could act as armor if a burning building collapsed on the firefighter and it could soak up water that was doused on each firefighter to protect him before he dashed into the flames.

I met Carol and the boys the next night in the passenger lounge at Tachikawa Air Base. She had a story of her own to tell. Her parents were children of the Depression and had lived through the war at home in Aurora. They had never traveled and, though resigned to her leaving with their only grandchildren, whom they doted upon, still saw the Japanese as the enemy. They were unaware that American service families lived in "Little Americas" overseas. Her father asked, "What will you and the children eat?" A meat, potatoes, and gravy man, he remembered the war propaganda of bucktoothed, bespectacled midgets surviving on rice and looking like ads for *Starvation* magazine. They then insisted that she go ahead and leave the children with them, where they could get a good American upbringing. After overcoming that hurdle she managed to get out of town with her brood intact and climbed aboard a commercial flight to San Francisco, where they changed to a military-contract jet flight to Tokyo. It was all servicemen and families, and they stopped in Hawaii for refueling. They were told that they could expect a three-hour layover, but as she was feeding Tim forty-five minutes later they called the plane. David was nineteen months old and Tim just three months. Her mountain of carry-on luggage was spread out around her on the floor and she nearly panicked trying to make it to the gate, with bits and pieces falling off as she skittered toward the passageway. David, carrying little pieces and running along behind on his short toddler legs, was encouraged by his mother but falling behind. He never cried or stopped. A young sailor went back, scooped him up, and took charge of him until they were reunited in their airline seats. Over the next eight hours Carol became airsick. While Tim slept most of the way, she had to waken David every hour and take him back to the bathroom while he stood by and watched his mother be sick. She knew the baby would stay asleep but was afraid David would wake up, discover her gone, and become upset. She felt it was better to take him with her. When she asked the flight attendant for something to help her stomach, the woman said, "You should have done that before you got on the plane. Nothing will help now." Carol landed without having had any sleep and continued to be ill on the bus ride around the end of the field. The only hope she had was the sight of a lit Coca-Cola sign she saw on top of a building on the other side of the perimeter fence. So, our reunion was not what I had expected. Carol had no color, and the thought of a two-hour car ride just made her more sick.

There were no Christmas trees in Sagamihara, so I cut a large pine branch from an evergreen growing on a post and stuck it into a foam block in a low, wide-mouth vase. We decorated it with strings of popcorn and set it on top of the bookcase. Carol, poor woman, could not believe the house I had rented. Fifteen feet by twenty and made of two thicknesses of plywood, with no insulation, it was in a neighborhood of identical miniature dwellings that were separated by cement block walls three feet high. We were the only Americans except for two houses across the narrow street that were occupied by Army sergeants and their Japanese wives, one of whom spoke English.

We had a living room nine feet square with large sliding glass doors that made up one wall. We also had two bedrooms—the master was so small that our American double bed touched three walls. In our tiny kitchen, one could stand in the middle and touch all the walls. The bathroom had a deep, sunken mosaic tile bathtub that resembled a buried oil drum and was impossible to use with small children. The stove and furniture was issued to us by the Quartermaster Corps warehouse on post. Naturally, it was overstuffed and very out of place in that dollhouse. In the center of the living room floor was a space heater which had a copper tube that ran along the floor and out through a hole cut in the window frame to a drum of kerosene. The fuel was gravity-fed and pooled in the bottom. A lighted piece of paper started it with a flash. The smell of unburned fuel hung in the house. Though a mild climate, in December there was snow on the ground which generally melted by noon. Carol, also an optimist, thought the place was charming. It wasn't; it was cold and very damp, but we were together again and that was all that ever mattered to her.

Life at Camp Zama was filled with challenges for her. Army wives are a breed apart. They not only raise families and care for their strange husbands, they also blend into any community with an ease that defies description. Hot water, essential to young children, was provided by a hot water heater which lived in an outhouse attached near the back door. It looked like an iron cylinder for bottled acetylene gas but was filled with water and had a nearly enclosed pan at the bottom. Kerosene dripped onto the plate and was lit with a match. Carol could never get the match to stay lit because it was always drowned by the liquid. She invented her own method. She allowed the fuel to fill the pan and overflow onto the cement floor, then simply lit the spillover on the floor, which eventually made its way to the main charge six inches above.

One day she lit it and went back into the house. Soon a passerby banged on the front door, waving his hands and yelling. She thought he was some kind of nut and closed the door in his face. Then, very excited, he appeared at the rear kitchen window along with several others. She opened the back door and found the back of the outer house on fire. Everyone in the street climbed the little wall and helped put it out. Japanese rarely called the fire department because they had to pay the firemen before they would work on the fire.

Looking out the front windows, we had a perfect view of a misty mountain—O Yama—framed by the cute houses. One quiet evening Carol told me, "I have a perfect title for a book about this place: 'There's a mountain at the end of my street.'" We also had a public bathhouse on our street. Many young people lived in rented rooms and worked in the big city. They frequented the bathhouse, as did some poorer families. It was a good fifty yards from our place and so the crowd that gathered outside was not really nearby. Many people worked late, and after dinner and a few beers they would go as a group to the bath quite happy around nine in the evening. By ten o'clock, embraced by a couple more beers, they would return home clean, socialized, and ready to start the rat race again. In bunches of four or five, the men, arms around each other or holding hands, would sing themselves home. Wave after wave would pass by. Between the clacking and clicking of the wooden shoes and their renditions of the Japanese version of "Home, Home on the Range," we got little sleep.

There were no door-to-door salesmen in Japan, but one day someone dressed all in white like a nun came to our front window. That was not unusual, often small bunches of local folks—old women and children, sometimes teenagers—out of curiosity would stand against the sliding doors, faces shaded by their hands, and look in. They would smile all together, as if in approval, then leave, giggling. They merely wanted to see how Americans lived. The people loved everything western. Seeing the nun, Carol went out the front door and around to greet her. She was in bleached gauze from head to foot and her face was covered with a veil. She rang a bell that was concealed under the flowing layers of her clothing. Nearby in the street other women, passersby, were pointing at the figure and saying something to Carol, but she couldn't get their drift. As Carol approached, the lady backed away, turned, and continued down the street, ringing her bell. No one approached her; indeed, they made a path for her to pass through. She was a leper.

The Signal Command was a very interesting place to work and filled with very competent people. The drafting section was nearly all Japanese. They worked in a large open room, one wall of which was lined with windows that offered a splendid view of the valley and mountain ridge behind. In the morning the countryside was always covered in mist, the lush, dark, pointed trees giving an impression of a gray-green painting slightly out of focus. I worked with one man in particular, a Mr. Yashita, who was in his forties. We became friends on my many visits as he changed blueprints for me time and time again. He was young enough to have been involved in the war, so one day I asked him if he had been in the forces during the war.

"I came from a well-to-do family, sir, from the south, and came of age to serve in the spring of 1945. My family was well placed in the government and they decided that I should go into the forces as a pilot. I was not happy with their selection, but one didn't defy authority in those days. I was sent to school not far from here, Atsugi Air Base, and since I came from prominent people I was given the honor of being a kamikaze pilot. I was interested in surviving the war; it was nearly over. But I couldn't dishonor my people. I was trained in a very short time because they only taught us how to take off and fly in formation. I learned how to read a compass and dive at targets. Our landings were never more than putting the plane on the ground safely so that we could go up again the next day and follow a compass heading. There was no doubt about what was expected of us and we received more ideological training on the code of the warrior than on the operation of the airplane. Many were reluctant to crash their explosive-laden planes into American ships operating off our southern coast. But we would all do our job and join our honored ancestors if that was what was required to save our homes and families. On graduation day I said good-bye to my mother and father, who were very proud of me. My mother was distraught and my father reserved but resigned to the sacrifice. I thought I saw regret in his face, that it had come to this. My heart was broken.

"I was in the lead plane, the only one that carried a passenger. A navigator sat behind me and it was his job to direct us out to sea on a bearing that would take us and our limited gas supply over the American fleet. At the last landfall he was going to parachute out and go back for another flight, leaving me with the responsibility to complete the mission alone. I was very young, just seventeen, and when I saw Mount Fuji in front of me I decided not to lead all those friends of mine to their death. I was not a good pilot, I was merely a pointer of airplanes. Mount Fuji was so large that I could not miss it and decided to fake engine trouble and make it sputter by turning the switches on and off. The navigator couldn't see what I was doing and, knowing that I was not good enough to land safely, jumped out. I headed for the mountain and crash landed on a forestry road. I was a better pilot than I thought. I was injured but the plane didn't blow up. I was still in hospital when the war ended." I had met, probably, the only surviving Japanese kamikaze pilot. His coworkers called him Chicken Kamikaze.

1st Lt. Jim Thomlenson was our idol. He had saved a crew member during an airplane crash and was wearing the Army Commendation Medal, a real honor. He looked like a hero, tall, dark-haired, with a movie star smile, and the colonel gave him a top job, as the officer in charge of the communication center. Identical to thousands of centers operated by all the services all over the world, the center ran twenty-four hours a day, seven days a week. Because the military is spread out around the globe, often in very remote areas, voice communication was most unreliable because the techology required a higher degree of sophistication and was subject to frequent breakdowns. Teletype, a relatively straightforward current-on or current-off techology that produced black letters on white paper, was very reliable and, in addition, produced a record copy, which was very important in military operations. The Army runs on paper, and most of it is in the form of teletype messages. Even phone conversations were always confirmed by message later if action was required. Therefore the message center was very important for the receiving and sending of thousands of messages a day. All traffic was encrypted to prevent the enemy from picking it out of the air and reading our every move. If the Russians could merely read our traffic they wouldn't need spies; it was all there. Once the messages were typed onto the line, the original, which was not scrambled, had to be destroyed in a very precise fashion. The night shift did the destruction in the basement, employing a special incinerator that was used only by the com center. The room was locked by vault double door.

In those days, military women were found in only a few branches of the Army—the Army Nurse Corps, the Medical Service Corps, and the Women's Army Corps—but female soldiers worked in many fields, mostly clerical, and therefore the com center had at least 20 percent women. Where other branches declared that they would not permit women in their ranks, the Signal Corps had found them to be great telephonists and message handlers. The men who worked with them, especially the young ones, naturally found the com center's staffing appealing, especially far from home. Fraternization was strictly prohibited between officers and female enlisted soldiers. Lieutenants in particular were warned because, young and mostly single, they were the most likely to behave badly.

One late night Jim decided to stop in and check on operations. Sgt. Margaret O'Leary, a topkick of the first order, was in charge of the shift of twenty soldiers who were typing messages and making distribution. A very strong personality, she and the lieutenant didn't really get on. Jim was rather easygoing and always joking around. Margaret was a professional and had worked very hard to get where she was, always competing against men who clearly had the edge within the institution. Part of the crew—four female soldiers who had been sent to the basement to burn several thousand old messages—was not present. Jim told the sergeant that if she needed him he would be in his quarters, and left after only a token visit.

As he walked away, he realized he'd never been in the burn room during operations. He had only inspected it for cleanliness during the day. So he went down into the dark, deserted basement. The long, dimly lit corridor was wet and slippery. At the far end the green metal vault double doors were closed, just as they should be. The troops, he'd been told, liked to do the burning with the doors open because it got too hot in the little room. The doors must be closed when they were burning highly classified material. It could not be safeguarded if the doors were open, and some could fly out into the hallway. The doors had a standard black-dial tumbler lock with sixty numbers in white. It was a little hard to see, but he got the combination right the first time. Wondering if he'd catch the crew reading or napping, he swung open one of the heavy metal doors. But they were working, all of them. In the nude. The chamber was so hot that they had all shed their clothes and were throwing gobs of paper into the open mouth of the furnace. Momentarily all five stood still and looked at each other. Jim closed the door behind him from the inside, both for security and decency. But, rather than run for their clothes—no one had said they couldn't burn with their clothes off—they stood their ground.

"Girls, I know it is very hot in here, and it isn't really a bad idea to keep your uniforms clean and away from the fire and smoke," he said nervously, "but, really, this is out of order."

The boldest of the four said, "If you are going to stay in here, you'd better get your clothes off, sir." Faced with four unashamed young women, something his Catholic background at Xavier University had never prepared him for, Jim lost his head. Two of the women helped him off with his things. They figured they were probably in trouble, so if he was co-opted, how could he punish them? Jim's Adonis-like physique in uniform was revealed to be a bit pudgy, really on the order of the Pillsbury Dough Boy. Their giggles had a leveling effect that fraternization rules were meant to prevent. But Jim felt completely free for the first time in his inhibited Christian life and frolicked with the girls in the heat of the fire by the dim light of the single naked lightbulb.

They were like naughty children playing Indians in front of a campfire, hooting and hollering, when Sgt. Margaret

O'Leary entered undetected through the steel doors. She was not amused. Very soon after, Jim and his family left Japan for the States and his last tour of duty, at Fort Slocum, home of the Army chaplain school.

One night while Carol and I were enjoying a movie at the post theater, the film was stopped and an officer came out on stage and made an announcement: "The President has ordered that all military family members in Vietnam will be evacuated immediately and sent to Japan. Essential personnel report to your units." Back in the States that probably did not get a mention in the nightly news, but out there it meant war. It had an effect similar to the announcement made in December 1941 among military support groups forgotten along the Pacific Rim. That proclamation had a direct effect on me. Within a month I was on a classified mission to Da Nang, Vietnam, to help with the installation of the first tropo scatter link down the country to Saigon. It was a short trip but very enlightening.

That year a lot of things were happening in the world, but I missed them. The Beatles stormed America and the Mustang was introduced. While the culture at home was changing over from the Beat Generation to flower children, we were suspended in time to the Americanized music and culture of World War II. Our only link to home was the Armed Forces Radio station, which carried no Huntley-Brinkley reporting, only entertainment. The most popular show was *Hawaii Calling,* with Webly Edwards. It opened with the sound of the sea breaking on the beach at Honolulu. It was all steel guitars and waving palm tree music. Webly would say, "From the warm beach and swaying palm trees of Waikiki, Hawaii calls." He had been saying that since before Pearl Harbor and that he was still saying it was proof that we had won the war and prevailed in the Pacific. It was a touch of home, or at least of home the way you would like home to be.

We were more than knee-deep in Japan and its people. A

friend told us about a good baby-sitter, a woman librarian for the Army hospital just up the street. Her name was Kimiko and she was in her late forties, I suspect. She had a great deal of trouble pronouncing our name and was very interested in its origin. In a way it was like her own, one from an ancient culture, which seemed to please her. She came from a very old and powerful family of monks who had a history that went back to the beginning of Japanese time. When she was a girl she had been well educated and betrothed to a young man she had never seen. She went through with the preparations dutifully, but on the morning of her wedding she ran away out of girlish fear, thus committing a great sin and dishonoring her family. When she was found she was banished from home. As a "spinster" with no dowry, all that was left to her in the 1930s was teaching. After the war the new government required that the old ways be changed. Teachers were no longer allowed to tell their students that the emperor was a divine ruler who was infallible. Instead the teachers were to help bring democracy to their ancient homeland. "I could not do this," she told me, "so I must find new work." It was said not in defiance but humbly, for she believed in the Chrysanthemum Throne. Well educated, she spoke near flawless English, with a bit of a British accent, very charming. She was five-feet-one and very slight—it looked like the wind could blow her away. Rather dark-skinned for a Japanese but with high, prominent cheekbones and gracious ways, she could have been an aristocrat. She loved children, especially small children, and Carol was to have one more within six months.

Children are a national pastime in Nippon. The Japanese venerate the old; they *worship* the very young. Fathers and mothers spent all their time with the child from the moment it was born. Brothers and older sisters constantly carried and played with the baby. The infant was never left alone, and even slept with members of the family rather than in a crib by itself. It was always well dressed, like a doll, in layers of bright clothes, and someone was always detailed to amuse it. In short, they were spoiled. They rarely cried because they were perfectly cared for at all times. Then one day, around the age of four, that all stopped! The child cried but no one came. He or she was still loved, and all essentials were done for it, but no more special attention was lavished upon the little critter. The shock to the psyche was so great that the child modified his behavior and joined society as a fellow player, there to support the group rather than its own selfish ends. I was told that things had to be that way because the Japanese were confined on those small islands and the people had to pull together if their culture was to survive. It appeared to work; rarely did I ever see a person alone. The Japanese socialized very well, smiled, and were always upbeat and helpful. "It is a disgrace not to have many friends," Kimiko confided. "In Japan we join teams to help the group win. In America you join teams so the group will help *you* win. That is why your President Kennedy is my favorite American. He said, 'Ask not what America can do for you, but what you can do for America.' Do you think he learned that during the war, from the Japanese?" I didn't mind missing out on what was going on at home, when I had a chance to know people like Kimiko and many others too numerous to mention.

Kimiko approached Carol with the idea of teaching four Japanese college girls conversational English. She had been their teacher and wanted to expand their horizons. It was from the girls that we learned why Kimiko had been very late when she was invited to Thanksgiving dinner, which was so out of character for her enormously polite ways. Their first question was, "Why is it fashionable to be late to an American social event?" They had read it in a magazine. Kimiko obviously didn't understand that "late" meant no more then fifteen or so minutes in case the hostess is not really ready, not two hours. It was a good starting point for

Carol to begin her lessons, but she had to be careful not to cause Kimiko to lose face.

The four girls were Miss Yamada, Miss Naito, Miss Nishiyama, and Miss Tashioka, all very eager at eighteen. By then we had moved out of our Japanese house and into an American "fourplex," a house built for Americans by the Japanese to US standards. It had two bedrooms and a bath upstairs and a living-dining room combination and moderate-size kitchen downstairs. The outside was a washed orange stucco. There was a dark, rounded tile roof and a front porch just big enough to keep the rain off while opening the door. It was situated in a U-shaped arrangement of two more identical structures with a park of tall pines in the middle. The open end of the quadrangle was for parking cars at an angle along the street side. There were a dozen or more similar arrangements within the Sagami Hara housing area, which was enclosed with a barbed wire fence and guarded by local police who stood at the two street gates day and night. We were in no danger, but the security kept the curious outside. Inside, our compound was Little America, with a commissary, four seasons convenience shop, gas station, and fire department. No *benjo* ditches; all the sewers were kept underground, and sidewalks wound through the area, wide enough for people to pass. There were green lawns and streetlights. It was nice to have central heating, but the flavor of living in a foreign country was lost except for the Japanese maids and baby-sitters, who were as numerous as the residents and treated like members of the family by their employers.

Satsuki, Kayoko, Toshi, and Shizuko were very shy when first presented to Carol and me in our western-style living room. They came in assorted sizes. Toshi was Carol's size and Shizuko was nearly as tall as me. They were charming and very courageous to reach out like this into a western house that was as foreign as our name, which none of them could pronounce. The four of them huddled on the three-person couch, sitting on the forward edge of the cushions and giggling as they each spoke a few words in English and covered their face with their hands. Their grasp of the language was surprisingly good, and I was truly ashamed that I had acquired only a few words and phrases of Japanese. Kimiko played big sister and helped the reluctant ones to speak to me, a man and officer, who was quite above their station. Carol got the two boys, the perfect solution to break the ice. The girls loved children and had never seen blond, blue-eyed boys before. Boys are highly prized in Japan. Our two were very friendly and loved attention. Soon they were up in the laps, one for each pair of guests. The women asked a million questions about American children. The kids had brought down the cultural barriers, without a crash, and conversation began to flow.

Although Carol did shop in the big stores she didn't buy much there. Japan is a country of tailors and dressmakers. Traditional Japanese garments are complex and often have to be taken apart to be cleaned. Then they are sewn back together. American wives would buy fashion magazines or have their mothers send over pictures of the latest creations for fabrication. Each military wife used a little dressmaking shop, hidden away in a tiny town down some back road, that had been handed down to her by her sponsor. Whenever an Army family changes station, the gaining command appoints a sponsor. That officer and his wife are responsible to see that the new members of the command are cared for right from the beginning and made welcome. We will never forget the kindness of the first lieutenant and his wife who were our sponsors. They cared for us as if we were their own family. They even fed us when the month was too long for the pay of a second lieutenant. We were to see them many times during my Army career. They always remained good, helpful people. Among the ladies of the command, passing along shopping tips was a most important service and came before giving advice on schools for the children and baby-sitters. Our sponsor's wife, Tilly, shared her dressmaker with my wife. In those days, the social life of an Army officer demanded that ball gowns be worn several times a year.

Mrs. Hanogi in Fukuoka, hidden away in a shop the size of a large phone booth with no front door, was our treasure. She spoke not a word of English, which didn't seem to bother the ladies who shared out her talent. Big business was conducted regularly, done with pictures clipped from *Vogue, Harpers,* and even *Seventeen.* The price was scrawled by Hanogi San with a black crayon on the back of ornate wrapping paper. It was so simple, what else was needed? Oh yes, all the American ladies "spoke" Japanese: they could all say, without an accent, "How much is it?" and "Yes," "No," and "Okay." I met plenty of Americans who were reluctant to go out on the economy and mingle or travel in the country, often because of the language barrier. The cure for culture shock proved to be shopping. But I never met a lady who didn't throw caution to the winds when told about a dressmaker tucked away in a dark alley in an unpronounceable town three hours away. Clever tricks were taught by the sponsor's wife. One: Show the picture; say, *"Dai jo bu Deska?"* (Okay?), while smiling and nodding your head. Two: The dressmaker will then bring you one bolt of cloth after another until you say *"Hai"* (Yes). Three: She will lead you to the rear of the shop and you stand while a girl takes your measurements. Four: Say, *"Sore wa ikura desu ka?"* (How much is it?). She will then write the price on a piece of paper. Five: Say, "No, *Hanogi San"* and shake your head while you write a smaller figure. Everyone understands the word "no" even though no is *"iie."* Six: She will point to a date on the calendar, which hangs on the wall of all shops, for the fitting.

I am told that this method was devised by our State Department officials in Tokyo when making trade agreements and is still in use today. Hanogi San made two dresses for Carol. It was amazing to see what my wife would put up with. The shop was freezing in the evening, warmed only by a miniature space heater, which I monopolized. With business done on the pattern and the selection made over the bolts of silk, the ladies would go into the back of the cooler, the dressing room, separated from the shop front by a thin curtain, and disrobe for measurements and fittings. They never once complained about conditions. That is how good the prices were.

One evening I was waiting just outside in the cramped street, taking in the smells of the market, the *benjo* ditch, and the exhaust from the motorbikes, which always gave off a cloud of light-blue smoke, when the earthquake of 1964 hit. I had been in quakes before; we felt little ones every few days. At first I thought the quakes were firing on the American artillery range because there was always a big bang in the distance. On other occasions there was shaking that came after the bang. Everything would vibrate, or there might be a slight swaying, and then it was over in a few seconds. They were so commonplace that no one even addressed one if it occurred during a conversation. The worst we had experienced was in the Japanese house, when the bed moved across the floor and touched the only wall it had not come in contact with. We just held on and rode it across the room.

But the big one in 1964 was bad. The cardboard shops tacked on to the fronts of the homes, which made up one block of the main street of Fukuoka, began to come apart at the seams. With pins in her new lilac floor-length gown and in slippers, Carol came running out into the street. We watched the houses sway in unison, one tight against the other, each giving its neighbor some degree of support. The locals were quick to recognize a bad one and joined us in the middle of the street. The power went out and we retreated to our car which was parked in front of the store. Gathering children as they went, people ran from buildings and stood in groups in every open area. Most shelves were emptied by the shaking and swinging. Within moments it was over and things were picked up and returned to normal very quickly. The center had been in Alaska, thousands of miles away. But the same fault runs right into the northern-most island of Hokkaido. Checking on communications that evening, I found that we had lost all contact with Alaska. Radio towers were down or twisted in the wrong direction and undersea cables were severed. Hard to believe that in modern times, an entire state could be incommunicado.

The summer Olympic Games came to Japan that year and we all got into the spirit. The bike races went past our housing area and so did some of the long-distance runners. The country was in a fever. The Japanese saw the games as an opportunity to show the world that they had emerged from the war and joined the partnership of nations, so the games consumed everything and everyone, and great cele-brations were planned everywhere. The people were told how important it was that all visitors be treated as personal guests and shown every courtesy for coming the great dis-tance to honor the country with their presence. Along with many other service personnel, I volunteered to help with the officiating. I picked fencing. I had been on my military school team and liked the speed and grace of the sport. I was assigned to help with the scoring. Competition took place at Wasada Hall, on the north side of Tokyo. I put on civilian clothes and boarded a train for the center of the city early one hot summer morning. The train was packed, of course, but I squeezed in and rode with my nose touching the window on the sliding door for thirty minutes, happy that I was on the train at all; some hadn't been able to get in. I had been instructed to change trains for Wasada at Shin-juku *iki* (station). Shinjuku has to be seen to be believed. Rather than a large open vault with trains running away off the sides, it is a labyrinth. There were no signs in anything like the Latin alphabet, and although I had learned to recog-nize the characters for Wasada, I wandered up and down passageways. When I hit a turnstile, which was plainly an exit from the system, I rebounded back into the catacomb like a pinball glancing off a rubber bumper. Everywhere were endless tunnels filled with fast-moving, even running, citizens trying to get to work on time. I explored every level—there were at least six—with no luck. Not another western face appeared with whom I could share my frustration. Lost with another fool, at least we could have commiserated. I was alone in a sea of people. I expected to find the skeletal remains of some American lying against the wall with cobwebs attaching him to the white tile walls under a sign advertising Coca-Cola. His bony finger would be pointed up, betraying his origin.

Out of options, I stopped at an internal iron gate, afraid to penetrate any farther, raised my hand, and said, "Can anyone help me?" At once a businessman in a white shirt and dark gray suit, which was very well tailored, came over to me and bowed. I said, in nearly intelligible Japanese, good morning, I was lost, could he help me, I was going to the games at Wasada. He spoke no English, but he said *"Hai"* (yes) and took me by the hand. So there we went, hand in hand. I felt a little conspicuous locked in his grip, but very grateful. Back in the maze he spoke constantly, I guess to reassure me that he knew what he was doing as we walked in and out, up and up to the street level to an elevated train station. And there it was, Wasada, as plain as mud but decipherable. I broke from his grip, bowed, and thanked him profusely. He smiled and returned my courtesy. But he didn't leave. When the next train arrived five minutes later, he took me to the automatic doors and pointed for me to enter. I did and bowed and thanked him once again. I had figured it out. No matter; the gentleman entered the car and stood next to me for several stations. We grinned at each other and I looked out the window, watching the vast metropolis spin by. One street looked like any other on the north side of town; there were few landmarks. A half a dozen stops later, over the low, gray tile roofs of homes and businesses, I saw the mammoth concrete dome of the sports hall approaching. It was a great ride and gave me an appreciation for the city of millions who have no lawns or trees, only wet streets little wider than my outstretched arms. Naturally, he got me off the train successfully and then took me down the steps to the street. We walked with him slightly ahead as he pointed the way with his free hand. The other was holding a very expensive black leather briefcase. He took me to an attendant and there at last bid me farewell. His smile was very sincere and his good work was unforgettable. When I told this story to others back at the camp, I found they'd had similar experiences. Come to think of it, in Italy a man ran in front of our car for three twisting blocks in Vincenza to get us back on the main highway, and he wasn't even Japanese. I hope Americans are as kind in our country to foreign guests.

Inside, I was appointed to hold the scorecard clipboard for one of the American judges during the competition. When each match was over I took the card to the official scoring booth and gave it to a statistician for entry into the record. I had a perfect view of every match, whether I was working or not. I was able to meet the athletes and listen to their banter about the sport and their competitors. America had only a slight hope for a medal, which never panned out, but that didn't really matter, I discovered as time went on. The competition and the chance to represent one's country was the important thing.

My leader that first day was particularly interested in the Russian coach, whom he had known most of his life. They had fenced against each other as Olympians before the war.

"Watch, he pretends not to know me." Wilfred Ohmes, the American Olympic fencing coach, nodded and smiled at his Russian opponent. Mr. Ohmes was correct, nothing came back from the stony-faced former athlete in his sixties who had gone rather to pot. Once a grand master, the

Russian could no longer strike a swashbuckling pose in tight black tunic and pants. Perhaps even a larger mask would have been necessary. "Sergei will ignore me for the first week, then at a social outing for officials, when he has shaken his KGB escort, he will be my old friend again. At least one-third of the bench are not fencers, they are agents watching fencers. They are watching you, too, Fitz. Soon they will know who you are and it will be entered into your dossier in Moscow. Sergei is a great coach, you know, Fitz." Here I could use my nickname again. "With a last name like yours, you must have some old-world fencing fraternity blood in you. Perhaps a Westphalian, or even a Heidelberg ancestor led you, unseen, to the sword in school, yes?" he said wryly. "Perhaps, Herr Ohmes, perhaps," guessing that he was speaking from personal experience. Finishing the questioning, he said, "In this ancient line of work, the sword is in the blood. There may be a hand on your shoulder, Lieutenant."

By late fall Carol was ready to deliver our third son. It was not presumptuous to predict that our Jonathan would be a boy; there hadn't been a girl born in my family for many generations. He turned out to be a little trickier than the other two. On a clear, bright Saturday five weeks before he was due, and with the gas gauge of the car on empty, he came to call at noon. Of the four and a half of us, only four were surprised. We jumped into the car and sped out the back gate for the five-mile drive down Suicide Alley, the main road frequented by gravel truck drivers, to the American hospital. While the brothers waited quietly, they were always good boys, Carol delivered. The birth was touch-and-go for a while, but in the end everything was fine. Carol had a baby announcement made that was a hit back in the States, brightening up dull, old Aurora. On the front it had five pairs of Japanese shoes lined up, big ones for me, a slightly smaller pair for Mother, and two child-size for David and Tim. Last, in baby blue, was a tiny pair for Jon.

Across the front were the words "Made in Japan." Inside, the name and statistics were printed in English, but along the side they were repeated in hiragana characters. Three healthy sons. God, I was lucky!

Army kids are lucky, too. They get to live all over the world and take their culture with them in our Little Americas. They have scads of friends because, being so far from home, everyone bands together and helps one another. Years later, when Jonathan was in high school in Frederick, Maryland, he was in a class filled with kids from the local community who, for the most part, had never left the county. Even the teachers' travel had frequently been limited. In class one day, Miss Levenson was explaining that other countries had different kinds of money, and one had to calculate the value in dollars before one knew how much it was worth. "In England, the pound cost two dollars twenty cents."

Jon raised his hand and said, "When I left there last year, it was down to one dollar ninety-five cents." They then went on to discuss the capital of France. Only Jon knew that it was Paris, having been there many times.

"Class, what is the Leaning Tower of Pisa and what country is it in?" Not a stir from the children, except for a comment about pizza. My son raised his hand again and answered. "That's right. Have you been there, too?" He had been at the top when it rang ten. "Where does edam cheese come from, class?"

Jon said, "I had some in the cheese market in The Hague, the Netherlands, Holland, that is, Miss Levenson."

"What country uses shillings other than Great Britain, anyone? Jon, do you know that one?"

"I used them to buy *pommes frites* in the Tyrol of Austria, skiing last year."

"Well, class, let's switch to the other side of the world. How many of you have heard about Japan? Jon, I suppose you have?"

"I was born there, Miss Levenson."

I had taken on many extra-duty jobs, mostly because I was the youngest officer in the command, but some I sought. I sat on minor boards, investigated misconduct and security violations, put on parties, conducted tours, coached children's teams, and helped out with people-to-people programs in the Japanese community. I was not unusual, many others were just as active. When the chief of the Signal Corps, Major General Gibbs, came on a tour of the Far East, I was appointed to be his escort officer, or traveling aide-de-camp. His executive, Colonel Reed, a tall, thin, active man, was his only other companion. The general was all a senior officer was supposed to be. Very distinguished, with graying hair and a small cavalry mustache, he was very bright. His experience had begun in the Army before World War II, during which he won a Bronze Star for Valor as a signalman with the infantry. His father had been chief of the Signal Corps as well, just after the first big war. He was quiet and liked to listen and question rather than lecture. He had encyclopedic knowledge of communications and the art of war. He put me and all who came into contact with him at ease. I was never afraid that I would say the wrong thing and set him off.

My promotion to first lieutenant came while I was with Colonel Reed and he asked if he could do anything for me. I asked that he intercede for me with orders back to jump school and assignment to Special Forces. My job had been cut from Japan and I would have to leave. He was an influential man and true to his word. My request to be transferred to Special Forces came through and I received orders to return to the States for airborne training. Special Forces was a new formation in the Army, one praised by President Kennedy and bound to play a big part in Vietnam, which at the time didn't look like it would last very long or employ many troops. I wanted to go back to Vietnam for the combat experience. After all, I was a professional soldier, not an armchair crank. I was very much afraid that only a few lucky guys would get there before it turned into another stalemate like Korea. I wanted the credibility that goes with experience. Special Forces were not the Rangers, but they were special troops. All volunteers, they were put out in teams to train and organize indigenous people for combat so they could protect themselves and their families from outside forces. Communications was one of the skills needed in SF.

Carol's girls were very unhappy to be losing their teacher. They had grown together and would miss exploring the contrast between East and West very much. Through Kimiko, Kayoko asked us if we would bring the children to her home in the city for a luncheon one Sunday. It was a very great honor she had bestowed on our family. Kayoko assured us that all the other girls would be there, as well as her mother and father. We accepted and were happy that we were welcomed by people who appeared very different from us yet proved to be the same. We had learned a lot from our girls. On the appointed day, we drove because it was too difficult with the boys, all under three, to take the train. I had been given a map, and with the help of one of the happy gods of Nippon we found the street, which was just wide enough for our car to pass. Once we were there, Kayoko's brother, a student dressed in a black uniform with a shiny billed hat, like a yachtsman, took my keys with a bow and drove my car away to a place big enough to accommodate it. He was gone a long time.

The Tashiokas' neighborhood was like the one I had seen around Wasada Hall. Outside, plants were grown in pots and window boxes; every bit of ground was occupied by necessity. Even cycles were hung up by the front wheel to save space. The two-story houses appeared to be made of large playing cards leaning on one another. The structures had been shifted so often by tremors that nothing was truly perpendicular. Most homes had glass windows, but Kayoko's house was very traditional and had double front sliding doors paned with opaque white rice paper.

There was much excitement as the girls came pouring out, giggling and laughing, picking up the boys and circling around. Kayoko was the only one of the four to be in traditional dress. Her kimono was a creamy white, with big colorful flowers in red and green splashed all over. Her stacked black hair was stuck through with decorative gold and enameled pins that looked like heirlooms. Hobbled by her skirt and wooden shoes, she clumped out onto the street behind the others. Dressed as a young lady, she was more correct and formally greeted us. We exchanged bows and Carol presented Kayoko with flowers. The entryway was at the pavement level and made of concrete as far as the broad wooden step, where we sat and removed our shoes and exchanged them for slippers. I was in suit and tie, Carol in a fuchsia-pink wool dress. The second sliding double door, which concealed the living area, was pushed open by Kayoko's mother, an elegant lady in her late forties who inclined her head to one side slightly as she spoke while her daughter translated. Her kimono was of brown and white stripes, edged down the middle with a wide, black silk border. Under it was a white blouselike garment that set it all off. Her hair was gray, only a little black still showing, and put up with hidden pins. She was a slight figure, not even a hundred pounds. With graceful hands she accepted a second set of flowers from my wife. We had been warned by Kimiko that the greeting would be long and involved, and saw that it was wise to let the family lead us through the customs slowly. Much was made over the children, who were so used to being handled that they were perfect ambassadors. Little English was spoken, and the few words of Japanese we had been working on were used over and over again. Mostly there were smiles because we were all delighted to be in each other's company and knew that the opportunity wouldn't last much longer.

The going-away party progressed as we were taken into the main room and introduced to the head of the household. There were no western items except for the television, which was pushed into a corner next to a lacquered book-stand. It maintained a special Oriental look because standing on top of the plastic case was a stuffed gray goose, a former family pet which eclipsed the set by its sheer size and ferocious mien. Kayoko's father had nothing ferocious about him, but it was clear that he was the master as he was formally introduced by his lovely daughter. The introduction was to me. For the moment the men were in charge. His English was halting but correct. At his request, I sat next to the little man on the floor. He was most cordial and smiled, thanking me for teaching his daughter and for all that we had done for her. "I was a soldier in the war, sir. I am very sorry. We were mistaken. Please accept my apology."

I had thought I was prepared for that day because I had spoken to our State Department liaison officer about how to conduct myself as a guest in the home of a Japanese family. But he had not mentioned anything about coming face-to-face with a veteran, who, in front of his family who respect him greatly, accepted personal responsibility for a world war. How could I accept such a gesture? I could not say, "Well that's okay, don't do it again." I could not blame him for history or his part in it. I was less than two months old when the war began and there I stood as a representative of the Army that had defeated his nation. I said, "You were a soldier, like me, sir"—I pointed to my own breast—"and my hope is that we will never see each other again in conflict." He accepted the words and all was well.

"I would like to invite you and your wife to join us in the tea ceremony," he said as he pointed to a paper screen that was drawn aside by one of the girls to reveal a corner of the room made elegant by its simplicity. The floor was covered with a clean straw mat, and in its center a square hole was cut where a small charcoal fire heated a black iron water kettle. He led us to our places, and the four adults sat while one of the girls who was not detailed to play with the children translated for the mother. Kayoko then appeared from behind another sliding screen, sitting on her heels. It began. Satsuki, our guide, was the only one to speak, which she did in a whisper. The mother and father watched their daughter proudly as she went through the ritual flawlessly. We asked no questions and made no comments, as I had been warned by the liaison officer about the ceremony's significance and what an honor it was to be given such a treat. The carefully prepared tea was bright pea-green, thick, and foamy. It had little taste. But in its making the young Japanese maiden brought to life a culture that I had seen little of in the hectic modern city. In the middle of all the crowding, street bumping, and train pushing, the real Japan was sucking me into its tranquility and tradition as time stood still. Perhaps that was what Kayoko's father had fought for in his youth.

Her father had been wounded in the war and after it pursued an education. He was a doctor working for the American Army in the infectious disease research center attached to the hospital where Jonathan was born. In all those years he had never had an American in his home. What conflicts must have lived inside this complex man.

Four six-inch-tall heavy wooden inlayed teak tables were pushed together in the center of the living room. Proper luncheon fare for Americans had caused great concern for the hostess. Kimiko had asked me a week beforehand what dishes were preferred. I told her that we liked Japanese cooking and looked forward to having traditional fare. "Are you sure, Lieutenant San? What about the children?"

"We are all in Japan, Kimiko San; your food will be perfect for all of us," I assured her. I was told that the family would likely have the food brought in from a favorite restaurant, plus her mother's specialities. Clearly, the Tashiokas expected all Americans to be big eaters. It was an afternoon feast. Nine adults and three children could not possibly have consumed the banquet. Not only was there a lot, but it was served in beautiful lacquered pans the size of hubcaps, each in a shiny black finish with red, orange, yellow, or gold figures on their two-inch-high sides. I had told Kayoko that I liked raw tuna and seaweed over rice, so one platter was just for me. The cold cooked lobster topped with thick yellow mayonnaise and a piece of black olive may well be the best thing I have ever tasted. Squid salad, octopus in vinegar, rolled vegetables in kelp served with bowls of hot sticky rice—each dish came with an explanation from one or all the girls. Just in case, a plate of American ham sandwiches cut into triangles was slipped in. To drink, Coca-Cola in six-ounce bottles with the logo in kanji characters filled the table and internationalized the meal. That was a celebration we have never forgotten. It was the best of good-byes.

When Kimiko came to our house for the last time, she gave us a framed twelve-inch kanji character in gold thread braided into a ribbon an inch wide on a black silk background. "What does it stand for?" I asked, knowing that I would be asked the question for years to come.

"It is a wish for long life and happiness," she said with her ever-present smile, but her eyes were filled with tears. I have had the ideogram translated many times in our numerous homes and it has never come out the same. We gave Kimiko a framed picture of our family, inscribed, "To our best friend, Kimiko." Those simple words have much meaning in Japan.

She would not go to see us off, as we were going home by commercial ship from Yokohama. In those days, American passenger liners in the Pacific were subsidized by our government. They were part of a naval transport reserve fleet to be used for troop movements if the need should arise. Any family that wanted to go by ship rather than airplane was welcome.

A Japanese driver took us to the dock at Yokohama in a big black sedan. It was fitting; we were first-class passengers. The tickets, in the inside pocket of my suit tailored from the Van Brothers Cap Factory in Taiwan, cost twenty-six hundred dollars. I had been provided one hundred dollars for tips, which were to be paid to those who took care of us on the sixteen-day voyage. Except for alcoholic drinks, everything was taken care of by the government. We drove out on the dock and our baggage was handled for us. Standing at the gangway were the four darlings, Carol's students, laden with flowers. A steward walked over and escorted all of us on board and to our cabin. The ship was the SS *President Cleveland* of the American President Lines. She was seven hundred feet overall, the largest in the Pacific, and painted pure white. Her smokestacks had a red-and-blue band with a white spread eagle emblazoned. The girls were giggling as usual and covering their mouths as the cabin steward explained the schedule for departure and filled vases with their beautiful bouquets. The tearful *sayonara* was almost too much to bear when we realized that we would never see them again.

Their final farewell was from the dockside as passengers threw colored paper streamers from the promenade deck to friends on the shore. We hurled a dozen or more to the young ladies, who caught them and held on. As the ship slipped her mooring and slowly plowed away, the paper links became taut, stretched, and broke. It was over. Our first real foreign adventure as a family was more fulfilling than I could ever have imagined. Foreigners in a land beyond explanation, we had thrived. It was so much more than a vacation holiday of a few weeks filled with sights that all ran together. We had been participants in their history as defenders of the island, and those two short years became reference points in our understanding of world affairs. We never looked at Japan in the same terms as other Americans during the boom in their economy and their domination of world markets.

I had never been on a ship before, but the chance to cross

the ocean was an opportunity I could not pass up. After her airplane experience on the trip over, Carol had needed no prompting to try another way. The days of American passenger liners in the deep Pacific were ending; only two, ours and her sister ship, were still operating. There was room for several hundred passengers in the first class, but only sixty were aboard because first-class passage was expensive. I could have bought a new car for the cost of our tickets. With one double bed and two bunk beds and a crib, our stateroom was big enough for the five of us. There was a writing desk below the two portholes, with personalized stationery. Below the red flag with four white stars in the corners and a white eagle in the center was our name, Lt. and Mrs. David Fitzenz, no hyphen, embarked aboard the SS *President Cleveland.* We started all our letters with the words "From somewhere on the Pacific Ocean."

The next morning it all changed. I awoke at seven to find Carol in the bathroom throwing up and the same color as the overcast and the rolling sea outside our porthole. Seasickness spread like a cruel virus, first to David and then to Tim. I ran around and managed to get Jon to his nurse before I was struck. Seasickness has to be experienced to be appreciated. We have all had the flu, colds, even car sickness. All are somewhat debilitating and very annoying. Some even come with a degree of delirium. But when seasick, I prayed for delirium. Worst of all, I was completely lucid and knew that if the ship didn't stop moving I would turn myself inside out. I also knew that it would not stop moving for fifteen days. At one point I knelt in the corner and pressed myself against the steel plates, trying to become one with the ship. It didn't work. I called the maid for something to give myself and my green family. She pronounced sentence: "Once you have it, sir, there is really nothing that will help."

"It can't be true. Try something, perhaps we are different," I pleaded. She came back with a plate of soda crackers and some aspirin. We all lay in our beds, looking at each other without seeing anything, feeling only the rolling, sliding, wallowing, and pitching. "Hopeless" is the only word that came to mind for our condition. If I'd been offered death, I would have accepted it for myself and all of my family. They would not have objected, they would have thanked me. Where was the joy of the previous night? When I thought of all the food we had consumed at dinner I headed for the bathroom once again. Then the steward, Hector, knocked and announced, "Boat drill! Everyone on deck with life preservers." He had it wrong, I didn't want to preserve my life. When he received no answer, he opened the door. "You must all come to boat drill. It is a rule, sir."

"We can't, we are all immobilized. We could go later. Tomorrow."

"It is very required, all passengers are going to be there. Order of the captain, sir." It sounded like a social occasion to me. "No, no, sir. Rules of the sea. I will help you." He pulled out the international-orange horse collars from under our bunks and tied the preservers on each of us, one after the other, as we sat catatonic on the edge of our beds. He enlisted the aid of the maid, who I vowed to get for telling us that there was nothing that could be done for seasickness. In my deranged mind she was to blame for our suffering. Between the two of them they got us out of the cabin and out on the boat deck. The stiff breeze straightened me up. It helped a little. Nothing remained in me to vomit so my stomach twisted into a knot and a headache formed between my eyes.

The only requirement in a boat drill was to appear, in life preserver, at the station assigned and listen to a lecture on safety while the crew lowered the lifeboats from the davits. I could do that, we all could do that, as long as we could sit down. The deck was wet from the spray and so were the chairs, but the cold dampness on the back of my pants felt good. Anything cool felt good. We all were feeling a little more human out in the air and we even spoke to one another. The topic was depressing though. "How are you?"

"Terrible, how are you?" It took a good hour, and the longer we sat there the worse it became. We had a reference point now that we hadn't had in our enclosed cabin. The horizon, thirty-two miles away, was perfectly even with the ship's rail for just an instant—on the way up and again on the way down. We were rolling a good twenty degrees. The sea and sky were the same gray-green as we. I couldn't believe that all those people scurrying around in front of us were perfectly all right, enjoying the outing, in fact. Why me, why us, and not them? The crew members were very wise; they left us alone. There is no possibility of intelligent conversation with a seasick person. We lingered on deck, unwilling to move even after the drill was over. Eventually Carol said, "I think we better go back to the cabin; the boys could catch cold out here exposed." I ached all over and my balance was fragile, but we made it back inside. Once in our beds we fell to sleep, exhausted by our efforts to comply with the rules of the sea. When we awoke about noon we were all better. We took no chances and ordered dry sandwiches for lunch. By afternoon the last traces were gone and we all had our sea legs. We put it behind us.

We stopped in Hawaii. It was startling to see the first land in nearly two weeks jump up out of the sea as we passed close to the rocks north of Kawai. We had the day free on Oahu and rented a car. I have never seen any place so beautiful. Green velvet columns like chimneys of the gods divided the island in two. The smell of orchids growing wild around a mailbox made me smile. What a place. On the ship that night they featured a tourist show from a hotel in Hawaii. It was a little plastic but the food wasn't. We would come back.

The remaining four days were sadder because we could see the end, and I was headed for jump school once again at

Fort Benning. My failure to finish two years ago had haunted me every day when I saw colleagues wearing their silver jump wings. Nothing would stop me this time. After landing and picking up our little car we headed east. Every mile made me more determined to complete the course successfully and get on with the road to war.

Nothing had changed in the curriculum at jump school. In fact it was as if I had not left. Most of the same people were still assigned. On my first day, a stick leader again, I mounted the thirty-four-foot tower with one thing in mind—to make the best blast out that door they had ever seen. I looked the jump master dead in the eyes and took the trolley straps from him with malice. I was mad—there I was going through the whole rigmarole again, when all I needed was one more jump. Within an hour I could be fully qualified and on my way, but, no, the cadre had no provision for that and I had to repeat the whole course, all three weeks. Of course, they were right. I had lost some skill and physical ability, especially while eating my way across the Pacific. When the moment came, I jumped up and out, counted like a veteran and held a tight body position all the way to the end. When I returned for my grade from the instructor, he was leaning back watching the novices. "Ever done this before, Lieutenant?"

"Yes, Sergeant."

"Where?" he asked without looking at me.

"Here, Sergeant."

"Who was your instructor?"

"You were, Sergeant."

"I did a good job, Lieutenant. Go run the rope the rest of the week. I don't want to see you again." That was ground week. I spent the days running the trolley back to the tower. Tower week was the same, one quick jump from the free tower and I spent the rest of the time taking physical training and hooking up safety lines. Jump week was a piece of cake. How could it have been so difficult two years before? I guess everything is easy once you know how to do it. Graduation came in two parts. On the last jump the school commandant was out on the ground, pinning wings on those who were injured and not expected to make it to graduation that afternoon. Carol and the boys were parked on the edge of the DZ during that final jump. She wanted to see the end to the saga that she had suffered through along with me. David and Tim sat on the hood of the car and watched the six planes drop their human cargo. They were thrilled to see the sky filled with parachutes as the men came within fifty yards and hit the dirt with a thud. It must have made an indelible impression on David. He is a jump master today in the Rangers.

Graduation was conducted in an air-conditioned auditorium on main post. Carol was there in a beehive hairdo, very smart during Beatles mania. The commandant got a great laugh when he said, "Remember those guys who refused to jump the thirty-four-foot tower?" The laughter was almost uncontrollable inside. It seemed absolutely absurd that someone could be that afraid of something that seemed, by that time, so simple and natural to us all. I don't know how to explain it, but everyone felt it. Fear is carried by all in some degree, but it is always conquerable.

He also addressed the ladies. He was a handsome man of forty-five and a full colonel of Infantry. He had the confidence that comes from having made three combat jumps in Europe during the war. His rather thick snow-white hair, square face, and hollow cheeks were the perfect setting for a deep brown suntan. He was well respected by the Army. "There are no women in the Airborne and there will never be. They don't have the presence of mind to get it all together, they are not mentally alert." That got a laugh from the class, but not from the ladies, who only smiled a little and looked straight ahead. "I don't doubt their courage. They would make fine infantrymen. They would kill without remorse, you know." Another laugh rocked the hall, with all the women thinking the same thing: I would kill him without remorse. Then he thanked the ladies for their support of the men with the silver wings and asked them very sincerely to continue, "For without you behind him, he will find it hard to summon that courage day after day to do this dangerous job." He redeemed himself somewhat with that, but I could see that he would not be promoted to general; the man was a fool.

Chapter Six

*Leaving on a jet plane, don't know
when I'll be back again.*
JOHN DENVER

My one-year tour of combat duty in Vietnam was over. We stopped in Okinawa for refueling. I slept most of the way. My inability to sleep on airplanes had left me, I suppose because of my relief that the show was over. I had done what I had hoped I could do and been a player in an adventure that would become history. The flight home to San Francisco was uneventful for me and I reviewed the year with pleasure. I remembered the friends I had made and those who were lost.

For a friend, Rocky Norris, the flight home had been a real trip. He told me about it years later when we met one day in the old German officers club at Patch Barracks, Stuttgart, Germany. He was with me in the 173d, where he had been an Infantry lieutenant. Over a glass of mellow, chilled German wine he began, "I had been badly wounded out in the jungle only a month before I was to go home. They knocked me out with morphine, but I knew I was bleeding from many places and expected to die. The conviction came over me very slowly and calmly." He had seen many with wounds like his before and held their hand as they passed away in the mud. Now he thought it was his turn, for he knew that he probably wouldn't survive. The narcotic made him feel that it didn't matter. "Just let me sleep."

Fortunately, a medical evacuation helicopter was at hand and as soon as he was out cold, they loaded him up and flew him to a major Army hospital near Saigon. There they assessed his wounds, stabilized him, and put him on a waiting Nightingale medical evacuation flight that had one free berth. Within a few short hours of being shot through, he was on his way home. His plane stopped in Alaska to refuel and all the patients had to be removed from the aircraft during the refueling. Rocky was still out so they covered him with more white blankets, strapped him to a gurney, and rolled him out the back of the plane to the parking apron. The nurses in white uniforms stood loyally by their wounded for the forty-five minutes it took to take on the thousands of pounds of JP-4. It wasn't terribly cold in Anchorage but it was snowing rather heavily. The nurses hovered over the litter cases, brushing away snow and protecting them from it with their own bodies. It was then that Rocky woke up for the first time since he had been wounded hours before in the hot, humid jungle. He was flat on his back and wrapped tight in white. All he could see was a white sky and large soft lacy snowflakes drifting down and settling quietly on his face. There was no pain, in fact he couldn't feel his body. A pretty blond nurse noticed that he was awake and said, in a soothing voice, as she bent over his face and looked him in the eye from very close range, "You are all right now, we are taking care of you, there is nothing to fear."

He reached down inside and with a quavering voice said, "Are you an angel?"

"I'll tell you, Fitz, I thought I had died and gone to heaven."

I called Carol as soon as I hit the ground. She was expecting contact that day, our first voice to voice in a year. Her short-timer's calendar had also run out and my last audiotape had narrowed down my arrival to within hours. The relief in her voice was apparent. "I always knew you would come home."

My orders sent us to school at Fort Monmouth, New Jersey, home of the Signal Corps. A small post, it was tucked into the city of Eatontown, locked in the middle of a civilian community. Unlike other Army installations I'd been stationed at, there was no outlying field area that stretched to the horizon. Monmouth was an electronics factory of red-brick buildings involved in research and instruction, confined by indoor laboratory spaces. Only a half-dozen blocks square, the only open land was the golf course, with its Tudor-revival officers club in the middle, and a family housing area separated from the main campus by a mile of suburbia. It did have something special. It was only forty miles from the bright lights of New York City. To further the military education of the officer corps, each branch had a career course six months long which "regreened" field soldiers, bringing them back into the fold from the bad habits learned by expediency in the field. It was the beginning of fall and my course would not start until late January. Therefore, it was necessary to "snowbird," meaning we were to rest, recover, and perform rather light duties while trying to remain unseen, like a white bird on a field of snow. I was assigned to command N Company, a housekeeping unit charged with feeding, housing, supplying, and disciplining the 340 new soldiers who were attending the electronics classes that would turn them into radio operators, field telephone and telegrapher technicians, and cable linemen.

I had a small permanent party of sergeants who made sure that students got to class on time and were looked after. The majority of the soldiers were draftees, just like the ones I had had with me in the war, only younger. They all knew they were going to Vietnam, so I spent much of my time walking and talking on daily visits through the billets. I had beds for nearly two hundred. But since the school was expanded to double sessions, one from nine to five and the other from eleven PM to seven AM, we ran a hot-bed system. While some trained, others slept, and before the beds were cold the other group took them over. Clean linen and hot meals were always a problem. There were six white, World War II–era two-story barracks buildings within the company area, and they were in the worst shape I had seen in my entire Army experience. Built with green wood in 1942, it had shrunk and warped over the years so that the windows couldn't be opened. The floors were rotted, the latrines were a disgrace, and the furnaces were moribund. At the end of each open forty-man bay were two small rooms for the sergeants. The wall dividing them was made of planks nailed to two-by-four studs. The pine had shrunk and there were spaces between the boards that I could stick my hand through. The construction looked more like a lattice than a wall.

My first sergeant, Lemar Warner, was a wonder. He ran a good solid operation, always in conference with the sergeant major at battalion over improvements of any kind. He was the first of the a new breed—not a graduate of World War II, he was more manager than killer. Not at all lean nor particularly athletic, he was big but quiet. Wearing thick straight black hair a little longer than the standard, he was the intellectual equal to anyone. I once said that I would like to be an aide to a general so I could find out how the Army runs. Warner knew how the army ran, and if I observed I could learn much of it from him. He taught me that job knowledge was power. When in conflict with higher ranking adversaries, they could be overcome when confronted by the introduction of facts and figures.

His other talent was knowing that all men are motivated according to their needs. Not everyone has the same needs, because personalities differ. "Captain, learn the personal details of people, watch them react to situations, and then pick the right man for the job. Everyone has flaws, so play to the strengths and sometimes overlook the flaws, which one is probably unable to correct due to time or inclination. Stay within the standards and offer higher standards. Many will rise to the challenge. Care for everyone according to their needs and don't worry about yourself. In the end you will win."

To illustrate, we had a mess sergeant, Levander Scruggs; SFC Lee Scruggs as he preferred to be known. Feeding the troops six meals a day was a daunting task. There was no room for failure; badly fed men are poor students. Running a kitchen twenty-four hours a day, seven days a week, with a multitude of cooks was a Herculean feat. My mess hall was the consistent winner of the commanding general's award, which was judged every quarter. There were twenty-four mess units in the population and Scruggs was always in the lead. I ate at least once if not twice a day there and often had visitors from higher headquarters as my guests. Not only was the food good, the atmosphere was convivial. Scruggs believed that it was all in the package. Great food tastes better if the dining room is properly lit, the walls and fixtures are decorative, and everything and everybody is clean and neat. Service was equally important, as was the attitude of his staff. He was a bachelor and lived within the company rather than in NCO quarters across post, where his friends enjoyed time away from the job. He was dedicated. He was also flawed. At least once a month he would go on a drinking bender that lasted three to four days. In essence he would be absent without leave, AWOL, a court-martial offense. Top overlooked that minor detail, keeping it from me, which was wise. If I had known I would have had to take action. But that year the office of the commanding general announced a special unit competition for Christmas, which included food preparation. It caught Sergeant Warner off guard and came at the beginning of his mess sergeant's December binge. After receiving details of the challenge in the morning briefing with the battalion commander, Major Briggs, I called a meeting of my staff. There was no hiding the absence of Scruggs, and when I asked to see him the next day I was told the reason for his absence. I told Top, "You have twenty-four hours to find him before it becomes a matter for the military police." Warner's search of Scruggs's favorite haunts, which had always before been fruitful, provided no joy. The first sergeant, a man of great ability, asked for the exclusive use of the majority of my junior sergeants. Then he went to the local liquor board for the names of all the bars in a fifty-mile radius and sent his boys out to find the mess sergeant. He equipped the NCOs with copies of the mess sergeant's glossy eight-by-ten photo that hung on the wall next to his culinary awards. I was afraid that the sober picture of the man in his uniform and decorations would not remotely resemble the drunk slumped over a bar in a den of darkness. Alerted to the danger of Sergeant First Class Scruggs's dishonoring the NCO corps of mess stewards, many of whom were his fellow drinkers, the mess stewards from the other mess halls joined the search. Even though he had bested them before, and many would like to take the prize which was within reach without his performance, they evacuated the fort on some pretense and drank their way across New Jersey. The next morning I was served breakfast by Scruggs. "Where were you, Sergeant?" I asked, hoping for a reply that would prevent me from pressing charges.

Before Scruggs could answer, Top rested his coffee cup on the table and interjected, "It is a sad thing, sir. His mother was taken ill night before last and he went to her bedside. He left me a note on my desk, in the small hours, but I overlooked it. My fault, sir."

N Company won the Christmas dinner trophy.

In the new year I gave up my company and joined forty captains who had just returned from Vietnam for the career course. Several had been in the 69th Signal Battalion with me and war stories flew hot and heavy. Exaggeration was the rule. Our favorite instructor had us all beat. Mr. Abby

Abbinnowski, who taught basic electricity, had been a foot soldier in 1944, and he dispensed the theory of the technical side of the huge radio rigs while championing the cause of the private soldier. He had dug his way out of the neighborhoods of Philadelphia and looked like he should have been a street vendor with a pushcart. No beauty, he was brawny with great thick hands and black wavy hair that was too young for his years. Only a thick mustache, running with gray, gave a clue to his true age. When he smiled, which he did at the end of each sentence, he revealed a jumble of white teeth that should have been corrected by braces, but his immigrant parents could not afford them. Because of the wit and wisdom he dispensed, he was the kind of teacher that everyone remembered. Larger than life itself, he was an actor, comedian, mentor, and friend.

Abby was a private soldier in England prior to D Day. I could imagine him as a tall, dark, young, happy-go-lucky prankster imitating the British accent in pubs and kidding the girls. His unit, the 4th Infantry, was going ashore in the first wave. He had been in the country for nearly a year by Spring 1944 and was thoroughly "browned off" with the repetitious training. At the bottom of the rank pyramid, little attention was devoted to his morale, and he was weary, carrying sixty pounds of ammunition that he never fired and provisions that he never consumed. At least twice a week and later three times a week, he road marched the twenty miles to the docks and went aboard a Navy transport for a pseudo-trip to France. After an uncomfortable night on a tossing, flat-bottomed troopship in the English Channel, he and his fellows would return to dock. The wet twenty-mile walk back to the barracks in the rain seemed endless. "It was draining me of my spirit," he told the class. "Remember, you young officers, soldiers are smarter than they look. I took all that food, ammo, dry clean clothes, extra boots, blankets, and bandages and got rid of them. I stuffed pillows in my pack and paper in the pouches. The next march was a breeze. It was the first week of June. The ship returned to England empty this time. So it was that I arrived on Omaha Beach, defenseless but light as a feather. It was a very long day."

Within the class I had credibility because I wore the patch of the Army's best-known combat unit, with its blue-and-white AIRBORNE tab on top. In addition, the Bronze Stars and the Air Medal, for numerous combat flying missions, helped divert attention from my lack of book learning and electrical engineering knowledge, which the others had in abundance. I also wore the paratrooper wings of the Army of the Republic of Vietnam on my left breast. The 173d twinned itself with the local South Vietnamese army paratrooper regiment, and we set up a jump school for it near Saigon. In order to keep up our jump pay, we jumped with them several times, not combat jumps but qualification jumps into safe areas. I went along to record the liaison on film. I remember loading up with little men so heavy with equipment that we had to lift them on board the C-46s. The airplane was strictly for cargo and built in the 1940s. There was no passenger door to jump from, so we exited the cargo doorway, which was so wide that I couldn't get a grip to steady myself before jumping. I was literally blasted out the door, then I bumped along the fuselage and caught a glimpse of the tail before I rolled over and headed for the rice paddies. The ARVN soldiers were so small and light that some went up instead of down when their chutes deployed above them. It was quite a sight, seeing my fellow jumpers above me drifting away toward the South China Sea. When I landed, the drop zone coordinator, Capt. Johnny Luck, said, "Fitz, get a picture of that. I think we are going to have to shoot them down."

At Monmouth the only real field training was given at the pole farm a block from the classroom building. Outside the little cream-colored wooden shack filled with climbing equipment was the pole orchard. In front was a sawdust pit which held forty blackjack telephone poles thirty feet high. Normally used to train the signal pole linemen who strung communication cables from one to the other, that day we were to be introduced to the art of pole climbing. I had seen it done many times both in and out of service. It doesn't look hard, just a little scary. The poles had no metal rungs. They were slick, creosote-covered pines, ten feet apart. The job required "climbing irons" strapped to the calves. Their sharp steel spikes protruded two inches below the soles of our combat boots. A wide, worn leather safety belt was wrapped around my waist by a grinning old sergeant who was enjoying every minute of his chance to show an officer just what it meant to work for a living high above the ground. It was true, the linemen were taken for granted, sent up those poles in all conditions with little thought for the danger by the tasker. It was a good idea that we learn how difficult the job was.

After a demonstration by experts who literally ran up and down the poles, it was our turn. Gloves were essential because no one ever sanded a telephone pole, and every inch of the rough surface was home to the mother of all splinters. At first all we had to do was gaff in and stand a foot above the ground. Leg strength was what that was all about. I hit the pole at an eighty degree angle first on one leg and then the other. I was up and leaning back on my safety strap. "Just stand there for a minute, climbers, get used to the feel of the pole and the grip you have with the irons," our instructor said through his megaphone. "Lock your knees, sir, or you will tire too fast," my personal teacher said from behind me, pulling me back away from the black sticky shaft by the back of my belt. It was true—it was hard to hold on. The megaphone then played the dirty trick we were all dreading. "Start up slowly one foot at a time, be sure that your gaff is good before you release the other foot." It was not fun. I wanted to hold on to the pole with a bear hug, but

I was assured that that would only make the gaff come out prematurely. Six feet off the ground one of my classmates slipped out and slid down until he hit the ground with a thud. Large splinters were broken off by his fall and pierced his thigh like hypodermic needles an inch thick. We all froze in place as he was walked to the shack. "Don't do what he did. Lean back and lock your knees, keep the gaff in, kick it in as you go." All good advice but very hard to do.

We were stopped at twenty feet. "That is high enough for a great game of volley pole." Our chief instructor blew a whistle and threw a white leather ball to me. "We'll let the paratrooper start the game," the now-jovial instructor announced. To catch it I had to remain away from the pole, knees locked, or it was splinter city for me. "Throw it around, the game doesn't end until each of you have caught and thrown it at least twice." What a game. There were plenty of near misses, and several gaffs came out only to be reset immediately by ever weakening players. I sweated right through my fatigue uniform—this was much harder than it looked. It took a good half hour, which seemed like an entire afternoon. Climbing down was harder than going up and several more hugged the evil-smelling column and were introduced to the splinters in the soft underarm flesh. I was as weak as water when I felt the sawdust, my knees were unresponsive, and I wobbled to the shack. The last words from mister megaphone were, "Remember today, gentlemen, when you send a soldier up a pole on a dark and stormy night filled with lightning and other hazards."

On dream sheet I had requested assignment to Germany and command of a company. I knew that the war would soon be over, so the Cold War in Europe was the place to be for the future. I didn't get it. That is why they call the form a dream sheet. Campus unrest caused the Army to assess carefully the quality of the instructors on the ROTC training staffs they had put into four hundred colleges and universities. The program was producing nearly sixteen thousand commissioned officers a year of good quality, but students not in the program—and very often the civilian faculty as well—were beginning to protest the war. Their easy targets were the regular military who strolled around the campus in uniform when not in the classroom as assistant professors of military science. Many ROTC staffers had requested the assignment as their last before retirement. Though highly qualified, the handful at each school could easily "go native" and lose the military edge the Department of the Army wanted them to present to set good examples and inspire leadership. The result was that all the career courses would send their Vietnam returnees to take over ROTC positions and put the Army's best foot forward. It was a good plan. The program would be strengthened to insure that only the best students got commissioned and sent to lead our troops during time of war. I tried very hard to avoid ROTC though; it was a good way to bury a career.

The Signal Branch gave me a list of good schools to pick from—MIT, Tennessee Tech, Texas Tech, Notre Dame, UCLA, Stanford, University of Washington, and University of Nevada, Reno. I selected Reno. We packed up our three sons and all our stuff and headed west. It was just another move—one of twenty-two we would complete in thirty years. We would live on Stead Air Force Base, a defunct training facility ten miles north of the city. It was a small base with plenty of housing, some of which had been retained for the instructors from the ROTC detachment.

I reported in and we were met by our sponsors, Jim and Audrey Conners. He was a senior captain of Artillery and she was from Detroit. Since my wife's extended family was from Dearborn, Carol and Audrey hit it off right away. The Conners had three girls a little older than our sons. Jim had been back from Vietnam for two years, where he had been an adviser to the Vietnamese Army early in the war. They were black, well educated (both had degrees), and very helpful. We stayed at their house, next door to our new quarters, until our furniture could be delivered.

The university was small, only a thousand students, mostly from in state. The corps of cadets was large because attendance was mandatory for freshmen and sophomores as it was a land-grant college. The juniors and seniors attended by choice, and graduation from the course meant a commission as a Reserve second lieutenant. The result was that we provided the Army with nearly a hundred new officers a year. The fifteen officers and sergeants were a great bunch of professionals, but we had our flaws. Lt. Col. Billy Reardon, a chemistry major in college, from one of our finer Jesuit institutions, was a devoted drinker. He lived down the block from me in a large house once occupied by the base commander. Forced by low pay to find an inexpensive way to support his and his wife's habit, he built a still in the attached double garage. Who says you never use what you learn in college? He was proud of the boiler, coils, and vessel, which looked like a laboratory for a Hollywood horror movie. All his spare time was spent in improving the output's quality and quantity. I learned quickly not to ask him for any decisions before noon, when he mellowed out. One day he got a panic call from his wife. "Honey, the fire department called and said they are coming at one o'clock for a routine inspection. What do I tell them about the still?" I was free that morning and Billy grabbed me for the high-speed run to the quarters. The open flame under the cooking pot would not favorably impress the firemen, but the smell would give the whole thing away even if they didn't intend to look into the garage. We took our Army truck and backed it up to the overhead door, and while he took the still apart, with little care I loaded it into the back of the vehicle. We both knew that procedure from years of unit inspections. Put the stuff on the road and return it when the inspection was over. He nearly cried when he saw his creation piled up like so much junk. Even the vat, emptied out on the sand behind the house, took a beating during the teardown. As we drove back to the college, Billy was distraught and stopped in his favorite bar for a pick-me-up. "Fitz, how could this happen to me? All my work, all that production, lost." He was inconsolable.

The firemen never showed. Billy was angry, and he took it out on everyone but the colonel. Two weeks went by, and repeated calls and visits to the inspectors didn't produce any joy. The supply sergeant wanted his truck back but it remained out of his reach. Driven by high over-the-counter prices, Billy could no longer afford the lapse and reinstalled the still to its former glory in the corner of the garage. I was waiting for another call, but at least his old humor returned. Then it happened. "Honey, the firemen are here and they want to see you right away. Come home." With head low, he drove home in the afternoon, stopping for a drink on the way.

"Colonel," said the chief inspector, a man with a considerable beer belly, "we can't have this. You will burn the house down one of these days." He was out of business. Operating an illegal still, even in Nevada, was a serious offense. "The boys and I think we can make it safe if we install some modifications. Do you mind?"

The colonel was delighted. "I would appreciate your advice, gentlemen. Perhaps a gallon a week would make it worth your while?"

"It's a deal."

My students were the sons of ranchers and professional gamblers. I met many of them and was surprised to find that Hollywood had not only misrepresented the military with stereotypes, it had done the same with gamblers. I was impressed with their conservative business approach to what I thought was a devil-may-care activity. It may have been the age of flower children and hippies, but not in Reno. When those who professed the undying benefits of free love arrived in disreputable vehicles and began to panhandle inside the gambling halls, steps were taken. Local officials picked up the happy souls and took them to a local park. There, the Reno barbers volunteered their talents and provided free GI-style haircuts. They were invited to return monthly for a "trim and a brush," no charge. Back on the streets of San Francisco their mere appearance struck terror into the hearts of their friends. The civil libertarians threatened to sue but the issue never came to court. Problem solved.

Because of the war there was one extra duty activity that none of us wanted, but we knew we were the only ones qualified to perform it. One of the corporal works of mercy from my Catholic background, burying the dead, took on new meaning. As soldiers, sailors, Marines, and airmen returned from war under the flag of their country, we were called upon to complete their military careers. That duty was performed only by the officers of the detachment who had been in combat. During previous wars, notification was by official but impersonal telegrams. Not this time. Notification of the death of any serviceman whose next of kin lived within a hundred miles of our station was given to the colonel. One of us was then assigned to notify the family. My first time out I had to go to the home of a soldier in the afternoon and tell his mother. There was no time to lose because we wanted to be there before a letter reached home from a buddy in Vietnam. As a rule it could be done within forty-eight hours of the death. I would have preferred that both parents be at home, but time was of the essence. Notification was always made in uniform, and I was provided a driver and military sedan for the task. The task had to be and look official. Pranksters might otherwise play cruelly and attempt to imitate us. That car with US Army on the side, driving slowly into a neighborhood, the driver looking for house numbers, was like a death knell. Folks shied away as I approached and stopped.

The house was a small ranch-style home in a middle-class area of similar dwellings. Number 1043 had a neat lawn of brownish desert grass with a basketball backboard nailed above the garage door. It hadn't been long since my charge had been in the driveway with his friends, playing and shouting. All the fun, travel, and adventure I had enjoyed as a professional officer was about to be paid for. I had spoken to others who had performed the duty, but nothing would prepare me for the moment when his mother opened the door. Understanding that, I rehearsed my lines for hours beforehand in the office with the door closed. The concern on my face would be genuine, as I had also lost men—boys, really—under the worst of conditions. I couldn't describe the scene, nor would they really want to hear about the last moments. The movies were too clean, and in real combat rarely were there memorable words from the stricken, who were often gone before anyone reached them. There on the doorstep of the home, the only place on earth where their son was still alive, I was about to end his life again. Until I spoke the words, he was alive in her heart as he had always been. I knew I would see the dread in her eyes the moment she saw my green Army uniform. I was the harbinger she feared most. Each of us who had the duty saw his own wife or mother confronted by the specter and tried desperately to find the right words. Feelings ran deep on both sides of the threshold.

A lady of small stature in jeans, a printed blouse, and medium-length dark hair opened the door at the second ring of the bell. She had a dish towel in her hand and was about to do battle with a door-to-door salesman when she looked up into my eyes, which widened as her mouth paused, open.

"I am Captain David Fitz-Enz, United States Army. Ma'am, are you Mrs. John Randolph, the mother of Private James J. Randolph?" That had to be the opening line, there was no way around it. Before I reached the next sentence, her hands flew up and covered her face. "My God, no!"

"I am very sorry, ma'am, but I must tell you that . . ." She never actually heard the end of my statement. I continued, just for the record, then my voice trailed off. I was silent. We were told never to touch anyone.

"Oh no, oh no," she said. If only I could have said "missing in action," I could have left some hope with the poor mother, but he was gone. "Come in," was all she could manage.

"Is there someone I could call, a neighbor?"

It wasn't necessary; the lady next door came in behind me and went to her friend. "Is it Jimmy, Mary?" The mother shook her head as she grabbed at her face and ran both hands into her soft hair, pulling. I stayed, standing, in the middle of the room, hands clasped in front, holding my hat like a shield. The newcomer put her friend on the wide couch and looked at me for words. When none came, she asked, "Are you sure?"

"Yes ma'am, it happened two days ago in Vietnam." Still directing questions while cradling her friend, she asked, "Does John know, her husband?" I shook my head. She turned to Mary, took her hands down, and held them at shoulder height. "I'll call him at work and tell him to come home, okay?" I was grateful for the help.

My sedan had aroused others to come across the lawn, and soon other ladies were in the kitchen, turning off things and making coffee. There was no hostility, only grief, thick and dark. The sunny day outside was blocked by emotion inside, as if someone had drawn all the drapes. When John Randolph parked in the drive, he knew from the olive-drab sedan and military driver what was about to descend on him in the living room. His eyes were filled with tears as he shook my hand with a limpness that strong working man had never used on another. I told him what I knew about the incident of his son's death. "Have you been there, Captain?" I suddenly realized how important it was that I had. He busied his mind with questions about my own experience in that faraway place his son had seen and written about. Some others listened to me while keeping an eye on Mary.

I drank a cup of coffee I didn't want. After an hour I told them about Capt. Arthur Riner, the survivor assistance officer, who would take over from me the next morning. "He will take care of all the arrangements, sir, and answer all your questions about the honors and burial."

John, a veteran himself, walked me to my car. "What can I say, Captain?" I was equally without words for a son who was probably more real to them at that moment than he had ever been.

It was important that the assistance officer, who received the body from the airport with an honor guard and conducted the military funeral, not be the one who made the notification; a certain amount of blame was naturally attached to the messenger and I was never seen again by the family. As the war went on it was necessary to assign two officers to the notification team, for their own protection.

I had the duty too often in the two years I spent in Reno before returning for a second tour to Vietnam. The worst was just before I left. There was no mother, which made the task look easier. The soldier's father lived out in the desert on a little ranch near Carson City. He was a retired lieutenant colonel and enjoying retirement on his own spread. His wife had died and I informed him that his only son, a captain, blond and blue-eyed like me, was a casualty. He was inconsolable and suddenly totally alone. There were no friends nearby, no family of any kind. Initially the soldiers were anonymous to us, but shortly after entering the house a picture would change that. That time the dead officer looked back at me from several pictures on the bookcase. He looked enough like me to be my brother. It wasn't coffee we drank that afternoon and I stayed to nearly dusk. My driver, Sergeant Anderson, joined us, and two old soldiers sat and listened to the former warrior reminisce about his days in the service and the love he held for it. Now it had taken his son. He understood that more than most but it didn't help.

The town fathers decided that Reno should have a local chapter of the Association of the United States Army. It is an old association that is well subscribed to across the country and made up of local citizens and active-duty Army; it looks out after government treatment of Army affairs. It is echoed by similar groups in all branches of the service. Leaders in Carson City, the capital, and Reno formed the chapter and named it for Gen. William Westmoreland. The general was asked to come to the inaugural meeting as its first guest and speaker. The governor was the host and our senior and junior cadets were guests, along with the Army officers from the university. The general was honored the night before at a reception in an old frontier bar and restaurant in Virginia City. It was a rough-and-ready place, Nevada style, rather than the post atmosphere that one would expect for so distinguished a visitor. There was sawdust on the floor and the menu was barbecue steak and beans served on tin plates. Dressed in mess dress blue uniforms, the general and his colonel aide-de-camp stood out from the others. The lieutenant governor asked if he could see the general's blue cap, which was encrusted with gold scrambled eggs and band, just before he was to be honored by the governor. The white-haired four-star gave him the hat and the recipient took it, stood up on a table, and nailed it to a wooden beam. "Thank you, general, there will always be a part of you here in Nevada," he said without apology. The general smiled, chuckled a little, and said, "You are welcome, sir, but it seems I have given you my aide's hat by mistake."

The next day at a local American Legion hall his speech was very good, and our cadets were invited to meet the great man, one by one. I had seen him from a distance many times in Vietnam and taken his picture in the field during combat operations. I stood in the back of the hall with my wife, Carol, and the colonel urged me to go forward and say hello. But the general was busy and we hung back, as the other officers and wives went up to the stage after the cadets. When it was all over we stood with the colonel and staff in the parking lot in a cluster and waited for Westy to come out and get into the governor's car so we could give him a salute as he left for the airport. We had great respect for the man who had shouldered the political and command burden for all of us in the armed forces. We were a good fifty yards away, near the parking exit, and watched him get in a limousine with smoked windows and start on his way. As the car rolled by it suddenly stopped, the electric window rolled down, and his aide stuck his head out and beckoned to our group. We were all a little bewildered. No one moved. Then the colonel, our senior officer, and his wife started forward the ten yards to the side of the car. With that, General Westmoreland popped out of the far side and came around the back and toward our group. The colonel stopped nearly where he had started and we all came to attention. The general stepped past the colonel, whom he had spoken to at length at several of the earlier receptions, and came up to me and my wife. "Hi, Fitz, how did you get here?"

"Just lucky, sir," I said, knowing how informal the man really was. He introduced himself to my astonished wife and spoke of the days with the 173d, a unit just like the 187th that he had commanded in Korea. I don't honestly believe that he recognized me, but the patch of the Airborne Brigade and my natural nickname, which he saw on a black-and-white tag stuck to the breast pocket of my uniform, was all he needed. Or perhaps not. It was a kind gesture, the thing he was always known for throughout the Army. My stock went up in the eyes of my contemporaries and their wives. As the youngest officer there I needed all the help I could get. Years later at the War College, I had lunch with him in his retirement and never mentioned the kindness he had shown. I did not want to shatter my illusion. What a great leader he is.

I took my cadets to Fort Ord, California, for an introduction to the summer camp they were about to attend. Camp is six weeks of basic training given the summer before commissioning. I wanted to get them over the culture shock of boot camp by letting them see their first Army installation and live for two days the way they would at camp. We gave them one day on the rifle range for familiarization with the big M-1 rifle. The second day was on the leader development course, to see how they would cope with field problems. We stayed in a training company that was out of cycle and so had no Army privates mixed in with our impressionable college students.

I will never forget the company commander. Capt. Jonathan Wilson was the only officer in the unit. I had breakfast with him in the mess hall while I watched my boys playing kitchen police, or KP, scurrying around under the direction of the regular cooks. Johnny was back from Vietnam a year. The first eight months were spent at Valley Forge Army Hospital recovering from a wound in his left arm. In the movies a soldier winged in the arm is returned to health shortly and goes home to a hero's welcome, fully recovered from a flesh wound. It is like shooting the gun out of the hand of a bad guy—nothing, really. The reality of a wound is felt by the owner for life, though the owner might not talk about it or even show it in daily life. They haunt and hurt. I was lucky, never wounded. But a couple of hundred thousand were. Johnny looked normal but rarely used his left hand. A bullet had ripped the muscles off his lower arm below the elbow, leaving the bone untouched but exposed. Even after reconstructive surgery the hand was nearly useless. There was little circulation to the fingers as well and it hurt, bad, all the time. He always wore a glove on it, to keep it warm, he said. But the expression in his eyes I will never forget. Though only twenty-six, he had lost his youth. He and that Purple Heart would live with pain the remainder of his life. His great fear was that he would no longer be able to remain on active duty. He was a professional soldier, and the thought of having to leave while his buddies stayed on to thirty years hurt as much as his arm. I hope he made it. We needed him as much as he needed us.

The next school year was just like the last and I was getting restless for the regular army. So were my contemporaries. With the exception of our air defense officer, who had vowed to complete his twenty years without service in combat, we all volunteered for another year in Vietnam. None of the wives were happy with that move, but they knew it was coming. As a volunteer I could pick my unit and I opted for another tour with the Airborne. This time there would be no slip-up and I could get the unit of my choice. Signal Branch in Washington, headed by Lt. Col. Fred Fellows, called and confirmed my assignment before we left Reno. Moving the household never becomes routine, but at least it is done first-class by the Army. Carol found a town house near the boys' school in Aurora, Illinois, within a mile of her parents, and by July I was packing all I needed into one bag for my return to the war. That night was momentous to the world. Not because I was going back to the fighting but because the astronauts had landed on the surface of the moon. We watched and packed, packed and watched. By the time those three heroes returned to this planet, I would once again be surrounded by heroes.

Chapter Seven

You can't fool the troops, I would advise you
not to try, but you can gain their respect and if
you do, you will have acquired something that
money can't buy.
ADMIRAL ERNEST KING

My first tour had begun with a twenty-one-day voyage across the Pacific with a unit during the initial buildup. The war was old by the time of my return and everyone was a replacement. It had been in my nightmares for the last year. There I was, in the jungle with an infantry squad, taking pictures as before, watching the enemy run back and forth through the lens of my still camera. When they got within ten yards, I let the camera swing on the cord around my neck and began to fire my rifle. I fired and fired but no one ever fell. They never came any closer but they wouldn't go down either. It was like an arcade game at the county fair, the one where the ducks ride across the range pulled along by a bumpy chain, clicking and clacking, but won't go down even though the bell sounds a hit. I couldn't see the faces of the VC, hidden under the metal brim of their helmets, but the rest of them was very clear. They crouch and run, hide and jump up, fire and yell. It goes on and on, in vivid color with stereo sound. There was never a conclusion, no one on either side was hurt, and then I would wake up in a terrible sweat, the bed soaked. Well, Carol wouldn't have to put up with that for a year, and I would miss the warm bed and the friend who always understood.

The second time, I was going over on a plane just like the 707 that had brought me home less than two years earlier. My seatmate was a young captain on his first excursion. Vernon Eberly, Signal Corps, was six inches taller than me and looked like a top-flight end from his football team at Ole Miss. Many officers in those days came from the college athletic programs because they were encouraged to enroll in ROTC to keep safely out of the draft. The officers who taught the program at the school and the coaching staff were birds of a feather. Most army officers are naturally interested in athletics, it goes with the profession. Like the coaches, we too are great team builders; as Wellington said, "The battle of Waterloo was won on the playing fields of Eton."

On the long flight over, scared that he would not be up to this more deadly game, he asked all the classic questions. I told him I had had the same fears and brooded over them for the duration of my voyage before my first tour. He had the advantage of the jet age and would quickly be in the thick of it, perhaps within hours. Somehow that didn't seem to calm him. I liked Vern immediately. He would survive. In fact, he and his family stayed in New Jersey with us in the spring of '74, he was one of my students at the seminar for brigade commanders in '88, I had dinner with him in Germany the night the Gulf air war started while on my way to Saudi Arabia, and he took my place as the chief of staff at the Defense Communication Agency in '91. That kind of contact and camaraderie has done a great deal toward making our army the best in the world.

We landed at Cam Ranh Bay, an American air base and seaport protected from the enemy by miles of guarded perimeter, more than a hundred miles north of Saigon. It could have been a resort in peacetime, a beautiful blue lagoon surrounded by miles of near-white sand so fine that I sunk in up to my ankles. But it looked more like an invasion port in Normandy. The only things missing were the barrage balloons. Dozens of commercial ships sat at anchor and half that number were unloading onto lighters or snug against the docks. Fairly small, gray Navy boats plowed in between, guarding the resting steel vessels whose sides were scarred with streams of rust. Not a pretty sight but a necessary one, serving the needs of hundreds of thousands of American, Korean, Australian, New Zealand, and Vietnamese troops. Leaving the plane, the hot humid offshore wind brought the smells of the Orient. Sweet foliage, charcoal fires, rotting garbage, and open sewers told me I was back again for another year of fun, travel, and adventure. That time, however, memories were attached to the vista at the top of the mobile stairs. I knew again that I would survive. I doubted I was wrong about that and trusted in my luck. Napoleon, when told about a new officer who had a top-notch record, listened to the fellow's supporters and when they had finished, he said, "Yes, but is he lucky?" I had always been lucky.

I was also secure. I had a set of orders in my hand returning me to the 173d Airborne Brigade while most, like Vern, were there for potluck. The officers were housed in a BOQ exactly like the enlisted barracks except for the sign outside that placed it off limits to enlisted men. Next door a similar building was used as an officers club. It had a long bar and soft chairs. A giant stereo system played music tapes donated by the crews of the airliners that brought us. It was just a place to wait while processing went on and on.

We were told that only two days would pass before we shipped out to our units. I was more than ready to leave and walked down to the beach and back several times between appointments and lectures about health and safety. I took a shortcut back in the late afternoon and, rather than walking on the wooden sidewalks, I crossed the area between the two-story wooden barracks buildings that were identical to the ones at home except for the open sides and insect screens that went the length on both floors. Armed guards had been posted as darkness fell. They were fresh out of training camps in the States and very jumpy. The sergeants had warned them that they were not at Fort Dix; a real enemy was out there watching their every move. That was certainly exaggerated; we were half a mile from the outer fence and experienced guards were out on the line, along with roving patrols.

Suddenly I was challenged in the twilight. "Halt, who goes there?" I could tell from the high-pitched voice that cracked with youth that the guard was nervous.

It was no time to play around; the kid would shoot my head off if I didn't play it by the book. "Friend," I answered in my best and firmest American accent. Then there was a long pause as he tried to remember the next instruction. I decided not to prompt him and perhaps scare him into pulling the trigger. I could just hear his court-martial. "I thought he was the enemy because he tried to trick me. So I shot him." Finally it came. "Advance friend and be reconnoitered." He was scared. The proper challenge was "Advance and be recognized," not reconnoitered. I walked up to him and showed him my ID card in the glow of the firelights on the end of the building. "Thanks, Captain. I hope I didn't make you mad."

"No, soldier. Well done. If you stay that alert you will be fine. May I pass?"

"Oh, yes, sir. Have a nice day," he said now that he was all unwound.

My final interview was set for the following morning, to be followed by a flight to the Airborne at Landing Zone English up the coast. "Captain Fitz-Enz, is your name spelled right?" said the Adjutants General Corps officer. "We need to have it correct for graves registration."

"Why?" I said. "Did I die, or do you know something I don't know?"

"Oh no, sir, it is just that not all your records have a hyphen."

"I know, Army computers can't handle it."

"Sir, have you ever thought of having the spelling changed. It would make it a lot easier. It is rather peculiar."

I had been there before. "I will think about it. Have you ever thought of having your name changed, Lieutenant? 'Smith' can be rather confusing." I shouldn't have antagonized him. "Sir, you are going to the Fourth Infantry Division." That was a straight leg outfit, not Airborne—how could that be? I had it all arranged back in the States. I pulled out my copy of the order to the 173d. "I have valid orders. I am a volunteer. You know I get the privilege of picking my own unit."

"Yes, sir, but there have been a lot of losses in the Fourth and we are sending nearly this whole planeload to bring them back up to strength."

"But I am a paratrooper, a special skill." I could see it was no use, but it was worth the fight to try to stay out of a line division where draftees served rather than Regulars. By noon Vern and I were seatmates again on our way to Pleiku, in the central highlands, home of the "Poison Ivy Division," the 4th.

The countryside around the capital of the province was mountainous, and the jungle of the south had changed to large hardwood trees and more open undergrowth. The city we drove through was like Bien Hoa only larger. Blue, pink, even some dark-yellow stucco houses crowded the paved streets, which had a layer of red dirt over the top. The city was poor but the markets were full and one could buy most convenience items from open-front shops or street venders who sat on the curbs with their goods spread out on blankets. Vietnam was not a starving country; the economy seemed vigorous, food was plentiful, and the people looked healthy. Clean, beautiful, large-eyed children played happily on the sidewalks with toys from Japan. Bicycles and motorbikes were the prime means of transportation. The only motorized vehicles were Lambrettas, three-wheeled motor scooters, open boxes on the rear filled to overflowing with goods or people. Smoky exhausts and open latrines gave the city an unforgettable odor. Ten miles outside of town was Camp Enari. It was named for Lt. Mark Enari, who had been killed defending his wounded soldiers. The compound was a huge square cut into an open plain with a cone-shaped hill that jutted up eight hundred feet, providing an excellent vantage point and radio relay position. The outer barricades were six miles around and dotted with watchtowers, barbed wire, minefields, and bunkers. The main gate looked like something out of the handbook of Attila the Hun. Twenty thousand men were housed inside the crude fortress, which was not for fighting but a home base for troops out on operations. In the year to come, I would spend little time within its confines.

I was given a private room in a bunker belonging to the replacement company. The place smelled like someone had pissed on the sandbagged walls. It was the rainy season, during which, each day for an hour or two, it rained harder than anyplace I had ever been. Everything was mildewed. A green fur grew on the black metal bedstead of my army cot. I was expecting to spend only one night there and that was fine with me. I was not going to be a combat photographer this time. My duty was going to be in the division signal battalion, providing communications to the units away from camp and links to higher headquarters. The next morning Vern and I went to see the battalion commander, who was also the division signal officer. He had an office in the division headquarters, a series of small wooden buildings whose outer walls and roof were protected by rows of wet sandbags. It was a one-block walk along the duckboards, which lifted us above the mud which ran through the camp like rivers. Inside I met the assistant division signal officer, Maj. Ash Beauregard, my old friend and sponsor from Japan, who'd been a lieutenant the last time we served together. I was beginning to suspect that my change of orders might not have been based on the replacement needs of the 4th. He jumped up and greeted me. "Hi, Fitz, long time no see." It was nice to meet a friend in a new unit; I felt a little more at home. We talked of old times and Vern felt a little left out, I am afraid. Then the other shoe dropped. "I heard you were here, Fitz. Welcome to the 124th Signal Battalion," said the commander, Lt. Col. Fred Fellows, former chief of Signal Branch and the man who had given me orders for the Airborne Brigade. It was plain now, he had gone through the files before he left Washington and picked the officers for the next year to fill up his own command.

"Nice to see you, sir. I'll bet the unit is full of people I know." It was; classmates from the career course were everywhere. That time good connections had worked against me.

"You see, Fitz, I wanted an officer in my battalion who was former 173d; they are our neighbor and I knew you would be perfect if I ever needed a liaison on operations." Sure enough, I was the only paratrooper in the officer corps within the 124th.

"I know you would like a company-commander job but all three are filled. I have a special problem and you are perfect for it. I need a very aggressive officer with a good combat record to go to the cavalry squadron. It is a real fighting unit; you will like it, I know." Naturally, Ash agreed with the Old Man.

"What is a cavalry squadron, sir?" I had never been assigned to an infantry division before. The 4th was made up of nine infantry battalions, four artillery, one tank, and one aviation. Then there were the eyes and ears of the division, the cavalry squadron. It was a special unit of combined arms: three troops of mechanized (ground) cavalry with tanks and armored vehicles that bristled with machine guns; flame-throwing armored personnel carriers; an aviation troop of helicopter gunships; an infantry platoon; and a communications platoon that linked them all together. In the cavalry, companies are called troops. The squadron had about six hundred troopers. Its mission was to screen the enemy from the other units and perform reconnaissance. It also had more firepower than any other unit in the division and was known to take on the enemy first, before other elements could be brought into the fight. In a way it was a miniature of the Airborne brigade I had served in on my last tour. "They haven't had a platoon leader for three months, since Captain Lamb was wounded," he told me, pleading his case. I would not be the only signal officer in a combat unit—each of the other line battalions had one as well. The remainder of the signal officers, twenty-five, served in the 124th, which was providing long-line communications to the fighting battalions. "Of all the line-unit jobs," Ash said, "the Cav is the best!" Ash turned out to be right.

I took my wet bag, left the replacement company, walked across the muddy track to the airfield where the 10th Cavalry aviation troop kept its aircraft, and reported in. It was the home of the Shamrocks, their call sign on the radio, and I got a room for the night before flying forward. The 10th Cavalry is one of the most famous in the Army. Begun in 1866 at Fort Riley, Kansas, it was formed to protect settlers as they moved west. It was unique back then because, except for the officers, it was all black. Made up of former slaves, non-freemen, the 10th's troopers fought the Indians, who gave them their title, Buffalo Soldiers, as a mark of courage and respect. The Indians thought the 10th's troopers resembled the buffalo, when covered with dust from long rides. Lt. John J. Pershing was known as "Blackjack Pershing" for his service with the regiment and he kept the nickname his whole career. The 10th fought in the Mexican campaign with by then Brigadier General Pershing, went to Cuba and climbed San Juan Hill with Teddy Roosevelt, fought in France during World War I, and went ashore at Omaha Beach in 1944. Harry Truman had done away with wholly black units in the early fifties but the 10th had turned all white prior to the 1917 campaign. The 10th was integrated in Korea, and in Vietnam it had black officers as well as black troopers.

The first man I met was the motor maintenance warrant officer, Chief Noah Twohorses, an American Indian. He was called Chief not because of his heritage but because that was his rank, chief warrant officer. "Captain, let's go see the supply officer. You need a kit if you are going on operations." The supply room was a one-story wooden shack filled with the things of war, everything from tank parts to toilet paper. The boss was another warrant, Chief Winslow P. Moses, a black officer. His cavalry predecessors would have been proud. Feeling that soldiers waste them—a belief not uncommon among supply personnel—he guarded the supplies as if they were his own. Supply rooms in the Army are famous for "horse traders" who add their own methods to the established bureaucratic acquistion practices. When the system doesn't deliver on time and because the unit cannot operate with "due out" slips, the supply officer is expected to become creative. There was a saying, "It don't matter, it's all OD" which, roughly translated, means, it isn't stealing to circumvent the system when it fails because it's all Army supplies, and even though it doesn't reach it's intended destination it is consumed by people who need it and are authorized to have it. Of course, such reasoning is wrong and only adds to the burden of the Army supply system, but it has been used at least since Hannibal crossed the Alps.

Chief Moses was a recalcitrant fellow not intimidated by senior officers, and he encouraged them to fend for themselves at times. I was used to that; on my first tour, when I wanted an M-16 rifle rather than my authorized weapon, a .45-caliber pistol, I had to visit a field hospital and help myself to one from a stack of rifles left in the open by medics bringing in the wounded. They would be of no further use to the men who'd been issued them and the misappropriation didn't really matter—it was all OD! The Cavalry all wore .45s because there was no room for a rifle in the tanks or armored Cav vehicles, where machine guns were mounted. They carried them in shoulder holsters rather than on a pistol belt because any bulk around the waist got hung up when they crawled in and out of small hatches. It gave the troopers a different look, like gangsters and tough guys from the movies, and they liked that. I was issued all the uniforms and kit I needed by one of the young sergeants, who reminded me of Fagin's errant children.

"I need something to put in this shoulder holster, Sergeant." A rather simple and unnecessary request, I thought.

"You will have to talk to the chief about that, sir. He handles the weapons personally," he said, knowing what was about to happen. I strapped on the empty but handsome new black leather holster for effect, hoping the chief would get my drift—that is, What's wrong with this picture?—and walked to his beat-up wooden desk in the back of the shop. He looked up from his paperwork with complete unconcern. "Got a problem, Captain?" He remained seated, a minor breach of military courtesy. It was going to be a battle of wills, which I thought was totally unnecessary. "No problem, Chief. I need a pistol. I am going forward in the morning." I added that last bit in case the previous signal officer had remained in base camp and therefore hadn't really needed a weapon. I didn't want to know how he had been wounded; it was bad luck to ask. Perhaps he'd been hit in the eye, like a friend of mine in the 124th, when he opened a bottle of champagne. It was very embarrassing for him in the ward. Surrounded by the truly wounded, he had no Purple Heart pinned to his pillow. He found it hard to get sympathy from the pretty nurses, as well. But I was a different breed, and Chief Moses should know that. "We haven't got any. Maybe next week, sir."

"Do you use your phone a lot in this business, Chief?"

"Sure do, Captain, couldn't live without it," he assured me.

"Does it ever go out and stay out of order, Chief?" I asked rather pointedly.

"No, sir. It is great. Always works. Why?"

"Well, Chief, my experience tells me that you could have chronic problems, you know, water in the lines, and the signal battalion might not have time to fix it with all the other high-priority troubles in the rainy season. I have influence in the Signal community and could help if anything went wrong, if you get my drift." I went over to the wall and fiddled with the fragile wire connection.

The old fox's attitude changed. "I really would like to help you," he said, standing up now, "but I just don't have one to give you, honest," raising his right hand as if about to swear on the Bible, appropriate for a guy named Moses. It had flashed across his mind that the loss of his telephone would seriously hamper the supply function and he wouldn't be able to prove that I had anything to do with it. Behind him on a nail hung his own pistol, a mistake.

"Tell you what, Chief. I could guarantee good phone service from my friends in the Signal battalion if you lent me your weapon for a week—you know, until mine comes." He reluctantly gave me his, a nice one with all new parts. It was unloaded, as I would expect. "I would like six clips and a box of ammunition."

"Sorry, Captain, I don't have any clips or ammo. They sell clips downtown in Pleiku, and you can gets bullets out at Blackhawk, our forward base." Another battle.

"I don't have time to buy clips on the black market, nor should I. I bet you have a clip in your desk drawer, for this one. Right, Chief?" Reluctantly he opened the top drawer and took it out and handed it to me. It held only five bullets instead of the normal load of seven. I didn't relish going out with only five but I could see there was no point to continuing this battle of wills on my first day in the unit, so I said thanks and took it.

Maj. Pat Long walked into Supply behind me. He introduced himself as the new S-3, operations officer, the most powerful position in the unit outside of the commander. He was a little taller than me and very thin but wiry. His face was lined and deeply wrinkled, which made him look older than the thirty that he must have been. I stepped back, my business concluded, and stuffed my gear into a waterproof bag and listened as Pat started down the same road. I lingered because I wanted to get to know my new boss and I also wanted to witness the fight guaranteed to take place over his new weapon. Pat was also on his second tour and he asked for a rifle rather than a pistol. He would spend lots of time on the road in a jeep and preferred a personal weapon that would reach out farther than the fifty feet a pistol could manage.

"You aren't authorized one, sir; the officer's weapon is a pistol."

"Okay, I'll take one for now."

"Sorry, sir, the Captain took the last one." The crafty old devil had begun the battle all over again. He expected the major to take mine. Pat was not about to play. "Where is yours. You really don't need it in base camp, do you?"

Pointing to the one safely in my holster, the chief said, "The Captain has it, sir."

"What an outfit," the major said in disgust.

That directly reflected on the old chief's pride as the squadron supply officer. "Sergeant Stokes, give the major yours," he said. He and Stokes could probably lay their hands on two pistols within minutes after we left. Pat and I knew that.

"Yes, sir," Stokes replied as he gave up his weapon. "But I don't have any rounds," he told the major.

Pat turned to me for help. "Have you got any bullets, Fitz? I am leaving in a few minutes to go to Blackhawk by chopper. When are you coming out?"

"I want to look at the aviation troop communications today and won't be coming until tomorrow morning." I handed him my clip of five.

"Okay, give me three and I will give them back when I see you tomorrow," he said, snapping the first three off the top of the thin, black metal holder.

"It's a deal, sir. See you tomorrow." I took the remainder and stuffed them back into my pocket. What a war this has become, I thought as I walked with Major Long to his helicopter.

The next day I met my pilot, a nineteen-year-old warrant officer named Lipscomb, at the helipad for the forty-mile flight over enemy territory to my new home. The kid was wired, as we say, full of himself, and we strapped into the quick light observation helicopter (LOH). It had space for a pilot and copilot in front, who were surrounded by a Plexiglas bubble, and space behind for two or three passengers. It was a tiny thing that looked and sounded like a bumblebee. Unlike its big brother, the Huey, this one you strapped on your back, more of a personal flying machine. They never assigned a copilot to the LOH and I sat in his place, up front. "You are going to have to fly this thing, Captain, if I get hit," he announced over the radio intercom in my aviation helmet. I had learned to fly "fixed-wing" in the ROTC aviation program that I ran at the University of Nevada, but I could see that it wouldn't be of much help in the whirlybird, where everything seemed foreign to fixed-wing operations. There was a stick between my legs and pedals on the floor—after that it was totally different.

With great ease we lifted off in a swirl and were out over the perimeter in seconds. At about a hundred feet altitude, the pilot followed the road toward Pleiku and veered off to the south just as I caught sight of the big airfield I had landed at two days before. "You have two choices, sir. We can fly nap of the earth, or at three thousand feet—anything in-between is vulnerable." "Nap of the earth" meant fifty feet at a hundred miles an hour, treetop level.

"Let's stay down." The wrong choice. The theory was that at low level the enemy couldn't get off a shot before we were out of range. My decision gave the pilot carte blanche, just what he wanted. His idea of nap of the earth was "the lower the better." We followed the road, and pedestrians hit the ground as we passed over them at twenty feet. He whooped and hollered and I dug my glove-covered hands into my knees as everything rushed by like lightning. It was a private amusement ride for him and a lesson for me in the art of giving a pilot instructions. We dipped and popped up between large army trucks and the young drivers waved, wishing they could take my place.

I was beginning to think I was getting too old for war when an LZ Blackhawk loomed up on the right. The pilot skidded the craft on its side in a hard left turn and, at full speed, slipped it under telephone lines that were twenty feet off the ground. I expected the rotors to hit the heavy black cable and stop the prop dead, but he missed it, pitched up to clear the front gate, and put the LOH down like a baby carriage in the middle of the dusty quadrangle. "Thanks, Lipscomb. Remind me not to fly with you again" were my parting words as I took off the helmet and left it on the seat. He gave me a thumbs-up and all I could see of his face sticking out from under his sun visor close to the microphone was a big toothy smile.

I reported in to Major Long in the operations bunker. "Fitz, can I have your two bullets? I have to go out to see B Troop on the road."

"Yes, sir." We traded like that for two days until one of us remembered to find a supply. I vowed that on my first trip to An Khe, thirty miles down the road, I'd work my hospital trick and pick up a couple of rifles for us.

LZ Blackhawk was a roadside fort built to contain a headquarters for the battalion-size unit that protected the highway between Pleiku and the major American base at An Khe. It was a half-block square protected by barbed wire and sandbagged bunkers with the Headquarters Troop ACAVs parked in between, guns facing out. The ACAV was an armored personnel carrier with the top off. It mounted a .50-caliber machine gun in a turret and one .30-caliber on each side. In addition, it carried a soldier armed with a grenade launcher. The crew of five was designed to scout and bring heavy fire on anything in its path. They were operated in company with other ACAVs and tanks.

The firebase was kind of a "circle your wagons" arrangement with large living and working bunkers aboveground in the middle. It had been built years before and melted into the mud during the rainy season. History said that it had been attacked before because it stuck out in the clear terrain next to the major highway.

My problem was that I had never been a signal officer responsible for communications at the battalion level. I was trained for long-haul communications, big stuff on large trucks that sent multichannel traffic between command posts, not portable FM radios connecting the operations center with small units, detachments, and individual aircraft. I had rarely operated small radios before and was totally out of my depth. The Signal Corps had worked a deal with combat units to replace all the battalion communications officers, who were experienced line officers, with guys like me. In years to come it would give us an appreciation for the problems at low level so we could do a better job at our normal positions on the battlefield. It was a great idea that I totally supported, but they didn't provide any training to us in that first year of the experiment. I figured it was best not to tell anyone that I was bewildered by it all. Perhaps my platoon sergeant could keep me out of trouble until I learned.

The BOQ was a heavily sandbagged building, thirty-by-twenty, with eight double rooms just big enough for two Army cots and a footlocker. The walls were made of artillery ammo boxes, plain wood with long strings of black lot numbers stenciled on the sides. The roof was also sandbagged, which made the place look like a demented igloo. My roommate was Lt. Ross Campbell, whose father was in the State Department and stationed in Thailand. He was big, a linebacker, with a square jaw and gold-rimmed glasses that perched on the end of his nose and caused him to tilt his head back to see through them. His nose, which was small and upturned, would have been more proper on the face of a woman. Clearly it was not meant for his face at all. Ross was quiet, thoughtful, and concerned. Most cavalrymen tended to be very outgoing and brash. I was interested in the character of the unit, and he had been with it for six months.

"We have been very active. Colonel Rislip, our old commander, volunteered us for every job no one else wanted," he said ruefully. "It cost us lives and equipment, but we are the killingest unit in the division." He said it without pride, which surprised me. I was not surprised at their record; the attitude of the Cavalry combined with their large family of heavy equipment caused them to shine over the dull infantry. "Well, Fitz, Rislip has gone back to the States to a glorious career and we are left to pick up the pieces. Our vehicles are spread out and broken down all over the Corps area. Some we dragged in here and piled up in the motor pool. Some were turned in as no longer serviceable and others are combat losses. My platoon has one tank and three ACAVs, less than half my authorization, and they should all be deadlined. We are sitting on this road because we can't go anywhere else. You have a real challenge, captain of Signals. Most of the radios are down and hardly anyone has a combat vehicle crew helmet with a microphone that works."

I broke in. "How is the new boss, Ross? Any good?" I was hoping for some encouragement.

"He is no fighter like Rislip, but he appears to be more interested in appearance than anything. One of the good old boys, West Point, friends in high places, getting his ticket punched before going back to Washington."

I had heard it before. Battalion command is the most important command post, the stepping-stone no one can miss if he expects to gain high places. At the same time it is the last place a senior officer can really influence the action and personally care for the soldiers. The system for selection to battalion command depended on who one knew rather than how qualified one was. Some turned out great, others didn't, and their failure to lead cost lives. In the years to come, those of us who had suffered under the good old boy system buried it. Our protests and reviews of wartime records led to a central selection system in Washington, made up of a board of senior commanders who would have to live with their choices. Since the late 1970s on to today, all brigade and battalion commanders have been chosen based on their performance and experience. That was one of the most important lessons learned in the Vietnam War.

Ross walked me to the command post for my first encounter with the commander of the First Squadron, Tenth Cavalry—1/10 Cav. "Remember, Fitz, one-tenth Cavalry, nine-tenths bullshit," were his parting words, which brought a grin even to his weary face.

Lt. Col. Marion Culpepper, a gentleman of Virginia, was standing in the bright light of the map board which covered one wall of the bunker. The enclosure was twenty feet square and filled with small field tables and telephones. Along the opposite wall was a shelf of radios, all of which were in constant operation. Situation reports, calls for logistics, instructions on movement, and intelligence reports all vied with each other for someone's attention. The operating environment called for selective hearing, a trait the military should probably breed for. Mentally one could block out the radios that were not of concern and eavesdrop on the one that mattered at that moment. The colonel was deep in thought and I was in no hurry, so I stood off to the side taking in what I could before he spoke. He was no more than five-feet-eight, but because he was so slight he looked taller. Thick straight black hair well streaked with dull gray was full and looked younger than his deeply wrinkled face that was weathered by the sun. There were no laugh lines in the corners of his eyes. His left hand was on his chin and stroked it slowly. He knew I was there, I could feel it, he just wanted to make me wait, to see if I would interrupt. I was in no hurry, my Type B personality told me, I was there for a year. But I could tell that he was not the kind of man who liked that sort of attitude, so I decided to don my Type A act, which I had used before. The Army loves hyper personalities—they look like they are going to make something happen.

I won the waiting game. "You must be that new Signal officer with the funny-sounding foreign name. Am I right, sir?" His Virginia accent and phrasing were right out of *Gone with the Wind.*

"I am only foreign to you, sir, because I come from the North." That caused him to look at me for the first time. There was a sparkle in his eye—he liked my repartee. I, too, had read Margaret Mitchell.

"Captain," he turned his entire body from the map, "oll ah wont from youu is loud and kleer communications at oll times. You ar desmissed, sir." He returned to his map and I left the room. A chill ran down my back. "That is a myghty toll ourder, sir," I said to myself in my finest Hollywood accent. It sounded more like Yosemite Sam than Rhett Butler.

On one of the deteriorating bunkers was a sign, COMMO. Only sixteen men were in the platoon according to Sergeant First Class Henderickson, the platoon sergeant. The bunker had a dirt floor and across the center were three heaps of equipment, each the height of a man. Everything was caked with mud and looked like it had been buried. Clearly it was all busted. "The colonel made us dig it up on our last move; we wanted to just leave it behind," he assured me. If that was my men's attitude, we were in real trouble. I was counting on Henderickson for help and he was destroying equipment rather than turning it in or fixing it. Some of the items I had never seen before. They had come out of tanks and were used to change frequencies and electrically match the antenna.

"Who is your best repairman, Sergeant?"

"Specialist Albert, sir. He was a plumber in civilian life." Albert had been a radio operator in the Infantry, and when he discovered that the enemy knew that the operator is always next to the officer and therefore a perfect target, he talked Henderickson into teaching him radio repair in his spare time. His knowledge of how water flowed was analogous to electricity, and his desire not to be shot made him an attentive student and dedicated repairman. I made him my driver, and as we went along, with a nod and a wink he taught me all there was to know about tactical communications. No one ever caught on.

One of the line troops was at Blackhawk "C"; "A" and "B" were down the highway at LZs Action and Schuller. Of course, those were just the command posts. The troopers and tanks were spread out over many small bridges and stuck up in the mountain pass at a thousand feet. It was there, during the French occupation after WWII, that Mobile Force One Thousand was wiped out by Viet Minh units. That was on everyone's mind and we were determined that the 10th Cav was going to reverse history on its ground.

Charlie Troop was commanded by Terry Worth, a prematurely gray senior captain. I needed a mentor and he took on the task. He let me go out with him on search and destroy missions, clinging to the back of his turret. Terry was a professional—he put out his own people and gathered intelligence rather than depending on the higher headquarters to tell him who he was facing. One night he came to me at about eleven and said, "Stick with me, we are going to be attacked at midnight." I had been to the nightly briefing and nothing was said there about activity. All day he had been slipping motorized elements into Blackhawk one at a time and deadlining them in the motor pool. After dark, by some miracle of motor pool black magic, they were all healed and slid into openings between the bunkers. When the ground attack came it was no contest; the heavy machine guns and tanks equipped with spotlights surprised the enemy and broke up the attack with no casualties to us and heavy losses to them. I watched two enemy infantrymen run into the fuel dump and hide behind a black rubber bladder which, at night, looked like a big rock. One shot from a tracer exploded the rubber rock like a roman candle. The next morning I checked out the location. The only thing that remained of the two men was two left feet, both bright green. Hiding behind big, black American rocks was not a good idea. From then on Terry was known as Gray Fox, another character from the American Civil War.

Our colonel would have loved to own that nickname, but he was more administrator than warrior no matter how hard he tried to change roles. The fact of the matter was that we needed a good administrator to put us back into a serviceable condition, but he wanted to fight. The commanding general decided to move the headquarters to An Khe, where the repair shops were located, to start the rebuild. The Boss was very unhappy with the move because it made him look like a maintenance officer rather than a combat commander, but the move was essential. It put him in a bad mood. He found a place that suited him down by the stream that ran through the camp. Streams have one very bad characteristic—they are always the lowest point in the area. In the case of An Khe, it also put us directly behind Hong Kong Mountain, a cone-shaped peak a thousand feet high and on a straight line to Action, Schuller, and Blackhawk, nearly fifty miles north on the other side of the Mang Yang Pass. That was asking a lot of radios designed for a thirty-mile line of sight. I was not invited on the reconnaissance team that picked our site, but the colonel was. When we set up the command post radios they couldn't reach Blackhawk and barely contacted Action. It was certainly not going to be loud and clear communications, as specified. I told Pat Long we had to move up the road two hundred yards to an abandoned command post across from the motor pool. "Sir, I tested the radios from up there on the rise and I am good to Blackhawk."

Pat knew the value of good communications and he didn't like it down by the water with all the mosquitoes. He called the Old Man on the road and told him what I proposed. Within ten minutes the Old Man came storming into the command post and yelled at me, throwing his steel helmet on the floor. "Who is commaden this here squadron, me or the commo officer, sir?" My explanation made no impression. Pat tried to back me but he caught hell. Finally the commander turned to me in front of all the people in the room and directed me to make the communications operate that night or I would be relieved. He stalked out.

"Pat, there is only one way. I have to install a fifty-foot telephone pole part of the way up this hill and run a transmission remote to you."

"Do it, Fitz."

Before dawn I located a new telephone pole and set it in the muddy ground with the help of a power-auger borrowed from the Signal battalion. It was raining with lightning flashing. Private First Class Zimmerman, a former pole lineman from the telephone company in De Kalb, Illinois, was the only one capable of climbing the pole and installing a six-foot steel mast with an antenna on top. Or as he called it, "Captain, you want me to climb this pole in a storm and attach this here lightning rod to the top?"

"It's okay, I'll go with you."

"Well, sir, two fools is better than one."

It was the pole orchard all over again, from my days at

Fort Monmouth. He went up first and I followed. The pole was wet and the coating of black sticky creosote made it slippery. Together we climbed to the top, trailing a rope which was attached to the antenna on the ground. The other members of the little platoon watched and planned to pick up the pieces. We were wet clear through and cold from the mountain air. Spotlights from tanks kept us illuminated on the big black shaft. It took an hour to screw in the bracket and haul the pieces to the top. When it was all over and we were on our way down on rubber-band legs, Zimmerman said, "When we leave this place let's not look up and remember we have to come back and get this son of a bitch. Just leave it, Captain. I'll steal you another one."

The decision to fight the war with the Regular Army and draftee soldiers rather than making a commitment to the conflict by bringing in the Army Reserves and National Guard, thereby involving the nation, was the President's. Because of the draft-exempt categories for students and others, the active Army was filled with many unqualified personnel. Many were high school dropouts, and a large number of category-four people—those who had very low IQs—were pushed through basic training and into combat units. They required a great deal of supervision which, in time of war, was a luxury we could not afford. Even a technical branch like mine received its share. Mine was PFC Grif Hornby. He was a good kid, always happy and eager, but life was a challenge for him. At nineteen, "Horny," a handle he *liked*, didn't believe in bathing and kept his area of the bunker in total disarray. He was always happy as long as he didn't have to do anything other than clean equipment or drive the jeep. He was unable to read or write but, to my surprise, had a high school diploma. One of the other soldiers, a dropout, had to read him his letters from his mother and write his letters home, which were dictated in appalling English. Horny would boast to his mentor about having graduated from high school, which never ceased to irritate me.

One day I was hard-pressed to get the encryption codes out to the troop headquarters at the firebases. Horny was my only choice. I stuffed the pages of code into big brown paper envelopes and scribed on the outside of each a single letter, A, B, or C. Off he went in the jeep, up the road, attached to the end of a motor convoy. The next day I paid for my mistake. The units were in C, A, B order as he passed, and since he could not tell the difference between the letters, dealt them off the top.

When a later President offered the Army a smaller all-volunteer force with no category three or four recruits and a reduction from one million to seven hundred thousand, the Pentagon jumped at the offer. The new high-tech army of the eighties could not stand any more Hornys. Having said that, I must add that most of the draftees were great soldiers, some were very well educated, and many had college degrees. It was not unusual to find that the company clerk had a masters in English and was putting in his time like a good citizen, serving his country. As a rule they were encouraged to attend Officers Candidate School in the States and spend two years as lieutenants before going into the Reserves in their hometowns. The draft had advantages and disadvantages. By the end of the war five million had served in the Southeast Asian theater, most of whom were drafted.

A Troop was in the worst shape. The first sergeant told me that they had no idea how many troopers were assigned to it. Its records were so screwed up that they didn't even know who was on leave and who had rotated home at the end of a tour. The troops' equipment was nearly all inoperable. In the previous thirty days, *three* commanders had been relieved by the squadron commander. The job was even offered to our logistics officer. It was a plum to have command of a troop in combat, but he turned it down. At last a captain from the division headquarters, Jorge Ramirez, took command. On his second tour, Jorge was a combat veteran from the 1st Cavalry Division. Married and with five sons, he was capable of handling any challenge. Small, almost diminutive, he was an optimist. The holder of the Silver Star for gallantry and a Purple Heart, he carried the kind of credentials needed. I liked him and his attitude; anyone who could smile in that position was worth loyalty. One week later the Old Man got mad at him and told Pat Long he was going to relieve the new commander. The five of us, the officers of the headquarters, went to see Culpepper that evening. We pledged to help Jorge in every area, but we could not stand to have another relief. The Boss backed down.

One afternoon, while on the road, I got a call from the colonel to meet him at Firebase Action, which was only minutes away from my daily trek down the highway. When I arrived he was waiting for me in the troop command post. Outraged, and in front of officers and enlisted, he demanded that I fix the two radios in his jeep. "Huow do youu expect me to command when the radios don't wurk, Captain?" I had two good radios in my jeep and offered to exchange them and take his back to my repair shop.

"No, sir, youu will personally go outside to ma vehicle and repair them where they are, yourself!"

"Colonel, I am no radio repairman, nor should I be. I have good technicians who can do the job and will return your radios by dark." Our equipment was interchangeable— I had well over a hundred of the same type throughout the squadron.

"You are not listening, sir." He pointed out the door. "You, and I mean *you,* go out there and fix 'em on the spot. That is an order." The threat was plain: if I didn't, he would relieve me of my duties. I was getting very tired of being threatened. The assemblage was mute. Even the troop commander avoided my eyes, with embarrassment.

I climbed the dirt steps into the hot sun knowing that I could not fix anything. I didn't have Albert with me. I was doomed. I sat down in the back of the dusty jeep and went through the motions. His driver had abandoned his post and

I was alone. I have always been lucky. It made up for my name, which the colonel delighted in mispronouncing. As I sat there I noticed that the antenna cable had not been connected to the front of the transmitter. Even I could do that. Ten seconds later I mashed the transmit button and went out to all stations. It worked perfectly. I called the headquarters of the division, the squadron, and each troop. I knew that he could hear my calls from inside the damp, crowded bunker. I hammed it up a little, running long checks on both radios. "How do you hear me, all stations? Check in." It was beautiful. Inside again, I walked with the god of communications, Mercury, visible at my side. "Loud and Kleer, sir. Anything else?" I won that battle, but I knew he would win the war.

The Cavalry lives on communications. Unlike the Infantry, which generally clusters and often uses hand and arm signals or lays telephone lines when stopped, mobile elements in vehicles must have radios. Therefore, even though the signal officer and his platoon are not fighters, they are vital to the Cavalry squadron. Like the motor maintenance officer and his platoon, our services make it possible for the unit to accomplish its mission. To restore the 10th Cav to full combat effectiveness, it was necessary to go to unusual lengths. I therefore decided to go to Nha Trang, a US coastal supply depot forty miles to the east, where the 4th Division maintained a small liaison shop of one captain and several sergeants who expedited the shipment of critical supplies directly to units. I took Albert along as my driver; officers were not allowed to drive themselves. We threw sandbags on the floor of the jeep to protect us against road mines. It didn't really work but everyone did it and it made us feel better. We were armed to the teeth with pistols, rifles, and a grenade launcher. The highway was known for ambushes, and since we were traveling alone, the road-control folks tacked us onto the rear of a truck convoy. Otherwise we could just see ourselves in hand-to-hand combat with a swarm of VC. Of course, that had never happened in a con-

voy. Transportation Corps gun trucks were spaced every fifteen vehicles. Now the Transportation Corps ranks *below*
Signal Corps when it comes to fighting prowess. But in
Vietnam, where there was no front line, everyone outside of
a base camp became vulnerable. Thus the gun truck, merely
a platform for defensive weapons. Its evolution became an
art form at An Khe. Through some sleight of hand, ten-ton
bridge-carrying Corps of Engineer trucks had been pro-
cured by the convoy control people. They were menacingly
large stake-body vehicles, high off the ground and shod with
bulletproof tires. Massive armor plates had been welded to
the sides and back with narrow ports cut for machine guns.
At least six .30-caliber muzzles pointed outward and one
heavy .50-caliber was mounted on a turret behind the cab.
The driver had similar plates surrounding him with slits cut,
allowing him just enough vision to see the road.

The men who rode those warhorses—that had names like
Road Warrior, Hell on Wheels, and my favorite, Charlies'
Nightmare, painted on the sides in brilliant colors—were
more interesting than the machines. When drafted soldiers
were sent to the Transportation Corps as truck drivers, they
had mixed feelings. Happy to be out of the firing line, yet
chagrined to be so far from the fighting, they were picked on
by the combat branches as near-noncombatants. But out
there on the highways throughout Vietnam they earned
many decorations and often had more than their fair share of
contact with the enemy. I had seen them many times on my
travels in our sector and they looked like wild men, covered
in dust, hunched over their guns ready for a fight, as they
protected their fellows in the cargo-hauling business. They
were the elite of the Transportation Corps and walked
around base camp with an air of superiority, like infantry
soldiers. Their eyes said, "I have seen the devil and spit in
his face."

That day the convoy commander, a Transportation Corps
captain, found a place for us behind The Grim Reaper,

which had a painting of a silver scythe with blood dripping from the pointed blade. We would eat his dust, since the windshield of our jeep was tied down flat on the hood, but I liked being tucked up near his bumper. When we pulled out at dawn the trucks were piled with equipment that had been destroyed beyond repair. A few of the Dragon Wagons, tractor trailer trucks that hauled armored vehicles, carried twisted and burned-out 10th Cavalry tracks. Other smaller trucks were filled with broken bits of unserviceable equipment destined to become scrap metal. On the return trip the fifty trucks would carry new equipment, including tanks and armored personnel carriers, machines meant for war.

It was downhill from our camp to the sea, a drop of a thousand feet to the coast and the blue South China Sea. Each day the trucks made the run to the seaport and by night they were back, enemy or no. We sent up a dust cloud as the train of trucks went through the tiny village that bore the same name as the camp. Kids waved and the soldiers threw candy and gum to them, a tradition with the Transportation Corps that began with the Red Ball Express of WWII. At a known ambush point the convoy commander gave the signal for the gun trucks to cut loose with machine gun fire to test their weapons. A mile before we entered the zone belonging to our ally, the Korean Army, a VC rocket-propelled grenade team fired one at the lead cargo truck. It missed, went over the top, and exploded in the trees. The convoy shot ahead and the gun trucks went into action, raking the hillside with devastating fire. We stayed with the main body while the bullets stripped the foliage from the jungle.

The Koreans picked up the protection mission and we rolled on unhindered. "Well, sir, we can relax," Albert said as he stripped off his flak jacket and helmet and unloaded his weapon, which was stuck between us on the floor. I must have look very puzzled and he explained. "The Koreans don't permit anyone to shoot at their road. When they catch an enemy soldier, they impale his mutilated body on sticks and leave it along the road as a warning to what it means to cross them." Even the little bridges were clear of defensive positions. The only Koreans I saw were smiling comrades every few miles who waved to us from the tops of their combat vehicles as they passed. I waved back and soon took off my protective gear, put my feet up on the dashboard, and enjoyed the sunshine as we rolled on to Nha Trang unmolested.

I rode up to our liaison section and found that Capt. Larry Susman, Quartermaster Corps, our 4th Division expediter, was buried under a mountain of paper. I had come to get as much radio equipment as possible but I had no paperwork to support my needs. I was an amateur at the military art form known as resupply, and Larry became my only hope. "I will supply you with some combat loss figures by armored vehicle. That should get your foot in the door. From then on it is up to you and the storage-yard people to work out the details." Nha Trang was not only a port filled with commercial ships, most of which were manned by Koreans and Filipinos, it was also a depot of enormous size. Yard after yard, each fenced in and guarded, lined the roads nearby. Huge forklifts with giant rubber tires ran along at high speed, dropping off metal shipping containers, which were often stacked three high. Larry directed me to 7-B, the electronics cantonment. There I met with the only US type; the others were all stevedores from Asian countries. He was Maj. Reed Stephenowski, Signal Corps, who though not a field communicator had branched out into electronics development and supply. His red hair was cut short and his eyes were tired from looking at reams of computer printouts which told him everything but what he wanted to know. The large blue computers that lined the floor of the only building in the sprawling yard suffered from garbage in, garbage out.

"Fitz-Enz. I think I knew someone by that name in college at Virginia Tech," he said as he rolled his eyes to the false ceiling covered with white perforated tiles.

"I doubt it, sir. There is only one family in the US, and my brother lives in California," I assured him. But he persisted, sifting through the card catalog of his already overloaded brain.

"On to business," he said. "My problem, and therefore yours, is that I don't know what I have. The drivers bring the stuff in all day and my people never get time to tear off the bill of lading for input to the computer database. Only about one-third of the items ever gets recorded. Let's see, you want a radio, FM, field, vehicle, with mounts, and antennas. . . ."

The conversation reminded me of the time I went to the Quartermaster furniture warehouse in Japan to get a high chair for our new son. The clerk said, "Okay, you want a 'Chair, high, baby,' right?"

The major punched in the code from a listing and the computer replied, after much straining and beeping, "Zero Balance."

"We don't have any. Sorry."

"But you must have, it is a common item," I said in desperation. "My troopers need them. They can't operate out there without good communication. You know that, sir."

"Well, you're right. They are probably out there, but I don't have anyone who can find them in all that mess." Great, even the "officer in charge" called it a mess. "I'll make a deal with you, Fitz. If you can locate a stock of radios like the ones you want, I will split it with you fifty-fifty. But you have to give me the location and the bills of lading attached to the sides of the ones you don't take."

What a great system! It was an invitation to steal, and I accepted it, along with Sergeant Albert; it was a task right up his alley. He and I spent the rest of the day crawling over and around sodden packing crates out in the open and found more snakes than radios. Once he stuck a long wooden stick with a nail in the end around a packing case, right in my face. A dead greenish-red snake was impaled on it. "I never saw one like this before, not even in Louisiana."

I jumped back into my skin and said, "If you don't stop playing with those snakes, I will leave you home next time." We found a crate of antenna-matching units and one of connecting cables, as well as two boxes of auxiliary receivers. He even found enough whip antennas to refit the whole squadron, very important items, but no joy on the radios. We knocked off around eight in the evening and put the paperwork into the computer as promised. I spent the night in Reed's air-conditioned quarters on the beach after a great meal in a local seafood restaurant.

His room was twenty-by-twenty with two hospital beds and two large American-size refrigerators stocked to the brim with beer. He had a set of Quartermaster furniture complete with rugs and a television set which was receiving the new Armed Forces TV rebroadcasts of the news from the States. They kept going on about the astronauts back from the moon. I had seen them lift off the night I left and had heard little since. Reed complained about being separated from the action of the division and cried in his refrigerated beer over his exile. It was difficult to commiserate.

The next morning Albert bribed one of the Asian workers with a bottle of whiskey, and that worthy led us to the mother lode. There it was, a Conex container full of new push-button AN/GRC-12 tank radios. With the help of another bottle of booze, Albert returned with a trailer and we loaded it to capacity. Before I left, I not only passed on the location of the cache but suggested that the major employ a good sergeant, like mine, to help him master the intricacies of managing a modern storage depot. Back home in the bosom of 1/10 Cav, I was hailed as a true cavalryman. My reward was much more than I could have hoped for. Colonel Culpepper had been transferred back to the States, to the

Armor school. Nothing more was said. If that man had stayed on long enough to give me an efficiency report, I was sure my career would have ended and I would have been transferred to the ice cream plant at Cam Ranh Bay to make butter brickle.

The new radios were my introduction to the new commander, Lt. Col. Radford L. Knox, who had just arrived from the post of chief of the Armor Branch in Washington, D.C. He was old-looking (to me in my twenty-eighth year) though he couldn't have been more than forty. Shorter and heavier than me, most of his hair had long since disappeared and the little that remained he had shaved off; it was a nuisance to play around with a fringe in the heat and humidity. As a new guy he was constantly sweating, so he dried his head with a green towel that hung around his neck. He smoked a cigar, which was out more than it was lit. But, most important, there was a leprechaun sparkle to his eyes that made me think that everything was going to be all right. I could see that he wanted the command and that he was going to enjoy the 10th Cavalry. To him command was not a burden to be endured but a privilege. He spoke plainly and called everyone "stud." I spoke first in our interview, which took place in a space that he called his office, a room the size of a bathroom that smelled like one, which was off to one side in the command post. There were two metal folding chairs with a rickety field table between us. Seated on one rusted chair, he leaned on the table for support with his hands folded, like my father in church on Sunday.

"I will take care of all of your communication problems, sir." After thirty days of twenty-hour operations at one crack, I had all the confidence I needed. I was also in no mood to hear any more about "All I want from you is loud and clear communications."

He looked me straight in the eye and said, "I believe you will, stud." I credited my short positive interview to a pre-briefing by Pat Long. We had become friends over the past difficult month, even if I was just a signal officer with two extra bullets.

I did not dismiss Colonel Culpepper from my mind. I had learned a lot from him. Nearly all the lessons were negative and I vowed not to do the things he had done if I ever got the chance to command. He had been sullen, and a commander can't inspire without optimism. He was short tempered; that only caused those around him to conceal bad news that never got better with age. He was openly critical in front of others; that suppressed freedom of action. A mean-spirited commander did not make people stop and think, he repressed their creative impulses. But mostly he displayed a lack of job knowledge that could not be covered up by imposing his rank in the settlement of differences. But he *was* decisive; there was no dithering, which wasted time and resources. Clearly he was predictable, readable—there was no doubt what would be his reaction. Men must know how their commander will react. He never played favorites, dividing the camp into the haves and have-nots. Lastly, he had high standards and drove them home. Americans like to be associated with success: they want to be a part of a winning team. But his greatest legacy was that he mistakenly thought he could fool the troops into believing that what he did was for their benefit and that of the unit and cause. They never believed it. They believed, through witnessing his daily actions, that he was solely interested in his own future and nothing else. A commander is always in view, talked about and dissected, the center of a very small universe. He holds the fate, the future, of his men in his hands, a grave responsibility.

Lieutenant Colonel Knox lost no time, but rather than make a speech he gave specific assignments to each of his key people and each night at the briefing for all to hear they reported their progress, or lack of it. The mission was simple: he had gotten a "stand down" from the commanding general, which meant that although we still had responsibility for highway security, for the time being that would be done by two troops rather than three, along with several infantry companies. The squadron's energy would be directed to working on its equipment, which was brought into base camp and rehabilitated. For the most part, the troopers were added to the An Khe defense force to help guard the eighteen miles of perimeter to stop the handful of VC that infiltrated at night to scatter charges around unit base camps. Knox's first move was positive; he gave us a mission we could accomplish. Most of our energy could be devoted to fielding totally serviceable fighting tanks and ACAVs.

It put the burden on the motor maintenance officer, Ordnance Corps captain Hamish Patrick Gill III, a red-faced Irishman who loved his work. Besides me, he was the only non-Cavalry officer in the squadron. He preferred Pat, but everyone called him Gilly. He was born in Ireland and brought to our country as a baby by his parents, musicians who played in the Boston Philharmonic. He was also musical and planned a career on the stage after his three years in the Army. He was good at everything, with a zest for life which was infectious. One morning I was having breakfast with the staff in our meager mess hall when Maj. Pat Long asked where Gilly was. No one knew. The major went to the enlisted table and asked Gilly's tank-retriever driver. Young Sergeant Roper jumped up and said, "Sorry, sir. I forgot," and ran out, leaving his breakfast to congeal. Sergeant Roper ran across the road and along the wall of rusted corrugated steel shipping containers that held our supplies. Rather bored, we all got up and peered through the insect screens and watched his frenzied attempt to manipulate the combination lock on the outside handle of a heavy metal door. After several tries he pulled open the door with both hands, and out popped Gilly. There was some shouting and hand-waving; clearly the captain was not a happy man. They both crossed over to the mess hall while the sergeant continued to apologize. The behavior was bizarre even for an Ordnance officer, according to Pat.

"Here he is, sir," Roper reported to the major. "It's all my fault." Roper had locked him in the night before but forgot to release him in the morning.

Gilly took a seat and a cup of coffee. "I have been yelling for an hour, sir, but that lame-brained driver of mine forgot to unlock the door." To be locked in a steel box all night apparently seemed perfectly logical to Gilly; he offered no explanation. We all had little cubicles in the BOQ; no one had ever noticed that Gilly wasn't using his.

"Have you lost your tiny mind?" Pat interjected. "You could suffocate in that metal coffin."

"No, sir, I cut several slits in the side, well, small ones, for air." Then he explained more fully, seeing that we all thought he had lost his grip. "Recently I received a letter forwarded to me by my folks that proclaimed that I was the recipient of the estate of my great uncle, for whom I was named, since the old man had no male heirs. It is a cool half a million and a pub in County Mayo. I am not taking any more chances. No marauder is going to pitch a satchel charge under my bed."

Our troops were still out on the little concrete bridges over the meandering stream that accompanied the highway. They ran the road during the day and set up at night on the bridges to prevent explosives from being set during darkness. A tank and two ACAVs made up each team and they sat nervously in the dark, night after night. One evening around midnight, one of the teams fought off an attack and took several casualties. A relief column was sent out from LZ Schuller but could not make much progress because mountain fog had set in. We were all glued to the radio in our squadron tactical operations center, listening to the A Troop radio net as the defenders called pitifully for medical aid. There were two wounded, and the remainder of the dozen men feared another attack. Knox called for a medical evacuation helicopter from division, but they were all grounded. The fog was so thick outside out TOC that the sidewalk disappeared within ten feet. Then the medical service aviation company called and asked for the situation and exact location. We also gave them the fog density report all along the route. It was hopeless for a dustoff to fly to the rescue. The relief column was going to take at least an hour. To our surprise, one of the grounded crews said it wanted to try. During extraordinary events men do extraordinary things. They never should have been allowed to go because they were endangering a four-man crew to save two men.

"That is why we have medals, Fitz," the colonel said. "There isn't money enough to pay for that kind of service. The medals come after the fact because, as a leader, I must do something to identify acts that go beyond men's natural instinct to protect themselves. It is all that can be done, give them the title of hero. The men of that crew have compelled themselves to risk their lives for fellow soldiers who, though they don't know them, know them. If the crew survives this mission they will do it again tomorrow."

The guard at the front gate was told to open it and leave it open. He did as he was told and a few minutes later a helicopter flew by at an altitude of six feet, hoping to follow the road to the highway. At every outpost along the highway, troops set off red pen flares to mark the route. The reports came in, "Dustoff just passed by heading north, visibility fifty feet." The relief column was flown over less than a mile before the stricken bridge. At the point of attack a track was on fire and the flames aided the chopper's landing. The return trip was no faster and the crew had used up most of its fuel flying low and at times even hovered in desperation. Once inside the fence at An Khe, they landed on the main road and were met by a ground ambulance: they would take no more risks flying on to their airfield. The chopper could be recovered in the morning when the fog cleared. "No sense in taking chances," the pilot broadcast.

I had my own track, an armored personnel carrier with a red-and-white Cavalry pennant painted on the sides with a big yellow 10 underneath. It was a type 577, big and boxy, crammed with radio-relay equipment with a repair bench along one side. It was unarmed and I traveled in it with armed tracks and tanks to field locations when we moved the headquarters. It wouldn't be long before we were finished with the stand-down and would return to the standing cavalry mission of reconnaissance and screening for the main divisional force. Sergeant First Class Henderickson, the commo platoon sergeant I had misjudged at first, was doing a great job now that he had a chance to succeed. One day on some pretense he walked me over to the motor pool and when we reached my newly painted track, he didn't have to point out his improvements. There, mounted in front of the top hatch, was a .50-caliber heavy machine gun complete with armor shield. "Sparks," the nickname given to all commo platoon leaders, was painted on the gun shield. He had even added a padded jeep seat welded to the top deck. "You won't have to look like a supply truck anymore on road marches, sir; you are now the commander of a combat vehicle," he proudly proclaimed. It looked a little silly, the only one in the Army. If there was a firefight on the road, though, there was nothing silly about having another heavy gun. Of course, to fire anywhere but to the front I would have to jump out of the seat and follow the gun around, but what the hell. My new battlewagon was the talk of the troopers and I took a lot of kidding about being a pseudo-cavalryman. My sergeant's innovation was an attempt to join in. Others found it comical and suggested I write the Armor school about the much-needed improvement we had made. I even sent a picture of it, with explanation, to Colonel Culpepper, but he never answered. The man had no sense of humor.

I couldn't wait to fire the gun and talked Jorge Ramirez, at Schuller, into letting me come out and fire on his range. My arrival at A Troop amused the crews no end, but they took me and my guys out on the little range for practice. It was a real adventure to sit up on top and fire the large gun at targets hundreds of yards away. The .50-caliber machine gun dated back to before World War II but was still respected for its accuracy and punch. To the surprise of the watchers, I had fired it at ROTC summer camp and knew how to service it. Before we went home I had the driver teach me his job, which was strictly against policy, as officers were not permitted to drive. A real menace to traffic, I ran the machine in a wavering fashion back down the highway and through the front gate, past the military police without detection, but I stopped it rather too suddenly in the motor pool and nearly threw my driver off the top, prompting the colonel to yell from nearby, "Who the hell is that maniac? Get me his name!" As he approached I popped my head out of the driver's hatch, took off the crew helmet, and put on my own, with the captain bars sewn on the camouflage cover. "Oh, its you, Fitz. I didn't think a cavalryman would drive like that." He smiled. Nothing else was said and he walked off, shaking his bald head.

Every officer has extra duties. One of mine was as investigations officer. That is, I was in charge of any paperwork that required making a report to higher headquarters but that was not directly connected to the combat operations of the squadron. Within that category was "wounds caused by other than enemy action." The most odious task was reporting on accidents. Just before the refitting was completed, a soldier was accidentally killed by his best friend at a sleeping bunker at one of the pumping stations that serviced the fuel pipeline that ran from the port to Pleiku. The pipeline pumped alternately both aviation and diesel and was laid along the side of the highway aboveground. One evening a mounted patrol returned. The troopers dismounted, unloaded their rifles, ate chow, and went to the bunker, where cots and their personal gear waited. They spent the early evening listening to AFN radio and music tapes and prepared for the next day, or took turns through the night manning the firing position at the gate. While the three men were sitting and talking, one decided to clean his weapon. He got rags, oil, and a cleaning rod out and laid his M-16 on his lap to start the breakdown process. He somehow snagged the trigger of the unloaded weapon and it fired. People are always hurt by unloaded weapons, I found. The bullet went through the body of his best friend who was perched nearby. He died instantly. The next morning I was dispatched to investigate.

Private Billy Morris was the shooter, and he sat on his bunk in the same position he had occupied the night before. He was distraught. I had asked the chaplain to come along and help both of us through the interview. Our chaplain was a very popular man. A Baptist from Mississippi, he was under thirty and known for his happy ways and concerned manner. He looked more like a carnival barker than a stern man of a vengeful God. Rather plump, his red face and blond curly hair were more in character for someone wearing a straw hat and selling snake oil from the back of a wagon. The troops called him Chappy. He was a man of the people and particularly liked for the words he had painted in white letters four inches high on the metal plate just under the windshield on his jeep: A DINK A DAY FOR CHRIST. I asked him if that quote came from the Bible. "No, Captain, it is a corruption from the holy wars, the Crusades, roughly translated from Latin," he assured me. I was amazed that he could get away with the mobile billboard and wondered why no reporter had picked it up and splashed it across the headlines of the antiwar newspapers. Of course, the troops loved it. The officer corps and the division chief of chaplains ignored it.

Private Morris was too young to be in such a mess. While

Chappy sympathized with him, I asked the obvious question. "Billy, why was the gun loaded in the bunker? You know that it is policy to unload when you go through the gate."

He didn't raise his boyish face. "Sir, I never did, because if we were attacked in the night, I was afraid that in the dark, you know, in the middle of the night, the enemy could come into the bunker and I would not have a chance to defend myself."

"Billy, nothing like that has ever happened here inside the compound. There are several lines of defense before anyone could get to you in your bed."

"I know, sir. But I have always been afraid of the dark, and I needed some assurance that I could get to it. I rehearsed it in my mind many times. That is why I sleep with the rifle in my bunk." Clearly, he was still a little boy, afraid of the dark like one of my sons, and Vietnam really was full of boogeymen. Several thousand of our best and brightest young Americans were lost by accident in the eight years of war. The battlefield is a very dangerous place, filled with items of destruction that threaten not just the enemy.

Within a couple of weeks of our new commander's arrival, with the help of all the king's horses and all the king's men, he had put Humpty Dumpty back together again. We were sent back into action. Our new mission was worthy of a great fighting unit: We were to screen the flank of the division along the Cambodian border. In addition to providing early warning of a major attack, we were to prevent the enemy's rolling across the frontier in the fifty tanks he reportedly held on the other side. The enemy had never used tanks against us, but we knew they had the capability. And NVA troop-carrying helicopters made in Russia had been seen on occasion on our side of the border. Our aviation troop was tasked with their destruction. We were to block Highway 19, the only road to Pleiku, the provincial capital, and conduct search and destroy operations. Our base camp was to be LZ

Meredith at the head of the famous Ia Drang Valley, the site of a great battle the year before. It would be a ninety-mile road march for the headquarters, which picked up its three ground-mounted troops as we headed north and west. The motor maintenance shops would be dropped off at Camp Enari on the way. Delta Troop, the aviation outfit, would remain at Enari, since it was policy not to leave helicopters at night on a landing zone. The LZs were too remote and too vulnerable to attack, and even daily maintenance was so complex that it could only be done at base camp.

What a kick, riding in an armored column behind my own gun on top of an armored track. I was part of the first element along with the scouts and flamethrowing tracks. There I was, the Signal Corps in action! Well, the idea did amuse the others. We stopped at Enari to top off with fuel and meet up with the tanks for the final forty miles to the border. Once we were back on the road, the dry-season dust boiled up at me. We had no choice but to stay tucked up behind the scouts. I wear contact lenses. Even though I was wearing protective goggles, the microfine dust sifted inside and felt like needles under my lenses, so I took one off. I was able to keep one myopic eye open while the other, with the lens still in place, was kept closed but free from dust. I figured that in the event of contact, I would open the good eye and close the bad one to shoot. Thank God we didn't meet any unfriendlies.

When the track stopped and the dust settled I found myself on a hill in very open country. The jungle was sparse and low, more like brush, and the view was beautiful. We were on the old Catecca Plantation, owned by a Dutchman since before the turn of the century. Originally it had spread over Vietnam and Cambodia but had been abandoned some years before. I was told that the plantation was also famous as a private hunting preserve and that Teddy Roosevelt had once bagged big game there. The master of the move had been our indomitable logistics officer, the S-4, Maj. Jack

Sanhurst, a sprightly man who had been enlisted and was nearing his twenty years of service. He was a favorite of mine. Professional down to his tanker boots, he nonetheless was a jewel of good humor and common sense. Small, I doubt he had a muscle in his body. The picture of male pattern baldness, he was a match for the squadron commander, and Jack often pointed out, "We look like brothers," while smoothing imaginary hair from his eyes and giving way with a few chuckles. He was Pat Long's running buddy and Jack's offhand comments always made Pat laugh. We were relieving an infantry battalion on the site and Jack rapped on the side of my track. "Fitz, come down here, I have someone who wants to see you." That sounded ominous. When I hit the ground, I found Capt. Chip Traeb, my wife's cousin from Detroit. His father, Stan, a paratrooper from WWII, had been an inspiration for me. A million miles from home, and there was Chip in the middle of nowhere, standing boot-top deep in the dust.

Meredith was the Christian name of the wife of the commander who had established the camp, years before. I am sure she was pleased to have something named in her honor, but if she had visited it, she might have changed her mind. Miss Meredith's namesake was less than a football field in size, with outer limits marked by sandbagged bunkers that had suffered from the weather, a minefield, and lots of entangled barbed wire in rust-red hung with old tin cans containing marbles to act as warning devices. They were burning off the latrine pits as we arrived and the smell was memorable. The camp was on a small hill beside the road and dominated the valley. To the east was a high ridge that crested several miles away, and to the west was the intersection of the only road north and the site of an abandoned camp called Jackson Hole. That road led ten miles to Pleijarang, a Special Forces camp that had an airstrip. Ten miles farther west was the border with Cambodia, which was

watched over by the Duc Co Special Forces camp. We were
not allowed to cross the border, even in hot pursuit, but of
course the enemy had no such restriction.

Living conditions were not bad. All the enlisted were in
underground bunkers covered by logs and sandbags. The
officers were all aboveground that is, the half dozen of us—
and Chappy decided that we should have similar accommodations. None of us had the time to dig in, so Chappy and
his two assistants had the visiting engineer bulldozer, which
had come to cut an enormous hole for the four headquarters
operations center tracks, dig a second hole for a BOQ. For
two days he and others filled sandbags and lined the dirt
walls with empty wooden artillery-shell boxes. Chappy also
built Adirondack chairs and a bar. When it was finished he
had a housewarming and the good Baptist stepped completely out of character and became the bartender. Everyone
contributed one bottle, the price of admission, from the
"Class VI" alcohol store at Enari. He announced that whenever officers went to division base camp, home of all non-
combatants, they would not be allowed to land at Meredith
without ferrying in one more bottle for the stock. Fair
enough; we all agreed it was only a proper penalty for the
day off while others stayed behind to defend South Vietnam
from the Red Ho. The colonel ordered all the officers to
move in. He however would not; he preferred to live in a tent
next to the TOC. Pat Long and Barry Norton, the S-3 air officer, didn't like the risk taken by the Boss and insisted that
if the Boss could be so foolish, so could they. My tent,
which had room for four, emptied out, and I also refused to
move until the Old Man joined us all underground. The
colonel grumbled something about how our loss wouldn't
matter and left it at that. I sandbagged the hell out of the
sides of my tent, as did my two neighbors, and we all sat im-
movable in an attempt to get the Old Man to protect himself.
It didn't work and the next four months we all hoped the

Gods of Canvas would keep us safe. It wasn't really that risky; at the first shot we would bolt into the underground TOC anyway.

Chappy and I became a pair known to every trooper sitting on a tank or strongpoint as we drove the roads in the new area. While I gave out new crew helmets—I swore the crews used them as footballs—and fixed microphone cords, he gave out the Word of God and condoms. Pimps from nearby small villages drove the roads on motorbikes with lovely young girls and tempted our warriors well beyond their Christian resolve.

The sector was rather quiet and little enemy activity was in evidence during the day, but they owned the night. In an effort to include the Aviation Troop in with the tanks, Colonel Knox had their Cobra gunships stop and refuel at Meredith, a first for our pilots, who'd been tied to Enari in the past. It was a brilliant stroke. The Cobra was a real killing machine and carried two pilots, one behind the other (the copilot rode in front and normally controlled the weapons) in the sleek narrow ship, which had tiger teeth painted on the nose. They were fast, well over a hundred miles an hour, equipped with rockets and machine guns, and a 20mm cannon was mounted in the nose. Guns like those could change the complexion of any battle. No one other than qualified crew members were allowed to fly in them.

The first day on station, the Delta Troop commander, Maj. Robert Strowbridge, a burly, audacious flyer who strapped the machine to his back rather than merely climbing on board, invited the Old Man to take the gunner's seat. Knowing he was breaking the rules, which our commander loved to do, he climbed in and took instruction on how to operate the weapons systems. They lifted off in a cloud of dust and the Boss fired all the systems out over the perimeter into the range we had prepared to test tank guns. The troops standing on the tracks and tanks loved it. When he set back down, the colonel walked over to a private perched on a nearby machine and said, "How would you like to take my place for the next run?" The soldier was delighted. The Old Man walked the trooper over and stuffed him in the front seat of the war machine. The major then swung the ship out over the range and the kid fired the machine guns at the empty oil drums, tearing up the countryside with red tracer bullets. Pat turned to me as we watched the men on the ground, who had their eyes glued to the common soldier at the triggers of the skimming chopper. "Fitz, that, my boy, is leadership!" With a simple act, the colonel proved to the troops that they were worth everything to him and that he had them always in his thoughts.

The colonel worked on all of us in one way or another. At night he held training sessions in the TOC for every officer who had dinner with him. I was always there and sat in the background as the cavalry officers worked out the answers to the tactical problems he dreamed up. He used the map board, a list of units available, and estimates of what the enemy was capable of doing. After hearing Barry Norton's solution to one problem, the colonel turned to me and said, "You have been listening, Fitz. What would you do?" It was as if he had stuffed me into that Cobra. I saw the connection. I gave an alternative which wasn't of any consequence and the colonel expanded on it to give it some credibility. As we left, Pat said, "More leadership. How does it feel?" It felt great.

Within a week of the first sessions, I sat with Pat in his tent one night drinking some of his scotch from the cut glass tumblers he had brought from home. "Sir, you, Barry, and John Herman take turns manning the TOC during the night," I said. "After a couple hours of sleep you are expected to work nonstop the next day. You all look dreadful. How long do you think you can keep it up?" There was only one satisfactory answer to the question; they would keep it up until the end of the tour, at the end of their year. I continued, "Do you think the Old Man would let me take every fourth shift

and give you guys a little break? I would have plenty of
help—enlisted radio operators, intelligence boys, and the artillery liaison team are in there as well. They wouldn't let me
go too far astray. I would only run it for the first few minutes
of contact until the Old Man appeared. I could handle it!"
My hand sweated around the glass of good whiskey as I
waited for the turndown.

Without hesitation Pat said, "Sounds good to me. I'll ask
the Boss."

At breakfast the colonel said, "You have the duty tonight,
stud." It was that simple. He threw a pair of miniature gold
cavalry sabers across the table, one of his sets, that had a
number 10 above the crossed blades. "But you will have to
take off those damn Signal flags; they scare the troops."

My first night on duty was quiet. The tactical operations
center consisted of four 577 armored personnel carriers
backed together into a pit, two on each side, with a wooden
plank floor in the center covered over by logs and sandbags.
The one entrance was down a set of steep stairs made from
wooden ammo boxes. At the top was the colonel's tent, Pat's,
and mine. The Central Highlands are hot during the day and
cold at night. On my bunk was an arctic sleeping bag so I
had never really noticed the cold. By two in the morning I
was freezing down below and was lent a blanket to wrap up
in. The radio operators kept in constant contact with the
troop headquarters and their patrols. The intelligence boys
monitored the division net and took in the teletype estimates
all night long. The artillery kept track of the harassment and
interdiction (H&I) fire from batteries within our area. Something was always happening. The three 175mm guns at our
location fired at least every hour. They were the largest in
the Army inventory and could shoot twenty miles. One was
next to my tent and I got so used to the shooting that I slept
right through the barrages. The artillery liaison officer was
Running Bear, his radio call sign so descriptive that it
was used instead of his name, which I can't remember. He

was fresh out of school at Fort Sill, Oklahoma. Very young, he had a new wife whom he wrote to as Little White Dove, which he'd borrowed from a song popular at the time. He would study the maps of enemy activity from the day before and create a measles map of red dots which he confirmed with the operations officer, Major Long. After midnight a dozen or more targets were fired on by the guns all around, at intervals. Enemy prisoners of war said that such H&I fires were very effective and hindered their night movements. At times the targets were inspected by our patrols, which often found blood on the underbrush.

On my next tour Pat took the night off and went by chopper to the officers club at Delta Troop on Camp Enari. At one o'clock we got hit with a probe of our perimeter. I got in the thick of it, moving tanks to supress the intrusion. I was very excited while telling Pat all about the fray when he returned. It happened again two weeks later, when we received heavy machine-gun fire at the crossroads and I dispatched a platoon and called for supporting artillery fire. "Now look, Fitz, I have to go the division tonight, let's not have any more shenanigans—the only time we get attacked is when you are on duty. What does that tell you?"

"Beats me, sir."

That night we had heavy movement in the area and the colonel told me to call out the aviation gunships from base camp. It was fairly early so the pilots and Pat were all in the officers club watching a movie. Two of the pilots blasted out of base camp in Cobras and came up on my radio. "Long sends greetings. What the hell are you up to?"

"We have heavy activity on the road to the west," and I gave directions and the friendly dispositions.

The lead pilot was "Stinger" Savage, a captain and our hottest shooter. "I got a problem. My fuel is low. Must have taken the wrong bird." He had been in such haste that he neglected to check it out on takeoff.

The colonel said, "Our boys are a little too eager to help

out." He was clearly pissed off that they could only stay on station a few minutes and he took a chopper in the morning to check out the operation of Shamrock, their call sign, something he had neglected. Long came out on the morning flight. The two spoke briefly next to the bird and the Boss left in a huff.

Pat stopped to see me just before I went to bed. "You are getting a reputation for drawing lead."

"It must be the sound of my voice. I still don't talk like one of you cavalrymen, sir."

I got a night off back at base camp. Pat said he wanted to see if they would attack in my absence. They didn't. The next morning Stinger offered me a ride out in his Cobra. By then I had had many flights in the LOH and had learned to fly them for my own preservation. Even though the man in the Cobra's front seat does not usually fly the aircraft, there is a stick mounted near the right armrest. Stinger put me in the front seat. I was wearing the flight suit from my first tour, which made me look very impressive, I thought. He showed me all the firing controls and how to use the stick and pedals in case I was required to fly. I couldn't keep from grinning as he went through all the procedures, which amused Stinger no end. "Now get serious, Fitz." I did my best to concentrate. Fun, travel, and adventure, that is what I had signed up for and that was what I was getting.

Three feet off the ground, we taxied out to the active runway and zipped off with power and grace, not like in the underpowered bumblebee I was used to flying. At altitude, six thousand feet, I got my first lesson and took the stick. Flying from the front seat, stretched out at the very front tip of the narrow fuselage, unable to see any portion of the chopper I controlled, it felt like I was sitting on the end of a diving board. The Cobra's controls were very sensitive and I found that just a little squeeze in one direction or the other caused the machine to respond radically. Stinger handled the cyclic, used for controlling the pitch of the blade and the Cobra's speed, bringing us to a hover at altitude. I was amazed at the precision of control. He took over above Meredith and did some aerobatics, finishing with a hammerhead landing at the firebase. The severe dive pointed us straight down at Barry, who was sitting outside his tent. At two hundred feet, Stinger pulled it out and set it down with ease. When I popped out, Barry said, "Now he is an aviator as well. What else can we expect from this boy wonder?"

"You can expect me to get back into this thing and go back to Enari; this is my day off." On the return trip in the Cobra I got to fire on the range. It was so much more sophisticated compared to my days lying on the floor of a Huey gunship while the door gunners, like ghosts from the days of the B-17 waist gunners, sprayed without the benefit of a real gunsight. In the Cobra I just pointed the sight that swung down in front of me, then squeezed the trigger; the servomechanism did all the work.

We landed back home and Stinger slid it over to the fuel pit. "After the talk I had with the Boss last week it has to be topped off." Then he added, "The colonel told me that after the other night when you and I had that fuel problem, you should get a chance to appreciate the Cobra."

I saw it all clearly—the ride was part of my training program, signal officer to cavalry officer in one tour. That was impossible. "This is going to be a hot refueling, Fitz. You hold it in a hover while I get out and put the gas in."

"No, man, no," I spouted into the intercom.

"There is nothing to it, just hold it steady." He turned the controls over to me. I froze at the controls as the engine roared. When he jumped off the skid on one side it unbalanced the bird, which slipped to one side. I corrected for the movement, that is I overcorrected. It swung back. I overcorrected again, and it swung out even more. Soon the Cobra was swinging side to side. Stinger dropped the nozzle and jumped back on the skid and into the cockpit. He managed to take back control and put it down. "Well done for your first time," he said. Sweat was running out of my every pore. My grip on the stick must have been white-knuckle under the aviation gloves. "Let go! It is okay. Just let go of the stick!" my pilot ordered.

Combat is a funny thing. Each morning, girded in flak jacket and a steel helmet, one of the four shift officers would get in a LOH, sit on an armored plate, and, armed with a machine gun, perform an early morning reconnaissance of the local area. Above him would be two Cobras and a chase ship to pick up anyone shot down. A box of white phosphorus grenades was attached to the outside of the door and if he saw any enemy from the altitude of fifty feet would drop a grenade to mark the spot with thick white smoke. The gunship would come in behind and hose down the area. It was dangerous, goading the enemy to fire at the low-flying intruder. At six o'clock in the evening one of the same officers or the colonel would take the same helicopter out alone, no helmet, no flak jacket or armor plate. Armed only with a Browning pump-shotgun he would hunt peacock, which is nothing more than a very big pheasant, for the dinner table. One day the peacocks got their revenge. While hunting in the treetops the eighty-five-mile-an-hour chopper met a thirty-mile-per-hour peacock, head on. The collision broke out the LOH's entire Plexiglas bubble, which crashed into the trees. The only real casualty was the peacock. It was delicious.

Just before dark we would put out snipers who would take up concealed sites along the road and wait with "starlight scope" night-vision devices for the enemy to attempt to plant antitank mines in the highway. It was nerve-racking work and the snipers had special training to operate alone. Once an hour we would make a radio call to see that they were all right. They wore a headset rather than use the speaker, which would have been heard for a mile at night. They would not speak into the microphone, but press the transmit button once for yes and twice for no. In the TOC the operator would ask questions and listen for the breaking of squelch, the interruption in the static always present when no one was transmitting. The sound was a "tch" when the button was pushed. I was on duty when the radio operator said, "Something is wrong with post number one, Captain. I asked him if everything was all right and got a 'no' back. I asked if the enemy was nearby and got another 'no.' I asked him if he could speak into the radio and tell me what the problem was and got another 'no.'"

I was also concerned. "Ask him if he has moved location."

The answer was *tch, tch.* I told someone to get the Boss and Major Long. They were there in a flash, knowing that I didn't cry wolf and half expecting trouble anyway since I was on duty.

Pat said, "Are you at it again, Fitz?" which I expected. We were all perplexed and repeated the questions for the colonel's benefit. The "no" answers came back again.

The colonel said, "Ask him if he is hurt."

Tch, tch. Long said, "He is all right, no enemy, he can't speak, hasn't had to move, and isn't hurt."

"Ask him if he wants us to keep transmitting to him," the colonel directed.

Tch. We were all bewildered—this had never happened before.

Pat picked up the microphone. "Do you want us to come out and pick you up?" *Tch.*

Knox said, "Get a tank and two ACAVs out there right now!" Within ten minutes the sniper was safely inside the track and on his way to the TOC. He came clattering down the steps with all his equipment and reported to the commander. "Well, stud, what the hell is going on?"

"Sir, you aren't going to believe me, but there was a giant tiger sniffing my boot."

"Why didn't you shoot him?"

"What if I missed, sir?"

Terry Worth and his C Troop were laagered for the night twenty miles south at the mouth of the valley. The Gray Fox was working with his own intelligence sources again and was sure he was astride the main enemy supply route into Vietnam from Cambodia. He had little fights for several days and had killed a half-dozen VC, one of whom was a paymaster carrying gold leaf, which was used to pay for big items. The cache of equipment was sent to our firebase for the intelligence boys to look at and analyze. I went through the stuff as well, out of curiosity, to see what they carried. The gold leaf was in books, like postage stamps, in very thin sheets. One of the items hit me hard—a picture of a young woman and a child about the same age as my youngest son. That was the first time it came home to me that the enemy were soldiers, just like me.

First thing the next morning Terry climbed on a track and rode down the hill from his camp a quarter mile to a stream that had a small wooden bridge that crossed it at a narrow point. He dismounted on the near side and, while the crew stood guard, walked across the planks with his towel and soap for a long-awaited bath in the cold water, which was deeper on the far side. When he got to the distant supporting post, he draped his towel over the top and started to take off his shirt. That triggered the hidden enemy company, which had set up an ambush. Terry was shot through—an AK-47 bullet entered at his belt buckle and exited his back, on the left side. He was down and not moving as the track stormed across the bridge and stopped just ahead of where he lay. Two troopers dropped the track's back gate to pick up their wounded commander while the others returned fire and radioed for assistance.

On the hill, three things happened at once. The remaining tanks and tracks rushed into the battle, his platoon sergeant called for a medical evacuation helicopter, and the squadron, at Meredith, was advised. While Terry's track backed up the hill, still facing the enemy and firing, the morning resupply

Huey was coming in to his laager position on the hill. The battle raged below while Terry, given only the most rudimentary first aid, was loaded into the chopper for transport to the hospital at Enari. He was off the battlefield within five minutes. Colonel Knox sent Capt. Barry Norton to the site by helicopter to take charge and to assess the situation. Delta Troop was turned out, and four hunter-killer aviation teams were dispatched. A Troop was prepared to move in to reinforce them, a trip that would take two hours, at best.

Terry was right, he had disturbed the enemy, but they were about to pay for the ambush. Barry, an extremely competent officer, was appointed acting troop commander. He pushed the armored force forward and broke the ambush. The enemy scattered; they couldn't handle the shock action of the tanks. The new troop commander took over a very well-trained and cohesive organization and they responded to him as if there had been no change of leadership. Their blood was up; the Gray Fox was loved by his troopers. More than a little revenge was involved in the fighting. Each time an enemy cell tried to stop and reconstitute, Barry brought in artillery. The Cobras on high said it was like shooting fish in a barrel.

It was the first time I had seen the squadron in full action and I sat far away in the operations center, listening to the radios and watching the headquarters map portray the situation while the others put their skills to work. As A Troop came up, Knox maneuvered it into a blocking position and the force in contact with the VC drove the fleeing enemy into their waiting arms. The colonel sat in front of me in the TOC and took a moment to describe the action to me. It gave him a chance to summarize the battle, which helped both of us. Major Long pushed all the right buttons, acting out the colonel's instructions and offering advice along the way. To my surprise the Boss did not stir from his seat when the helicopter returned from dropping off Barry. He sent Running Bear out with one of his artillery controllers to give direction to the guns from a thousand feet above the field of battle. In similar situations I had seen other commanders, in the past, take to the air and sit high above and add confusion rather than help. But Knox had trained his troops well and he let them do the fighting. By nightfall the long battle was concluded, we didn't count bodies, only gave an estimate, but it was clear that the Viet Cong line company had been 70 percent destroyed and made combat-ineffective.

The following day the commander made two stops in his command-and-control helicopter. The first was with Barry, to hear his account of the battle and talk to the men. He took several Bronze Stars for Valor along and presented one to Barry and several to those who had been key to the operation. The second was made toward evening at the hospital. Terry had survived the vicious wound and the Old Man sat with him and told him the story of his gallant troop in action, which he now missed so very much. Terry suffered for years from his wounds but managed to recover enough to command a battalion and, later, a brigade. I saw him only once in those years, and he was the same as he was in the turret of his command track at Blackhawk, a leader, a professional soldier, and a friend.

When Colonel Knox returned in the morning, he brought with him our new squadron surgeon. We had not had one for a long time. Capt. Dr. Vinnie Calimaggio would be the leader of the medical section, which consisted of a sergeant first class and six corpsmen in the headquarters and several more corpsmen attached to each line troop. He was billeted with me in the tent. He had heard of the fighting the day before and had already toured the base hospital, seeing to those who had been wounded. He was a little shaken to find that rather than remaining at Enari, he would live and work in the field like the rest of us. A true noncombatant by the rules of the Geneva Convention, he could see that he was needed at our advanced position but would be of more help in a field hospital where the facilities were adequate. With us, all he had was pills and potions and a very limited medical track which was normally handled by the sergeant. But the colonel had other ideas. He wanted the doctor to see the troops in the field, where they lived, and return with an assessment of their general health. Men don't get stronger in combat, they weaken. He also wanted to show the troops that a real doctor was nearby in case one was needed. Knox was a believer in preserving the force and never risking life if risk could be avoided.

Doc was a chubby little fellow with dark hair and, for a surgeon, rather fat hands. From the laugh lines around his eyes I was sure he had a great sense of humor, but that evening he was sullen. All his questions revolved around the danger of being so far forward. I couldn't blame him for his anxiety. Outside of how to salute and wear his uniform, he had not received any real Army training. A doctor in the Army has no responsibility outside of medical matters. I confess I didn't make it any easier for him, telling him some of my most gory stories. By bedtime he was more scared than when he had arrived. He didn't undress or take his boots off when he got into his sleeping bag. In the morning the others were not any more helpful at breakfast and they turned him over a couple of more times: he ate very little. It was the standard "new guy" treatment, which we overdid a little. Doc, however, was no novice to blood and conflict. He had taken his residency at the general hospital in Newark, New Jersey, during the civil riots of '68. More composed that evening, over one of Pat Long's big scotches, he said, "Fitzin, that isn't Italian, is it? You aren't one of those northern Italians from the Tyrol, are you? There is a town that sounds like that near Innsbruck."

"Well, you are getting pretty warm, Doc. I do have some connection there, back a couple of hundred years."

Doc's first evening only lent credibility to the war stories we had fed him. We had movement in the wire along the orange sector, which started around eleven and persisted. The guys in the bunkers called in on the crank telephones. "I can hear them but can't see anything," a starlight-scope user reported. We thought the cause must be some small animal looking for food in the grass. But it persisted.

Pat Long said, "Get your rifle, Fitz, and meet me at your track." An unusual request; what were we going to do, two officers and one rifle? We sat next to the small front opening of the bunker and listened along with the others. Something was out there, just inside the lighted perimeter, in the dark, close to the inner edge of the wire.

I expected Pat to have that side of the defensive line open up and rake the wire with bullets, but he had something else in mind. He pulled a flashlight out of the baggy side pocket of his field pants. "Pass the word to the sector," he said, speaking to my platoon sergeant. "Tell them to put their weapons on safe and not to fire until we are back inside."

"Are you going out there?" I asked with more than a little wonder in my voice.

"No, *we* are going out there. It is our own wire, after all." I wanted to tell him that was crazy, but it was no time to be the voice of reason. I knew I must go in order to keep what credibility I had gained over the past months. I could barely see his face in the gloom as he outlined the plan. "We are going to walk through the wire's edge and see if there are any sappers crawling up to put charges in place prior to a ground attack." *Walk,* I thought, with our guys' weapons on safe—that only protects us from our own people. "You stay right against my left side while I shine the flashlight on the ground. Follow the beam with the muzzle of your rifle and if you see anyone, shoot him. They won't be expecting us out there with them and they will freeze rather than try to move away."

All I could say to his audacious plan was, "Right." We stepped into the wire, which was knee-high at that point, and began to walk bolt upright slowly along the front. Even the troopers thought it was a foolish thing to do as they watched. They were ready to snap off the safeties and cover the party that would come out to pick up our bodies.

There were no VC in the wire, we discovered. The troopers must have been mistaken. Pat shone the circle of light on one of our claymore mines, sitting on its two-inch-high wire stand. The plastic-covered, concave, command-detonated antipersonnel mine was filled with metal ball bearings packed in front of plastic explosive. When activated on command through an attached wire by the men in the bunkers, the claymore's C-4 explosive would propel the ball bearings in a thirty-degree arc away from our camp. "Just as I thought, Fitz. Someone has crawled in and turned it around." He was right, the mine now faced the men it was supposed to protect. If they had activated it in an attack, it would have fired directly into their position. Pat reached down and turned it back to the west. In the next few minutes we turned them all back around and went back to our starting point. "Tell everyone to take the safeties off, but I doubt we will be attacked tonight," he told my sergeant.

In the TOC, Pat told the colonel what had happened. "You took the Signal officer with you? Good thinking!" He laughed.

"Yes sir, I figured he couldn't miss from three feet." Pat smiled at me.

Colonel Knox turned to me. "You are a reckless officer, Captain." That was a compliment in the Cavalry.

I was riding in the chopper with the commander when word came over the radio, "We have a casualty near LZ Precarious." There were no details. The Boss changed course and headed for the little clearing cut in a thick wood on the edge of the Cambodian border. We were there in minutes. No action had been reported. We set down in the middle of a circle formed by the vehicles of the 2d Platoon of C Troop. It was another accident. They had found an abandoned village that contained a rather deep well. The platoon leader thought that it might have an entry into a tunnel complex near the bottom, so he decided to throw two grenades into the pit. When he pulled the pins at the same time by twisting them, thumbs through the rings, they went off instantly instead of after the normal four-second delay. His body was nearly destroyed, but that didn't matter; we knew it was Lt. Ross Campbell. He had been my roommate back at Blackhawk, my first friend in the Cavalry.

"This one is yours," the stunned colonel informed me. He meant that I had to do the accident investigation report and question the witnesses while the Old Man went among the troops to quiet things down. Most of us carried the baseball-shaped fragmentation grenades on our belts. The first rule was, never accept a grenade unless you personally took it out of case. There were several kinds of fuses, and one that had no built-in delays was used for booby traps and trip wires. Somehow Ross had picked up that kind. The troopers were shaken, and the Old Man decided to bring them into Meredith for a stand-down. Ross was a leader who would be hard to replace in the hearts of his platoon. He rode back with them and I was dispatched by air to Enari to do the report.

On the way I got a call from the TOC. It was Pat. "There is an enemy platoon in black pajamas raiding the village of Roe Doc." That was on my way. "Get over there and direct B Troop to the target. Delta is also on the way. Put them into the action." It couldn't have come at a worse time. I was not the one for that mission, but there was no time to stop off and give him the chopper. The young warrant officer pilot took it down to treetop level and we approached down a narrow river that wound toward the village. I cleared my mind of the report, and the sorrow at the loss of my friend, and rode well forward in my seat, rifle stuck out the side. I felt like the cavalry riding to the rescue. The dark trees were a blur outside as we reached eighty-five miles an hour. Our nose was nearly touching the muddy water as we rounded the many bends and the chopper lay on its side to make the turns.

As we neared the huts on the tiny outcropping, the people on the docks pointed to the north. I was first on the scene, but the foliage grew dense beyond and hid the ground. We buzzed around in tight circles looking for figures in black, knowing they could see us better than we could see them. My blood pressure was high and my heart was pounding in my ears. I heard the radio call of the aerial gun team coming in from the west. "I have you," the scout reported.

"Break off. We will take it."

I was disappointed to be called out of the action; I wanted some revenge for Ross. I wanted to get into the thick of it, then and there. I lingered and was told again to get out of their way. He was right, I was not equipped to indulge in single combat. We broke off and went up to fifteen hundred feet, where we watched the ground troop coming in, dust plumes rising from the spinning steel tracks where they made contact. Then the ground commander took over and we were out. We went on to Enari and the business of writing a report that saddened me.

Strowbridge liked the Old Man very much; they both lived on the edge. The major was only happy when risking his life and the colonel when risking his career. Born rule-breakers, they conspired to cross the border, insuring that no one in our unit—more important, at division—knew about the incursion. The commander wanted to look at the tanks division had told him about, and the major wanted to show the Boss that his aviation capability could do things the three ground troops could not. One night, dressed for hunting, they took off in search of "tigers," not a surprise to any of us. Naturally, nothing was said to division. They slipped across the border between the two Special Forces camps, which were twenty miles apart. The risk was of the highest degree. If they were shot down they would never be seen again. In that situation, death would have been the easy way out, but they both must have had capture on their minds. They had no intention of staying long. Like all good commanders, our boss wanted to see for himself just what danger his troops faced. He was violating a presidential order and if successful he could never tell of the exploit; that would mean the end of his career. He believed in civilian authority over the military, but he also believed that his organization needed to prepare in order to consider himself a worthy commander. He must have laid awake at night weighing the risks of the adventure.

The two cavalrymen were back before dark with a tail full of arrows. Long guessed where Colonel Knox had been. "Someone must have armed the tigers, hey, Colonel?" His suspicion was confirmed the next morning in his mind when an American captain from the Duc Co Special Forces camp begged an audience with the Old Man. His native patrols of montagnards, the aboriginal people who ranged on both sides of the border, reported seeing a lone American helicopter in Cambodia. The Boss must have had the whole picture confirmed in his mind. Nightly training of the staff increased and discussion of a potential enemy armored force was prominent. He asked the commanding general to come out one night and join in our tactics sessions. Not long after that two trucks loaded with explosives arrived at our front gate. Something was up. B Troop was moved to Duc Co. The troop moved out in strength and set up on the very edge of the border, which was nothing more than a line scratched in the dirt. The countryside was open there and one could see a mile or more into Cambodia, across terrain that looked exactly like that on our side. There were no houses or signs of life, in fact, one could easily have crossed over without noticing if it hadn't been for a weathered sign that read DOUANE, French for customs.

I had no role in the affair and concentrated on other projects. That is, until I got the word that the Boss wanted to see me at Duc Co. I had taken the ten-mile drive many times while looking after our elements strung out along the unpaved road. Road mines were always our main concern, so my driver kept our wheels rutted in the recent tracks of tanks that had successfully made the trip. We continually checked in on the radio so our location and progress could be tracked. I passed the SF camp across the road from a tiny dirt airstrip and went straight to the border, where the engineers were advising the troopers, who were digging holes and planting mines. The mines were aluminum canisters three feet high filled with fulminate of mercury, a very powerful explosive. There were sixty in all.

I was watching the work when the colonel directed me to join him at the troop commander's armored personnel carrier. There I met with newly promoted Capt. Frank Frisbee, who was famous for getting his track stuck between two trees. "I have a mission for you, Fitz." The words I had learned to hate. An engineer lieutenant, the adviser on the project, pointed to two small black metal boxes sitting on the lowered tailgate of the commander's track. "All the charges will be in by nightfall. They are fired by a radio triggering device." He pointed to the two electronic devices at my feet.

I got the picture; "radio" was the secret word. Knowing that it would do no good, I nonetheless said, "What has that got to do with me?"

"This is as far as I go, Captain; I don't know anything about communications."

"I don't know anything about radio detonators," I replied.

The engineer went on, "If it were a blasting machine or standard fuse I could handle it, but not radio control. I have never seen one before. Have you?"

"Never," I assured them all, looking the colonel straight in the eye, daring him to challenge my lack of knowledge.

"Well, it is time you learned. It is 'signal' equipment, isn't it? Radio is your bag." The Old Man kept eye contact.

There was no way out. "Yes, sir, it is. How do I test it?" They all shrugged.

I fooled with the boxes the remainder of the afternoon and found it was quite simple to get the firing lights to correspond between the two. My driver, good old Albert, and I set the receiver-detonator into a shallow hole in the sand and connected the firing wires, which led in series to the buried charges with only the tiny antenna sticking above the ground. I gave the transmitter to Frank and told him to put it in the turret. It was done. When those Russian tanks came rumbling across the line, all he had to do was release the safety and press one button, a red one of course. If he waited until the enemy column was in the middle of the field I assured him that he could set off one enormous explosion. Everyone was pleased. I nearly forgot about the "doomsday" machine, as it was called, during the next month.

I was watching my guys cleaning radios with soap and water and drying them out in the sun before going at their repair when Frank Frisbee came rolling up to my fix-it shop at Meredith. Covered with dirt and with most of the buttons undone on his jacket and pants, he was the very definition of shabby. Happy as usual, he made small talk for a while and I asked him about communications in his unit. He had the usual problems, broken microphone cables and weak radios, which could be corrected with a little operator maintenance. But detail like that was beyond him; Frank was a cowboy, a lovable slipshod of a man.

His crewman walked over and handed me the doomsday machine.

"Oh, yes." Frank cleared his throat of the dust accumulated on his ride in. "Fix this while you are at it." It was just flattened black metal, no longer resembling the box I had given him the month before.

"Fix it? I can't even identify it. What have you done?"

"Well . . ." he chuckled a little and flashed his biggest smile. "We had a little accident."

"Exactly who is included in that 'we,' Frank?" I refused to take the mangled fragment in my hands and therefore share in the blame.

He finally went to the point. "It was sitting on the back of the track."

"Did it get up out of the inside of the turret and wander off?"

"Well, you *are* making this harder for me, buddy."

"I hope so, Frank."

"You see, we were getting ready for the night and we thought it would be better to have it where we could reach it, you know, in case of a night attack."

" 'We,' Frank? One of your troopers is responsible for destroying government property?"

"Not exactly, Fitz. Let me finish. I kind of picked it up and put it on the deck. It must have been jarred off when the driver backed into the revetment, and he drove over the thing."

"Well, Frank, you got the 'it' right; it certainly isn't a radio detonator anymore." I looked at the black pancake he took from the driver and thrust toward me.

His tone became much more conciliatory. "Can you fix it?"

"No, Frank. No one can fix that. Not even God."

"Fitz, the colonel is going to be awfully pissed off."

"But, Frank, the general is going to be even more pissed off. I already checked about getting a backup unit, and there isn't one in the whole damn country!"

Action continued and our tanks were used more and more. The open country of the Catecca Plantation was one of the few places that could accommodate the sixty-ton M-48/A3 Pattons. One can't really appreciate the size and brutishness of a tank until given a chance to ride in the top turret. Of course, true appreciation can probably only be found in an enemy who has been chased down or rolled over by its immense presence. The main gun was a 105mm cannon complemented with a coaxial-mount .30-caliber machine gun. In addition, the tank commander sported his own personal weapon, a .50-caliber machine gun. The biggest problem with the tank in Vietnam was that it did not float. In an attempt to prove otherwise, B Troop bogged one down and drowned it. To come to the rescue, Capt. Hamish P. Gill III was called out of his uncomfortable conex container two weeks shy of the end of his tour and the claiming of his inheritance. He was not alone. He rode into the remote site, well within bad-guy country, with his right-hand man, Chief Noah Twohorses, on an M-88 tank retriever. B Troop provided three ACAVs as an escort. Even so, the site was rather isolated and Gilly was not happy. In essence, the M-88 was double a tank in size but not in weight. It was a tow truck for tanks and not a fighting vehicle, and was armed with only one M-60 machine gun, housed in the driver's hatch above the covered crew compartment. Its lightly armored sides could accommodate five in a pinch, if they all sat down. There Gilly and the three-man enlisted crew headed by Buck Sergeant (E-5) Roper, his keeper, and the chief were all packed in for what they hoped would be a routine recovery.

The tank had tried to ford a stream and almost made it before the engine flooded. The only thing to do was to haul it out and take it back to Enari, where they could dry it out and assess engine damage. It was all pretty straightforward and within an hour the sodden tank was up on the road and ready for the tow home. Gilly rode in the turret of the stricken tank, the safest place to be, while the chief and his crew connected the heavy cables and ran the twin tank engines of the retriever up to full blast. Gilly directed that they waste no time getting home before dark. With the ACAV escort in the front and rear, Gilly sat alone in the tank, on the commander's seat, only his head showing above the hatch. The incident drew a great deal of attention, and helicopters hovered above from time to time, and other elements of the troop came by to take a look and make a joke or two. The activity also aroused the curiosity of the enemy and they easily determined the retrograde route and set up an ambush with a few infantry and a team with a rocket-propelled grenade launcher, RPG, sufficient to knock out any ACAV and capable of damaging a tank.

The enemy sprang the trap, clearly pointed to kill the lead ACAV, but the round sailed over the top and impacted in the trees. The handful of infantrymen fired to keep the tracks buttoned up, so they had difficulty finding the RPG team. But Gilly knew that even though his tank's engine was inoperable, the main gun and the electrical mechanism to operate the turret were in good order. That was a technical detail missed by the enemy, who thought that it was truly out of action. Gilly, too, buttoned up. Then he clattered down inside the compartment and loaded a main-gun round, which was as long as a yardstick, into the breech. Back up in the closed turret, he looked for the RPG team through the vision blocks.

Meanwhile, Twohorses, a very big Indian indeed, knew he must come to the rescue of his friend, whom he was bound and determined to see survive. He pulled the only crew weapon in the compartment from the bracket on the inner wall. It was a .45-caliber M-3A machine gun, called a grease gun because it looked like one, which dated from World War II. Small and compact, it had a folding stock stamped out of gray metal. The weapon was designed for tank crews; only twenty inches long, it could be passed through the small hatch. It held a thirty-round straight magazine with short fat bullets that had a great deal of punch, even if it was rather short on range and accuracy. There was no safety, and the chief wracked the first bullet into the chamber and headed for the overhead hatch that would let him out the top of the still moving machine. The grease gun may have been small, but the chief was not. As he squeezed his bulk through the hatch, the trigger snagged, and before he could release it, the grease gun spit six rounds into the metal crew compartment with a deafening sound. The bullets sprayed directly into the floor and were embedded in the plates.

"Watch it, will you, Chief!" Roper yelled as the crew flattened themselves against the walls. Twohorses dropped back to the floor four feet below. "Sorry, boys." Then he exited with the gun above his head. To his horror he saw two VC on the tank going for the .50-caliber machine gun mounted on top of the turret. He fired half the magazine at the tank, which was invulnerable to its little bullets. The VC however were softer targets and both were killed. The big man danced out on to the back of the heaving M-88 and jumped down. He caught a fender of the towed tank and climbed on to take a position on the side of the turret to prevent other enemy soldiers from mounting. As the column rumbled on in the dust, it slowed as ACAVs slipped off to the side and engaged the enemy. Nearly blind inside, Gilly grabbed the firing handles, which also were the controls for swinging the gun, incidentally knocking the chief off the tank as he traversed the tube. Undeterred, Twohorses jumped to his feet, caught up, and remounted. He nearly fell as the tank jerked along on the tow cable. Once back on top, he wrapped an arm around the barrel of the cannon just as Gilly fired at the hunter-killer team in his sights. The kick of the barrel dislodged the chief and he was dumped off a second time. The RPG team was able to get off a shot that glanced off the rear of the tank retriever before Gilly destroyed them. Realizing it was hit, Roper stopped the M-88. What was left of the enemy ran off and the engagement was over. The chief was bruised but not at all broken. Gilly came up in due time and found the chief staring down into the open engine hatches of his beloved M-88. The captain went to his side. Twohorses was inconsolable. "They killed Little Joe, Captain, they took his head clean off." Little Joe was slang for the auxiliary generator crammed into the engine compartment. The only casualty. Soon after, Gilly left the Army and went to Ireland, where he took over his uncle's pub, fulfilling a lifelong dream. I saw him there in 1976, in Westport, and had a drink. The only thing he changed was the name—it is now The Two Horses.

We had an infantry platoon as part of the Headquarters Troop. The platoon leader's position called for a genuine infantry officer to lead the forty-man contingent. We filled the job with an armor officer who had been to the infantry school. In reality, there was no branch in the Army called Cavalry. After the demise of the horse, the name "cavalry" was changed to "armor," and Armor branch included the tank outfits as well as the former cavalry units, which were mounted in lighter armored vehicles. However, the officers who served in units called Cavalry refused to wear the symbol of the Armor branch, which had the front view of a tank superimposed on the old crossed sabers. It was a matter of pride, and the official Army turned a blind eye to the variant.

The Blues, as the infantry platoon was called, after its branch color, were inserted by helicopter and used to augment the armor force in dense terrain. The colonel found it advantageous to create a second platoon to augment the Blues. It was composed of cooks, mechanics, signalmen, and supernumeraries, twenty-five in all, and I was to be the provisional platoon leader. Even before it could be trained it was called out. The auxiliary platoon's creation was a surprise to me and Pat Long until the day came when the Blues were inserted and became surrounded. Rather than call on a regular infantry outfit to come to the rescue, Colonel Knox thought it would be faster to create one internally. We all met at my track and were issued machine guns, rifles, and grenade launchers. As Pat Long outlined the operation, for the first time in the war, I was deeply scared. Pointing to the map, he described the predicament, the location of the friendly units, and that of the enemy, a force of about one hundred that had been surprised in its base camp. My platoon was to be inserted behind the Blues, then move a quarter mile for a linkup and reinforcement at their present position. What worried me most was the possibility of getting my men lost in the woods and therefore isolated. Pat assured me we would be well directed from the air by the Old Man.

I outlined the plan to my three makeshift squad leaders, one of whom was my faithful platoon sergeant. "If you say so, Captain," was his only response. He too was scared to take on the responsibility.

One of the mechanics was opposed to the whole undertaking and as I briefed the men on the plan, he was open about that. "I don't want to go out there led by no Signal officer." No one joined his protest, and I was surprised at how trusting the other twenty-four were. We loaded up and waited alongside the helipad for pickup. I was nervous and went over and over the task and tried to anticipate what pitfalls I could lead the platoon into before we reached the Blues. Once we had linked up I planned to follow the direction of Capt. Les Morrison, the platoon leader of the Blues and a friend in whom I had complete confidence. We sat for hours and I sweated it out. Major Long came over near four o'clock. "You can stand down, Fitz. The tanks have broken through and we won't be needing your marauders." It was the best news I ever received. It was true that I had been with many infantry platoons in combat during my first tour, and had learned a lot, but that was no job for amateurs.

The colonel came storming into the TOC. "Major Long, I have relieved the B Troop commander." He went on at length about what a stupid son of a bitch he was and how he had risked the troop for the last time. I was relieved that it wasn't me he was after; Colonel Knox was something to see in full rage.

"That is just great, sir. Who the hell are you going to replace him with?"

"I don't care, anyone could do it better than Frisbee." It was true, but a replacement commander for a cavalry troop was hard to come by. They had been looking for someone for a month, but no one at division wanted the challenging job and there were no spare captains in the squadron.

"Fitz, I want you to take command of B Troop until I can find a permanent replacement."

"Yes, sir!" It was actually easier than being an infantry platoon leader in a way. Rather than being out in the woods all alone, I would be surrounded by a small staff that wouldn't let me go wrong. Long took the Old Man to one side. "You can't do that. He would be lost!"

"Nonsense. He is better than Frank any day and he has done it for two months."

Long stepped back in. "The troops won't like it. They know he is really a Signal officer."

The colonel ignored Long. "Pack your bags, Fitz, you are going out tonight."

Pat walked me to his tent. "Look, Fitz, nothing against you, but this is not a good idea."

"What should I do, sir, refuse to take command?"

"No, you can't do that, but tell the Boss you are going to need a lot of support. You know, make him realize that it is a bad idea." I was truly in the middle and didn't know what to do, but I trusted the colonel's judgment. Pat threw up his hands as he often did when trying to keep the colonel out of trouble. Then he briefed me in detail on operations and told me not to do anything unless he approved the action first.

Before I could get to B Troop that night, Pat found an infantry officer in the division operations center who said he would love to command a cavalry troop. Once again I was saved from embarrassing myself with duties that were clearly over my head. Of course, I would have had a grand obituary: "Signal officer killed when he led a charge that no one followed while commanding a cavalry troop in combat."

Christmas morning was hot and humid. I was sitting on the edge of my bunk when a terrific explosion went off behind me on the far side of the perimeter. The colonel sent

Barry Norton to see what was happening. "Fitz, go to the cook tent and make sure it isn't anything to do with dinner. Whatever happens, don't let them stop cooking." While I protected the turkey, Barry found that a tank, which was on guard, was undergoing some maintenance. A motor warrant officer and his master sergeant had been working on the firing mechanism when they apparently set off a main gun round in the storage rack. The tank was fully combat loaded and awash with ammunition of all kinds in addition to a full load of diesel fuel. The crew was not present and the two men were trapped inside the bowels of the tank. One of the rounds in the rack of thirty ruptured the fuel tank, then the whole vehicle was enveloped in flames. Boxes of machine-gun ammunition began to cook off and explode from the heat and sent hundreds of bullets in all directions. Barry was told by a soldier nearby that the men were still inside.

"With complete disregard for his own life," the citation would later read, he climbed on the back deck of the track and then onto the ball of the turret. The top hatch was open and so was the gunner's. Flame and smoke billowing in his face, Barry went headfirst inside, grabbed the chief, pulled him up to safety, and rolled him off the side into the arms of others. The chief was bleeding from a neck wound, the most serious of many. Captain Norton then went back into the loader's hatch and found that the sergeant was on the floor deep within. "In spite of the fire all around him," the citation went on, "he entered the inferno and pulled the second man to safety." The sergeant's back was injured and he was unable to help himself. With the men clear, Barry jumped into a fuel tanker truck parked next to the burning tank and drove it away as its tires began to smolder from the heat. "He then directed his attention to a fire that had started in an ammunition bunker filled with mortar rounds and bags of powder, extinguishing the fire." The tank burned for two days. Christmas dinner, however, was saved.

Before New Year's, Colonel Knox met me at the side of

the helicopter after my morning recon. "Fitz, you are a lucky fellow. Your name, though misspelled, is on the promotion list to major." I had been so cut off from the world that I didn't know a list was due. I was more than pleased. Barry Norton's name and several others in the squadron were also on the list. That is a great thing about the Army—it is so big that it is common for all qualified officers in a unit to be promoted. Therefore there is little need for backstabbing and sucking up, which is a way of life in business, where only one in a work group of many will get the big promotion. Promotion meant that I was going to be a field grade officer, one who wears the gold scrambled eggs on the brim of his hat. I had been on active duty only six years and because of the war, promotions had been accelerated.

It also meant that I would be leaving the squadron, because my billet called for a captain. After the party that night in Chappy's bunker, which flowed with champagne rather than the usual beer, the colonel asked me to come to his tent. He was in his cups, as was I, and he paid me a compliment. "Fitz, if you would consider changing branches, I can fix it. If you do, I will give you command of Headquarters Troop." Though he was clearly a little unstable from the hospitality of the chaplain, I felt he was sincere. It was a very attractive offer and one I should have taken, but I declined. I had made a good start in the Signal Corps and that was where I felt I belonged. When I told Pat Long in the morning, he was amused.

Chapter Eight

Another one of those personnel rules applied to me now
that I had completed half of my second tour in a combat
unit. I was authorized to pick any other combat unit in the
country and receive a transfer to it. No one was allowed to
stop the paperwork, and approval was automatic. I loved the
excitement and the attitude of the folks in the Cavalry, but
there was no place for me there now that I was to be promoted. The 4th Infantry Division was not airborne and
therefore held little appeal. I requested to be transferred to
173d Airborne Infantry Brigade, which was adjacent to us
along the coast, just north of the Korean forces. My request
prompted a visit to Meredith by the commander of the 124th
Signal Battalion, Lt. Col. Fred Fellows, the guy who had
picked me up upon my arrival in country the previous summer. I had seen him often in his office at division headquarters, where he was also the division Signal officer and
headed the communications staff organization. My request
passed over his desk, since he assigned all the communications officers in the division. His arrival was quite unex-
pected. He hadn't visited the Cavalry squadron since
assigning me to the job, which was not unusual; I couldn't

remember one visit from any staff officer. It seemed they were always too busy to come forward. We sat together outside my tent in the shade of a few banana trees, in wobbly folding beach chairs purchased at the open-air market in Pleiku.

"Fitz, aren't you happy in the division?"

"Sir, I am very happy in this squadron, but I don't want to serve in a straight leg infantry division signal battalion." Fred was not Airborne qualified and I knew he didn't understand the appeal of being in an all-volunteer outfit like the 173d.

"What would it take to make you stay with us?"

I shot for the moon—what did I have to lose? "I would accept the appointment to be your battalion operations officer, the S-3." That was the best major's job in the Army, very career enhancing, which was always given to the most experienced field grade officers. It read well on efficiency reports because the S-3 ran the battalion day-to-day and made the majority of the operating decisions. It was the 3's task to deploy the men and material into the field and provide the plans that governed all commitments. The S-3 was the heart of the eight-hundred-man battalion and operated on his own, with the approval of the commander, who was responsible for everything the men and unit did or didn't do. Several senior majors were vying for the coveted spot, but I put my bid in anyway. Because I was on the promotion list, my rank was now "captain, promotable," abbreviated to Capt.(P). Lists in the services could go on for a year or more before the recipient was allowed to pin on the rank and receive the new level of pay. It was a kind of limbo.

Finally, Fred asked, "You will stay in the division and withdraw your request for transfer if I give you the job—is that what you are saying?"

"I will, sir."

Without hesitation he said, "You have it. I will expect you in a week at my headquarters. Welcome aboard." He had

called my bluff. I would be stuck in the leg outfit for the remainder of my tour.

My departure party in Chappy's Bunker Bar was a happy
affair, and I received three going-away presents. The first
was a captured shovel painted black, with a silver plaque that
read: TO THE BIGGEST BULLSHITTER IN THE SQUADRON. Others
got captured rifles, but they said I couldn't hurt myself with
a shovel. The second came from Pat Long—a letter opener
in the shape of a miniature cavalry saber, with the words
1/10 CAVALRY, VIET NAM engraved on it. I still use it. Lastly,
the colonel gave me a set of nickel-plated cavalry spurs to
wear with my dress uniform. "Like all cavalry officers who
have served in combat since the beginning of our regiment
in 1866, you have earned the right to wear these spurs." I
have done just that over the years, though the practice is
strictly unauthorized by uniform regulations. Once, years
later, at the War College, I was challenged by a fellow
colonel and cavalry officer as I stood at a reception in a dress
mess uniform piped in the orange of my Signal branch.

"Where did you get the right to wear spurs?" he asked.

I noticed that he, too, had a set clamped to the heels of
his shoes. "First Squadron, Tenth United States Cavalry,
Vietnam." He probably thought I had changed branches after the war.

I moved my footlocker filled with the treasures from the
squadron to the Signal headquarters. Although I had asked
for the job, I was not a happy man as I stood on the helipad
with several other captains and lieutenants waiting for a ride
to inspect the signal site on Dragoon Mountain. I felt I had
deserted my buddies in a line cavalry unit for a support element, the Signal battalion. I was sullen, which didn't endear
me to my new comrades, but I couldn't help it. They were all
crying about how hard their life was at base camp. "You
guys are lucky to be in a noncombatant unit like this." It was
a stupid thing to say and it would haunt me for the next six

months, but I didn't really care if I was liked in the new unit or not; as the S-3, I had the hammer and I wasn't prepared to listen to carping.

The compound of the 124th was well within the safety of the huge base camp at Enari and had been handbuilt by members of the battalion over the previous four years. As a promotable captain I was given field grade quarters. That meant a private room in an air-conditioned building made of tin with concrete floors and my own adjoining flush toilet. I'd had worse quarters in the States. It would have been embarrassing to have friends from my old unit see my new digs. There was electric light and a real sprung bed with a mattress and white clean sheets. I preferred my old sleeping bag and threw it on top. I felt guilty. I had a real office next to the commander's and anterooms for my staff of two officers and eight enlisted men who ran the battalion control van that was stuck on the end of the building.

My experience as an assistant S-3 in the Cavalry working for Major Long and years before in the 69th Signal gave me the job knowledge I needed. First thing I did was tape my short-timer's calendar to the inside of the center drawer of my wooden desk. Less than six months and I would be home with my family again. Carol had been sending audiotapes of conversations at the dinner table, which made me feel I was there in spirit. She was happy that I was no longer out on the line. I didn't allow myself to think about them during hard times, but they always crept back into my thoughts during quiet moments. I had sent her pictures of me and my friends covered in dirt or sitting on a tank. She had reciprocated with photos of the boys at birthday parties. Now the end was in sight and I wrote more often and talked about our next tour, which I had requested be in Germany. There I asked to be assigned to the highest staff they could find; I needed time to come back to civilization and pay back the family time that had been wrenched away by two years in Vietnam. Branch had sent me orders to Headquarters European

Command, in Stuttgart, not far from where my forefathers had walked the streets of villages across the border. Perhaps there my name, a burden in the States and to the unhyphenated computer world, would not cause problems.

In Vietnam it was still with me when I met the commanding general on the mountain as he checked out the living conditions of our crews in the numerous radio rigs at the top. "With a name like that, where do you come from, Captain?" In front of my delegation, I told him the quickest, most abbreviated story I could. He, of course, was not really interested and just used it as a ploy to see if I could express myself coherently in the presence of the two stars gleaming on his helmet. It was, however, a chance to explain to him the essence of the lines of radio communications that spread out from Dragoon Mountain, like an unseen spiderweb, to every element of the twenty-thousand-man division. The links suffered from weather, terrain, temperature, breakdown, enemy interference, and lack of operator proficiency. He in turn explained to me and all those around the importance of communications to him. "Fitz, without loud and clear communications I cannot command this division. Nor can anything else be accomplished without it." That was true, but he could say the same about many other services provided by the Combat Service and Service Support units within the command. The Army in the field is a team, and some players are more important than others, but all are essential to victory.

Capt. Don Ewing, my assistant S-3, and I were birds of a feather. He had just completed six months as a signal officer with an infantry battalion. We spoke each other's language—we were both glad to have survived the line. His background was far more interesting than mine. A half-dozen years older than me, he began his career in the Air Force as a security policeman guarding airplanes in England, where he married and homesteaded. She was a beauty, from Wales. When the war in Vietnam started, he transferred to the Army Infantry. He was known for his karate skill, which surprised anyone who saw him. Though six feet tall, Don had small, sloping shoulders and a natural paunch caused by the worst posture I had ever seen. He was cocked slightly to the right side and walked as if he had no bones. He had plenty of black hair and a beard that required shaving twice a day, which he didn't do. Though in his thirties, his face had fallen into a double chin. Yet his eyes were as bright as buttons and he was never found in anything other than a smile. In fact, when things were very serious and he was caught in the presence of a senior officer, he would have to go into an act to appear deeply concerned. His first tour in the war, two years before, had been with the 1st Infantry Division where he was a lieutenant platoon leader for twelve months. "If you survive that, nothing else bothers you, sir." I believed him. He was the only captain who called me "sir," though it was not necessary. But Don was a professional when it came to soldiering. Only when we were alone, out of the job, did he use my name, and then it was always David, "a good Welsh name," he would say. Our friendship lasted a whole career. We were students together at Command and General Staff College, Fort Leavenworth, where I came to know his wife and lovely daughter, the pride of the Hunt Club. When I was a special assistant to the supreme allied commander in Europe, Don was the inspector general for all Signal matters in the theater. I had held the same job in the States a few years before and we exchanged the secret handshake on occasion.

We were fortunate to have Lieutenant Colonel Fellows as our commander. Unlike most battalion commanders, who were permitted just six months to make their mark, Fred was allowed to spend his entire year in command. He was not an expert in communications but he had the confidence of the commanding general and of the division staff. Fellows was a good politician in the best sense of the word, absorbing the bad from above without passing it down the line to his people. He had put the 124th in tip-top shape by using the talents of his people and supporting their efforts. A very mild man, he was a listener and known to take recommendations rather than put forth ideas of his own. The troops liked him and his officers respected his authority. In the officers mess was a wooden Adirondack chair with wide armrests. Someone had carved lieutenant colonel's leaves and painted them silver where Fred's hands rested. It was his chair and no one was to sit in it when he wasn't there. Not knowing the tradition I did once, and was told later that anyone caught doing that or wearing their hat at the bar would pay by buying a round of drinks.

Shortly after I joined the outfit we were notified that the division would be moving to Camp Radcliff at An Khe. It was rumored that the American troops were going to be withdrawn and we were preparing by moving eighty miles closer to the coast. I knew An Khe well from my early days in the Cav, so the recon there to find a new home was no problem. We picked out an old artillery compound built by the 1st Cavalry Division years before and began the move that would take a month to complete. Our Camp Enari was to be turned over to the Vietnamese Army and we were not allowed to take anything out of the buildings other than furniture and equipment. The loss of the flush toilets was mourned by all.

With troops from the division spread temporarily between two homes while continuing operations, the Signal battalion and other combat support units were required to mount day and night foot patrols. That had not been done before, since the combat units had sufficient troops and used patrols to train new replacements. In an effort to prevent the enemy from surprising Camp Radcliff, patrols spread out for several miles in all directions. The Signal troops were reluctant to take on the task, but one sergeant volunteered and took the duty for the first month. He would take out a group of six and be gone all night. In the morning he would return, clearly drunk. When I reported it to the battalion executive officer, Maj. Cass Miller, the exec said, "He is famous for it. He always stinks of liquor during debriefings. I have searched him myself before they leave and have never found the source of the alcohol. I have changed his exit point at the last minute and his patrol area, in case he picks it up on the way out or from a stash in the field. No matter what precautions I take, he comes back intoxicated."

I told Don about it and he asked to take the next inspection at the mounting of the guard. It took place in front of the headquarters building, while Miller and I watched from the stoop. Captain Ewing had completed the search and checked to see that all the members were properly prepared for the patrol, when he asked the sergeant for his canteen.

Major Miller whispered to me, "I always check his canteen for booze. I have even poured out the water and had him refill it in my presence."

Then Don asked the sergeant to give him the cleaning rod from inside the butt of his rifle. The wily captain opened the top of the water bottle, which was filled to the brim, and poured the water out on the ground. Then he took the narrow steel rod and punched it into the empty flask several times. The sergeant closed his eyes as Don poured it out a second time. Out ran Johnny Walker Red Label, in quantity. "Go fill it with only water this time, Sergeant." The crafty drunk had filled condoms with whiskey, knotted them, and slipped them into the slender mouth of the canteen.

In a way I got my wish to return to the 173d, which was responsible for the strip of land along the coast and the adjoining mountains. They had a special problem and Colonel Fellows asked me to fly out and see if I could help. It meant spending only the day, since he gave me a Huey helicopter to make the one-hundred-mile journey. I was eager to see how they were doing and what I had missed. They were set up at LZ English in the valley. Their signal officer was Maj.

Bob Heartenetti, a generous man with a full head of black curly hair cut down to white sidewalls. He sported a bushy moustache, the first I had seen in an Airborne unit. It hid a badly scarred lip, the result of a piece of shrapnel, which made it impossible to shave. He was kindness itself and offered me a cold beer from a cooler next to his field table. I wanted to catch up on the goings-on, and he wanted me to tell him stories from my days in the original brigade. He had a copy of the yearbook to which I had contributed and we went through the pages over the second beer. He had been assigned to help out on the current edition and I steered him to the photo company in Saigon, suggesting that they be brought up for a week or two to take pictures.

"The reason I need your help today is because of our inability to establish a good relay for our combat radios," he said. That was limiting the ability of the infantry units to move and still stay in contact with the artillery in the valley. The brigade had changed composition since I was a member. It was no longer an international force. That had ended on my last operation several years before when the Australians and New Zealanders had broken off and formed their own force. The two American battalions had been expanded to four, which made it even more formidable.

I had brought along a combination of radios and antennas boxed together, which I had used in the mountains to the east but no longer needed. We picked a spot on a high ridge that had an ARVN camp and I left Bob to fly up and install the equipment. He remained at English and when we turned the radios on, he was able to get through to his deployed elements. I said good-bye on the radio and got back into my chopper with a couple of my great technicians and headed home happy. Ten minutes later the big prop spinning above our head began to shudder. That had happened to me before—the last time it was caused by the pilot flying through the kite string of some children playing next to our landing spot. The nylon string twisted around the rotating main shaft, just below the blades, and was spooled down into the ceramic bearings.

The red master warning light, the "Jesus light," flashed on as we were at a thousand feet with hostile land below. The vibration told the crew that it was time to set it down before we came apart in the air and took on the aerodynamic characteristics of an Army footlocker. The pilot headed for a clearing while the copilot radioed in our position. We were armed, but what did that matter? We were alone and far from friendly lines. The pilot put the chopper down hard. He shut it down and we all jumped off and moved out in a circle of four, facing the major points of the compass, while the crew inspected for damage. My aircraft commander was beside himself when he discovered the source of the trouble—several bullet holes in the end of one of the blades. The machine was not really flyable. Help might be on the way but so were the people who made the holes. The crew chief came up with a solution. He pulled out a roll of "hundred mile-per-hour tape," like duct tape only OD green and much stronger. While one man pulled the end of the blade down as close to the ground as he could, another climbed on the pilot's shoulder and wrapped the tape around it, covering the holes.

"Is that going to hold?" I asked, not believing that such a low-tech solution could solve such a high-tech problem.

"Would you rather wait for roadside maintenance, Captain?"

"Not me; let's go." At that point I would have accepted anything to get us out of that menacing clearing. We all climbed aboard and he tried it out in a low hover. The blade was certainly unbalanced, but what the hell! We "wap-wap-wapped" all the way home. Duct tape: the handyman's best friend.

The following morning I found a present on top of my desk, left by the patrol that had come in after dawn. It was the head and last foot of tail of a giant boa constrictor. The mouth had been propped open by a new yellow wooden pencil. It was as big as a Rotweiller's head, eyes open and blood seeping out the back onto my blotter. Sergeant Felps, my former drunken patrol leader, was standing by with an explanation. "Captain, now you know why I drink when I have to stay out in the jungle all night." I sympathized. Once while trying to sleep in the pitch dark on the ground during my first tour, a boa constrictor had crawled over me, thinking I was a log. The weight was terrific. He was clearly traveling away and I didn't want to disturb his concentration by moving. Perhaps he was after someone else, poor fellow. In addition to the snakes, night feeders, there were many kinds of giant spiders and scorpions who found people resting and had their way with them. The enemy was not the only hazard.

"Sir, we found a small cave just before dark and Specialist Allen went in on his hands and knees. It was no more than a cubbyhole. He didn't see anything until he turned on the flashlight, and there it was, staring him in the face. He said he could feel its breath; the smell alone propelled him out, backward like a shot. We thought he had found VC, and we all pointed the muzzles of our rifles into the opening, while I tried to make sense of what Allen was babbling about. His description of the monster made me think it was some kind of dragon—you know, sir, like the Chinese have in parades. Allen didn't get a good look at the body. I got a long stick and poked it around. I heard hissing, and a kind of guttural groaning. I was afraid it would come out and find us at night, and I didn't want to shoot in blindly; we might only wound it. So, sir, I threw in a grenade. We knew no one would believe me; they would say I had the DTs. So here it is."

"Sergeant, you shouldn't waste this on me; I'm only a captain. This is a prize worthy of a colonel; let's put it on his desk, a going away present."

It was true, Fred Fellows's year was up, and within days

the new commander, Lt. Col. Anthony Holman, fresh from the Pentagon, would arrive. He was Virginia Military Institute, came from the Department of the Army General Staff, and needed the position to go any higher. He was, however, fully field qualified. To my surprise. Familiar with the unit, he had held all the officer positions in a Signal battalion before. On his first tour in Vietnam he had served in the 1st Infantry Division as operations officer and later as battalion executive officer, and our unit was a copy of the 121st Signal, down to the last radio and cable. He was eager. The difference between the two men was that he was a talker, not a listener. I feared that his having a captain (P) rather than a senior major as operations officer would upset things, but it didn't matter. It turned out that Holman was a one-man band. He had good ideas and knew how communications worked, always a shortcoming of Fellows. Just forty, he looked younger. His red hair accented by dark sideburns was thick while the rest of him was tall, slim, and very athletic. He was a runner. Most things seemed to amuse him and he laughed quite easily, finding humor in most minor tragedies, which in a unit like ours occurred twice an hour. Something was always out of order when ten wideband radio sets were running twenty-four hours a day. If it wasn't that, it was wet cable and scrambled phone lines. In an environment like Vietnam, command was less operating than an attempt to control disasters. A unit without communications was a unit that could not be supported in a life-and-death struggle. He took the job seriously but was not good in a crisis, and that was when other colonels and generals began to compare his work with that of his much-liked predecessor. He was used to success and became very irritated when his work was criticized from above. Colonel Fellows had always rolled with the punches. Holman just got punchy.

He supported me, which I appreciated, when the company commanders complained that I was taking too much authority. He waded into the troops like a bad feeling and talked down to them. He demanded that he check each radio rig before it went out on operations, which I thought was a great idea. The companies thought that he didn't trust them. However, he proved several times that equipment was out of order and would have had to be returned immediately for repair once it got to some remote site. It wasn't his job knowledge that they questioned, but his manner. He put everyone on edge. Morale was going down fast but the efficiency of the unit improved. Even Major Miller, the unflappable, showed signs of tension.

In my office, AFN, the Armed Forces radio station, was always playing in the background. The young announcer said, "US and Allied forces have crossed into Cambodia this morning in the III Corps area and are continuing operations. The incursion was authorized by President Nixon and will continue for thirty days." That was the best war news I had ever heard. For years the enemy had slipped across the border and licked their wounds while resupplying in a safe haven. The President's decision may have provoked a disaster at Kent State, but in South Vietnam it was welcomed and would result in the saving of many American lives. We had never been allowed to pursue the enemy across the border, a restriction absolutely untenable in warfare. We were in the II Corps area and I wished we had been allowed to cross as well. By nightfall the colonel called me to his quarters in an old house trailer, which he shared with the two majors, and told me to prepare the battalion for movement to Cambodia. The next morning we, too, would strike.

That meant moving the entire fighting force of the 4th Division over a hundred miles and into contact with the base camps of the enemy, which had hitherto been sacred. When the troops heard the news, morale was restored. Every man wanted to go. We would carry the war to the NVA rather than playing cat and mouse. By eight in the morning we were all back on the highway to Pleiku and beyond. The bulk of the fighting elements would go all the way, while the division would set up its main field operations center, the hub, at the corps headquarters. There, an American three-star was in charge of all Allied forces in the Central Highlands, an area that covered one-fourth of the country. His compound was Old French, filled with stately pink stucco buildings covered with red-tile roofs. There were twenty or more, all good size, some reaching three stories. Behind the main headquarters was a soccer field where I put ten radio trucks and antennas in place and fired up the new tactical operations center. An Khe would remain our rear area for logistics support.

While standing with a young captain, Bill Konen, a company commander, we watched the complex come to life as the wire platoon ran lines into the new headquarters, which was set up in a former ballroom. We were facing each other when he pushed me aside, took a half-dozen running strides forward, and grabbed a soldier standing on the edge of a trailer that held a large generator, which he was attempting to start. The private, having trouble, poured raw gas into the carburetor, the gasoline flashed, and the soldier was engulfed in fire. From my sitting position I saw Bill grab the flaming body and yank it off the trailer four feet above him. He rolled the soldier in the dirt and beat at the flames as several of us helped put out the fire. The soldier was black and most of the fuel had splashed on his arms, which took the majority of the fire. I had never seen anything like it. The skin on his forearms had curled up like burned newspaper, into crisp wafers. He was unconscious, thank God. Another accident—why were there so many?

Captain Morgan Smythe, an old friend of Don Ewing's from his days in the Infantry, was the signal officer for the corps headquarters. He was a rare bird. Like Don he had come up through the ranks. His father was an engineer from England who had emigrated to Canada after the war and later married an American, settling eventually in Albany, New York. As his father was a former officer of the

Yorkshire Light Infantry, Morgan therefore was born to his father's sword. The son was a natural soldier, but after a close encounter with death on his first tour, for which he received the Silver Star for Gallantry, he changed branches to the Signal Corps. He looked like Cary Grant but spoke like a New Yorker. Always upbeat, he offered to share his rather nice quarters in the "pink palace," the name given to the officers quarters. It was a quadrangle of rooms that opened onto a central courtyard that was shaded by palm trees. The pink palace had its own little club and veranda and was in the middle of the compound, quite safe.

Don and I took Morgan Smythe up on his generous offer and moved our packs into the cool, spacious room that had high ceilings with a spinning overhead fan. It was more like a set from Rick's Place in *Casablanca* than a hill in Pleiku. As evening approached, Don gave me the bad news. The commandant, some American "light colonel" (lieutenant colonel), didn't like having our invasion of the 4th Division staff upsetting his operation. He ruled that we should all be quartered off the compound in rat-infested buildings with great holes in the walls, nearer the main road. I was pissed off; I needed to be close by the soccer field. But the order stood, and all the sleeping quarters in the pink palace were off-limits to us. I got to bed down in a room that had a hole in the wall so big, I didn't have to go out in the hall to enter my neighbor's bedroom. The place smelled bad and there were no screens on the windows. The only comfort was a sandbag revetment surrounding us.

At six in the morning I was awakened by the sound of a 122mm rocket attack, big stuff fired from miles away. The Russian-made rockets impacted as lethally as artillery rounds, with plenty of fire and smoke. There was a good side to the attack, though—they were after the headquarters, not the BOQ where we were staying. The rockets were well over us and racing toward the hill. Don and I sat on the sandbags and smoked a cigarette, just watching. It was quite a sight as the rockets slammed into the thick concrete walls of the pink palace. Twenty screamed overhead, but no ground attack followed. The unguided rockets were easily dodged and the attack was just a diversion to draw troops away from the main effort in Cambodia.

In due time we drove to the soccer field and found that no one was hurt. One empty truck had taken the splash from an explosion, which covered it with little pieces of hot aluminum from the outer casing. Another had taken out the little club across from the room where we were to stay. We went to see the damage and how Morgan had fared. He and a beer were perched on a wall outside his room. Rooms were smoldering all around.

"Where were you during the attack?" Don asked the rather debonair officer.

"Oh, I was in my room." He pointed fifteen feet away, to his quarters that no longer had a roof. "I took cover under a couple of mattresses. I came out though when I realized my new tape recorder was on the table." He pointed to the only item he had saved. "You fellows want to hear the rockets?" That's right, he had recorded the attack and explosions on his Super Sony. He started the recording at full volume and people started to run for cover again. He smiled wryly.

We stayed at Pleiku only a few days before the division commander decided that fifty miles from the border was too far from the action. The main field headquarters and the majority of the staff would remain at Pleiku while a much leaner key-personnel staff would go forward to the Special Forces camp with its four-thousand-foot dirt runway at Pleijerrang. It was on the edge of the low mountain range that separated it from Meredith, my old home. I split the radio equipment mounted on trucks and took some out on the road, along with the twenty vehicles that would comprise the commanding general's forward command post. Without communications gear there would be no forward command post. The rainy season was about to start and much of the soil had become a powder which hung in the still air and heat. I relaxed on the road. My driver, Sp4. Abraham Simpson, was not as much in favor of the incursion. He was concerned about road mines, having seen the wrecks of vehicles dragged into Enari all twisted, minus their passenger, whom he suspected would look the same. "Mines are not a problem if you stay in the tracks of the vehicle in front of you. If he made it, you will make it. If he hits a mine, you stop!" That was the theory of mine warfare I told him. "Oh yes, never volunteer to be the lead vehicle." Abe did not see the humor, there in the driver's seat, gripping the steering wheel tightly so if he did hit a mine he had hold of something. It was like closing your eyes real tight just before you run into something—it softened the blow.

Abe didn't see the humor in anything. All my little jokes about wild animals and enemy patrols on the border seemed to make him tense. Abe had been raised in Iowa by his grandparents, who were retired farmers. I had the feeling that there was little amusement in their home on the prairie filled with the religion which kept the bad weather from ruining the crops. I remembered it well, having worked on a farm in Illinois as a boy. "Don't tempt God by showing how you are enjoying yourself or he will smite you for your sin of pride," were words to live by in my hometown.

My farm boy was in no danger but he was clearly not happy. "I hate the Army. When I get out, no one will ever know I was a soldier," he vowed, not taking his eyes off the rut in front of him.

"Nonsense," I assured him. "In years to come you will join the American Legion or the Veterans of Foreign Wars, put on your cap with gold trim and insignia, and march in the Memorial Day parade." That only made him madder. "Do you think all those guys in your hometown who go to the Legion hall on Saturday night enjoyed service life? They are all like you, but time softens the edges. You and your comrades will spend endless hours telling lies about your officers, the food, and the fun it was to drive jeeps."

My own cheery mood was about to be shattered. Our convoy approached the airfield and halted, awaiting instructions from the headquarters commandant as to where we would fit into the new tangle of tents and trucks. A couple of hundred yards away, Chinook cargo helicopters were loading infantry in great batches for movement to the battle area across the border, which was within sight. They were taking battalions rather than the usual companies, and there was heavy traffic as open trucks stuffed with heavily burdened soldiers rolled out to meet the choppers. A half-dozen banana-shaped birds were loading as a stick of four came back empty and began to settle down along the apron. A truck, fully loaded, jostled along toward a loading point when it disappeared into a cloud of dust created by a landing chopper. Suddenly blind, the driver stopped in its path. I could see the collision coming from my vantage point on the ridge, but was unable from that distance to do anything about it. Abe and I watched as the big cargo ship settled into the back of the stationary truck, crushing some of the men with the fixed extended landing gear. Then the Chinook fell over onto its side as the pilot felt for the ground in the cloud of dust he had created. While the engine roared, the giant blades flailed at the ground like a bird beating itself to death. There was no fire. I can't imagine why, but perhaps enough damage had been done to please the god of war. Many were killed and more injured. No reason for it, just another tragic accident.

My radio vans, carrier equipment, patch panels, and terminals were in the process of installation, but all was not well. The radio shots were marginal, and I called on Don back at Pleiku to establish a relay point somewhere in-between. That first night we were called upon to man a section of the perimeter. It was a burden and I stopped all work on communications. We resumed in the morning, very tired men running wire to all the elements of the headquarters. By nightfall Colonel Holman arrived and was upset by our lack of progress. Rather than accepting congratulations on the great job we had done, he received complaints. I was sitting in the battalion control van, an officelike affair with telephones hooked to each of our elements, coordinating, when he opened the back door. He yelled, "What the hell is going on, you sorry bastard?" and threw his steel helmet at me. It missed, clanged against the back wall, and ricocheted into Simpson's lap. Rather than give it back, Simpson kicked it under the table as the colonel continued to rave. He had clearly lost control. After asking all rhetorical questions, he slammed the metal door and disappeared.

The four of us in the hut doubled our efforts. As evening approached he returned, one for his helmet and two to call me outside and talk. He had calmed down. "I have solved your biggest problem, Fitz." Impossible, I thought: he was my biggest problem and he was still here. "A friend of mine is the commander for the sector next to ours and he has agreed to man our defensive positions tonight so you can finish the work of wiring everyone up."

"That is great news, sir. Thanks, I needed that." By morning we were done and everything was working at last. After a couple hours of sleep I walked around to see if all the customers were happy with our service. The headquarters commandant, a major, came storming toward me. Without a greeting he started in. "Did you know that no one was in your bunkers all night? Fifty yards of open territory, they could have run through here and killed us all!" I explained what I had been told by my boss and he said, "That man is an idiot! You can't believe a thing he says."

I went hunting for the Old Man with blood in my eye. I found him in his tent, where he was having two enlisted men dig a personal foxhole for him next to his bunk—the height of bad taste. One, a good officer digs his own hole, and two, he didn't need a hole to hide in during an attack. He should be up with his troops fighting on his sector of the perimeter. It was my turn now. "Colonel, didn't you tell me not to man our positions last night, that you had it covered?" He smiled rather sheepishly and chuckled while he drew back away from me. "I knew you needed the troops to finish installation, so I invented the story that you were covered." I couldn't believe the lie. The man was a dangerous fool who had violated the oath to protect the force that he had taken upon assumption of command.

When the troops found out what he had done, they were outraged. Later that day the colonel said that Major Miller in the rear was not supporting us properly and left to fix it. Word on the grapevine was that the general had ordered him out of the field.

I received a call that the corps commander wanted to speak to the CG and he didn't want anyone to overhear the conversation. I asked our general to leave his headquarters tent and come into the radio hut. I dismissed the operator and for the few minutes the talk would take, operated the equipment myself. All I could hear was our end of the conversation, and the Boss had sworn me to secrecy. When I handed him the operator's handset, I forgot to tell him that he must push the button on the device to transmit. That caused a little confusion for a moment. It turned out to be a three-party call. The three-star corps commander, my general, and the President of the United States, from his office in Washington. White House to foxhole. I was proud. It had never been done before over tactical systems and I couldn't tell a soul. Years later, however, when I was commander of the battalion that operated the Moscow Hotline, I was able to say, "It isn't the first time I have provided communication to a President," leaving it at that.

During the nearly thirty days we spent on the operation, my soldiers came up with a package of communications built into a conex container and helicopter-lifted it into the battle area. It was unique. Dubbed the Tactical Information Center, it accompanied the tactical operations center farther forward. My boys named it the TIC/TOC. The result of our attacks across the border was a historic breakthrough and the enemy was completely surprised. One Viet Cong doctor we captured said that when our troops walked into his underground hospital, all he could say was "Who are you?" When told that they were Americans, he said, "I was assured that we were completely safe, that your government would never permit soldiers to cross the border!" The only enemy I experienced on the operation was the weather. It was the beginning of the monsoon season, which started only a week after I arrived. At first it was welcome—temperatures dropped to human levels and the dust turned to mud. But I'd never seen rain like this. It came in torrents several times a day, while at other times it merely poured. I had given Simpson my rainsuit to pack in the jeep but now that I needed it, he could only find his own. No matter what I threatened him with, he could not come up with it. So my careful planning did me no good and I stayed wet to one degree or another for the duration. I vowed I would get him for that.

Thirty days later I was back, along with the division, at An Khe. While I was away, my end of the tin office building had been abandoned. Each morning from then on, when I came in, the green blotter on top of my desk had a blob of greenish-yellow crystallized stuff soaking into the middle. I would scrape it off into the wastebasket. It was the consistency of wet glue and nearly stuck to the ruler as it plopped into the container. After this happened a couple of times I figured that the night crew was playing some kind of joke and waiting for me to rise to the bait. "Abe, find out what this is and have those guys cut it out," I instructed my driver. He asked around the next morning, carrying it around on the blotter. "No one will admit to anything, sir." Half a dozen of my troops along with Don Ewing trucked in and gave their opinion before I cleaned it off one more time.

That evening Don and I were going over a plan about ten o'clock when he jumped off his chair and yelled, "What the hell was that?" There on my blotter was a newly deposited blob. It had come from the open rafters above. Don was pointing at the offending spot in the ceiling from across the room, where he had landed after two or three giant steps. He pulled my pistol from its holster on the unpainted plywood wall. I looked up from my standing position, and looped over the beam above me a horned, scaled tail hung just above the light. It extended three feet and switched back and forth slowly. I pulled my flashlight out of the drawer and shined it up. Leering down at us was a lizard five feet long, its sharp claws wrapped around a two-by-four. The light disturbed it so it hissed before walking the beam like a circus performer, balancing with the swishing tail, into the darkness in the direction of the colonel's office. "Well, at least he is heading in the right direction," Don observed. We figured he was eating mice and bats and perhaps we could induce him to enhance the Old Man's blotter as well.

"We will make this our little secret. Okay?" I suggested.

The next night was the colonel's birthday and the adjutant had planned a party in our officers club, which was also our mess. There officers young and old gathered in the evening and listened to the Boss tell war stories of his first tour with the 1st Infantry Division. The party was well attended, nearly every officer was there, and a lot of beer was drunk and the obligatory cake with candles was presented. Shortly after the ceremony I left for my office; I had work to do for a deployment. I hadn't been there more than fifteen minutes when there was a terrific explosion in the clubhouse, no more than fifty yards away.

I ran out onto the concrete stoop and noticed that the lights had gone out in the club. Then the colonel came running toward me and pushed by. "You son of a bitch! You did it, didn't you?" He went straight to the phone and made a call. "Someone has tried to kill me, at my own birthday party." While he spoke he looked at me. Behind me stood my crew of three enlisted men who had been reviewing the plan that they had helped write. He must have suddenly realized that I had been working and probably had plenty of witnesses. "Sorry, Fitz. I am all het-up. I thought it might be you since you were the only officer not inside." He looked deranged.

"What happened, sir?"

"Someone threw a grenade against the outer wall of the club." I asked if anyone was hurt. "No, the sandbags must have absorbed the blast."

I grabbed the big man by the upper arms—he was babbling. "If they wanted to kill you, sir, they would have thrown it *inside* or through the window of your trailer. It was just a warning!"

"I know I am unpopular, but why a grenade?"

"Sir, grenades don't leave fingerprints." The colonel then ordered B Company to fall out, had the men armed with loaded rifles, and had them stand with their backs to the club, on guard, while he continued with the party. Within the week he was gone, transferred to a hospital in the States. I don't know why he came apart as a commander. He had been brilliant as a staff officer for fifteen years. At first I thought he was a coward, but I finally concluded he was not. I had only seen one coward in my two years in Vietnam—a young sergeant who was hiding during an attack while everyone else was moving forward. I can only conclude that the colonel's undoing must have been the burden of commanding hundreds of men in combat and feeling that although he had trained all his life for the job, inside he knew he was not up to the responsibility.

One of the untold stories of the war was the enormous effort made by every unit I was ever in contact with to sponsor a local village. I saw it in the 173d, where troops who had precious little time away from combat duties spent it among the people, helping to make their life better. The Army called it the "People to People" program. Soldiers taught English, dug wells, cleaned up water supplies, built sanitary latrines, gave medical treatment, donated money, and showed American movies. The 124th Signal adopted a Montagnard village of nearly eight hundred men, women, and children who lived as aborigines much like our own American Indians of two hundred years ago. The warriors wore loincloths and the women sarongs made from brightly colored cloth woven from the hair of goats. At ceremonies they carried spears and shields, but they hunted with rifles. They ranged over several countries, living in villages of stilt-houses with thatch roofs. Our village had a good tree, under which the elders made all governmental decisions. On the other side was a pit where the bad spirit lived. That was avoided by everyone. We had a group of nine volunteers who lived there full-time in a metal building that the unit had erected some years before. Sandbagged and bunkered, it was like a castle keep. There, a warrant officer led the effort and provided military training and arms to a Montagnard platoon that provided protection against the marauding Viet Cong. The warrant was loved by all the villagers, especially the kids, because he gave them candy and showed them American cartoons before the feature film in the evening. The adults liked the animation as much as the children and couldn't begin to fathom the James Bond and Matt Helm films, which were as fantastic to them as *Star Wars* would be to us years later. One morning after a favorite cartoon had been shown for the tenth time, one of the elders came to Mr. Lack, our warrant, and said, "America must be a wonderful place. Could you teach our cow to speak like the one in the film. I would like to talk to her and find out what her problem is. She has stopped giving milk."

At Radcliff, the sole base camp for the division once the incursion into Cambodia was over, there was a thousand-foot mountain with precipitous sides so steep that in wet weather only helicopters could resupply the relay site at its top. At the very top was a flat space so small that it could only accommodate a few metal huts, but it was key terrain because from its thousand-foot elevation, our radios could reach eighty miles in any direction. As a result it belonged to the Signal battalion and I appointed my assistant, Capt. Don Ewing, as the mayor of the outcropping. No more than twenty soldiers lived there full-time. Most liked the duty because it was a vital mission and they were rarely bothered by high-ranking officers or inspectors. Getting laundry done was the biggest problem because all the water had to be trucked to the top or brought in by air. The tiny mess hall had its own cook, but there was no place to put the garbage. The latrine was the worst-smelling one in the whole country, but it was a little cooler up there and the wind blew the smell away sometimes. It wasn't the kind of place to write home about, but it had its charms. A fat black cable had been run up the mountainside, connecting the radios to the keying lines in division headquarters. That enabled the center to talk directly to units on operation. In the process two line trucks had gone over the side of the winding road, their hulks barely visible in the jungle that was beginning to overgrow them.

Our assistant division commander was a one-star who, like all that class, wanted to become a two-star. Brigadier General Crandle was a nice guy but a little tense. For some reason known only to him, he decided to visit the top of Hong Kong Mountain. Perhaps he wanted to show his gratitude to those who stood the lonely sentinel. I sent Don up to be in place well before the general's lunchtime landing, to insure that all was well and brief the men on how to treat the important man. Don could handle any situation and was cool in the presence of stars. He told me the story after the event, that night at the bar in our officers mess.

"Fitz, the place looked great. The troops cleaned up themselves and the camp. The meal was steaks and baked potatoes, prepared outside on a charcoal fire. The general arrived right on time. There was a heavy crosswind and the chopper pilot had trouble landing on the small pad. Rather than coming straight in against the wind, like our regular re-supply guy does, he tried to set it at hover and let it settle. Well, it didn't work and he slipped to the side and nearly took out several antennas with the tail rotor. He tried it again and the prop wash from his blades caused a tremendous down draft and blew trash from the dump all over the place. Dirt, dust, paper, cardboard, tin cans, old magazines, and chunks of tar paper stripped from the roofs all went flying around like missiles. I had the troops all lined up, and they were pelted with garbage, potato peels, rotten tomatoes, melon rinds, stuff like that. When he finally got on the ground the place looked like a hurricane had hit. But you know, Fitz, he didn't seem to realize that he had caused the chaos. He was in my face from the beginning. I tried to get a word in, but you know generals. He suddenly had assigned himself a mission. He was going to straighten the place out, like some irate squad leader. He stormed off after reprimanding the men for their personal appearance. 'You all look like rat bags,' he told them. The chopper had also fanned the charcoal fire, and when we got to the mess hall, the cook was spraying the porch with a fire extinguisher where hot coals had been flung. Dinner was off but it didn't matter, the general was on a roll. He dashed between the buildings where the twenty or so keying-lines were strung, and some of the troops were using them to hang their laundry out to dry. A wet shirt flopped up in his face and he grabbed the clothesline with both hands and tried to rip it from its mooring. He would have done it, too, if it had been a real clothesline. But the wire only gave a little and then rebounded and threw him on his back. That's when he lost control. 'Tear these clotheslines down! Don't just stand there, Captain.' I could have explained that they were the keying lines that connected the division headquarters to all of its fighting elements in combat, but I was sure he wasn't interested. So I said, 'Yes, sir,' and called for the men to get out their pliers and we cut them all. 'Now get this mess cleaned up. I want all this laundry off the hill today. This is supposed to be a communications site, not a home for washerwomen.' I, of course, agreed with him and thanked him for his visit as he stormed back to the chopper waiting on the pad."

"Well, Don, that explains why the commanding general called me earlier. He said he had lost the ability to command his division and could I find out what the hell was up. Before I could get back to him the aide-de-camp called and said it wouldn't be necessary and asked me how long before we would be back in operation."

Not surprisingly, I never heard a word from General Crandle about the state of Hong Kong Mountain. So being a rather outspoken officer, I asked him at the division evening briefing if he found everything to his satisfaction on his earlier inspection. You see, he wasn't in my rating chain. All I got was a quiet "It was fine" as he turned away. The division operations officer, Lieutenant Colonel Farris, came up and put his arm around my shoulder. "You know, Fitz, you shouldn't tease the general like that. He is still smarting from being called a bonehead in front of the entire staff this afternoon by the commanding general."

All things end, good and bad. After exactly three hundred and sixty-five days I was standing next to my buddy, Capt. Vern Eberly, dressed as we were the day we arrived, in suntan uniforms, all our jungle fatigues left behind to be burned. We were waiting for the C-123 from the north to come in and pick up passengers for a flight to Cam Ranh Bay. Our short-timers' calendars were all colored in and our good-byes said. On the manifest at Cam Ranh Bay, for the flight to the United States, I was listed as Eng David G Fitz. Even so, I answered, "Yes, sir!" and got on board.

Vern had spent the year as the radio frequency control officer and assistant to the division signal officer in the headquarters of the division. At mid-tour, however, a crisis occurred and he was sent for two months to be the signal officer in an infantry battalion. He was reluctant to go out on the line because when I and others of my kind had visited once a month to get our new frequencies and call signs, we pumped him up with stories that curled his straight brown hair. It was great fun, about all we ever got, and he dreaded the day of our arrival, when he would have to sit and listen to tales of bullet holes in the canteen or shrapnel that scratched a helmet. We always brought him little presents, bits and pieces of smashed radios, and in great detail acted out the scene that had caused the carnage. When he returned from his time on the line, he treated us to similar lies, which got us involved in one-upmanship. We all knew that when we got home no one would be interested in or understand these vignettes and so they would have to be tucked away. They would only be let back out of the bag when we were seated in an officers club somewhere or over a desk at a distant staff job, when a fellow warrior would drop a strange-sounding name, then out they would pour. Ribbons, badges, unit citations, and shoulder patches could be read like a résumé by any veteran. From fifty feet away I could tell you the life story of any soldier just by seeing him in his Class A uniform. More important, by the absence of telltale markings, I could see what he hadn't done. It became important—often the credibility of opinions or pronouncements was judged against those telltale insignia. It kept people honest.

Millions served honorably in that war, even if they hadn't gone by choice. Today they live quietly and will mention that they were there only if pressed. At Frederick, Maryland, in 1981, I played tennis with a group of men in a league for a year before I found out that my partner had been in the 25th Infantry. I feel that those of us who stayed in the military had far fewer problems dealing with the private horrors of war because we were surrounded by fellow sufferers who coped. Their example helped others and we went about the task of changing the Army to the fighting force it became in the Gulf War, where only a very few were hurt on the side of the good guys.

When I attended the Command and General Staff College in the mid-seventies, it all bubbled over. Reform was in the air in the office of the chief of staff of the Army, in Washington. My class of nine hundred majors, all of whom were in the top third of their peer group, had spent years in combat as lieutenants and captains. We knew the frustration of war, because we had fought it at its most basic level, the company. Shortly after the year of study began, which concentrated on the history of warfare and would mold the future of distant conflict, our chief of staff sent twenty-five two-star generals to spend a couple of days with us and discuss the conduct of the Vietnam War. He warned them that they might be in for a tough time. We were all students and not beholden to any of them. Our commandant suggested that we remain professional, or at least civil, as one or more generals spent the day in our classroom of forty. At first the give-and-take was cordial, and during the break, since many of us had known these men, we reminisced and recalled old friends.

In my section, it all fell apart when a two-star insisted that all reporting of maintenance failure was true and accurate. That did it. We all had experienced the chicanery that was required to make the figures look good while we were compelled to circumvent the system in order to stay operational. The general ordered one man to "Shut up" when he strenuously disagreed. The section wouldn't take it and got up en masse and took a break in the cafeteria. When the fifteen-minute cooling off period was over, the section refused to return. Soon the snack bar was filled with other sections in similar conflict, and the college was brought to a halt. There was far too much at stake as far as we were concerned. It was time to change the Army, and this was the spark that began a revolution. I think the chief of staff of the Army knew exactly what he was doing when he sent his stars to visit, and he got what he wanted. From that day, I think, grew reforms, including central selection of commanders, realistic standards of readiness, the restoration of integrity, the study of ethics, and the establishment of professional goals. It took fifteen years and the slow but steady promotion of those majors, but the result was the force that, with the help of the Army Reserve and National Guard, produced a victory truly historic in its conservation of human life, the Gulf War. An Army is people with arms, not arms with people.

Chapter Nine

*What's in a name? That which we call a rose
By any other name would smell as sweet.*
Shakespeare

My name has always been an issue. It was either too difficult to spell or impossible to remember. On occasion it has become a topic of discussion. When I'm asked to explain, eyes soon glaze over, and I have learned that it is rarely a serious inquiry. In my hometown people were used to it and it was never important. Aurora, Illinois, was settled by immigrants from Alsace, which has been a province of France during my lifetime. In my grandfather's time it had been annexed by Prussia after the Franco-Prussian War. John Baptist Fitz-Enz had escaped as a student on his way to a Prussian military academy. His family thought that he, the youngest of six sons, should be a soldier; there had been soldiers mixed in with civil servants in my family for many generations. Well-off relatives in Prussia had enrolled him because his father, a poor gardener in a chateau on the Rhine, could not afford to educate him during the depressed days of the 1880s in France. But when John's train stopped in Hamburg on the way north, the sixteen-year-old took the money intended for school expenses and hopped a boat for America. He arrived in New York harbor dressed as a cadet.

Living with relatives in the New World, he worked in a brewery driving a beer wagon and later as a fireman for the

Burlington Railroad. His fortunes changed somewhat when he married a widow with a splendid house. She was an immigrant from Luxembourg and ten years his senior. They had only one son, my father, John Arthur, whom he called A'ter. Grandfather never lost his thick accent. When I asked my father about our name he was evasive. As a second-generation American he was not interested in the old country, he wanted to be known as pure American and had taken the hyphen out to anglicize it. He hoped to pass for a Fitzpatrick or Fitzmorris.

As a teenager I attended, as my brother had before me, a school run by the Benedictine monks. It was a military academy named in honor of Blessed Marmion, the abbot of Maredsous, in Namur, Belgium. I attended as a day student, going home each night, but one-third of the eight hundred in the corps of cadets were boarders. It was a remarkable school that provided a curriculum based on the seven liberal arts and the classic form of education. It added a great deal to the small midwestern industrial town, built like a rock on the foundations of the Industrial Revolution, consumed with heavy manufacturing. Several days a week I would pass my grandfather's house and stop on my walk home, resplendent in my gray cadet uniform. There, grandmother would trot out sugar-coated molasses cookies and milk for her growing grandson, and Pa would tell me the continuing story of his family. When I asked my grandfather about our name it brought the old man to life; his son had been bored by the story.

He was more than fond of beer and by afternoon my grandmother would advise me to take anything he said with a grain of salt. We sat in the parlor on hard, leather-bottom lounge chairs, and the white embroidered doilies on the back and arms would scratch my hands and the back of my neck. Against one wall was a cabinet with a hinged top. I always started my visit by winding up the Victrola inside and playing his favorite record, "Josephine." While Gramma supplied an unending stream of cookies from a cold crock in the cellar, he drank beer out of a deep-blue-and-white mug with a hinged pewter cover. His sister had sent it to him from Stuttgart. On the top were his initials cut in with a gothic scroll and the words "Z 70, Geburtstag v, d, Schwester 'Josefine.'" His favorite story was his own. Even though he had lived in America since 1889, his Alsatian accent was very strong and came out under a wiry mustache. He always wanted me to kiss him once on each cheek, on arrival and departure, but the bristles scratched my face and I grimaced under their assault. But his face was warm and so were his large hands, working hands that had shoveled coal for the Burlington Railroad for nearly fifty years. In his eighties, he was wracked with rheumatism and walked with a cane. His frame was stooped and his legs bowed, but his round head was erect. I was surprised that he didn't need glasses. "If you drink a lot of beer, you will never need glasses," he advised me.

"When I was sixteen, just like you, David, the Prussians," he hesitated and spit tobacco juice into a brass pot at his feet. Every poorly aimed shot was followed with the expletive, "Prussians!" It was obligatory, like crossing yourself upon entering a church. "The Prussians had taken over our country and everything was done in German. I was attending the church academy in Colmar along with my brothers. There were six of us boys and one sister. My family had a military tradition and we lived in a small chateau just outside the town, where our people had been for many generations."

My grandmother couldn't stand it and broke in, "His father was the gardener."

Pa neither confirmed nor denied the interruption. "My relatives from Prussia demanded that one of us be sent to a military school in Berlin and I was chosen. I didn't want to go and leave my family and France for those butchers in the north, even if they were my relatives. But my father agreed, and I was sent to a tailor in Strasbourg to have my uniform made. It was blue with a red collar and white piping. The buttons had the German eagle and I added the French shooting cord that I had won to the shoulder with the French medallion on it to show my opposition. I had money for the first time in my life and I took a train north. I had not chosen to go, David, and so I did not have to arrive. When I got to Frankfurt, I bought a ticket for Hamburg instead, and then another for America. All I had with me were my uniforms, and there I stood like a soldier on the deck of the ship and saluted as we passed by the Statue of Liberty in New York."

Gramma scoffed. Her husband had not been in steerage and the great statue had not been erected at that time. A short argument ensued and he reminded her that it wasn't a Luxembourger who built it, but Bartholdi, an Alsatian.

"Come, David, I will show you." In a small den off the dinner room which had a smell of antiquity was an ornate trunk. A little enraged that his story had been scoffed at in front of his grandson, he tried to bend down but couldn't reach the black iron clasp on the front. "You open it and we will see if it isn't true." My grandmother watched from the dining room. She was proud of the little old man. There in tissue paper, surrounded by mothballs, my grandmother had preserved the tunic of the old academy. If nothing else the smell of that preservative will stay with me forever.

But all that didn't explain the name and I pressed him for its origin. "We are the only people in town with the name, even though the town is filled with families from Alsace. Why is that, Pa?"

"David, we are French and our family were civil servants as well as soldiers. Civil servants beget civil servants and there was no need to leave home as long as we continued to employ each other. You will find our name wherever the ruling class employed people to run their property and principalities. Once Alsace was owned by the crown prince of the Habsburgs, who lived in Innsbruck. There is a small village near there called Fitzen where that branch set up housekeeping for the ruler. As functionaries we have survived the changes in government." Could there be any connection with the Billatchs, my grandmother's maiden name, from Ober-Innsbruck?

My grandmother spoke softly from behind her knitting, "None whatsoever," she said in perfect English, very slowly.

The old man looked at her slyly. "No, our people were not horse thieves or deserters."

She came right back, "No, your people were little men in big hats who thought they were somebody."

He continued making the stories bigger. "In Holstein you will find another little town with the same name which was a spinoff of a member who went north and became the Von Enz and administered the lands of one of the junkers."

"How old is the name, Pa?" I asked, hoping to put a start to the whole story.

"It is as old as Christendom, David. We are all descended from Henricus de Vitzen, a member of the Teutonic Knights, one of the military orders who fought with King Louis on the fifth crusade in 1245 that conquered Egypt." Another trip to the old trunk ensued. There was a letter from his brother, who worked in the French provincial government of Mulhouse. At the top of the rather stiff, off-white stationery was an embossed symbol. Holding the letter in his shaky hand, he pointed to the emblem which held a heraldic wolf springing, sable. "It is the shield of the Vitzen, your namesake." There it was at last!

That bit of information sent me straight to the great library in our military academy, which was the pride of the Benedictine fathers. My Latin professor, Father Alquin, told me that Vitzenz was the form for "victorious." The books told me the story of the fifth crusade and of how the Teutonic Knights, one of several military orders, had three branches. One served in modern Lithuania against the remnants of Genghis Khan's horde from the east that destroyed many Christian communities. Another hugged the northern coast of Germany and Prussia, warding off Vikings. The third was known as the German branch and was formed from provinces in the south, Alsace and Burgundy. It was the tales of the Teutonic military order that spawned some of the stories of German epic brought to modern people in the operas of Wagner.

A day came when I stopped in and my grandfather was in bed. He had been out most of the night drinking and his wife had gone, at the request of the bartender, to bring him safely home. She was still upset with his behavior and offered to tell me a part of the story that he had overlooked. "There is another shield you should see that comes from a few hundred years later." She took a piece of paper and put it in front of me on her spotless kitchen table and drew a simple shield with a chevron and three stars. "This is from the branch of the family that is closest to your grandfather, I am sure. You are old enough and should know the whole truth, like your papa. David, one of the Von Enz wandered through Alsace before he went back north. He was a rascal like your grandfather and left behind a whole new branch of that sainted family. He had a son, John, who was born 'on the wrong side of the blanket,' the sinister," and she folded her arms and nodded her head to make the point. His illegitimate offspring couldn't be a "Von" Enz, it was not possible, but he needed a name in order to succeed, so the church provided him with one. He became The Fitz-Enz. Fitz is very old French for "bastard."

Index